EAST PARK

150 Years of Compassion

MOYRA HAWTHORN AND IAIN HUTCHISON

EAST PARK

Published in 2024 by
East Park School
1092 Maryhill Road
Glasgow G20 9TD
Scotland

British Library Cataloguing in Publication Data
East Park: 150 Years of Compassion
A catalogue record for this book is available on request from the British Library

ISBN-13: 978-1-7395575-0-8

Typesetting and design by Dice Design
Cover colour photography: Pete Copeland
Printed by Bell & Bain Ltd, 303 Burnfield Road, Glasgow G46 7UQ

Contents

The Authors

Moyra Hawthorn is a qualified Social Worker and Music Therapist. She has worked in a range of settings including with abused and traumatised children, young people and their families, and latterly in a residential short-break service for those with complex additional support needs. Moyra has also worked in research, training and consultancy at the Scottish Institute for Residential Child Care (SIRCC), which became the Centre for Excellence for Children's Care and Protection (CELCIS), where she completed a PhD on Survivors' Narratives of Historical Institutional Child Abuse. She has published on a wide range of subjects. She was a member of the East Park Board of Trustees 2013–22.

Iain Hutchison is a historical researcher at the University of Glasgow. His work focuses on disability history, health history and Scottish social history. He wrote *A History of Disability in Nineteenth-Century Scotland* and *Feeling our History: The experience of Blindness and Sight Loss in Edwardian Edinburgh, the Lothians and the Scottish Borders.* He was the lead author of *Child Health in Scotland: A history of Glasgow's Royal Hospital for Sick Children* and he was the editor, with Martin Atherton and Jaipreet Virdi, of *Disability and the Victorians: Attitudes, interventions, legacies*. He was awarded his PhD in History by the University of Strathclyde and he is a Fellow of the Royal Historical Society.

Abbreviations

BI	Baldovan Institution, Dundee
BMJ	British Medical Journal
CALM	Crisis Aggression Limitation Management
CAMHS	Child and Adolescent Mental Health Service
CELCIS	Centre for Excellence for Children's Care and Protection, formerly Centre for Excellence for Looked After Children in Scotland
DOE	Department of Education
EIS	Educational Institute of Scotland
EMS	Emergency Medical Service
GASS	Grant Aided Special School
GCA	Glasgow City Archives
GML	Mitchell Library, Glasgow
GRI	Glasgow Royal Infirmary
HMI	Her Majesty's Inspectors of Schools
HMSW	Heatherbank Museum of Social Work
HNC	Higher National Certificate
JASS	Junior Awards Scheme for Scotland
MEF	Mediterranean Expeditionary Force
MTHGC	Minutes of the Trades House of Glasgow and Committee
NHS	National Health Service
NRS	National Records of Scotland
RHSC	Royal Hospital for Sick Children, Glasgow
SCOPE	Social and Community Opportunities Post-Eighteen
SED	Scotch (later Scottish) Education Department
SHS	Scottish Human Services
SIRCC	Scottish Institute for Residential Child Care
SMART	Specific, Measurable, Achievable, Relevant and Timebound
SNI	Scottish National Institution for Imbecile Children, Larbert
SOED	Scottish Office Education Department
SOEID	Scottish Office of Education and Industry Department
SQA	Scottish Qualifications Authority
SSSC	Scottish Social Services Council
SVQ	Scottish Vocational Qualifications
SWOT	Strengths, Weaknesses, Opportunities and Threats
THGA	Trades House of Glasgow Archive
UCL	University College London
UDA	University of Dundee Archives
VAD	Voluntary Aid Detachment

Foreword

In commissioning this book, the trustees of East Park School were conscious that for this charity to be still in existence 150 years after its foundation, and to be still delivering its services from the same location and in the same community of Maryhill, Glasgow, Scotland, was a remarkable fact, and worthy of exploring, recording and sharing.

East Park: 150 Years of Compassion is an account of an organisation, often warmly referred to as a Glasgow institution, which was formed in the second half of the Victorian era and which continues today, in good health, as we approach the conclusion of the first quarter of the twenty-first century.

It is a book that charts a story, a history, of inevitable change. This is a story that places the continual evolution of a small but significant charity in the context of 150 years of societal change, of community development, and goes to some length to understand the policy directives behind changes in education, health provision and social care over time, not least bringing us up to date with current, rightly expected, high standards for the education and care of children and young people who present with the most complex of support needs. The book shows that East Park has, on more than one occasion, had to confront major challenges to its continued existence. That such challenges were overcome reflects on the resilience of those committed to delivering its charitable mission.

The trustees have sought to provide a readable account that will appeal to a wide audience – those with an interest in the local history, those involved in the provision of education and care services, and those who welcome a good read. It is punctuated with often surprising snippets that inform and incidentally entertain, for instance, the background to the annual Glasgow taxi drivers' outing to Troon.

A subtitle that emphasises compassion is no accident. The reader will find out about the progressive values that East Park today seeks to embed in its work. Compassion may now be viewed as an old-fashioned word, but nevertheless it is considered applicable as an instinctive emotion behind the involvement of so many with East Park over the years. This is not to imply that current managers and trustees are in denial that in its 150 years there will have been dark periods for some of the children and young people entrusted to East Park's care, where indeed compassion was not apparent. The book addresses such matters and brings readers up to date with the recent development of the Redress Scotland Scheme, a national collective effort endeavouring to address the experience of abuse by children while in the care of institutions and organisations across Scotland before 2004.

On its 150th anniversary, readers will learn about a mature, confident and committed organisation, now geared towards providing the most professional and compassionate education and care to children and young people with complex support needs, especially those with autism.

We believe the authors have successfully risen to the task of recording a fascinating history. The book's completion should be seen as a tribute to staff and the many children and young people who have passed through the doors of East Park over the years. Today, children and young people, each unique and with latent talents, but who face the utmost challenges in their interactions with everyday life, can expect an environment where commitment, compassion, and indeed love, are to the fore.

Gerald I Wells
Chair of the Board of Trustees
2018–23

Kieron O'Brien
Executive Director
2017–present

Acknowledgements

The research and writing for this history took place over a two-year period during 2022 and 2023. Many people have assisted the authors during this time, to whom we owe grateful thanks. At East Park School, we were guided by a mentoring committee and give thanks to Kieron O'Brien, Gerry Wells, Geraldine O'Neill, Catriona Campbell, Marjory Devlin, Kiran Kaur, Tom O'Connell, Kim Pollock and Heather Welsh. We also thank Lauren Balfour, Lynda Gallacher, Peter McLanachan and Diane Taylor, who frequently received and supported us during our visits, but also all the other staff behind the scenes with whom we did not have direct contact. Additionally, we thank former personnel Linda Gray, May Henderson and William Livingstone, and former members of the Board Ken McChlery and Alex O'Hara.

Much of the research took place in East Park's own archive, but not exclusively. In particular, we therefore express gratitude to East Dunbartonshire Leisure & Culture Trust – Museums, Alyson Purves of Girlguiding Glasgow, Elizabeth Howie of Girlguiding Ayrshire North, Sandra McCallum of Girlguiding Ayrshire South, Glasgow City Archives, the Glasgow Room of the Mitchell Library, Laura Stevens of Greater Glasgow & Clyde NHS Archive, Friends of Glasgow Royal Infirmary, Aurora Segnan of Maryhill Heritage, Alan Willoughby of Scouts Scotland, Tom McKendrick for providing information on the Clydebank Blitz and for helping to identify the work of Ian Fleming, and University of Dundee Archives.

Oral and written testimony has been an important resource to the project. We are therefore especially grateful for narration of memories and experiences to Amy (pseud.), Lauren Black, Elizabeth Elgey, Keith Greene, Elizabeth Hunter, Maura Morran Kaur, Michael McCreadie, Jimmy McIntosh via Sean Bradley of Thirsty Books, Jay McInally and Hannah McIntyre, Peter McLanachan, Tommy Mullaney, Mairi Smyth, Elizabeth Thompson and Bryan Tolland.

Some of the children who died at East Park and at the Country Branch during its first century were buried in the Glasgow Necropolis, the Western Necropolis and Haylie Brae Cemetery, Largs. Gerry Wells undertook valuable research of the Glasgow Necropolis burial lairs. Thomas McQuilkin of Glasgow City Council helped track down 'lost' graves in the Western Necropolis, and Fiona Porter of North Ayrshire Bereavement Services directed us to the Country Branch grave in Haylie Brae Cemetery. These sites echo a sad side of East Park's history and we thank Gerry, Thomas and Fiona for their investigations.

For assistance in numerous ways, we are grateful to Daniel Autumn of

Capability Scotland, Bill Black, Elena Billinghurst, Julie Breadner – specialist speech and language therapist, Ailie Davie, Michelle Devlin, Liam Feeney, Karen Ferguson, Ruth Foster, Lesley Gray, Pamela Greenhow, Fiona Harrison, Carol Kerr, Stephen Lally, Amy Little, Jim McDermott, Stephen Mann, Evelyn Mellan, Lesley Nutton of Cerebral Palsy Scotland, Margaret Orr, David Pool, Tim Simmons, Barbara Simpson, David Traynor, Lesley Watson, Jean White and the staff in the residences, Skye and Lewis, Arran, Barra, Harris and Robertson House.

All photographs in this book are from the East Park archival collection unless otherwise credited. We thank those outside bodies for facilitating use of the images in their collections and for granting the appropriate permissions. And we thank the Fleming family for granting permission to reproduce the depiction of the Kilmun Street bombing.

In bringing the book together we particularly thank Ian Brooke, not only for his editing expertise, but as a talented sounding board whose guidance has been invaluable. We also thank Simon Pledger of Dice Design for laying out and designing the volume that is now in your hands.

Moyra Hawthorn and Iain Hutchison

Introduction

Walls and railings, secure gates, a tower piercing the skyline. These are some of the features that defined the view of East Park from the increasingly bustling outside community on Maryhill Road in the late nineteenth century. In the twenty-first century, walkers passing behind East Park encounter a very different environment, notably the Forth & Clyde Canal's towpath that lines the bucolic waters of a once-bustling inland marine highway. It is an area of relaxation and quiet contemplation, the presence of East Park being almost a world away. On Maryhill Road, East Park's presence is proclaimed in a blaze of bright, welcoming colour that announces without ambiguity that here is a place of hope and joy, a community that provides support while nurturing independence in the lives of its young people.

East Park opened in 1874, its aim being to receive children, not only with physical impairments, but with a wide range of disabling conditions, children 'rescued' from families unable to cope with poverty that was further challenged with the arrival of a child with a debilitating health condition. Before the acquisition of East Park cottage was ever contemplated, a constitution was drawn up by a gathering of 'Gentlemen' who declared their plans for a philanthropic body to address a newly identified need in Glasgow: 'The Association proposes to confine its attention to children who seem to be Incurably Infirm, Deformed or Imbecile'. The word 'confine' suggests that this enterprise did not wish to be overly ambitious, and indeed the last category, 'imbecile' children, was dropped early in the Association's existence because of its swift appreciation that its initial self-imposed remit was too broad and that two residential institutions for mentally impaired children already existed.[1]

The forms of impairment being experienced by East Park's first children in 1874 are mostly unfamiliar to us today, not least because we have become accustomed to the benefits of medical breakthroughs such as the discovery of penicillin and of the availability of healthcare for all through a National Health Service (NHS). Opportunities for medical treatment and nurturing care were very different in the late nineteenth century and it was left to philanthropically minded members of the comfortable classes to make interventions that might benefit marginalised individuals, especially children, who were unfortunate victims of circumstance.

East Park was intended to be a temporary place of residential provision, it being founded as a necessary expediency by an Association whose aim was aiding children in their own homes. If admitted to the East Park Home, children's ailments and infirmities might, with careful medical and nursing intervention and a nutritious diet, be improved, while outside, a confident imperial city, Glasgow, endeavoured through social reforms to banish the poverty, disease and squalor that were hallmarks of a rapidly expanding industrial metropolis. Of course, it did not work out that way. East Park's capacity was regularly expanded over the following decades, yet still there were waiting lists of those being referred for admission.

The creation of the NHS, more than seven decades after the opening of East Park, was the milestone event that should have ensured 'total' state medical treatment of children with disabling impairments. Consequently, the arrival of the NHS almost marked the demise of East Park as an independent, charity-supported endeavour as it faced 'nationalisation', as critics of the new NHS termed it. The circumstances of East Park's survival as an independent entity from the mid-twentieth century are explained in this history.

But survival in 1948 was only one stepping stone in East Park's journey to its one hundred and fiftieth anniversary in 2024. By the close of the twentieth century, independent living in the community, with support where required, had widely replaced long-established practices of institutionalisation of certain members of society, a practice that the noted thinker, Michel Foucault (1926–84), called 'the great confinement'.[2] In Scotland, this change was marked by, for example, the closure of such institutions as Lennox Castle hospital, near Lennoxtown, a place that had been the long-term residence for people with certain mental challenges.

Over the decades, East Park has had to adapt to changing circumstances, values and health conditions. Children fitted with calipers as a consequence of polio are no longer familiar to us, polio itself having been eliminated from most parts of the world. Today's East Park children are very different from their nineteenth-century counterparts. Now they are young people with complex additional support needs being nurtured in order to enhance their quality of life while mostly living in homely environments, but who come to East Park for specialist support and education.[3] East Park has often had three aspects to its purpose – provision of health support, delivery of focused schooling and training, and offering a comfortable home. Each has supported the other two and, while the balance has periodically adjusted, these three areas have long been the hallmarks of East Park. But over 150 years, East Park has had to embrace change so that in the twenty-first century care and education are balanced by strategies to provide its young people with 'independent' living.

The story that follows explains the nature of East Park's fifteen-decade evolution.

It is a story of an 'institution' and a story of Glasgow. It is also a story of a particular type of childhood experience.

Tracing East Park's history

At the core of the research needed to produce this history of East Park has been its in-house archival collection. In particular, key sources have been its printed annual reports that were produced for public consumption, especially among the extensive networks of subscribers who provided diverse strands of funding to support East Park's work. Additionally, the minute books that recorded the deliberations of the directors and committees of East Park and of the Association, for many years in handwritten script using pen and ink, have been important in revealing some of the inner thinking of the people who sustained the functioning of East Park and managed the necessary fundraising. The annual reports collection that recorded one and a half centuries of activity in the support of children with disabilities is not totally complete and a missing minute book has also contributed to omissions in the East Park archive. However, research has been aided by an annual report collection in the Glasgow Room of the Mitchell Library and by some other external sources.

The annual reports of philanthropy-led associations such as East Park, which in nineteenth-century Scotland included a scope that ranged from animal welfare to hospitals and infirmaries, tend to exude positivity. Their aim was to draw upon public largesse, to encourage contributors to form long-term attachments, and to perhaps increase their level of annual support over time, culminating in the creation of legacies so that even in death, their support continued. Therefore, the initial pages of annual reports narrated progress, success, and ambition for the future – a balancing act that, while showing with positivity and optimism what was being achieved in ameliorating social ills, also strove to emphasise that much remained to be done, by highlighting crises in society and among its poor, in order to keep donations flowing. This, of course, in the case of East Park was not just to maintain support for the consequences of social adversity on the children it received, but to adapt to the changing nature of these circumstances – combating the effects of rickets, tuberculosis and polio in the nineteenth and much of the twentieth centuries, to enabling twenty-first- century children to have lives of fulfilment while facing the challenges presented by circumstances calling upon complex support.

The format and style of East Park's annual reports have changed over the years, early editions being noteworthy because of their comprehensive nature, their reflection of the religious values and inspirations of the day, and being uninhibited by modern conventions of bestowing privacy. Subscribers' names, addresses and level of contribution were fully detailed, as were the personal details of children who were showcased, with the aim of pulling on heart strings and purse strings. By the beginning of the twentieth century, some degree of protection of children's identities and medical circumstances were exercised in the annual reports, while the intervention of two World Wars that, among other things, were marked by paper shortages, ushered in a trend towards brevity, which diminishes, but does not remove, their value to the historian. For five decades, annual reports were produced in the autumn and reported on the previous twelve months. In 1924, this changed to a calendar year system, annual reports appearing in January to give an account of the preceding year; for example, the annual report dated January 1930 gives readers an overview of 1929. Further changes occurred at the dawn of the twenty-first century, when the reports altered to reflect a 'financial' year running from April to March. With revised governance a decade later, the annual reports were replaced by trustee reports.

Minute books, in contrast to the annual reports that were made widely available in the public domain, were intended to record the activities of a small group of people, namely East Park's directors, and some senior officials such as the visiting medical practitioners. Through the early decades, this group consisted of public-spirited *men*, and minutes were written as an internal record of the deliberations of what was an elite group within the organisation. Women and their endeavours were undoubtedly taken for granted, yet their work and commitment were essential to fulfilling East Park's ambitions and achievements. It was the women who were charged with raising the finance to make it all possible, of providing the maternal touch in roles ranging from home visiting to leading children's activities at East Park, and to knocking on doors in affluent areas to promote the role of the Home and solicit donations.

While male Board members often met in a city centre office remote from the Home in Maryhill, it was women who filled gendered roles as nurses, teachers and domestic staff. The responsibility of the matron was all-embracing and, although in course of time, matron's summaries appeared in the annual reports, in the minute books their difficult multitasked role was often dismissed with the brief sentence, 'the Matron delivered her report'. Minute books are also inconsistent in their reporting, so that a topic of discussion at one meeting might not be followed through in the written account of subsequent meetings, while subjects of delicacy were either not recorded at all or were written with intentionally vague and euphemistic phraseology. Indeed, it is challenging for historians to piece together what minute books do not say, either because of negligence, or because of directors' desire to sanitise recording of the finer detail surrounding moments and events that might have caused unpleasantness or discomfort.

For six decades, there was a second East Park Home. This was the East Park Country Branch located on the edge of the Ayrshire town of Largs. Here, children benefited from fresh sea air, air that contrasted with that encountered in increasingly industrial Glasgow, and where they lived in an adapted mansion with spacious grounds. The Country Branch was particularly beneficial to convalescing children. Furthermore, with the evacuation to Largs of the children living in Maryhill due to the outbreak of the Second World War, Largs really was, through the early 1940s, 'East Park Home'. There is therefore a chapter dedicated specifically to the story of East Park's Country Branch.

The experience of childhood at East Park is particularly challenging to trace in a story where the children should be centre stage, but who are seen (such as in annual report photographs) but not heard. Because official records concerning children are generally closed for one hundred years, the challenge of discovering childhood experience is further inhibited. It is one of many aspects where research of outside records has been helpful, but particularly where personal testimony has been invaluable. In writing the personal experiences of the children, and also staff, where these occurred within the last hundred years, anonymity, such as by the use of pseudonyms, has been adopted, except where the individual has given express permission for their identity to be shown.

Writing East Park's history

The chapters of this book have approached East Park's history by following two strands. They consist of chapters that pursue a chronological approach, tracing different phases of the 150-year story. However, these chronological chapters are supplemented by chapters that pursue a theme-based strategy in order that, for example, the experiences of children, nurses and teachers can be better understood and acknowledged.

This strategy has been used to showcase some of the early charitable endeavours of promoters of East Park, but also the competition that they encountered, specifically from William Quarrier and his Orphan Homes of Scotland. It attempts to right a great wrong in the apparent poor recognition often afforded to women, the ladies who knocked doors to fundraise, and the matrons and nurses (trained and untrained) who cared for the children and who faced, sometimes extreme, difficulties on a daily basis. The teachers who strove to deliver education to children denied the chance of attending mainstream public schools are also presented.

While East Park's physical boundaries may be seen as a shielding barrier between children with disabilities and the bustling mainstream life of Maryhill, East Park has in fact had a long association with outside community life. This is demonstrated in a chapter that highlights the roles played by personalities from the worlds of show business, music and sport, individuals who have formed a sustained procession of dedication to the work of East Park that continues to the present time.

It will be noted that there were instances of some irregularity, some might even say carelessness, when East Park was referred to in official accounts as East-Park or Eastpark. Such aberrations will be apparent in the pages that follow. Also, in writing a history such as this, we have inevitably been confronted by jarring terminology. Terms such as 'cripple', 'imbecile' and 'handicapped' are now archaic and unacceptable. Readers will, however, inevitably come across examples where it has been necessary to include these in the text as they reflect eras when certain terminology was not thought pejorative. Just as language of the past can disturb today's readers, we are conscious that language surrounding impairment and disability continues to evolve and today's politically correct language may no longer be acceptable tomorrow. In their introduction to *The New Disability History*, Paul Longmore and Lauri Umansky consistently speak of 'people with disabilities' rather than 'disabled people' in their endeavour to rally a people-first approach and in their critique of 'historical examination of disability [through to the late twentieth century being] based on medical pathology [that] misinterprets or filters out a great deal of evidence'.[4] We have frequently used people-first descriptors, such as 'children with disabilities' rather than 'disabled children', while also attempting to reconstruct the experiences and lives of some of East Park's children over the decades, and to recognise that 'disability … is not simply located in the bodies of individuals. It is a socially and culturally constructed identity.'[5] However, variations in terminology used will be found in the narrative that follows, as it is also influenced by the likes of a publication by the Union for Physically Impaired against Segregation (UPIAS), where Mike Oliver refers to 'disabled people' on the basis that it is not impairments that represent the main cause of social exclusion of disabled people, rather the way in which society responds to people with impairments.[6] This is seen in terminology used in recent Scottish Government policy documents that refer to 'disabled children'.[7]

In addition to incorporating some reflections of children's experiences at East Park, the book contains several vignette panels where individual children's lives have been reconstructed. For more recent decades, the oral testimonies of former children have been invaluable sources. Past children often spoke of their East Park experience in positive terms, but if they voiced criticism of their perceived treatment, the book does not shy away from repeating some adverse views. Equally, more widely, it does not avoid revealing occasions of religious sectarianism, a trait that has long blighted west of Scotland society.

There have, of course, been instances where the formal records have been open to challenge as to their veracity, a tendency in all historical sources to which historians have to be alert. There are also absences from the formal records, just as there are failures to explain why certain actions arose, and this can necessarily result in 'putting the empirical together with the speculative'.[8] Historical investigations can therefore be confronted with conundrums surrounding 'what is not there, what is missing', Icelandic archaeologist Haraldur Thor Hammer Haraldsson highlighting that 'in the effort of filling these blank spots, where information has been lost to time … subjective insertions from the researcher might become inescapable'.[9] In this history, while we have benefited from a range of historical records, where there are gaps, an element of 'subject insertion' has been necessary in order to try to explain an action or event. Fortunately, there are few such instances.

We hope that *East Park: 150 Years of Compassion* goes some way to recording a serious social history of an important Glasgow institution. It is one that has not only survived numerous structural changes to the city and the society that surrounds and embraces it, but also tells a story that readers can identify with and will see as reflecting the evolution of, not just a collection of buildings lying in the shadow of the Forth & Clyde Canal, itself a mirror of social and economic change, but of the evolving nature of life itself.

CHAPTER 1
Education and the 'Association'

[There] were blind and deaf and imbecile children, and for these institutions existed,
to which they were sent. There were also the lame, the halt, the maimed, those
suffering from spine and hip-joint disease, and many covered with sores. For these, no
suitable institution existed.

William Mitchell, 1891

When William Mitchell, one of the most prominent founders of the 'Association for Visiting and Aiding the Permanently Infirm and Imbecile Children brought under notice by the School Board Educational Inquiry', penned these words in a fundraising appeal letter addressed 'To The School Children of Glasgow', East Park Home had been operating as a refuge for physically impaired children for eighteen years.[1] It provided residential care and also endeavoured to give education to its child residents according to their needs and abilities.

East Park Home for Crippled Children, as it was then called, opened in Maryhill in August 1874. The Association only preceded the acquisition of East Park Cottage by a matter of months, being set up in February 1874. The organisation's long title makes it quite explicit that residential care was categorically not on Mitchell's agenda at that moment in time. Indeed, in the early days and years of the Association, it made several notable adjustments to its objectives as Mitchell and his fellow directors became more aware of existing provision for children with certain impairments, and of instances where there was no provision at all.

Scotland: a nation in transition
The nineteenth century was a time during which Scotland was transformed from a rural, agricultural country into a predominantly urbanising industrial powerhouse. Extraction of coal, iron ore and other minerals, available in abundance in a diagonal line from Ayrshire in the west to Fife in the east, were key components to the development of heavy engineering using new innovations such as blast furnaces. Traditional industries, such as weaving, were also undergoing dramatic change as

handloom weavers were being displaced by the construction of large, mechanised mills driven, no longer by artisans' individual muscle power, but by water and, soon, steam power.

In 1801, the population of Glasgow was 77,385. The Barony of Gorbals was incorporated into Glasgow in 1846 and, in 1851, the population was recorded as 329,097. In 1871, it was 477,732 and, with further expansion in 1891 to incorporate burghs such as Maryhill, Hillhead and Govanhill, it had grown to 565,839. The addition of Govan, Partick and Pollokshaws in 1912 brought Glasgow's population to 1,008,487.[2] Although it was often boasted that Scotland enjoyed a high level of education and literacy, by the mid-nineteenth century this was open to challenge. One reason for this was the often informal and diverse nature of education, and certainly the absence of compulsion – quite simply, children did not have to attend lessons in a school.

An example of this can be found in the rural parish of Inchinnan, an agricultural community only ten miles from Glasgow. John Howie, schoolmaster, despaired at the irregular attendance at his school, which was particularly low at certain periods of the agricultural cycle such as the seasons for sowing crops and, later, harvesting them. These were labour-intensive activities when most tasks had to be done by hand. Between 1866 and 1869, for example, Howie expressed his frustration, with such entries in his logbook as: 'Some of the boys beginning to drop away, I suppose they are taken out to work on the farms',[3] 'A number of the older boys and girls have left to engage in farm labour',[4] 'Many of the children at outside work',[5] 'The parents keep their children from school on the most frivolous pretences',[6] 'Some more of the scholars returned from harvest work',[7] 'The attendance generally this session has been very irregular. The fault is chiefly attributable to the parents'[8] and 'Either the hay harvest or the fact of having a holiday on Friday is keeping at home'.[9]

Efforts to make Scotland into a more literate society gained pace when the Education (Scotland) Act of 1872 was passed. Attendance at school was no longer to be a whimsical activity shared with distractions such as children's participation in household economies and by their early recruitment into the workforce. All children between the ages of five and thirteen were now to be obliged to attend school, which is why, from the mid-1870s, grand sandstone school buildings began to appear in Glasgow and beyond. These new schools replaced small places of varied teaching and learning, which went under a variety of names such as parish schools, industrial schools and ragged schools.

Compulsory education meant that there had to be a system to ensure that children were indeed going to school. The 1872 Act inevitably had an adverse effect on some family economies, generating resistance. There were children in the poor parts of

Glasgow where parents relied on their ability to earn a few pennies to contribute to family survival in adversity. These were families who often lived in extreme poverty due to large families, low wages, unemployment and poor health. And, in the view of the comfortable classes, also due to ignorance, fecklessness, and alcohol dependency. Historian Richard Winters describes the middle-class perspective that was exercising increasing influence by the mid-nineteenth century:

> Throughout the 1850s and 1860s, the agitation for greater educational provision ran parallel with the growing doctrine of social responsibility towards the less able, fuelled especially by the evangelical energy of the Free Church. Numerous men and women from the churchgoing middle class of Glasgow threw themselves enthusiastically into the field of social welfare. Their contribution in terms of both finance and organisational ability cannot be overestimated. There was, nevertheless, a strong tendency to be paternalistic and moralising, an approach perfectly consistent with their beliefs. Their own moral outlook and values, they believed, had brought them social standing and financial security; their habits of thrift, hard work and self-help had raised them to a position from which they considered it a duty to transfer such beliefs to the working class. The aim was not simply, or even primarily, to control the working class but to give them an opportunity to better themselves. Many of the middle class believed that poverty was a direct consequence of immorality; only as the century progressed did increasing numbers come to regard poverty, unsavoury housing and poor health as the mainspring of differing moral standards. In keeping with their own views, the middle class considered the family unit as the basis of a strong and virtuous society.[10]

These values and objectives drove efforts to transform Scottish society. This was to be done through the introduction of compulsory education, but also through transforming the social realities of the working classes, from the perspective of the middle-class gaze, in order to bring such a transformation about. To ensure compliance with the new and compulsory participation in lessons, school attendance officers were appointed, their job being to hunt down children who were not attending classes.

Although it was not until 1890 that specific provisions were made, by law, regarding children who were deaf or blind, philanthropists had set up deaf and blind schools, beginning in the eighteenth century. Two residential schools for education or training had also been created by charitable bodies for children who were mentally impaired, namely Baldovan Institution, near Dundee, in 1855, and the Scottish National Institution for the Education of Imbecile Children (SNI) at Larbert, in Stirlingshire, in 1862.[11] Sensory and mentally impaired children might therefore already be receiving teaching or training that was considered appropriate to their needs and was suited to their capabilities. However, the 1872 Act was a first step towards creating a nationwide system that was to ensure that *all* children between the ages of five and thirteen were receiving basic education that equipped them with literacy and numeracy.

Therefore, from 1873, if children were not attending classes, it was believed by some sections of middle-class society that they must be the offspring of irresponsible parents. School Board attendance officers set out to trace absentee children to enforce parents' obligation to send their children to school. In pursuit of these 'delinquents', the officers found themselves visiting dwellings in the most impoverished parts of Glasgow. In wynds off the likes of the High Street, their paths took them to, for example, The Vennel where they found people living in squalor and severe deprivation in the likes of cellars with earthen floors and devoid of the most basic items of furniture.

The squalid living conditions of the lower orders were not previously unknown to the officers. Photographer Thomas Annan (1829–87) had painstakingly photographed these localities in the 1860s, while journalist Alexander Brown, under the pen name of 'Shadow', had both titivated and horrified respectable middle-class readers with an account of his exploration of the lives and living quarters of Glasgow's most deprived inhabitants in his *Midnight Scenes and Social Photographs: Being Sketches of Life in the Streets, Wynds, and Dens of Glasgow*, published in 1858. In his introduction to the reprint of Shadow's book twelve decades after its original publication, historian John McCaffrey noted that, even in 1976, the author 'manages to give the reader the contrasting impression of a city made up of areas that are now in close proximity physically but socially and morally miles apart'.[12] Such environments continued until the end of the nineteenth century, by which time the Improvement Acts of 1866 and 1871 had enabled the clearance of the worst of Glasgow's slums. This action was intended to make possible the building of new tenements for working-class people, with such amenities as enhanced space and a degree of indoor sanitary facilities. In 1877, the City Improvement Trust boasted that:

> The Trust is at present very much engaged in clearing out the remanent portions of many of the scheduled areas … A large amount of property is thus being cleared away, to be replaced by fresh buildings along the lines of new and airy streets, where they have long been sadly required.[13]

Photographer Thomas Annan captured the unhealthy living conditions of 1860s Glasgow in this alley off 118 High Street. (© CSG CIC Glasgow Museums and Libraries Collection: The Mitchell Library, Special Collections)

Locations in Calton, Townhead, High Street and Rottenrow were among those cited where the properties being replaced formed a 'densely populated and squalid locality'.[14] In reality, only the skilled working classes, such as artisans and journeymen-tradesmen, could afford the new dwellings being facilitated by the Trust's actions, while slum clearance exacerbated the wider working-class housing problem for low-skilled and unskilled workers and their families.

However, in 1872, while perhaps being conscious of the existence of extreme urban squalor, Glasgow's comfortable classes had little direct experience of these living conditions and the battle being waged by people at the bottom of the economic ladder to survive. This was especially so among the upper middle-class pillars of society who lived in and beyond the city in leafy suburbs, in villas or genteel terraces where they were waited upon by servants. This gulf was explained by William Mitchell in 1874 when he addressed supporters of the nascent East Park Home, telling them that he had '… discovered in his inquiries, the existence of woes which were perhaps imagined, but were not identified as existing in our midst'.[15] Of course, the circumstances of poverty that Mitchell was narrating to his refined audience were *not* to be found 'in our [their] midst', as was once the case when the city was closely packed around Glasgow Cross and before its westward expansion had made much of an impact. Early in the nineteenth century, many middle-class citizens lived in the upper levels of tenement buildings, while poorer people occupied cellars or street-level quarters. But as the city had expanded westward, the middle classes had relocated so that the two sections of society now lived in very different worlds, the poor inhabiting one of which, in 1873, Glasgow School Board was largely unaware, and which its attendance officers, in pursuing their role, were about to discover. Mitchell himself was living in some luxury at this time, sharing a sixteen-room dwelling with only his wife and mother-in-law, and being waited on by two domestic servants.[16]

The age of middle-class philanthropy

The later nineteenth century was a period of great prosperity for the comfortable classes whose wealth was fuelled by the growth of modern industry and by the benefits that came from exploiting overseas territories that formed the British Empire. Members of these upper middle-class elites had increasingly enhanced their public status by their involvement in founding and running charities for people who they saw as the 'deserving' poor. The deserving poor consisted of people whose misfortunes were regarded as of no fault of their own, such as disabled or orphaned children. Therefore, organisations such as the Glasgow Blind Asylum, founded in 1804, and the Glasgow Deaf and Dumb Institution, which was established in the decade that followed, took a particular interest in 'disabled' people, adults as well as children, offering occupational training and schooling. Institutions for people with mental troubles, which tried to offer therapeutic support through philanthropy, began with a chain of voluntarily funded 'royal' asylums, originating in Montrose in 1782. Glasgow opened such an institution in 1814, but its capacity swiftly became inadequate and Glasgow Asylum moved to new buildings, designed for both the poor, and the wealthy who paid fees for superior accommodation and care, at Gartnavel, in spacious grounds to the west of the city.[17]

Baldovan Institution, originating near Dundee in 1855, and the SNI for Imbecile Children that opened at Larbert in Stirlingshire in 1862, received admissions from

Glasgow and from across Scotland. William Quarrier (1829–1903) began his crusade of rescuing children whom he believed were orphans firstly from a base in Glasgow, but in 1878 founded his Orphan Homes of Scotland near Bridge of Weir, Renfrewshire. So Quarrier and William Mitchell, who founded East Park Home in 1874, were contemporaries. Quarrier quickly became well known and attracted significant largesse from donors who wished to demonstrate compassion and responsibility towards the unfortunate in society. Mitchell and Quarrier, while engaged in similar work, were to have differences upon more than one occasion, although both were driven by unswerving religious conviction.

These well-meaning interventions were nonetheless heavily laden with middle-class values. The middle classes wished to instil in the working classes their own ethos of respectability, thrift, hard work, temperance and godliness, and to remove the irrational rough culture that was their perception of the working classes, such as drunkenness, laziness, squalor and violence. Embedding literacy and numeracy among the working classes was part of this process, as aspired to by the 1872 Education (Scotland) Act. Achievement of compulsory schooling in Glasgow was to be the task of a School Attendance Committee, to which William Mitchell, formerly the proprietor of a calico printing business, was appointed vice-convener. It was in the

More than a decade after Glasgow school attendance officers began pursuing children absent from education, William Mitchell (second left) was one of the adjudicators questioning this young trio brought before No. 2 Committee of the Glasgow Juvenile Delinquency Board in 1886. The smallest child has no shoes. (Courtesy of Glasgow City Archives)

course of the school attendance officers' work that children were discovered, often in squalid conditions and environments in the city's poorest areas, and whose existence prompted Mitchell to be at the forefront of setting up a philanthropic organisation to address their pain, misery and deprivation.[18]

Who, where and what?

Plans to form a Ladies' Association for Visiting and Aiding Permanently Infirm and Imbecile Children were made at the inaugural meeting of the Association, which 'opened … with prayer' and was held in the Religious Institution Rooms on Tuesday 10 February 1874.[19] The prevailing middle-class values of godliness were apparent from the outset and religious conviction was key to sustaining the Association through its early decades. What is less apparent was the direction that the Association was to take in aiding disabled children.

Men, of course, in a patriarchal society, were at the forefront of establishing the Association, but their intention that their wives and daughters and other middle-class women were expected to do the footwork was clear. The ladies' role, 'either personally or by proxy', was to visit the homes of disabled children already identified, to report on the condition of their dwellings, the 'condition of parents whether poor or otherwise [and] whether receiving aid already', the nature of the child's infirmity and 'whether [the child] ought to be removed and if so whether parents are willing'.[20] The help needed in these homes, such as medicine, food, clothing, bedding or the visit of a doctor, was to be assessed by the lady visitors.[21]

A statement was drawn up detailing the aims of the Association. The notion that it might be termed a 'Ladies Association' was dropped, the female role, a few days later, being referred to as an 'Auxiliary of Women', but the goals of 'visiting' and 'aiding' were explicit, while the children to be sought out were to be 'permanently infirm'.[22] This last object seemed to rule out that any medical intervention should aspire to 'curing' a child, or indeed that children with a curable condition should even be considered.[23] Mentally impaired, i.e. 'imbecile children', were also part of the Association's self-appointed remit. It should be noted that, while the original 'Consulting Committee of Gentlemen' had five members, the Ladies' Committee had sixteen and a membership of thirty-one.[24] Additionally, the appointment of Dr R Wilson Bruce as medical adviser 'at a salary of £20 to £30' was made in April 1874, acknowledging that some level of clinical support was unavoidable.[25]

In initial investigations across three districts – 'Calton, High Church and Central' – it was reckoned that around 120 deserving cases had been identified, but it was expected that this number would increase by two to three hundred more once an additional nine districts were explored.[26] The young people whose circumstances were to be addressed were described as being of 'so distressing a nature, where poor suffering children are lying in weariness and sorrow in filthy rooms breathing polluted air, with little or nothing done to soothe or alleviate their pains'.[27]

The enormity of the task that the Association was setting itself up to tackle quickly became apparent. If institutionalisation of 'imbecile' children was considered the best form of aid, it made sense that they went to the two established institutions that were already caring for this category of child. Although a caveat has to be added, in that Baldovan Institution and the Scottish National Institution were almost always having to decline admissions because of insufficient space, and because they endeavoured to restrict admissions to children who were eight or nine years of age, and who might show improvement in their physical and mental wellbeing as a consequence of being accepted. The Association would expect to aid mentally impaired children from around the age of five, since its awareness of them would be stimulated by their obligation to attend school from that age. Its mission to focus on 'permanently' impaired children would suggest children for whom 'improvement' might not be realistically expected, therefore disqualifying them from help by some existing institutions whose goals were the amelioration of the child's condition as found at the time of their admission.

As home visiting by the ladies from such refined addresses as Park Circus and Wilton Crescent gained momentum, it was very soon concluded that the children encountered displayed various needs, but that there were three distinct categories. After initial home visits had been undertaken, on the positive side – and debunking the all-encapsulating middle-class perception that all working-class households were beyond redemption – there were fifteen families where the parents were providing caring attention to their disabled children without need of outside intervention. Next, there were twenty-two children who fell under the Association's original aim and required help in their own homes – urgently so. But there were also twenty-one children who needed a level of care that, the Association believed, could only be adequately aided by removing them to an institutional setting.[28]

In April 1874, at a meeting where a constitution was adopted by the Association, the case for a 'temporary institution' was mooted 'until such times as the Cottage Homes are ready, which it is proposed to erect in the National Institution promoted by Miss Clugston'.[29] Beatrice Clugston (1827–88), while serving as a member of the Association's Ladies' Committee, was also independently active in fundraising for a residential institution for people impaired by permanently disabling conditions. Meanwhile, a member of the Ladies' Committee proposed that, for very urgent cases who had already attracted the ladies' attention during their visits, 'some place might be taken for the summer months at the coast where a very limited number of those who could be removed might be placed for two or three weeks at a time'.[30] Additionally, the ladies, ever practical and, it seems, highly motivated, appealed for 'any articles suitable for children such as cribs, bedding or blankets, perambulators, clothing, also any little delicacies such as preserves, any old picture books or toys'.[31] To this, the ladies added that, 'as many of the children suffer from deformed limbs, bandages and supports suitable for such will be very acceptable'.[32]

In addition to the visiting and fundraising energy that was already being pursued with vigour, medical needs were to be addressed. To Dr Bruce fell the task of establishing an arrangement with a druggist for medicines.[33] It being already apparent that, in some instances, medicine alone would not be enough, one of the Association's gentleman supporters, William McEwen of Park Terrace, who described himself as an East India Merchant, 'pressed on the Association the necessity of removing at once to [Glasgow Royal] Infirmary cases where disease had manifested itself before allowing it to go too far'.[34] Tubercular disease of the bones, a progressive condition (as will be seen later in the case of Robert) requiring regular intervention and monitoring to prevent amputation and death, and the resetting of bones as part of the treatment of rickets, were two circumstances that would require periodic hospital admission of children who were the focus of the Association's investigation and concern.

'A cottage on the Maryhill Road'

After the initial flurry of activity recorded between February and April 1874, it seems that work continued quietly behind the scenes. Then a momentous meeting of the Gentlemen's Committee took place in the Religious Institution Rooms on 17 August 1874. This was 'for the purpose of considering a proposal to buy a cottage on the Maryhill Road suitable for the accommodation of about forty children'.[35]

While the ladies had undoubtedly been on the front line in aiding children and evaluating to what extent intervention beyond their own homes was needed, the notion of a temporary cottage in a rural setting for short-term periods of convalescence had obviously been overtaken by the extent and severity of what was being found in the impoverished dwellings of Glasgow's most deprived localities. However, the August proposal had not come out of the blue, the meeting being informed that one of their number, Thomas Wharrie of Largs, 'had been diligently looking about for suitable premises and that said cottage was the only place they had been able to fall in with'.[36]

This statement suggests, if a home was to be the way forward, that the 'cottage' being considered was presented with an air of some desperation. However, Dr Bruce had inspected the cottage and concluded that it 'would answer exceedingly well for the object contemplated'. The price asked for the building, which came with grounds of 1,576 square yards, was £1,450, with entry promised 'not later than 10th September [1874]'.[37]

The cottage's location on what is now Maryhill Road was in a relatively rural environment while being conveniently close to Glasgow. It is true that immediately behind it was the Glasgow branch of the Forth & Clyde Canal, a hive of heavy commercial activity, but the canal also served as a barrier to encroachment by future urban expansion. The Gentlemen's Committee therefore approved Dr Bruce's assessment of the cottage's suitability. It was agreed that the Association conclude the purchase, and a subcommittee consisting of Edward Collins, Thomas Wharrie and William Mitchell, with support from Dr Bruce, be formed 'for getting the cottage put into proper order and such arrangements and furnishings as are necessary for the reception of the Infirm Children'.[38]

Within less than a month, the deal had been struck and renovation work put in hand. Plumbers and a mason had been contracted and arrangements 'for certain repairs and alterations' were quickly set in motion. The long history of East Park Home was about to begin.

CHAPTER 2

East Park Cottage Home, 1874–5

… after my first visit among the Children, I noticed the case of a poor Child found lying in extreme suffering and misery, turning her little head from side to side. This dear Child is now in the Home, and, although paralysed on one side of her body, the sweet face and smile of Maggie McGill is like a ray of heavenly light cheering the labours of those who are interesting themselves in this work..

William Mitchell, 27 October 1874[1]

The encumbrances experienced by children, and their parents, that inhibited regular school attendance have been described in chapter 1. When these obstacles extended beyond poverty and overcrowded, often squalid, dwellings, the circumstances followed where ill health was ever-present. In some instances, this manifested itself in the various severely disabling conditions that the school attendance officers found in housebound children.

Hospital medical treatment of children in Glasgow had, to a limited extent, been provided by Glasgow Royal Infirmary (GRI), opened in 1794.[2] However, by the 1860s, GRI had been flagged up by both medical practitioners and the city's elites as totally inadequate, leading to calls for a paediatric hospital. This was a noble goal, but one that took two decades to achieve, the Hospital for Sick Children (HSC) opening on Scott Street in Garnethill in 1883.[3] So, when East Park Home opened in 1874, the same year that the Western Infirmary also opened its doors, focused hospital services for children had still not been addressed.[4] The HSC, which received 'royal' patronage in 1889, gradually built up a close association with East Park Home. The hospital began with three wards, two medical and one surgical, with a total of fifty-eight cots. The shared interest of the hospital and the Home in physically disabled children was apparent from the early days of the Garnethill facility.

From 1883, the surgeons at the HSC, opened a decade after the introduction of compulsory education and throughout efforts to demolish the worst of Glasgow's housing stock, were regularly treating cases of rickets and of tuberculosis of the bones and joints. Rickets arose through calcium deficiency. Children with legs bowed as a consequence of the condition were frequently found in the wynds off the High Street where they survived on poor diets and a lack of adequate sunlight to ensure they absorbed sufficient vitamin D. Treatment of the deformed 'bandy' legs that were a feature of rickets required surgeons such as William Macewen to break the bones and reset them. Tuberculosis of the bones often required limbs to be opened and for the disease to be scraped away from the infected bones and joints. The hope was that this would stop the spread of the disease and restore the child to good health, but repeat treatment was often required and, if success was still not achieved, it could result in amputation.[5] Children who had been 'crippled' by such diseases and were therefore considered to be permanently disabled, were among the nineteenth-century admissions to East Park Home.

Like many of the first East Park admissions, eight-year-old Teddy arrived at the hospital in 1883 in a 'dreadfully dirty and naked state' and already beyond hope of saving. To loosen the purse strings of its charitable subscribers, the hospital's directors depicted Teddy's situation in a manner that not only described his medical condition, but conveyed the usual middle-class view of the irresponsibility and fecklessness of the labouring classes in caring for their children:

> Sometimes the night nurse would take [Teddy] in her arms, and sitting by the fireside would converse with the dying child. On one of these occasions he said to her, 'I ken I'll no get better, but I'm no feer'd tae dee.' It was not permitted that he should die among his kind friends. His mother, a dissolute creature, appeared in a drunken state at the Hospital, provided with a piece of old blanket and a piece of carpet, and demanded her child. She was told that, if taken out, he would die in a few days, and her demand was refused. In a few days, she returned, with the same rags, but now accompanied by her husband. The nurse dressed Teddy in some old clothes and they took him away. One redeeming character of this dissolute couple was their affection for their child, and he was pleased to 'gang hame' with them; but to what a home! The nurse sought it out – a little room without an article of furniture, and on the floor, in a corner, covered by a few filthy rags, on a bed of straw and shavings, lay the poor dying Teddy.[6]

How much of the hospital's account of Teddy should be taken to heart is open to debate. The story may even have been 'created' for the purposes of dramatically depicting what the hospital was up against in serving the city's poor. It reflects the poverty found in the old town's alleys and closes, but the colourful description of this event also conveys the psychological gulf between the wealthy and poor of Glasgow. It accuses working-class poverty of being caused by drunkenness, while failing to appreciate that living conditions were so bad in the poorest areas of the city that public houses, generally well-lit, heated and furnished to provide an inviting environment, were a common refuge for people seeking escape from dark, damp rooms and cellars that gave the most basic of shelter. This did not necessarily mean that the public house was used for excessive consumption of alcohol. Furthermore, the middle classes, in their roles as business proprietors and employers, did not acknowledge that their profits were aided in part by exploiting labour at the lowest possible rates and by subjecting the labouring classes to casual and irregular employment when it suited them. The causes of working-class poverty, it might be argued, lay at the doors of the city's business entrepreneurs. Tensions within the working classes were seen both in their rejection of middle-class values and by adoption of the self-same values, notably by the skilled working class. As historian Callum Brown has argued, alienation of the working classes was further spurred by the middle classes' attempted appropriation of religious ideas and ideals, by their patronising slum-visiting, and by their use of religion as a means of social control, while nonetheless it was seen that 'evangelising did work'.[7] Likewise, historian Esme Cleall states that 'in many institutions, schools and asylums there was a joint emphasis on working on both the bodily and the spiritual wellbeing of the inmates'.[8] These trends and tensions can be seen in the early activities of the Association and the rhetoric expounded in the deliberations of the Gentlemen's Committee.

The gulf between rich and poor is shown by the narrator's decision to highlight the linguistic polarisation between the two groups, the upper middle class and the lower, unskilled working class. In disapprovingly describing the outcome of Teddy's treatment in the HSC, its first annual report indignantly reported on Teddy's removal against medical advice. His removal was firstly refused to the mother, but acquiesced to when his father arrived. This illustrates, and accepts, the disempowerment of women in Victorian Scotland and the dominance of masculinity. But the tussle over where Teddy should die nonetheless concedes that working-class parents, no matter how impoverished, loved their children and had feelings towards them in illness. As life ebbed away, they wanted them at home rather than have them die with strangers in a hospital ward, even those as compassionate as the night nurse who cared for Teddy. The boy was recognised as being in a terminal condition. The doctors had conceded that he could not be saved, yet the power of middle-class clinicians was strenuously exercised against the emotional needs of the child and his family until the boy's father intervened.

East Park Home for Crippled Children

On 9 October 1874, William Mitchell reported that 'on or about 10th Sept' the Association had taken possession of East Park Cottage.[9] Staff had been recruited. Notably, 'Mrs Jane McLintock had been engaged for six months as matron at a salary of £40 per annum, exclusive of her board. She was to reside in the house with her husband, but he was to be on no charge on the Association further than his lodgings.'[10] Other initial appointments were a kitchen maid at £12 annually, and two nurses at £15 per annum.[11] The focus of East Park was firmly on the health needs of the children being admitted.

Between taking possession of East Park Cottage and implementing repairs and alterations, it was also reported on 9 October that eleven children had already been admitted during the preceding four weeks.[12] Furthermore, the Committee members were informed that soon there would be twenty children resident and that an additional nurse would be employed.[13] With this background of frenetic activity, the meeting also discussed the Association's finances, and the arranging of a formal opening of the Home, which was to be on 27 October 1874.[14] Undoubtedly, the two topics were interlinked.

Weekly meetings at this time were attended by a committee of four men – Edward Collins, John McClure, William Mitchell and Thomas Wharrie – and chaired by Mitchell in his office at 134 Wellington Street. It was from here that the programme

The original East-Park Home building accommodated thirty children when Maryhill was a rural backwater.

for the formal opening was organised. Invitations were to be printed and sent to 'Members of [the] Committee, Lady Visitors and Principal Subscribers'.[15] Two [horse-drawn] omnibuses were to be hired for the occasion, and would depart from Clarendon Place, near St George's Cross.[16] The committee was clearly confident that the opening arrangements had been completed in good time since, a week before the opening, it expressed happiness that everything was set for the event, and it now concentrated its attention on practical matters – what to do with children who were blind, 'deaf and dumb' and 'imbecile'.[17] And what to do about the educational needs of the children now in residence at East Park.

Education of children had, of course, been the spark that, through a sequence of events and discoveries, brought about the establishment of East Park Home. Miss Thomson had accordingly been recruited as the Home's first teacher. It was a part-time position at a salary of £2 monthly.[18] How schooling would be delivered may have been one of the reasons behind the committee's discussion surrounding children with sensory and mental impairments. Consequently, individual committee members and their associates agreed to take responsibility for investigating alternative arrangements for these children. Blind children were to be the responsibility of John McClure, a Mr Hannah was to be invited to take on a role in respect of children who were 'deaf and dumb', and Messrs James A Campbell and Edward Collins were to pursue how best to serve the needs of the 'imbecile' children.[19] Children in these categories were to be the subject of negotiation with other institutions during the early years of East Park. However, the immediate priority for the full committee was the big event, the formal opening of East Park Home on Tuesday 27 October 1874.

The East Park opening ceremony

The formal inauguration of East Park Home, presided over by Alexander Whitelaw, newly elected Conservative Member of Parliament for Glasgow and, in 1873, first Chairman of Glasgow School Board, was conducted with due solemnity – reports and remarks being interspersed with prayer, the singing of Psalms 20 and 90 and hymn numbers 53 and 75, and concluding with a benediction.[20] A detailed report of the occasion covered such themes as the children being served – 180 from six districts had now been identified as 'unfitted through severe permanent bodily infirmity from attending School', the classification of children according to the nature of their impairments, and the acquisition of East Park Cottage Home. East Park's intended role had to be more fully formulated, the nursing and schooling needs had to be addressed, and the work of the Ladies' Committee and, of course, fundraising activities had to be maximised.[21] The occasion was held, as might be expected, at East Park, but apart from a description of the case of one child which, upon discovery, was used to elicit sympathy, the children seem to have been unseen and unheard throughout the proceedings.

The opening address did, however, concede that 'a large number of these Children are kindly and carefully attended by their own friends, and require no aid from the Association', again demonstrating the tension surrounding the middle-class perspective of the lower orders who, on the one hand, they saw as being ignorant, and indeed callous, towards their parental responsibilities, while on the other, the experience of the Lady Visitors showed that many poor parents demonstrated care and affection for their children despite their shared hardship and deprivation.[22] This is seen in a comment within months of the opening of East Park Home when two children were withdrawn by their parents and taken home. It was declared that 'there is only too much reason to believe that the motive was that the parents – who must be thoughtless, idle, and dissipated parents – were anxious to trade upon the infirmities of their children'.[23] It was implied to the meeting that the children were to be used by their parents to beg, their impairments being used to attract sympathy and spare change. But no actual evidence is offered to support this assertion.[24]

In being appraised of the children being encountered by the Lady Visitors, guests were told of the various cases for which the support of existing institutions was being solicited. Of those children for which the Association expected to take responsibility, the assembled gathering was told that:

> … [of] the Deformed, the Paralytic, the Lame, &c., twelve have been relieved from their sufferings by the hand of death. Twenty-four have been found whose cases were not quite so bad as represented, and most of whom it is hoped will by-and-by, with the aid of crutches, be got to School. Eleven have removed from the city. Or have left no new address. There are about thirty of the more recently discovered cases of which no correct analysis can yet be given. Twenty children are being regularly visited in their own homes by the doctor, and seventeen are now inmates of this Cottage Home …[25]

'The first child', it was reported, 'was admitted on the 16th of September.'[26] This was a mere week after East Park Cottage had passed into the Association's hands.

A total of seventeen children had been admitted during the four weeks preceding the formal opening, but the report goes on to say that 'time will not permit any sufficient statement of the interesting nature and character of nearly every one of these cases'.[27] This is disappointing since surely the children should have been centre stage at such an event rather than being absent. The singular exception is Mitchell's anecdote, quoted at the beginning of this chapter, surrounding the discovery of Maggie McGill. Unfortunately, further details of Maggie McGill, that 'ray of heavenly light', do not survive in the Association's early records, frustrating efforts to identify her life with any certain accuracy.[28]

In tandem with the residential role of East Park, the Association quickly embraced the healthcare needs of its first admissions. Dr Wilson Bruce was not only to visit East Park on an almost daily basis, but also to visit children under the Association's embrace who remained in their own homes. As mentioned in chapter 1, he had initially been appointed as a 'medical adviser at a salary of £20 to £30' but, no doubt because of his heavy commitment following the opening of East Park, this was increased to £50 a year.[29]

The catalyst for the formation of the Association had been the introduction of compulsory education. It therefore followed that schooling of children in East Park should also be given immediate attention, resulting in the appointment of 'lady teacher' Miss Thomson. She attended East Park three hours daily and, although the children were reputed to previously have been totally deprived of schooling, it was enthusiastically reported that, in the Home, 'many of the Children are being found most apt pupils, both at their letters and in knitting and sewing'.[30]

East Park Home had made great strides within a matter of months, but this caused anxiety to be expressed that the Association should not lose sight of its original aim, that of visiting and assisting disabled children in their own homes.[31] Despite 'the absence of many ladies from town' [on long holidays], Janet Moir (1815–97), as joint secretary/convener of the Ladies' Committee, added new impetus to the visiting programme, prevailing upon her Lady Visitors to do 'a double share of work' to compensate for those still enjoying the leisure of summer months.[32] Only six months had elapsed since the formation of the Association and only a month had passed since the opening of East Park when forty-four ladies were listed as distributing collecting cards, while other ladies were aiding East Park's 'clothing department' by, for example, each week devoting a day at the Home to engage in sewing.[33] Additionally, 'young ladies' were encouraged to visit East Park to sing or read to the children.[34] The reaction of the East Park children to the young ladies' serenading is not recorded.

'It was difficult to say …'

The opening event on 27 October was reported in the press with a fair degree of self-congratulation, expressed in the most modest of terms, of course. The energy of the Association in the few months since its formation was quite astounding, as were its achievements as 1874's autumn leaves prepared to fall around the villas of Glasgow's west end and in the park lands that followed the River Kelvin to Maryhill. Yet the Association remained unclear about its long-term role, and even if it would, or should, have one. Would the problems it was addressing be no more than a short-term intervention in a situation that might soon be fixed by expanding medical intervention and better social provision for the poor?

> [The Association] had begun the work on a modest scale, and [William Mitchell] thought they had done wisely. In mercantile affairs, the soundest concerns were those which had their rise from small beginnings – and the same principle would hold good in charitable institutions. It was difficult to say to what extent this Home might yet attain. Thirty was the number that could be accommodated; and let them all hope there would be no necessity for more room.[35]

Not only did Mitchell downplay the enormity of the Association's achievement so far, but he was optimistic that the current actions were to be a necessity of short duration and of limited extent. His reference to the use of sound business principles might also have been aimed at William Quarrier and his approach to expansion at his Orphan Homes of Scotland, which he had launched near Bridge of Weir on a 'cottage' principle, with villas of about thirty children, each under the care and supervision of house parents. Quarrier, always ambitious in his plans for expansion, would commission the erection of new cottages without the funds to pay for them, and sailed close to the wind in having sufficient provision to feed the children. If cautioned about his imprudence, he would respond by asserting that 'the Lord will provide'.[36] The Lord didn't provide directly, but Quarrier, always adept at promotion and publicity, survived his more cavalier decisions. It was philanthropic individuals and organisations that underwrote the success of Quarrier's Village rather than divine intervention, although Quarrier would have undoubtedly seen these as being the same thing.

While Quarrier constantly pursued expansion, as Mitchell saw things from the vantage point of 1874, he declared:

> The poor we will always have with us, and the Christian judgment of good people would always wisely determine the extent of this and similar establishments. But might they not hope that a brighter day might arise, when there would be fewer Homes required for the mitigation of suffering and misery; when there would be a more pure, full, and complete family life; when there would be homes really deserving the name, and characterised by all that is good in our conception of that hallowed name.[37]

In his prudence about the long-term role of East Park, it was also difficult for Mitchell to say that it was indeed the best place for all of the children who were being admitted, even at this early stage. 'Infirm' children, as in the Association's title, might encapsulate a diverse range of impairments, while the 'imbecile' category represented a quite specific group of children who were mentally impaired – 'imbecile' was a medical classification of mental impairment and not the pejorative term it later became. In early realisation of the necessity to balance prevailing need against current provision, the SNI, located at Larbert in Stirlingshire, was approached and, at a meeting with its directors, the Association was informed that 'favourable consideration' would be given to cases presented by East Park, although this would have to await the realisation of SNI expansion plans.[38]

The Glasgow Deaf & Dumb Institution gave education, training in communication through sign language, and tuition in certain crafts that might provide careers in adulthood to hearing-impaired young people. It declared that no children 'were admissible under 7 years [but] that the Institution is prepared to receive all other children on the list on very moderate terms'.[39] Very young deaf children received by East Park would have to remain there until they were seven, while older children not registered with a poor board as paupers would be received, although financial responsibility for them would remain with the Association. As with 'imbecile', 'dumb' was later to become a pejorative word, but at that time it simply referred to children who were profoundly deaf from birth or infancy who could not articulate. The Deaf & Dumb Institution offered to receive seven children from the Association. Fees had to be paid to defray expenses, but these could be negotiated according to circumstances: 'Each child cost the Institution about £20 per annum, but in the case of poor children we take £10.'[40] The Deaf & Dumb Institution went even further by saying that, in a few special cases, it would take £6 'but it is impossible to go under that sum'.[41] A deal was duly struck with the Deaf & Dumb Institution. Three girls were also admitted to Glasgow Blind Asylum, but an arrangement was concluded with Barony Parochial Board in respect of the Association's continued accommodation 'of a blind boy, John Ferris, who was too young to be admitted into [the] Blind Asylum and was at present an inmate of East Park Cottage'.[42]

On 2 February 1875, a year after the founding of the Association and only a few months after the acquisition of East Park Cottage, residents in the Home consisted of:[43]

	Boys	Girls	Total
Blind	1	1	2
Imbecile	5	12	17
Infirm, Crippled, Diseased	13	14	27
Totals	19	27	46

It was hoped that the seventeen imbecile children would soon be transferred to the SNI, leaving thirty children at East Park. Citizens active in philanthropy were often found to be spreading their energies and largesse around several organisations, prompting Mitchell to urge supporters of the Association who were also subscribers to the SNI 'to use their votes in favour of the children in the Glasgow district'.[44] The SNI admitted three categories of 'imbecile' children: those who were 'parlour boarders' from wealthy families who were provided with superior facilities for which fees were paid; pauper children whose more basic support was paid by parochial boards in their administration of the Poor Law; and children from poor (but not pauper) families who were elected in an annual ballot for admission and support by the SNI's charitable benefactors. Electors of this third category were accorded votes in proportion to the level of financial support they gave to the SNI, so that subscribers from Glasgow could potentially have a notable influence on the election of poor children.[45]

However, this is only a partial picture since, in the preceding twelve months, 226 children had come to the attention of the Association, with various outcomes. Among these, on the positive side, sixty-eight children were being successfully cared for at home by their families. Forty children were at home, but were being regularly checked upon by Dr Bruce because of the nature of their impairments and their delicate health. Furthermore, since the initial explorations by the Association, seventeen children identified as needing support had died. And, highlighting the mobile nature of Glasgow's poorer working-class families, ten previously identified children had already become 'lost' to the Lady Visitors, having 'flitted' from their last known address.[46]

As 1875 progressed, Mitchell addressed a spring meeting consisting of some fellow members of the Gentlemen's Committee and 'a full attendance of ladies'.[47] The tenor of the meeting was again one of self-congratulation. Beatrice Clugston was singled out for special recognition and it was apparent that her involvement with the Association was considered to be a feather in its cap because of her established reputation as a passionate and energetic philanthropist.[48] She had particular concern for those individuals whose support could not be expected to result in improved health, ignored by other charitable organisations, including infirmaries, which felt the need to demonstrate the 'successful' nature of their work by using 'cure' and a return to health as yardsticks.

Mitchell took pleasure in announcing how the proceeds from the Association's recent fundraising bazaar would be invested, estimating that the annual running costs of East Park were expected to be £800.[49] He took further pleasure in his intimation that the health of the children who had been admitted to East Park had 'much improved', to the extent that it was now intended to discharge four or five to their homes or to an industrial school.[50] This action would enable the arrival of new admissions identified by the Lady Visitors as needing urgent care, although the choice of 'an industrial school' is curious as this implies that these children were juvenile delinquents and, in the words of lawyer and researcher Christine Kelly, industrial schools were 'diversionary alternatives to imprisonment for young offenders'.[51] If the choice of an industrial school was made as a preventative measure in deflecting children from being tempted towards criminal activity, it perhaps reflected East Park's negative perception of the child's home environment.

The challenge now, according to Mitchell, was to maintain the momentum of this initial effort and energy which, as already noted, seems to have been challenging during the summer months when some of the ladies went on extended holiday and so placing extra demands on the more resilient of the lady visitors.[52] However, autumn came with the announcement of a setback. On 12 October 1875, the assembled committee members were informed that Mrs McLintock, East Park's first matron, was severely ill.[53] Jane McLintock, aged forty-four, had been increasingly debilitated by liver disease in recent months and died, less than two weeks later, on 23 October.[54]

CHAPTER 3

The Ann Ruth Bowser Years, 1875–1907

The many forms of juvenile infirmity – the maimed, the halt, the lame, the weak,
diseased, and helpless children – present a touching spectacle of human sorrow. …
Some [children] come every year only to die. This is somewhat discouraging.

William Mitchell, Annual Report, 1883

The first Annual General Meeting of the Association was held at East Park on 25 October 1875 and presided over by Alexander Whitelaw in his role as president.[1] The achievements of the Association in its first year were, however, overshadowed by the untimely death of Matron Jane McLintock two days earlier. The minutes of that occasion convey the sombre mood:

> The loss sustained by the Association through the removal by death of Mrs McLintock was alluded to by several speakers and it was resolved that the Association record in their minutes their high appreciation of Mrs McLintock's services to the Home and their sympathy with her bereaved friends.[2]

Among those 'bereaved friends', William Mitchell noted her husband, James, a 'colour manufacturer' to trade, although previously described as a drysalter – a dealer in dyes, glues, colourings and dry chemicals. At the time of her death, the couple lived at 181 North Street, close to Charing Cross.[3] It was unusual for Jane McLintock's role as matron to be assigned to a woman in her position in the middling classes, not only because it was considered unseemly for a married woman of her social background to engage in paid employment when she had a husband to support her, but because of the demands required of the occupation of caring for individuals needing residential healthcare and support. Hospital matrons in the late nineteenth century were responsible for all aspects of the running of their establishments, such as overseeing the care of patients, managing staff, and ordering all the food and other supplies. They required to be totally committed to what was a vocation rather than a job.

Although East Park Home had opened in the optimistic hope that it would only be needed as a short-term expedient in its provision of residential support for disabled children, the appointment of Jane McLintock's successor reverted to the convention of having an unmarried woman for the matron's role.[4] Ann Ruth Bowser was born in London about 1838/9.[5] Employed as matron at an annual salary of £40 with board and lodging, the gender dynamics between the Ladies' Committee and the Gentlemen's Committee were perhaps revealed on 6 November 1875 when 'Mr Mitchell intimated that the Ladies' Committee, after consulting with him, had appointed Miss Bowser as Matron at East Park Cottage Home'.[6] Was this courteous protocol, or was it the case that the final decision lay with the Gentlemen's Committee?

'Her arduous work had been in respects satisfactory', was how Bowser's role was described in October 1876, with the proposal that her salary be raised to £52 per annum after her first year at East Park.[7] This milestone was less than a month away. Two years later, her salary was further increased to £60 annually.[8] In the early years, Ann Ruth Bowser, it might be argued, was given only occasional recognition for her work in keeping East Park running smoothly, yet the lack of regular comments on her role is perhaps confirmation of her dedication and efficiency. That her task was not always easy was alluded to in 1877 when an unfortunate incident occurred, namely that 'at the Cottage Home the Matron had been robbed by a former servant of a considerable quantity of clothing and, considering the circumstances, the Ladies had recommended that five pounds be paid to her out of the funds of the Association'.[9] This gesture suggests that Bowser had lost the equivalent of a month's salary through the theft, while the incident was an attack on the benevolent nature of the East Park ethos. However, this was an exceptional incident and the nursing staff were regularly commended, such as in the warm summer of 1887 when children were frequently moved outside, so that 'their pale faces became quite tanned', placing 'much hard work on the nursing staff' who had to carry the beds.[10]

Dispersal of children with sensory and mental impairments

At the beginning of 1876, the Association continued to wrestle with what were the best arrangements for children with sensory and mental impairments. As it continued to be frustrated by the SNI's inability to admit 'imbecile' children until it had expanded its premises at Larbert, an arrangement was negotiated with Baldovan Asylum, an institution near Dundee that had been receiving mentally impaired children since its opening in 1855.[11] It was the highlighting by Mitchell of the 'sad condition [of] the imbecile boy [Robert] McLintock' that prompted the further development of an arrangement between East Park Home and Baldovan.[12] Joint action with the Board of Lunacy and the parochial board for the parish in which the child lived had resulted in his admission to Baldovan.[13] Further overtures were made by Mitchell to Baldovan through which he ascertained that it had five vacancies that might be secured at a rate of £13 10s per admission annually and this arrangement was concluded in consultation with Dr Bruce and the School Board.[14]

In its first year of operation, Baldovan accommodated eleven children, a roll that had increased to forty-one by 1874.[15] At the conclusion of 1875, it was announced that capacity had been increased to forty-six.[16] In that year's medical report, Baldovan's physician, Dr David Greig, further explained that there had been eleven new admissions during the year, with five discharges and one death, which suggests the possibility that all five additional places had been used to fulfil the approaches from East Park Home.[17] In April 1878, Greig reported the removal of 'Alexander McGilvray on 6 Feby, an inmate since 10 March 1876'.[18] At the same meeting, Baldovan's secretary intimated that he had received a letter from 'W Grant Paton, Secretary to the Society in Glasgow for looking after neglected children asking return [of] £3-10/- for unexpired board for George [sic] McGilvery removed on 6th February', the meeting agreeing to the refund.[19] The surviving East Park records do not name the five children moved to Baldovan in 1876, while the Baldovan minutes suggest that the name of the sponsoring body for McGilvray or McGilvery was not immediately familiar to its directors – perhaps compounded by Baldovan's confusion over the boy's forename – yet Baldovan's reference to W Grant Paton is confirmation that McGilvray was one of the Association's imbecile boys, Paton being the Association's secretary.[20]

Also in 1876, the Association noted its success in securing places in the likes of the Glasgow Deaf & Dumb Institution and the Glasgow Blind Asylum for some of the sensory-impaired children for which it had assumed responsibility in its initial enthusiasm to aid all disabled children.[21] However, Mitchell reported that he was aware of 'three Blind Roman Catholic children whose guardians would not avail themselves of the institutions provided for these'.[22] Smyllum, a Roman Catholic institution, had opened near Lanark in 1864 to receive orphan children and, in 1870, special arrangements were made to receive children who were blind or deaf. By 1881, there were twenty-seven deaf and six blind children in residence, but there were many Roman Catholic families who did not want to admit their deaf or blind children to Smyllum because of its distant location and the difficulty that this presented in enabling them to travel from Glasgow for visits. Equally, Roman Catholic families, and their priests, were not happy about the option of their children going to what they saw as 'Protestant' institutions where their children would be corrupted by being inducted into the ways and beliefs of the 'reformed' churches.[23] They were right to have these concerns, East Park Home itself being guided by the religious convictions of Mitchell and his colleagues, and where Sunday services were held in the Home by Protestant ministers and missionaries, and indeed by Mitchell himself.

Meanwhile, the Association continued to pursue its mission of rescuing children and raising funds to finance its activities. Cases were highlighted to promote the noble nature of its cause:

> The case of an imbecile child in Bridgeton was taken up. The child is gradually pining away for want of proper nourishment, the father has no work and is in Consumption [i.e. tuberculosis], while there is neither furniture nor bed clothes in the house and no relief from [the] Parochial Board was received beyond some medicine. Mr Mitchell expressed the hope that some lady present would visit the child and give what nourishment was required and also report on the case more fully … that the case might be laid before the proper parties.[24]

There is a sense that the Association was beginning to realise that it might have over-extended itself in assuming responsibility for children with a range of disabling conditions, notably where there were other institutions active in the sphere of mental and sensory impairments. In applying to these institutions to admit some of these children, any successes freed up spaces at East Park Home, but did not necessarily remove the Association's financial responsibilities towards the cost of maintaining those children. Accordingly, the Gentlemen's Committee not infrequently expressed concern that initial largesse from the Association's supporters should be maintained and that various additional fundraising avenues should be identified. In one such press notice to keep its mission in the public eye, readers were prompted to remember:

> … that these children are afflicted with incurable, or at least very severe bodily infirmities of various kinds, and are either orphans or are the children of poor parents, in whose houses they were found, in most cases, lying in misery. Special nourishment and medical attendance are required for them. The maintenance of the Home, in addition to the board of the children at various asylums, will require income not much under £1,000 per annum.[25]

Creation of East Park and making it fit for its intended role was a long-term financial commitment that had to be maintained. The appeal highlighted the shortcomings in the provision of relief under the Poor Law, while its mention of some of the East Park children being orphans was perhaps a portent of the rivalry that was to periodically arise between the Association and William Quarrier's Orphan Homes of Scotland.

Meanwhile, following another School Board Enquiry in 1876, more children were being identified as needing assistance, seven or eight being considered as candidates for admission to East Park, while there were 'some imbecile and idiot children, these the Ladies might visit and aid a little'.[26] The new survey and the experience to date of varied needs were perhaps key to the organisation's name being changed to the less cumbersome 'Association for Aiding Infirm Children'.[27]

The Association felt that its work eased the Poor Law burden placed on parochial boards, 'saving' children who, with their families, were living in such dire straits that they were not far from becoming pauperised and in need of poor relief, either as 'out relief' in their own homes, or in a poorhouse.[28] There were instances of parochial boards having families on their registers with children who were disabled and these children might therefore be sent to East Park as part of Parochial poor relief administration. Parochial boards therefore had a say in what happened to such cases over time. As children at East Park grew older and if they became more robust, some were discharged to their own homes, but poor relief cases might be sent to an industrial school, or be 'sent to the country', this being discharge under the widely used parochial system of 'boarding out'. This was a strategy where they were sent to a family in a rural location to live and where they would have the perceived benefits of a healthy country environment and settlement away from urban squalor and the bad influences of city life.[29] The recently opened Broomhill Institution for Incurables, the work of philanthropist Beatrice Clugston, provided a progression for children who were deemed to be outgrowing East Park and three children were admitted there in 1877.[30]

So, within three years of opening, East Park had taken steps to free up places for new admissions and to have a more focused approach by discharging sensory and mentally impaired children to specialist institutions and by transferring children who were entering their teens. Yet other challenges arose periodically at East Park when there were outbreaks of infectious diseases such as whooping cough, scarlet fever or measles. Outbreaks of scarlet fever occurred periodically, an instance in the spring of 1879 resulting in seven children being sent to Maryhill Joint Hospital, expanded upon in chapter 6. This outbreak marked the first occasion when Glasgow's urban expansion earned the developing community of Maryhill a mention in East Park's minutes.

It also was the first occasion on which the Association's ownership of a lair for burials in the Glasgow Necropolis was alluded to.[31] The Necropolis had opened in 1833 as a garden cemetery inspired by Père Lachaise in Paris, which had received its first interment in 1804.[32] Six children recovered from scarlet fever in 1879, but one

Emily's Story

Emily had not quite reached her fourteenth birthday when, at an East Park Board meeting on 1 September 1904, William Mitchell reported that Glasgow Parish Council proposed that 'Emily Gallagher [sic] – Armless Patient' was to be transferred to Broomhill Home for Incurables 'on trial when a suitable vacancy occurred'. Apart from a couple of earlier mentions of children by name when finances were being discussed, this is the first direct mention of a specific child in the East Park minutes. It is unfortunate that her name was recorded with such inaccuracy.

Emily Mary Callaghan was born on 24 October 1890 in the Calton district of Glasgow, one of the localities where Mitchell had been identifying disabled children in his original investigations in 1873. Emily's father, Michael, was a tinsmith and, with his wife, Margaret, they had eight children, of whom only five survived to adulthood, one of these being Emily, who was recorded as having 'congenital deformity of the arms'. Michael and Margaret, although remaining married, were estranged from the 1890s, Michael seemingly going on a downhill trajectory of lodging with his parents, boarding with strangers and finally dwelling in a model lodging house at the time of his death in 1924. Margaret retained the family home, while working as a winder in a weaving factory.

Emily arrived at East Park Home in May 1898 and, during her seven years there, it was claimed, she had enjoyed improving health and 'had been taught to sew and [to] write well with her feet'. Indeed, when East Park recorded Emily as 'removed to Broomhill Home; too old', she was fourteen years of age. From a twenty-first-century perspective, she was still a child, but in 1905 compulsory education finished at thirteen years. Upon her departure from East Park she was described as intelligent and having made good progress.

Receiving support under the Poor Law, it was the parish council that could dictate Emily's future support and she entered Broomhill Institution on 17 February 1905. In 1905, out relief of 28s per three months was initially granted, while Glasgow Parish Council was charged £18 4s 0d for her board at Broomhill. In 1908, her father applied to the Parish Council for her discharge to his care, but this does not appear to have been approved. The remainder of Emily's life evolved around Broomhill Institution, and upon admission she was described as 'well developed and healthy'. She may have spent periods at the two-room family home at 51 Marlborough Street, this being recorded as her usual residence. However, it was at Broomhill Institution that she spent her adult life, during which she had undergone surgery for bowel cancer. This had likely taken its toll, although her death at the age of forty-five resulted from heart failure. At East Park, Emily had learnt, by using her feet, to sew and to write and she was not intellectually slow. Should Emily have been institutionalised throughout her life?

child died, referred to in East Park's records only as 'the other boy', a sad reflection on the anonymity of children who had nonetheless inspired wealthy middle-class people to try to improve their lot. The first interment in the East Park grave had actually taken place in 1875. 'The other boy' was the fifth child to be placed in the grave and he was five-year-old James Tooley who died on 4 June 1879 and whose genealogy is summarised by Gerald I Wells in the panel on the Glasgow Necropolis.[33]

Victorian and Edwardian life in East Park Cottage

It increasingly became apparent that Ann Ruth Bowser was held in high esteem by the East Park directors, but, perhaps because she was an employee, she was not initially included in their meetings. For example, because of high demand for new admissions, when the directors decided to accede to her suggestion in the spring of 1881 that the East Park playroom be temporarily co-opted for use as a dormitory, she was not present to argue her case. While her proposal was unanimously endorsed, her request to the meeting was by letter, and its success was aided by its approval by the visiting surgeon, Dr Bruce, who was accorded the privilege of being invited to the gathering.[34] However, a turn of events saw an adjoining cottage coming on the market that year, an offer of £1,500 was made and accepted, and plans were drawn up for various alterations to be made costing an additional £300.[35] The physical growth of the Home and the wider expansion of the neighbouring Maryhill community are discussed more fully in chapter 18.

The extent of Bowser's responsibilities towards her expanding cohort of children deserves quantification. During the year to 30 September 1889, 110 children had passed through her hands, representing thirty-eight children no longer resident, and seventy-two then living in East Park. Of those who had moved on during the year, twenty-two had returned to their own homes 'much benefited', ten had been reclaimed by their parents, one had transferred to Beatrice Clugston's Broomhill Home, one had been sent to 'Saltcoats Home', one child had been transferred to

Glasgow Royal infirmary, and three children had died.[36] The ten children removed by their parents may be explained by a variety of reasons, including parents and siblings pining for their return to the family dwelling no matter how impoverished it might be. Some of these children were explained by Bowser as being 'very ill [and] were taken away by their parents with the desire that the last few days of the fading lives of their little ones should be passed under their own care'.[37] The three children who died had been cared for at East Park for some time and had been bed-bound for almost the entirety of their stay. They were James Prince, Lizzie Gemmell and John Currie.[38]

In his 1889 report, Mitchell had made reference to 'the varied interests of … children'.[39] By this, he meant the health conditions.[40] These were mostly rickets or various tubercular conditions, but the seventy-two prevailing cases at that moment were grouped as:

Paralysis	13
Spine disease	14
Hip joint disease	12
General struma (a thyroid condition)	10
Phthisis (tuberculosis)	1
Rickets and general weakness	20

In 1893, Dr Bruce optimistically declared that cases of rickets were in decline and represented only ten per cent of the conditions found among East Park's children, attributing this to 'the improved sanitary condition of the city … wholesome houses and open spaces'.[41] Yet, in 1908, this optimism appears to have been misplaced, Bruce reporting the 'high incidence of rickets', yet perhaps with less severity when he reported that 'after a few months' treatment in bed, [those children] were able to be passed into the classroom, and at the end of a year were fit to return to their parents'.[42]

The earliest surviving annual report, for 1880, lists thirty-one children resident with conditions that were classified as: scrofula – 1, paralysis – 4, spine disease – 3, hip joint disease – 2, sores – 5, rickets – 10, delicate/ill health – 3, cripple – 1, amputee – 1 and deformed – 1.[43] In 1908, which reflects the end of the Bowser and Mitchell eras, there were 131 children resident with conditions that were designated as: spine disease – 32, spinal paralysis – 7, spine and hip joint disease – 2, paralysis – 8, infantile paralysis – 6, infantile paralysis and spine disease – 1, hip joint disease – 10, multiple tubercle – 17, amputation of both legs – 1, knee joint disease – 2, chronic hydrocephalus – 1 and rickets – 44.[44] While statistics alone do not provide an accurate barometer of the children's well-being, it is nonetheless evident that city improvement was by no means eliminating one of the most prevalent of manifestations of juvenile physical impairment – rickets.

On more than one occasion, it was noted that some children received at East Park were in a terminal condition when they arrived and the best that the Home could do was provide a little comfort in their final decline. Annual deaths ranged from one in 1888 to fifteen in 1909, a period during which the occupancy of East Park rose from fifty-four to 131 children. Periodically, the death rates had gone into double numbers, but as with statistics for listing the nature of impairments borne by the children resident, death statistics can also be misleading, for example it being noted in 1898 that two children had died in East Park, an exceptionally low figure for this period, but also that two or three had been taken home when the end was close.[45] Echoing William Mitchell's rather despondent quotation that heads this chapter, in 1903, when six deaths in the Home were noted, it was added that some of the children were 'taken home by their parents, very ill, [and] died in a short time after leaving the Home'.[46]

Progress attributed to children at East Park in other spheres, notably their spiritual awakenings, is open to challenge. Religious revelation in the children generated great passion in Mitchell, an enthusiasm that also inspired Bowser and Bruce and was replicated in staff who provided care, including nursing and teaching, at East Park. In 1880, three of the four children who died had declarations of faith attributed to them. David Lavery was supposed to have declared, when asked if he would like to get better, that, 'Yes, I would: but I would rather go to heaven', while Hannah Quin is reputed to have expressed her readiness to 'depart and to be with Christ; which is far better'.[47] Jane Harvey, it was claimed, slipped into death reciting 'Let my sins be all forgiven, take me when I die, to heaven, Happy there with Thee to dwell'.[48] Were these true utterances from dying children, or was it rhetoric targeted at a pious, prosperous and philanthropic audience ever desperate to receive messages designed to loosen their purse strings in support of the Home?

Photographs of the children at East Park Home appeared on the covers of annual reports from at least 1880, when an image of Hannah Quin, who, as mentioned above, died in August of that year, was used, but which unfortunately has not survived the collation of reports into bound volumes.[49] From 1903, photographs began also to appear on the internal pages of the reports, which had a wide distribution as part of fundraising efforts. Over many pages, the reports listed the names and addresses of donors and were used as an instrument to encourage, increase and widen the scope of public largesse. The appeal of the assemblies of East Park's children to Victorian supporters and donors, as they were posed by the photographer, presents curiosities for the twentieth-first-century reader to ponder. This is especially so of the

The 'Giraffe Platoon' evoked imagery that children would associate with the Boer War.

first offering, in 1903, when, before the entrance to the Home, sixteen boys are lined up for military-style inspection, each bearing a crutch over his shoulder as if they had recently returned from battle in the Boer War, while a seventeenth boy, astride a giant toy giraffe, takes on the role of their commanding officer.[50]

Much might be made of the photographs that appeared over the years that followed, but the ploy of using the camera originated in 1879 when the directors decided that 'some photographs of children recently admitted should be taken for distribution among Lady Collectors and that Mr Mitchell arrange to issue a leaflet with photo or woodcut for Sabbath School Union Collection'.[51]

The pulling of heart strings and purse strings was the obvious intent, although the Association does not appear to have engaged in the dual before-and-after photographs used by some other charitable bodies to illustrate dramatic change between the time of admission and discharge – and that, perhaps, is to its credit. The Association did, however, in the narratives of annual reports, describe certain children who had experienced exceptional improvement in health circumstances. Jean Robertson, who became matron in 1908, in a way not characterised by earlier reports, gave details of two success stories. The first, a five-year-old boy, was not named but Edward Knobbs fits her description of a child arriving 'very emaciated and suffering from kidney mischief', who seven months later was discharged 'a strong, healthy little fellow, full of

Mary and Alex's Stories

Sister and brother, Mary and Alex Wright, were admitted to East Park on 8 March 1882. Mary, seven, was described by East Park as having 'rickets; great deformity [and] no education' and, after seven months there, she was seen as '[health] much improved; slow at lessons'. Alex, nine, was described as arriving with 'rickets; deformity [and] no education' yet a year earlier he had been recorded by the census enumerator as being at school.

The subsequent life journeys of the two siblings were quite different. Mary was later described by East Park as being able to read a little, but as being 'a dull scholar'. There had been some improvement in her health, but this was not sustained. She died at East Park on 26 March 1883 and was interred in the East Park lair at the Glasgow Necropolis. Alex, whose physical condition appears to have been slightly less severe than that of his little sister, experienced sustained improvement in his health in Maryhill, and was credited with being 'smart at lessons, knits well, very industrious', to the extent that, in 1884, he returned to his home in the Hutchesontown district of Glasgow 'able to go to school'.

The children's father, James Wright, was a journeyman blacksmith, but having a formal trade did not mean prosperity or a noticeable advantage over the unskilled working class. Their mother, Janet, had worked in textiles, in their native parish of Tarbolton, Ayrshire, but by 1870, the family, which included five older siblings, Margaret, James, John, Janet and baby William, had moved to Glasgow where they lived at various addresses in Govan Parish. Daughter Janet was five years old when she died in April 1871 from hydrocephalus.

The next year, 1872, saw the birth of Alex, and Mary was born in 1874. Then, in 1876, their mother died of a heart condition, aged thirty-five. Five years later, in 1881, James Wright was caring for his six surviving children, albeit that the two oldest, Margaret and James, were now adults and working. As 1882 drew to a close, James, now fifty-one, used the new year holiday as an opportune time to marry for a second time. His new wife was forty-eight-year-old Margaret Johnston, a widow from West Lothian, who brought a fourteen-year-old daughter with her. Did this have any bearing on the decision to seek admission to East Park for the two infirm children, Mary and Alex, earlier that year?

Mary died in East Park one year after her arrival. But, Alex, who East Park had seen as showing much promise leading to his discharge in 1884, was still with his father, stepmother and stepsister seven years later when he reached his nineteenth birthday. He was in employment as a wood carver, a craft that may have had its roots in his short time in the Maryhill home.

life and activity'.[52] The second was described as 'a little girl of five years (quite a baby)' with tubercular bone disease, for whom 'it was thought that an amputation of one foot would be necessary', but eleven months later 'marvellously rapid' improvement was being hailed, resulting in bandaging being dispensed with.[53] This child conforms with the description of Mamie (Mary Hughes), whose progress is described in chapter 7.

Towards the end of an era

Ann Ruth Bowser was sixty-eight years old when, on 7 August 1907, she died at East Park of carcinoma, a cancerous condition that she had been battling for the previous seven years.[54] For over three decades, she had seen East Park grow, through the addition of a series of adjoining buildings, from a cottage accommodating thirty children to an institution with a capacity of 130. The original cottage was now dwarfed by the addition of new buildings, but Ann Ruth Bowser had not been dwarfed by her task in ensuring that the Home ran smoothly throughout that time. Bowser's success in the stewarding of East Park perhaps deserves additional plaudits because there is no evidence that she brought previous experience as either an administrator or as a nurse to the role. She was the eldest in a large family that had relocated from England to Scotland in the early 1850s, her father, William Bowser, running an engineering establishment; at age twenty-two, she was at home engaged in 'household duties', and ten years later she was still in the family home with no occupation recorded.[55]

Dr Wilson Bruce, in attending to the health needs of both children and staff throughout that time, was probably closer to Bowser than anyone else, including William Mitchell, who had remarked of her death as being her removal 'to "The Better Land" to meet so many of the children whom she had so carefully nursed and attended'.[56] Bruce summed up Bowser's life in the following terms:

She was in many ways a remarkable woman. 'Thorough' seemed to be her motto, and she possessed a rare business faculty which, joined to other gifts and graces consecrated to the service of the Master and suffering children, eminently fitted her for the work to which she had been called. With a keen intelligence and observation she was always ready with a helpful suggestion, and seemed equally at home in the placing of a pillow or the fixing of a splint. Her interest in the children followed them to their own homes, and to many young people she had been for quite a generation both a counsellor and friend; several testified their esteem by attending the funeral service. She has gone Home 'bringing her sheaves with her'.[57]

While the kind words spoken by peers upon such occasions, as they sought solace through sentimental reminiscence and spiritual comfort, might be expected, it was perhaps the presence at her funeral of East Park children from across Bowser's three decades as Lady Superintendent (matron) that were a true guide to her stature and standing.[58]

Bowser's thirty-three-year tenure as matron followed the one year in post of Jane McLintock. History was to repeat itself in 1907 when Bowser's assistant matron, Eliza Jane Hendry, succeeded her as matron, but became severely ill in November that year.[59] Hendry had been appointed as Bowser's assistant in 1889, at which point the Home's capacity had increased threefold over fifteen years.[60] Born in the Strathbungo area of Govan Parish in 1865, Hendry had served as summer relief for Bowser in 1887 and 1888, after which she promptly progressed to the role of assistant matron.[61] After being laid up for some months, in 1908 the directors expressed regret 'to record the death of Miss Hendry, who had so recently been promoted to fill the position of Matron', adding that 'Miss Hendry's services to the Home extended over a period of twenty years, and the thoroughness which characterised her work, and the gentle influence she exerted over all, cannot but be productive of good in the future work of the Home'.[62] Eliza Jane Hendry was forty-three when she died from tuberculous enteritis, her short tenure and relatively young age being similar to that of the first matron, Jane McLintock.[63]

While Dr Wilson Bruce was to continue in post for a further decade, William Mitchell, no doubt shaken by Bowser's death, and by that of his wife, Jane, in 1903, retired from his own role as secretary and treasurer in 1908.[64] The loss of Bowser, of Mitchell, who died in 1910 at the age of eighty-four, and also Eliza Jane Hendry, marked the end of an era.[65]

East Park and Glasgow Necropolis

Gerald I Wells

The early trustees of East Park Cottage Home were men of substance. They would have approved of Glasgow's Merchant House establishing the Glasgow Necropolis shortly before Queen Victoria took the throne. The Glasgow Necropolis became the final resting place, especially up until 1900, for the wealthy and upstanding. Into this Victorian park scape, with its extravaganza of monuments, some of East Park's earliest, more tragic young residents were interred. Standard genealogical sources were used to compile these stories. Research has revealed the interment of forty-one children and one adult in four lairs (numbers 68, 71, 71a and 71b) in compartment *Iota* of the cemetery. A further four children were buried in two lairs (123 and 124) in compartment *Omicron*. The *Iota* lairs are congregated around a nineteenth-century 'East Park' gravestone. There is currently no marker on the *Omicron* lairs.

The first child to be buried at the Necropolis was Sarah Higgins, a child of the immigrant population seeking employment in Glasgow's booming industries. Born on 12 February 1864, at 120 Broomielaw, her birth certificate uncompromisingly declared Sarah as illegitimate. Her mother was Mary Higgins, born in Ireland and a cotton-mill worker. Three months later, Mary Higgins did marry, the ceremony taking place in the forerunner of the St Andrew's Cathedral of today in Clyde Street. Sarah's stepfather was Terence Quinn, a pit-head man. He also was born in Ireland.

Over the next eleven years, Sarah gained at least another five siblings, each child being born at a different address, including one in England. In 1872 and 1873, brothers Joseph Quinn and John Quinn were born at Maryhill addresses. East Park Cottage Home opened at the end of 1874, meaning Sarah was one of the first children admitted, perhaps by then in desperate circumstances. On 1 August 1875, Sarah died in the Home, with her death ascribed to 'hip joint disease', a condition she had borne for seven years. Using her mark, Sarah's mother registered the death, but did not bury her daughter. This was carried out by the Home and Sarah became the first of twelve children to be interred in lair 68 within compartment *Iota* of the Necropolis. Her name is the first inscribed on the East Park Cottage Home gravestone.

It is not known exactly when and why James Cree Tooley was admitted to East Park Cottage Home, but his life was tragically short. Born on 3 June 1874 at 18 Cornwall Street, Govan, he was the son of George Lawrence Tooley and Jessie Tooley (born Cree), who had married at their address at 77 West Street, Glasgow, on 28 June 1872. James' father, a journeyman letter-press compositor, was some ten years older than James' mother, a shirt manufacturer.

In November 1877, James' father died at Govan Parochial Asylum. His death certificate described him now as 'a pauper', and, in the language of that time, a 'lunatic', with his death attributed to epilepsy. Clearly, he experienced a massive change in his fortunes and his health in the short period after James was born.

Less than two years later, on 4 June 1879, James, aged five, died at the Joint Infectious Diseases Hospital for the burghs of Maryhill, Hillhead and Partick – later to become known as Knightswood Hospital – where he had been admitted, along with six other children, from East Park Cottage Home. An outbreak of scarlet fever was a serious risk to the children. James was the only one not to recover. Two days later, he was buried in lair 68 at the Necropolis.

Born on 13 September 1878 at 31 Wilson Street in Partick Burgh, George Anderson's birth was registered by his mother, Margaret Anderson (born Pyle), using her mark. His father, Thomas, was a journeyman slater while his mother was a cotton-mill worker. George's parents had married in 1867 at London Road in Glasgow's East End, living at that time at 32 Great Dovehill Street beside today's Barras market. At the 1881 census, the family lived in Kinning Park, by which time George was the fourth of five brothers. His eldest brother, twelve-year-old Robert, was now a mill worker, while nine-year-old James was benefiting from the now compulsory schooling. Two sisters were later added to the family.

In 1882, the family lost their youngest son, one-year-old John, through meningitis. Further tragedy struck on 14 June 1888, when George's father died as a result of 'internal injuries to head and chest', perhaps falling at his trade. George was nine years old. The family home during these events was in Calton.

In April 1889, aged ten, George was admitted to East Park Home for Infirm Children, when he was described as having 'spine disease' and no education. Each year, the briefest of comments on each child's health and education was included in the organisation's Annual Report. For George, these showed a decline in health, but some ability to read.

George died on 27 September 1891, a death attributed to 'spine disease for eight years'. He was buried two days later in lair 71b, the last of the forty-one children buried around the Necropolis gravestone. As with the eleven children before him, his name was not inscribed at the time.

CHAPTER 4

A Philanthropic Triumvirate: William Mitchell, Beatrice Clugston and William Quarrier

… if the philanthropist be poor, it procures him a comfortable livelihood, and many a good dinner at the table of the great; while if he be rich, it gains him a social standing which he would not otherwise possess.

The Bailie, 31 March 1875

Charity has been described as the act of passive giving, while philanthropy operated at a considerably higher level. Philanthropy involved giving on a large scale, but also embraced many wider commitments of a practical nature. These activities included hands-on roles such as organising, and coaxing others to part with their money. For example, within a month of the Association being formed, schemes had been set up to raise money, such as the appointment of a paid 'collector', while an appeal to Scots domiciled in London, and no doubt perceived as making their fortunes as a consequence, was already starting to bear fruit.[1]

In setting up the Association and becoming the guiding hand behind the establishment of East Park Home, William Mitchell (1825–1910) was a driver of philanthropic endeavour. In 1874, Beatrice Clugston (1827–88) had already established herself as a highly motivated woman in her identification of areas of Glasgow life where there were people needing support. Clugston and Mitchell quickly found themselves to be kindred spirits and worked well together in the early days of East Park Home. By contrast, William Quarrier (1829–1903), whose primary interest was orphaned children, was nonetheless, in ways, a competitor to Mitchell and his work with disabled children – because some orphan children were disabled and some disabled children were orphans. This rivalry was sometimes conducted through the letters pages of the Glasgow newspapers. What all three had in common was the deep religious conviction in which they found motivation and inspiration. All three, while enjoying various degrees of comfort by middle age, were not philanthropists as the disbursers of great wealth, but by being motivators, organisers, and cajolers of otherwise passive members of the wealthy classes to support the causes to which they supplied unbounded devotion. Historian Olive Checkland saw Clugston and Quarrier as being members of a very select group whom she described as 'activist philanthropists', 'forcing people to consider the needs of society'.[2]

William Mitchell

The Bailie was a weekly, two- to four-page 'magazine' that profiled local worthies. Launched in 1872, it continued in print until the interwar period. The publisher had a style of writing that liked to court a bit of controversy. In describing city celebrities, he would laud their vigour, entrepreneurship, innovation, generosity, good wit and bon viveur-ship. Equally, he would call them out for the failings he perceived in them, their pomposity, arrogance, stubbornness, and numerous other traits. To be selected as the subject of a guest profile in *The Bailie* must have been received with both pride at being acknowledged as a person of substance, and in trepidation of the writer's habit of cutting to the bone.

Mitchell was featured in 1886.[3] *The Bailie's* topic was education, the importance of results, and therefore 'the system of mechanical teaching'.[4] Success in schooling was gauged, argued *The Bailie*, by the increase in attendance over the fourteen years since the introduction of compulsory education and Mitchell, as vice-convenor of the Attendance Committee throughout that time, was automatically synonymous with any evaluation that was to be offered. *The Bailie* adulated Mitchell for his commitment to the post, his dedication and diligence. Mitchell, *The Bailie* claimed, was 'the most lucid and cogent speaker and the most thorough-going statistician on the Board'.[5] He was also 'a hard-working member of the Juvenile Delinquency Board. Convenor of the Day Industrial Schools in Rottenrow and Green Street, [and] a leading patron of the Kyrle Society …'.[6] The Kyrle Society was one of the many improvement societies active during the nineteenth century. Its aim was to make 'good, dull lives of honest men and women just a little brighter, to give them something to think and talk about, to show them that all pretty music and beautiful things do not belong to places where there is at least the temptation to evil ways'.[7] Effectively, the Society's goal of good conduct, intended to wean the working classes away from rough culture and towards rational conduct and temperance, to appreciation of 'flowers, music, pictures and books' and away from 'vice presented as amusement', fitted well with Mitchell's view of an ideal world.[8]

Much as Mitchell might aspire to a perfect world as epitomised in the Kyrle vision, *The Bailie* then alluded to Mitchell's own imperfections, his 'minor defects' as it called them:

> Our friend is not free from angularities. While possessing the greatly-desiderated Arnoldian quality of 'lucidity', he has not too in large measure this apostle's other endowment of 'sweet reasonableness'. His mind lacks judicial bent. Ever tenacious of his opinions, there is at times no power in the tongue of man to alter him from any project he has taken in hand.[9]

The Bailie writer nonetheless goes on to acknowledge his work, 'work ever without fee or reward, and oftentimes with very bitter attacks for his pains – [pains that] entitle him to the privilege of being entered in the Bailie's Book of Fame and Gallery of Celebrities'.[10]

Mitchell's views, in pursuing relief from poverty, poor housing and destitution as the gateway to children and their families being able to avail themselves of universal education, might be regarded as advocation of a socialist system because of their perceived radicalism in a time of the general middle-class view of the poor as responsible for their own misery. In 1885, he wrote:

> Education is the leading spirit of the age, but education is not food; education is not clothing; education cannot take the place of home comforts, home training, home influences. Children must have the natural and material wants of the body supplied ere the benefits and blessings of education can be either received or valued.[11]

Yet, Mitchell was also deeply conservative in his views. He opposed abolition of fees for education and believed that social hierarchy was a cornerstone to the good order of society. While his obituarist recorded that Mitchell was not an active participant in politics, he wrote that Mitchell was 'a loyal adherent of the Conservative Party'.[12]

Mitchell was driven by his unshakeable religious convictions, which might be seen as both radical and conservative. When the evangelical wing of the Church of Scotland left en masse in 1843, an unprecedented schism known as The Disruption, Mitchell was one of those who immediately committed to the new Free Church of Scotland, joining the congregation of Free St Enoch, where he married in 1850. When, in 1878 and 1879, East Park Free Church formalised its Session and Deacon's Court, Mitchell was there at the outset, becoming one of the Elders.[13] In the 1880s, he had a particular role in guiding new communicants, as befitted his other work with children and younger people, addressing them annually as they were received into the congregation. However, Mitchell tendered his resignation as an Elder at the end of 1896. His letter was left to 'lie on the table meantime', but it seems ultimately to have been accepted.[14] The reason for his resignation was not recorded, but earlier that year there had been a debate about introducing instrumental music into East Park Church's services which had resulted in divided opinion, ultimately settled by a ballot in favour of the change.[15] Simultaneously, a proposal had been introduced by the Free Church of Scotland and the United Presbyterian Church to form a union, this resulting in the congregation becoming East Park United Free Church from November 1900.[16] Had Mitchell taken umbrage over either of these developments?

In his assessment of the man, historian Richard Winters sums up Mitchell's persona as being:

> … a complex character whose motivation for charitable work is the product of varying forces, including his deep religious faith. Through the work of members such as William Mitchell, it is seen that the Glasgow School Board was as much involved with questions of social welfare as with education. The idea of social reform for William Mitchell encompassed questions of housing and health as much as education.[17]

William Mitchell was born in Glasgow on 22 November 1825 to Alexander Mitchell, a jeweller, and his wife, Jane.[18] William's life journey can be traced through the Decennial Census returns, beginning in 1841 when the family lived at 175 St Vincent Street, which was in Glasgow's Barony Parish.[19] In the latter 1840s, William was living in Bonhill in Dunbartonshire and working in the calico printing trade.[20] It was a locality that was a hive of industry, using dyes such as Turkey red and generating industrial output that produced wealth for the owners and toxic pollution for the many manual workers.[21] On 18 January 1850, he married Jane Neilson Alexander Turner at St Enoch Free Church.[22] The daughter of a Glasgow lawyer, Jane was three years younger than William, born on 2 March 1829.[23]

By 1851, Mitchell, still in Bonhill, was managing a calico printworks. With his young wife, he resided in Dalmanoch House, along with his widowed mother-in-law, the trio being run after by a sixteen-year-old servant girl.[24] Ten years later, the Mitchell trio had returned to the fringes of Glasgow where they occupied a six-room house and were again attended by a servant.[25] At this point, William was running his own calico printing business.[26] By 1871, two years before he was to take up his key post with the Glasgow School Board, he and Jane were living in a sixteen-room house at 18 Kew Terrace.[27] It was in what was a predominantly rural location at that time, and facing Glasgow's Botanic Gardens, which had opened nearby in 1843, ensuring an environment of greenery to nearby residents. Kew Terrace was to be the Mitchells' home for the remainder of their lives.[28]

Having returned to Glasgow, Mitchell now described himself as a merchant, and, from 1888, as superintendent of the Marshall Trust. Indeed, he had declared himself as retired from business in February 1886 when, at a meeting of the Association's committee held in his offices at 134 Wellington Street, it was recorded that, 'being no longer in business, he had no need for an office and he asked the Committee to consider whether … they could not make a contribution toward the rent of the office in which the Committee met and also whether they would engage the Clerk in Mr Mitchell's employment to do the Association's work under Mr Mitchell's direction'.[29] Whether his Committee colleagues thought this to be a bit of a cheeky request, or to be only fair, is not recorded in the minutes, but 'after consideration' it agreed to contribute £20 towards office expenses for the next year, plus £30 as salary to the clerk, John Eadie.[30]

William Mitchell as he was caricatured by *The Bailie*. (*The Bailie*)

He may have retired from the calico business, but Mitchell was not the retiring type. Apart from his various activities on behalf of the School Board Attendance Committee and in directing the Gentlemen's Committee (and the Ladies') in the support of East Park Home, it was with the Marshall Trust that he identified in terms of employment and profession for the final two decades of his life.[31] The Marshall Trust originated in the drawing up of a Deed of Trust in 1871 by Glasgow merchant, William Marshall, and his sister, Janet, its objective being charitable provision 'for the education, lodging, board, clothing, and industrial training … of as many destitute boys and girls who were at the time of selection resident in the counties of Lanark and Stirling … and who were orphans or fatherless …'.[32] The resources of the Trust could also be used for the education of certain other children of needy families and it included schemes of support for industrial training and higher education.[33] The ethos of the Trust obviously fitted well with Mitchell's personal outlook in advancing educational provision and in aiding children living in adverse circumstances.

Several trustees to the Marshall Trust were appointed to oversee its governance, one of which, the Trades House of Glasgow, had a representative. The Trades House noted in 1889 that the Trust was 'now in full operation':

> The Governors have adopted a Scheme whereby poor boys and girls, who are desirous to obtain the benefits of higher education, have their railway expenses paid to Glasgow from their residences in the country and other towns. A large sum is also expended in books and stationery.[34]

The terms of the Trust made funds available, by competition, to applicants from Glasgow, Lanarkshire and Stirlingshire.[35] In 1885, it was recorded that 'when the bequests emerged in 1880, the funds amounted to £190,535, and by judicious investment of them they now amount to £224,000, with an annual revenue of fully £8,000'.[36] In 1897, the Trust's capital fund rested at £277,872 10s 8d – no paltry sum. The extent of the fund's reach had been demonstrated a year earlier:

> The work of the Trust continues satisfactory, and the Governors take a very warm interest in the administration of the scheme. Last year 5,000 students received books and stationery; 551 scholars, grants for clothing; 135 senior scholars, bursaries of £10; 169 scholars, industrial grants of £5 for Technical Classes; 44 scholars, bursaries of £15 and £20 for Higher Education; 20 scholars, bursaries of £30 for the University; and 2,050 scholars got grants for fees in evening classes.[37]

Mitchell's post as superintendent of the Trust's very substantial resources and outreach does not attract comment in the Trades House reports except for his attendance at school examinations around 1903 and his decision to retire in 1907.[38] Mitchell's choice of his superintendence of the Marshall Trust as his primary occupation in census returns is explained by the large numbers of young people aided, suggesting it was a demanding job rather than a token appointment. That his name is largely absent from the surviving records is a positive acknowledgement that he carried out this role with diligence and efficiency.

An administrator whose input was obviously in demand, in addition to his other activities Mitchell was a director of the Glasgow Deaf & Dumb Institution and of the Society for the Prevention of Cruelty to Children, an advocate of temperance and served as a Justice of the Peace.[39] Mitchell, as did Quarrier, gave evidence to the parliamentary Departmental Committee on Habitual Offenders, Vagrants, Beggars, Inebriates and Juvenile Delinquents for Scotland.[40] As a teetotaller, he was forthright to the committee about his distaste for alcohol consumption, which he saw as both cause and consequence of lower-order life in general. While taking a slightly more lenient stance towards gypsies who were caravan dwellers, he was scathing in his condemnation of people he called 'tent-dwelling tinkers'.[41] He drew on encounters with these travelling people in Perthshire during holidays in Pitlochry, believing the adults were all drunkards and that the children received 'no moral training or teaching'. While advocating 'moral suasion' rather than punishment, he might be commended in his desire to level-up gypsies to a respectability recognisable to the middle classes, though his views might also be recognised as an intolerance towards travellers that prevails in the twenty-first century.[42] Historian Robert Fell considers Mitchell, stemming from his School Board role, as exhibiting class prejudice in his submission to the Departmental Committee. Fell describes views about travellers expressed by Mitchell in 1895 as being nothing less than 'vitriol'.[43] Mitchell was, of course, in his various duties, used to being interrogator rather than interrogated, and the commissioners were not shy about challenging his assertions, perhaps not least because of his declaration that 'My object is to have [tinkers] extirpated as a class, and absorbed into the labouring population.'[44] As *The Bailie* said, 'Our friend is not free from angularities.'

William and his wife, Jane Mitchell, had no children. Jane passed away after an attack of influenza and bronchitis on 22 December 1903.[45] The combination of bereavement and advancing years subsequently resulted in William reducing much of his involvement with East Park Home and elsewhere, and he died while holidaying in Moffat, Dumfriesshire, on 12 August 1910.[46] He was eighty-four. With his strongly held religious convictions, he would not have seen his demise as an end, but as a staging post on a progressive and continuing journey.

Beatrice Clugston

Philanthropist Beatrice Clugston was a contemporary of William Mitchell and they were similarly motivated in their compassion for the weak and marginalised, and in their religious conviction. The gradual ability of East Park Home to focus primarily on physically disabled children was aided by Clugston's charitable enterprises, most notably in her opening of the Broomhill Home for Incurables. Emily Callaghan, whose story is told in this volume, was one example of East Park child residents who in course of time moved to the Broomhill Home.

Born in Glasgow's Barony Parish on 19 September 1827, Beatrice was the first child to John Clugston and Mary McKenzie.[47] However, a paper trail for Beatrice Clugston between her baptismal record in 1827 and her appearance beside her widowed mother, Mary Clugston, in the 1871 census is fragmented. Mary Clugston was born in Jamaica around 1804. Mary's mother was Beatrice Morton and her father, Duncan McKenzie, was a sugar planter in the Jamaican parish of Hanover. Beatrice had just reached her eighth birthday when her grandfather received £95 10s 5d as compensation for the emancipation of four slaves in his service in Jamaica.[48]

Beatrice's father, John Clugston, died in Larkhall, Lanarkshire, in 1855 when he was fifty-five and Beatrice, the oldest of five children according to his death registration, was twenty-seven.[49] He was a master cotton bleacher whose assets at the time of his death were assessed at £2,627. In addition to his personal household assets of £217 plus £2 in cash, the equipment at his Avonbank bleachfield was valued at £2,233 and included a cow and calves; he had two ponies with harnesses and carts valued at £100 and £75 worth of shares in the Larkhall Gas Light Company.[50] By contrast, when his widow, Beatrice's mother, Mary Clugston (née McKenzie), died in 1881, her assets were detailed at a lesser sum, £1,142, extracts relating to John Clugston indicating a complex marriage contract stretching back to Mary's father, Duncan McKenzie.[51] By the time of the drawing up of John Clugston's will, only his wife, Mary, and daughters, Beatrice and Mary McKenzie Clugston, survived. His daughter Mary died four years later of typhus fever, aged twenty-four, and was buried beside him in Calton burial ground.[52]

Beatrice's humanitarian work began in the unattractive role of prison visitor in the early 1860s. Seeing prisoners' wives and families as victims, especially when they were confronted with ill health as well as poverty, she endeavoured to support them in Glasgow Royal Infirmary when they might become patients. This was put on a more formal footing by her formation of the Dorcas Society, in 1864, to provide help with clothing items and small monetary allowances following discharge from the GRI. Recovery for impoverished people dwelling in poor housing conditions was challenging and Beatrice's awareness of this led to her setting up the Glasgow

Convalescent Home in Bothwell in 1865, replaced in 1871 with larger premises at Kirkintilloch. In 1869, near Dunoon, she founded the West of Scotland Seaside Convalescent Homes. Convalescents' post-hospital care in one of these homes would, hopefully, return them to good health. But Beatrice was aware that this was not a possibility for some people, leading her, in 1875, to found, also at Kirkintilloch, the Broomhill Home for Incurables.[53] In addition to these activities, her energy contributed to the setting up of the Samaritan Society to assist patients in Glasgow Western Infirmary, opened in 1874, and raising funds for the planned Sick Children's Hospital that eventually opened in 1883. Furthermore, funds from one bazaar aided, via the Glasgow municipal authorities, the setting up of Belvidere, Knightswood and Govan hospitals for the treatment of infectious diseases.[54] East Park Home was a bazaar beneficiary when, in 1875, it had a table at an event organised by Clugston in the Kibble Conservatory, re-erected at the Glasgow Botanic Gardens two years earlier from the Coulport home of inventor, engineer and eccentric John Kibble (1815–94).[55] The bazaar raised £815 9s 9d for East Park, prompting the Association's committee to 'record with satisfaction that a valuable screen had been presented to Miss Clugston at the Bazaar from the ladies and gentlemen having charge of the East Park Cottage table in humble testimony of their appreciation of her energy and kindness'.[56]

Clugston was probably already experiencing ill health when, in 1880, she toured several English institutions on a fact-finding mission as she strove to create Homes to provide care for people in Scotland for whom there was no current provision. Her convalescent homes were already established, aiming to bring the likes of impoverished people back to moderate health as they transitioned from hospital treatment to overcrowded homes with environments of deprivation. Her Home for Incurables provided for a group unwanted by the 'royal' hospitals, which really only wished to receive patients who could be restored to health and not to have to care for the chronically sick who had no hope of recovery. Furthermore, mental institutions did not want to admit people who had epilepsy, so Clugston wished to provide for them too. Also, at a time when fever hospitals were just beginning to emerge (Glasgow's Belvidere Hospital opened in 1870), she saw a need for 'Homes for the Consumptive'.[57] She obviously did not foresee a time when all needs would be addressed and when her work would be fully accomplished.

The close link between Clugston and East Park Home under Mitchell's guiding hand is perhaps demonstrated in 1887, when a legacy of £100 was left to what was described, vaguely, as 'Broompark Home for Incurable Children near Maryhill'. The trustees of this legacy agreed that the intended recipient was East Park Home and, subject to the Association signing a discharge, the gift would be passed on to the Home.[58] Mitchell and Clugston saw East Park Home and Broomhill Home as occupying complementary roles and not as competitors.

Spinster Beatrice and her elderly widowed mother, Mary, remained as the only survivors of a once-large family by the time Beatrice had reached the height of her philanthropic work and in the 1881 census both ladies were listed as 'living on invested funds'.[59] Yet they were not wealthy, these funds being the proceeds of a bailout by concerned friends since Beatrice had impoverished herself by unfalteringly coming to the aid of others. The expression 'she would give her last penny to help someone in need' was more than just a figure of speech in the case of Beatrice. While she was spurring philanthropic enterprises such as Broomhill Home for Incurables to success and also helping distressed individuals, she had selflessly disposed of her personal resources to the extent that friends were driven to action on her behalf. She was therefore graciously provided with a house, *Northwood* in Lenzie, and other security during the last twelve years of her life as her well-being became delicate because of a heart condition.[60]

When Beatrice Clugston died in 1888 at the age of sixty-two, she was interred in Kirkintilloch Cemetery, where a poignant and impressive tombstone, the result of public subscription, was placed on her grave. Never having married, and her siblings having predeceased her, almost all in childhood, she had no immediate survivors. Her philanthropic work was her legacy and has been cited frequently over 130 years, keeping her role in aiding poor infirm children and adults at the forefront of public memory. But Beatrice 'the person' has rarely been discussed, most especially her roots. One unattributed source described her, in her early adulthood, with uninhibited candour, as 'short, dumpy, bossy and very religious'.[61] She cared for her mother until her death in 1881 at the age of eighty-five in the twelve-room *Northwood*.[62] Even although the Rev A D Morrison described Mary Clugston as 'a dear old Scottish lady', Mary's census entry shows her birth as taking place in Jamaica, the daughter of Duncan McKenzie, sugar planter, and Beatrice Morton.[63] When slavery in the British Caribbean was abolished in 1834, Duncan McKenzie appears, as noted earlier, to have had a 'minor' slave holding, receiving compensation for the loss of his four slaves hired from a William McIver.[64]

There are few depictions of Beatrice Clugston, so two images have been used frequently and repeatedly. These are a painting and a photograph. A caricature in *The Bailie* was probably based on the photograph, but not on the painting. There is a strong argument to suggest that the photograph reveals distinctive African features in Beatrice. This is in contrast to the painting, presented to her in 1882 'by a number of friends in cordial appreciation of her varied unremitting efforts in the cause of suffering humanity', by Scottish portrait and landscape artist Robert Cree Crawford

Beatrice Clugston as seen by the portrait artist. (Auld Kirk Museum, East Dunbartonshire Leisure & Culture Trust)

Beatrice Clugston's probable Afro-Caribbean genealogy is apparent in this photographic portrait. (Source unknown)

(1842–1924), which projects her in a pinkish glow and with an obviously narrowed nose.[65] This was originally a full-length portrait that hung in Broomhill Home, but a decision was taken in 1953 to 'trim' it to the small head and shoulders depiction that can now be seen in the East Dunbartonshire Museum in Kirkintilloch and depicts a 'Europeanised' Beatrice.[66] What did Beatrice's mother, Mary Clugston, look like, as it seems that her grandmother, Beatrice Morton, was what David Alston, in his exploration of the legacies of Caribbean slavery, terms a 'free coloured'?[67] Was Beatrice descended from a grandfather who was a participant in Caribbean slavery and a grandmother, after whom she was named, who was a former slave? Beatrice was a successful and passionate woman who rose to prominence in Scottish society, yet one who Alston would term a 'quadroon' in the time of her grandfather, while, in her own adult life, she moved in elite circles where she could flourish 'unchallenged by white relatives, [was] eager to succeed, [but where] colour, and shades of darkness, mattered' – or perhaps did not matter within the late nineteenth-century environment where she expended unlimited energy in helping the 'helpless'?[68] How did Beatrice feel about her Caribbean and African heritage – did it inspire pride, denial, indifference – what were her views of the unknown artist's portrait? Daniel Livesay, in his exploration of the complex dynamics of planter and slaveholder families where mixed-race children and grandchildren resulted, suggests that 'when family trees merged, most Britons either suppressed or forgot the African branch'.[69]

How did Beatrice and her mother, Mary Clugston, respond to this aspect of their heritage?

Today, Beatrice Clugston has become an icon, dating from her initial outreach to the families of prisoners and her setting up the Dorcas Society in Glasgow. Her achievements in creating the Dorcas Society, her convalescent homes and Broomhill Home for Incurables have resulted in her being remembered as the epitome of Victorian compassion. Her links with East Park Home have, by and large, not featured in this acknowledgement, while her little-explored family heritage makes her a fascinating subject at a time when Scotland increasingly is having to come to terms with its historic links with slavery.[70] More than a century after her death, the late *Herald* columnist, William Hunter, unstintingly acknowledged Beatrice's compassion, energy and generosity. But he was candid in his appraisal of her persona:

> She was short and dumpy. She talked a lot. She was bossy. Less than alluring were her looks. Often in her chat she became holy. She could quite wear out a drawing room party with her religious energy. If her name was hard to get the tongue round, it became, once learned, harder to forget.[71]

William Quarrier

If there was periodic antagonism between William Mitchell and William Quarrier, this was perhaps not the result of differences in approach, perspective or personal philosophy, but because they had very similar outlooks and beliefs. They had, it might be argued, parallel views on how society, the lower orders in particular, should be reformed, and they were both driven by their unwavering religious conviction, albeit as members of different denominations; Mitchell was Free Church, while Quarrier was a convert to the Baptist Church.

Much has been written about Quarrier, by himself, by his contemporary admirers and by those inspired by his legacy long after his death.[72] In recent times, Anna Magnusson has authored two volumes separated by a twenty-two-year interlude.[73] Her 1984 account was published by Quarrier's Homes and may be expected to place some constraints on Magnusson breaking the hagiographic mould of earlier books. However, she does cite Quarrier's 'strong and determined personality', which translates into him being 'a man who liked to get his own way and [who] was no diplomat'.[74] Magnusson revisited her history of Quarrier's in 2006. Although produced by an established Scottish publishing house, it was done in association with Quarrier's. Several additional chapters were added, one of which addresses 'Past Wrongs'. In recent times, various institutions have been investigated because of allegations of historical child abuse. In former times, appropriate behaviour towards children was defined in different ways, it employed ethics that are now critically challenged, and acknowledges abuses could occur because of a societal naivety from which the lid has now been removed. In the case of revelations associated with Quarrier's from the later twentieth century, Magnusson does however offer an explanation (but not an excuse) as to how such things could happen:

> Quarrier's Homes, like other residential institutions at the time, was in many ways a closed community. Although changes were being made, the men and women who looked after children were largely untrained and there were no police and security checks of the type which are standard today across all areas where adults have care of children.[75]

Innocent environments of care were remarked upon by Joan Black, a nurse at Glasgow's Royal Hospital for Sick Children from 1962 to 1988, who recalled that child abuse 'didn't come over our horizon'.[76] While recent revelations relate to long after the time of William Quarrier, the largely uncritical appraisal of the man has nonetheless continued, Brian Talbot, in 2009, a clergyman writing in a church history journal, continuing admiration of a unique character and a unique institution, but where we now know that checks and balances on certain behaviour were not in place.[77]

Greenock was William Quarrier's place of birth on 29 September 1829.[78] Unlike Mitchell and Clugston, he did not come from relatively comfortable means, writing that '... when a boy about eight years of age, I stood in the High Street of Glasgow, barefooted, bareheaded, cold and hungry, having tasted no food for a day and a half ...'.[79] At this time, he was living with his widowed mother and two siblings. As annual reports for East Park during the Victorian period show, sabbath schools were extremely active in communities across Glasgow and beyond, and Quarrier had some exposure to lessons in one of these, but it was at the age of seventeen that he was introduced to Blackfriars Street Baptist Church, which brought about the religious awakening that was to dominate the rest of his life.[80] In a rags-to-riches story, his apprenticeship as a shoemaker when aged seven marked the beginning of a journey that saw him establish his own shoemaking business by the age of twenty-three.[81]

His personal experience as a street child and his youthful religious awakening were the spurs that, in the 1860s, prompted Quarrier to establish shelters for street children. He increasingly engaged in philanthropic circles with the likes of Annie Macpherson (1833–1904), after whom he named a daughter, and Thomas Barnardo

(1845–1905). He claimed to have learned from their endeavours, but declared that he would not engage in the proactive fundraising activities of other charities, such as holding grand fetes and recruiting legions of lady collectors to undertake door-to-door soliciting of subscriptions.[82] In his quest to found a home for orphaned children, he engaged in what might be called blind faith: 'I would take it as a sign from Him that if He sent from £1,000 to £2,000 for the building of a house … I would go forward with it.'[83] He got his money, £2,000, and while he might have liked to have believed that it came from Him, the cheque was made out by a London-based Scottish philanthropist, Thomas Corbett.[84] The whole expansion of what became known as Quarrier's Village followed this pattern; Quarrier would pray, a wealthy donor would sponsor the erection of a new cottage, and Quarrier would thank God for his gift. His strategy, which all charities of the period employed in some form or other, was described by historian Olive Checkland quite simply as 'moral blackmail'.[85] Quoting an unpublished paper by Margaret McNay, even Talbot concedes that:

> Quarrier was happy to give God all the credit for the funds that came in abundance for his work. However, it would be inappropriate to deny that every reasonable means was employed in marketing and promotion of the work consistent with his religious principles.[86]

While Quarrier was inevitably 'a good man', proclaiming that 'we have no earthly object to gain in the work we have taken to hand', he was a man of determined, even inflexible, willpower.[87] *The Bailie* described him as 'one of the purest-minded and most earnest men living' but, unlike many of the reverential publications lauding the man, it was a journal that liked to shake the pedestals of the good and great.[88] *The Bailie* believed that Quarrier was 'imperious beyond everything. No rival is allowed to approach within bowing distance even of his throne', and 'the narrowness of his view, the intensity of his egotism, give serious cause for annoyance to the more earnest among us'.[89]

The rivalry that sometimes occurred between Quarrier and Mitchell might not have arisen as, on the face of it, Mitchell's focus was on disabled children, while Quarrier's was on orphans, but inevitably the two circumstances could overlap and, indeed, Quarrier had specialist care for infirm and disabled children on his list of ambitions.[90] This aspiration dated from 1864 and so the arrival of East Park Home in 1874 may well have rankled with Quarrier when he was writing his *Narrative of Facts* for publication in 1878, not least because East Park had preceded the fulfilment of his grand plan that culminated in his acquisition of land at Bridge of Weir for his Orphan Homes of Scotland in 1876 and the opening of the first cottages there

A young William Quarrier as seen through the eyes of *The Bailie* artist. (*The Bailie*)

in 1878.[91] An instance occurred in that very year when, in the pages of the *Glasgow Herald*, Quarrier advanced a plan for a cottage for cripple and invalid children to fulfil a need which, he inferred, was not being addressed.[92] An indignant response followed from Mitchell in the next day's edition of the newspaper, in which he wrote that Quarrier was well aware of the role already played by East Park Home and, perhaps in an effort to depersonalise his retort, he also advanced Beatrice Clugston's Broomhill Institution for Incurables in his letter, which, he wrote 'in addition to their large number of adults has many infirm youthful inmates'.[93]

The Orphan Homes of Scotland 'cottages' grew in number over the last four decades of Quarrier's life. The villas, each housing around thirty children under the guardianship of house parents, were laid out along wide avenues shaded by maturing trees and were everything that the wynds off Glasgow's High Street were not. As a self-contained village, Quarrier's had a shop, a school and, of course, a church. Daughters Isabella, Agnes and Mary also devoted their adult lives to the Orphan Homes; William, Arthur and Annie died in early childhood, while the last son, Frank, has not been traced.[94] Dedicated to his project, the village became home to Quarrier, his wife, Isabella, and other family members, and in due course they were buried in the cemetery behind the village church. William Quarrier died on 16 October 1903 and Isabella followed a few months later, on 22 June 1904.

The triumvirate

Mitchell appears to have grown up in relatively prosperous circumstances, Clugston less so but certainly not in poverty, while Quarrier's childhood was spent in absolute deprivation. All were driven by both compassion for the unfortunate and by their deep religious beliefs. Clugston and Quarrier dedicated their lives to their projects, while Mitchell, involved in a variety of spheres and no less committed, was arguably more widely 'spread' in his day-to-day activities. Perhaps it is for this reason that Clugston and Quarrier are marked by having entries in the prestigious, sixty-volume *Oxford Dictionary of National Biography* while Mitchell passes unmentioned. However, recognition comes in different forms and this he received by having an honorary Doctor of Laws conferred upon him in 1901 by the University of Glasgow for his work in advancing education.[95] The three, in their similar and different ways, presented their own unique strands of compassion and endeavour directed at children in late-Victorian Scotland. Their recognition is not so much for their personal monetary funding of support for marginalised children in and around Glasgow, but through their displays of drive and energy to marshal resources from the pockets of the wealthy, whether they be members of the landed gentry or doyens of industrial and commercial enterprise.

CHAPTER 5

Consolidation to Evacuation, 1908–39

Clinics in the City … did a great service in the training and education of mothers, in the prevention of carelessness, and in the removal of ignorance, which was so often the cause of the troubles for the treatment of which Children had to be sent to the Home. With the new environment created through the building operations of the Corporation, with better home conditions and the training of parents there would be less and less need for East Park Home. That would be no disgrace. The Home was a pioneer, and began a great work and had carried it out well.

Sir Robert Wilson, 31 January 1936[1]

1907 had been a watershed year for East Park Home. Matron Ann Ruth Bowser, having devoted over three decades to the Home, died in post and her replacement, Eliza Jane Hendry, was only in charge for a matter of months before she was overtaken by serious illness and passed away. 'Inability … to act on account of advancing years' had prompted William Mitchell to retire in 1908.[2] However, East Park's visiting surgeon, Wilson Bruce, continued to care for East Park's children and staff for another decade, retiring in December 1919 after forty-six years in this capacity.[3] The key directing role of secretary and treasurer was filled by William Bunting and he was to serve for four decades.

The post-Mitchell and post-Bowser years were years of development of care and education delivery within the confines of the now-expanded East Park complex of buildings on the Maryhill site. The greatly expanded Home had to undertake these tasks in times that were to be disrupted by war, pandemic and economic depression. It was, however, an epoch when, through various stages of deliberation and delay, East Park adapted to a setting that had changed from rural to urban, explained in chapter 18, and established its second Home at Largs, discussed in chapter 10. The interwar period was a time when education and nursing, especially for children with impairments, underwent change and development. Healthcare and education provision at East Park is explored in chapters 6 and 7. This chapter covers some other themes that demonstrate societal traits of the early twentieth century at East Park. It remembers some of the matrons who followed Ann Ruth Bowser's long tenure. It explores two aspects of commemoration – commemoration as a means of raising funds from East Park's charitable donors, but also commemoration of children who died and who were not placed in family graves, their last resting places in this period being East Park lairs in the Western Necropolis. The chapter also remembers William Mitchell's successor as secretary and treasurer, William Bunting. But firstly, the chapter discusses a form of controversy that many readers from Glasgow and the west of Scotland will be familiar with, the issue of sectarian sentiment, a prejudice that periodically found expression during East Park's first century.

Sectarianism

The three decades explored in this chapter did not begin with the Board covering itself in glory. The tensions between those adhering to the various Protestant denominations prevailing in the west of Scotland and followers of the Roman Catholic faith have already been noted.[4] Polarisation of the two religious persuasions of Protestantism and Catholicism occurred at East Park in 1909. By surveying the names of East Park's children, it is not difficult to surmise that there was a considerable mix, including many of Irish Roman Catholic heritage. Because of the severity of the medical conditions of the children, a small number of deaths occurred at the Home almost every year. The directors assumed responsibility for the burial of some of these children in certain instances, such as when their families were

Children are drilled in physical fitness against the background of urban and industrial development that was well established by 1908.

living in extreme poverty. The decline and death of a child resident in East Park had particular implications for Roman Catholic families.

A situation arose with the arrival of a letter from the *Glasgow Observer* newspaper. Founded in 1885, it served the Irish Roman Catholic community in Scotland and strove to protect and advance the interests of that community within an often hostile environment. One benign strategy used to bring this to the fore and to promote Catholic civic contribution was the *Glasgow Observer*'s eulogising of the efforts and tribulations of its members in their obituaries.[5] Upon occasion, the newspaper's editor was more direct and, in 1909, he raised the issue of access to Catholic custom and practice at East Park. In this instance, the editor asked the directors 'whether, in the case of Roman Catholic children being admitted to the Home, any facility exists for allowing such children to be visited by clergy of their own creed and whether, in the case of a child dying in the Home, a Roman Catholic Priest would be permitted to administer the last Rites of the Church'.[6] The response of Frederick Young, convener of East Park's management committee, was that 'no provision had hitherto been made for the instruction of Roman Catholic children in their own faith and, when … application was made for the admission of such children, the parents were led to distinctly understand that this being a Protestant Institution no exception would be made in the religious teaching'.[7]

There was no apparent challenge from co-directors to Young's assertion, but when a new constitution was adopted three years later at a directors' meeting convened by Young, there was absolutely no mention of religion or any such sectarian agenda.[8] This new 1912 Constitution was considered necessary because 'the powers invested … in the Directors … were framed at the inseption [sic] of the Home in 1874 and were found to be now inadequate'.[9] This inadequacy was an understatement because the 1874 Constitution was minimalist in its scope and, similarly, it contained no mention of the religious denominations of children who were to fall under its care. Yet, religious bias was perhaps automatically assumed by the dominant middle-class Protestant elites who tended to hold considerable power in late nineteenth- and early twentieth-century Glasgow – a power that was only significantly challenged by the election of socialists John Wheatley to Glasgow Town Council in 1912 and Patrick Dollan in 1913.[10] In instances surrounding the death of a Roman Catholic child at East Park, the inflexible stance expressed by Young and based on dogmatic principle seems particularly harsh and un-Christian, but it may explain those instances where families elected to withdraw terminally ill children from East Park so that they might die at home, no matter how impoverished those home surroundings might be.

If Young's views were laden with an entrenched perspective spurred by his personal values, he was not alone in expressing sentiments in this period that might be considered narrow and inflexible. Andrew MacDonald was a guest attending the thirty-seventh Annual Meeting and who seconded adoption of the annual report in 1911. He bemoaned welfare reforms that had recently been introduced by government. In doing so, as well as criticising welfare as removing personal responsibility, he laced his comments with rhetoric that scorned religious faiths in other lands and typified the British imperial crusade that was soon to be tempered by the sobering events of the Great War and post-war economic depression.[11] MacDonald argued that society was now facing something even worse than 'alien' religions in the Empire, namely state intervention at home.[12] 'Speaking not from any political, but merely from an economic point of view', he claimed, he 'deprecated the present clamour of everything being aided by the State'.[13] The meeting further reported that:

> He could not liken the worship of State administration to anything else than the worship of that great idol of the Hindus – Juggernaut.[14] When Juggernaut, or when the State entered, there was not the least doubt that it crushed some victim under its wheels. It might be a very good thing to have something to worship, but he was quite sure that both the heathen and Christian found more advantage if they worked for what they wanted instead of merely praying for it.[15]

Despite speaking 'not politically', it might be concluded that he was not a supporter of the ruling Liberal Party and he was not a supporter of recent welfare reforms that introduced limited state aid.

The rhetoric of this period, which pervaded the administration of many of Glasgow's charitable bodies, was notably middle-class, male, Protestant, conservative and imperialistic, and was embodied within the circles occupied by city elites in the early twentieth century.[16] Many members of these 'elites' opposed the welfare reforms occurring from 1906 under David Lloyd George's programme of social legislation and they had deep-seated views on such doctrines as social Darwinism, while religious sectarianism had become entrenched in the west of Scotland. East Park's constitution did not express support for religious sectionalism, but in the 'spirit' of the times, perhaps it did not have to. Historian Callum Brown has noted the prevailing tensions that arose during the early twentieth century, such as those related to the formation of the Irish Free State in 1921, and that prompted 'the major cities of Glasgow and Edinburgh [to be] scarred by the rise of sectarian politics and movements'. There was political polarisation of anti-Irish Catholic sentiment while, writes Brown, 'the Church of Scotland and the United Free Church entered a period of the most infamous sectarian bigotry, blaming Irish Catholics for weakening the

Robert's Story

Robert was born on 24 May 1905 and was approaching his sixth birthday when, in May 1911, he was admitted to Glasgow Royal Infirmary, where he was diagnosed as having tuberculosis in the right ankle. The infirmary surgeons worked on removing infection, but he remained in hospital. Four months later, the tuberculosis had spread and the infected area was drained. After this, it was optimistically proclaimed that his foot was 'looking well, almost healed, and having very little discharge'.

However, the disease continued to spread and an abscess in his left arm was incised. Robert's condition was not improving and, on 22 November 1911, it was noted that 'Teale's amputation of foot done'. Teale's amputation was a procedure developed in the mid-nineteenth century where two flaps of flesh, one long and one short, were left to seal the stump following the removal of a diseased limb.

Three weeks after the amputation, Robert was discharged from GRI and sent to Biggart Home in Prestwick. Biggart Home had been opened by Robert Biggart a few years earlier for the purpose of giving respite and convalescence to 'crippled' children. In 1911, East Park Home had twenty-four beds at Biggart Home at its disposal and here, it was hoped, Robert would benefit from fresh sea air and a nourishing diet.

Robert's continuing poor condition, remarked upon when he arrived at East Park in Maryhill in February 1912, soon saw him return to GRI. The tuberculosis that had resulted in the amputation of his right leg was still present in his left arm and was now detected in his right thigh and right arm. Through April and May 1912, Robert endured further 'excavations' and 'scrapings' until, on 10 June, the infirmary claimed he had 'greatly improved'.

Yet it was only in October 1913 that East Park was cautiously able to record that Robert was 'now improving, wounds healed and going to school'. Progress was slow, but two years later, in October 1915, East Park bade farewell to Robert, when it was noted he had 'returned to parents for school'. Now ten years old, it was his education that concerned his parents. And rightly so, because, while his health had finally been restored, his education level was 'Infant 1'. Robert had survived some pretty gruesome surgery, but his education had suffered severely. Yet Robert went on to have a full life, passing away in 1980 at the age of seventy-four.

Elizabeth Hunter
Children at East Park, 1937/38

Elizabeth Hunter, born in 1917, was a nineteen-year-old when she travelled from her home in Dumfries to take up nursing at East Park Home. Interviewed in 1999, she recalled her impressions of her time at East Park.

During the time I was at East Park Home, I learned quite a lot about myself … I got on very well with the children, with the different children. There was one girl. I can still remember her, Chris, because her arm was off here [pointing to her shoulder] and she had four fingers on it. And the other arm was a bit longer and she had a full hand on the end of this stump. And you should have seen her. I was amused by the way she could play the piano. Her shoulders were going down … it was most interesting and she thought nothing about it.

And then there was a lad that I remember – Hector. He had been run over by a train and lost both legs. His arms were alright and he was perfectly right. In fact, he was an ideal lad because he could make a pair of clogs. This was the sort of thing that a lot of these older children were taught at East Park. There was a workshop outside. And Hector could get about better on his bottom, in the corridor, because they were all polished floors, no carpets. And Hector used to tear about these corridors on his stumps, on his bottom, no bother.

And then we had an open day, one day. A benefactor had seen Hector and decided that he was such a clever boy at making clogs and he had a good brain on him. He was about fourteen at the time I knew him. And this benefactor thought it would be a good thing to get Hector legs, artificial legs, so that he could move about like an 'ordinary' human being. And he did this, but Hector wisnae happy with these legs. And we would hear him … we'd got used to being able to hear him skite-ing about in the corridor.

And we'd go into a cupboard for something or other – and there were his legs hidden. And this is what Hector used to do, hide these legs. I often wonder what happened to that lad because he was a delightful boy. He just seemed to stand out wi' the others.

It has not been possible to identify Chris (or Chrissie) with certainty, but Hector was born in Kincardineshire in 1924 (making him seven years younger than Elizabeth) and he was admitted to East Park Home in 1930. He died in Inverbervie in 1977 at the age of fifty-three.

Scots race'.[17] The tensions of this era are highlighted by what historian Irene Maver has called 'a convenient focus for anti-Catholic prejudice', namely the Education (Scotland) Act of 1918, 'which brought denominational schools into the state system … and for staunch Protestants this meant the distasteful prospect of subsidising Popery …'.[18] Issues surrounding sectarianism are returned to later in this book.

The Great War and 'Spanish' flu

Aside from such biases on the parts of Young and MacDonald, East Park's charitable outreach continued to look forward with enthusiastic energy and compassion. The growing number of children being accommodated at the Maryhill home gave rise to proposals in 1910 to establish a country branch. This was to be a drawn-out aspiration, not least because of the intervention of the Great War, but the directors perceived the need for such a facility that would potentially offer therapeutic benefits of clean, fresh air provided by a rural environment. So, in 1912, a 'temporary' arrangement was negotiated with the Biggart Memorial Home, Prestwick, to receive a cohort of children from East Park, a cooperation that was to endure for the next decade.[19]

In 1908, when Jean Caddell Robertson was appointed as East Park's matron, East Park Home had 131 children in residence, a figure that had increased to 151 by 1914, her final full year in post, this tally including children boarded at the Biggart Memorial Home.[20] It was a significant responsibility for a young woman whose duties had been carried out to 'the entire satisfaction of all associated with the Home'.[21] Jean Robertson's successor was Kathleen Jamieson, who was promoted from her post as assistant matron.[22] Jamieson was East Park's matron until 1926, when she tendered her resignation after eleven years in charge.[23] Both Robertson and Jamieson departed East Park through fulfilling the convention of the times, namely that women aspiring to respectability did not undertake paid employment upon marriage.[24] Both prospective brides left East Park with the hearty support of the directors. Kathleen Jamieson was succeeded by Mary MacEwen who, for the previous six years, had been her second in command and who now embarked upon two decades of overall responsibility for the running of the Home.

While the impact of war from 1914 had an effect on East Park, it was not a cataclysmic time for the Home. The aspiration for a second Home in a rural location, a country branch, was placed on hold 'in view of the unsettled condition of the country through the outbreak of the European War', this understatement of the impact of the conflict that was about to unfold reflecting the feeling in the early weeks of the war that it would all be over by the end of 1914.[25] However, by 1915, an increase in the number of younger children being admitted to East Park became noticeable, a consequence of household visits by the Home's Lady Visitors and their discovery that 'the homes of men who have joined the Army often brought to light

Baden-Powell launched the Boy Scout movement in 1908 and within a year his influence was apparent at East Park.

much hardships [sic] caused by the presence of a cripple or delicate child'.[26] We are left to ponder if such male departures for the trenches, at a time when military service was purely voluntary, was prompted solely by the jingoism of the time and societal pressures for men to take up khaki and rifles, or was a useful distraction for some fathers wishing to escape challenging domestic responsibilities, responsibilities that might be compounded by the special care necessitated by the presence of a disabled child.[27] In being 'distracted', they were aided, in the words of historian Ian Wood, by 'councillors, politicians of all parties, lawyers and employers [who] vied with each other to be seen on recruiting platforms, with men of the cloth also to the fore'.[28] In 1916, with conscription on the horizon, a poster headed 'Lord Provost's Appeal to the Young Men of Glasgow' epitomises the atmosphere under which young men were pressured to volunteer 'for the Good Name of our City, and the Honour and Safety of the Empire'.[29] It was initially single men who were being urged to sign up for military service, and not married men with families, but the sense of obligation permeated every strata of society.

At the 1915 AGM, Sir Matthew Arthur spoke of the war having brought 'a higher sense of duty', and a practical demonstration of this sentiment came from Catherine Thom, who had joined the nursing staff as assistant matron that year, but who resigned in 1916 in order to take up 'Military Hospital Work'.[30] East Park had little to say about the war during its final two years and indeed, in October 1916, vice-president James Graham announced to subscribers that 'the war … had made less difference to the work of East-Park Home than might have been expected'.[31]

While the impact of the Great War on East Park may not have been profound, minor war-related decisions were nonetheless made. One of these was prompted by the Educational Institute of Scotland (EIS), the trade union representing teachers, and it was this body's approach that secured a decision for the school staff at East Park to receive a war bonus of £10 annually.[32]

A prolonged 'event' that began in the closing year of the Great War and which, through phases, lasted until 1920, was the global influenza pandemic. Millions died, yet it was not the subject of newspaper headlines, news reports worldwide playing down the gravity of the virus and its consequences for large numbers of people – it uncharacteristically targeted healthy adolescents and young adults rather than the frail and elderly. Spain had not been a participant in the Great War and therefore reported openly on the presence of the virus among its population, with the result that the influenza pandemic became widely known as 'Spanish flu'.[33] UK government concerns about infection and death rates from the pandemic, and the effects on public morale in the aftermath of four years of war and high military casualty rates, were further compounded by the Bolshevik revolution in Russia in 1917. Consequently, there were deep-seated concerns in government that political turmoil aimed at creating new social orders, prompted by war fatigue and despair, and influenza deaths, might spread across Europe. Simply put, after four years of war the population was unsettled and this point was alluded to at East Park when its president, James Graham, said that '… at the bottom of [today's] unrest was a strong desire that the conditions of life generally should be better than they were before the war'.[34]

However, if East Park had come off lightly during the Great War, it did not escape the impact of the pandemic. It may not have made front-page newspaper headlines, but the virus was rampant within the community and it was attacking the young and the fit. Writing in some detail on 6 October 1919, the direct effects upon East Park were explained by visiting surgeon, Wilson Bruce:

> In the early months of this year [1919], during the epidemic of influenza in Glasgow, we had a trying and anxious time. Many of the children had high temperatures with chest complications, and in some a distinct pneumonia was present. Several deaths were due to that cause. Twelve of the staff were ill with influenza, inclusive of the Matron [Kathleen Jamieson], [along with] the specially trained nurse brought in to help during the emergency, and myself. Dr Vera Bruce took charge of the Wards till the outbreak ceased. Nurse Foster developed a double pneumonia and died after a protracted illness. The nurses who kept well during the epidemic gave willing and much appreciated help.[35]

Don't tell the referee: East Park's 1909 football team appears to have an extra player!

Perhaps people had displayed a mixture of stoicism and resilience, but these years of war, pandemic and then post-war economic depression were difficult ones, worldwide, nationwide and at a personal level.

As memories of war and influenza began to recede, the ages to which children might remain residents of the Home was a periodic topic of deliberation. East Park's records suggest that, in the years that mark the beginning of this chapter, children were discharged by their early teens or sooner.[36] The standard school-leaving age had been raised from thirteen to fourteen in 1901 and remained so until increased to fifteen in 1947.[37] While these criteria played a large part in defining 'childhood' in the first half of Scotland's twentieth century, at East Park, defining the years of childhood had been adjudicated as being until the age of sixteen, but were shown sometimes to be interpreted with some flexibility, such as by allowing an additional year 'for completion of workshop training'.[38] This problem of delineating childhood was highlighted by a tragic incident in 1923. Margaret Ross was recorded as being a young domestic servant employed by East Park when she was admitted to Glasgow's Western Infirmary, on 15 December, with burns to her face, body and legs, injuries sustained from an accident while she was making tea in the Home's kitchen.[39] In what must have been a slow, painful death, she succumbed to her injuries three weeks later. The registration of her death by her grandfather recorded that she was fifteen years of age.[40] Yet two and a half years earlier, the 1921 Decennial Census listing of East Park's occupants shows two children aged sixteen and one youth receiving industrial training, aged nineteen.[41] In other words, as an employee Margaret was younger than some of the children being cared for by the Home.

William's Story

At an East Park Board meeting in 1928, it was recorded that Dr Sloan raised the topic of 'the lad William Tyre who is now 19 years old and cannot be kept longer resident … and suggested that he might be employed as an extra outdoor-hand and messenger at a moderate wage and suitable lodgings might be got for him at Maryhill'.

Surviving records have several inaccuracies about William, including his birth at Renfrew on 6 April 1906 – which means that when Sloan remarked on the future of 'the lad' he was actually twenty-two, not nineteen. William's father, William senior, and his mother, Margaret, had three other known children, all older than William. Margaret died from phthisis in 1907, aged twenty-eight and when William was only one year old.

The nature of William's infirmity is not recorded, nor is the date of his admission to East Park, but this is unlikely to have been before he reached his fifth birthday. However, he first appears on the East Park school register in 1913 when he was seven. The capacity of William's continued presence at East Park in 1928 is unclear, but we know that his father had died the previous year of acute lobar pneumonia, and if his father had been ailing for some time, William's departure may have been delayed on compassionate grounds if he was performing some useful role for the home – and if track of his true age had been lost.

When William left East Park, he literally remained within the physical shadow of its buildings, moving into a tenement apartment at 1066 Maryhill Road, and it was from here that he began married life with Jessie McCarron, who was a laundress at East Park Home at 1092 Maryhill Road. At the time of their marriage, William was a gardener, a clue to a useful role that he probably played at East Park in 1928 and before. William's parents had an 'irregular' marriage in 1902, a 'marriage by declaration' that was presided over by two people, a commercial traveller and a traveller's wife. The godly influence of East Park perhaps ensured that William and Jessie's beginning to married life conformed more closely with the values of the Home, as they were joined through a wedding service in Ruchill Parish Church.

Jessie died in 1972, aged sixty-five, having been in declining health for a number of years. William lived for a further ten years, dying aged seventy-six in 1982. It would appear he had enjoyed a healthier life than his parents and it would be nice to think that no small part in this was played by the care received during his childhood and adolescent years at East Park Home.

Commemoration

By the early twentieth century, East Park had developed a variety of fundraising networks to provide a sustained stream of income to support the Home. Regular 'subscribers' included individuals and companies whose largesse was acknowledged in each annual report. Also active in contributing from commercial firms were employee groups, these often representing initiatives that exceeded corporate contributions, or indeed demonstrated support not replicated by company boards of directors. Employee participation in supporting worthy charitable endeavour was not uncommon, and was a conscious demonstration of working-class respectability that countered middle-class depictions of irrational rough culture among the so-called lower orders.[42] This working-class cultural divide, which evolved through the nineteenth century, is described by historian Anthony Cooke as 'the respectable middle and skilled artisan classes who formed the backbone … of campaigns for temperance … and self-improvement' (among other things), being spurred by 'a rich seam of anxiety but also … an equally rich seam of prurience about the behaviour of the lower class'.[43]

There were also 'special contributions' raised at specific events – examples from 1910/11 include £22 0s 3d from a 'Matinee at the Empire Theatre', £12 10s from a collection taken at Cathkin Park, home of Third Lanark football club, £3 10s from St Andrew's Reformed Good Templars, and one guinea from Glasgow Fleshers' Soiree Society.[44] Churches, sabbath schools and Bible classes formed extensive networks that made small annual contributions, while ladies' networks operated in localities in and beyond Glasgow where they collected from middle-class neighbourhoods, generally modest subscriptions but cumulatively making a significant financial contribution. There were also contributions of clothing, old and new, fruit, food items, prams, wheelchairs and cots, toys, books and entertainments.

An increasingly important money-raising scheme came from both the naming and endowment of cots. Naming seems to have originated without fanfare in 1888 with a ten shillings donation 'for maintenance of special cot for one year in [the] new building' under the name of 'Edie', while an undated building appeal, but believed to have accompanied the 1888 annual report, noted that commemoration through sponsorship of an East Park 'named' cot was a much more practical gesture than the likes of a stained-glass memorial window gifted to a local church.[45] Generally, 'endowment' of a cot was a more substantive commitment by the donor, effectively an undertaking to fund the care of the succession of individual children who, over time, occupied that cot. The appeal declared that 'the cost of maintaining a single cot is about £30. Two cots are already being maintained, one is "Edie's cot", the other by the children of Hillhead Parish Church'.[46] By 1939, 'Edie's Cot' remained

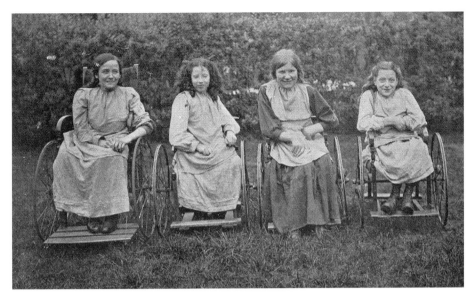

In 1912, four elegant young ladies enjoy a light moment, while their wheelchairs represent a variety of styles.

as the first-mentioned cot on a growing list of named cots.[47] The named-cot concept was a practice employed in other institutions, notably in voluntary hospitals.[48] Out of the carnage of the Great War, the Board saw an opportunity to actively promote the idea of cot sponsorship as a symbol of consolation for bereaved families. At its 1919 annual meeting, the Association urged that:

> … [to] perpetuate the memory of those who have fallen in the Great War, the Directors respectfully suggest that no more appropriate means than this could be found. … The Directors contemplate reserving one of the wards for Cots so endowed or named to be called the 'Honour Ward'. It is proposed that a brass tablet should be affixed recording the names of the donors and in commemoration of whom the Cot is endowed or named. A sum of £1,000 endows, while £100 will name a Cot.[49]

In continuing to publicise this idea a year later, the directors noted responses had not only come from an initial two families, but from Partick Thistle Football Club, and that £150 had been contributed 'towards the support of the Maryhill Charity Football Association Cot'.[50] At the end of 1939, there were nineteen endowed cots at Maryhill, a further fourteen endowed cots in the Country Branch, and there were over fifty named cots.[51] Furthermore, in 1935, 'The Mrs Katherine Cargill Ward' had been endowed for the figure of £5,000.[52]

Space in the East Park lairs in the Glasgow Necropolis apparently exhausted, in 1908 William Bunting purchased four lairs in the Western Necropolis.[53] There were a significant number of burials here until 1914, but with the final interment taking place in 1922. Although child deaths for which East Park had to assume responsibility had slowed, as economic depression took its toll on society and with optimism at a low ebb, in 1923 the directors decided to purchase an additional six lairs in a new section of the Western Necropolis – and also 'to secure the rights, if possible, of [an]other six adjoining lairs with the option of purchase later'.[54] The directors' sense of foreboding in the dark days following the Great War and the influenza pandemic were not, however, borne out. Only three of the lairs in this second section appear to have been used for a total of ten burials.[55] The last of these is a distressing illustration of a child apparently abandoned, or predeceased, by family, this being for Margaret Lee who died in 1963 of cardiac failure as a consequence of congenital heart disease. Matron Jessie Mackay Ross registered Margaret's death, her death registration poignantly recording that the identities of both her mother and her father were not known.[56]

These sad events had fallen out of memory until the research for the one hundred and fiftieth anniversary of East Park was embarked upon. While the first tranche of graves in the Western Necropolis had never been acknowledged by erection of a memorial stone, the second site had been adorned with a memorial recording the names of seven of the ten children buried there. Alas, like many other gravestones in the older sections of the Western Necropolis, it had fallen from its pedestal at some distant date and lay on a slope below the site, enveloped in undergrowth. Like the East Park graves in Glasgow Necropolis, the 2024 anniversary has provided an opportunity to acknowledge the identity of these forgotten children through restorative work to the grave sites.

Elizabeth Hunter
Nursing at East Park, 1937/38

Elizabeth Hunter, born in 1917, was a nineteen-year-old when she travelled from her home in Dumfries to take up nursing at East Park Home. Interviewed in 1999, she recalled her impressions of her time at East Park.

That was my first experience of being away from home. I remember the first day I was there. I never saw the matron. It was one of the other senior nurses that I saw and I was taken up to this room. I said, 'What about the morning?' 'Oh, if you are down at half-past seven at Ward One.' And that is all I was told. So, next morning I went down there and the children were all still sound asleep. I didn't know a thing about them.

Eventually, a senior nurse came in and just started to whip the blankets off the children, those in cots and those in beds. I thought it looked kind of cruel, the way they got them up. However, the children were obviously used to it and thought nothing about it. Those who could walk got their own clothes on. Even the wee nippers, you saw them putting their clothes on, inside out and back to front. I was immediately attracted to these small children. Some had facial disfigurement and some didn't speak very well. But they all seemed to be able to get out of their beds, so their legs were alright. But nobody … the nurses never told me anything about them. And next they went into the dining room.

We had nothing to do with them in the dining room. We had to make the beds and change some of them, of course. I think I had never seen cripple children before. Some of them were diabetic, and one or two with different types of children's ailments. I was a bit upset that I was never told anything about these children. And, if I asked, I was told, 'Oh well, you'll learn later on about what they're like.' After a short time, I began to think, 'No, I don't think I'm going to be as happy here as I thought.' I intimated to the matron [Mary MacEwen] that I wanted to leave. This was less than a month after I had started. She was a bit of a strict person, but very kind.

And then she said, 'Are you a bit frightened of those children?' I said, 'Well, possibly that's what it is with me.' She said, 'Alright, I'll take you round each child and tell you what's wrong with them.' And that was the beginning of the security I needed because this is what she did. And she spoke to each child she met in the corridor, and she would say, 'Well, that child's suffering from …'! They were all crippled children yet mentally they seemed to be alright. Speech was a difficulty with some of them. Or hard of hearing, but I didn't notice that because they could all speak quite well. That reassured me and I stayed on and was glad I had that talk.

But the thing about East Park Home, there was no training for any new nurses going in there. I had never seen a crippled child before and this is why I had difficulty at the beginning. But I wanted to get some training in children's nursing. So, the following year, I left to go to Edinburgh and took the Princess Louise Children's Nurses Training.

A seismic moment in 1927, when some of Maryhill's children departed for the newly opened Country Branch in Largs.

William Bunting (1873–1948)

This chapter began by flagging up, with the retirement of William Mitchell, the appointment of William Bunting as the new secretary and treasurer. On 6 May 1948, during a visit to the Country Branch, Bunting died suddenly from a heart attack.[57] In reflecting upon this occurrence, at the next directors' meeting, those assembled 'stood for a few moments in respectful silence' and recorded 'their high appreciation of his valuable services to the Home for over fifty years'.[58] At the Annual Meeting of Subscribers, held at East Park on 8 February 1949, his 'grievous loss by death' was recorded with the intimation that he 'had done a great deal for the expansion of the Homes at Maryhill and Largs'.[59]

In contrast to his predecessor, William Bunting, who served as secretary and treasurer for forty of those fifty years, seems to have been an unassuming man who quietly got on with the job in hand, to the extent that at no stage did he appear to have any great profile in the public eye. Aged seventy-four when he died, his home was in Cambuslang, where he had lived in comfortable circumstances from the early years of the twentieth century.[60] He variously described his professional life as 'school board clerk' (1896),[61] 'teacher of shorthand' (1901)[62] and 'secretary of an educational trust' (1905).[63] This trajectory possibly suggests a mentoring influence on the part of William Mitchell, but Bunting's 1911 census listing shows the enduring impact on him of benefactors William and Janet Marshall, discussed in chapter 4, as in this decennial survey he described himself as 'Superintendent of Educational

Endowment of the Marshall Trust'.[64] The 1921 census also declared that he worked for an 'educational trust', so maintaining East Park's link with the Marshall bequest.[65] His death registration in 1948 described him as 'hospital secretary', an interesting appellation since East Park had recently successfully argued that it was not a hospital and therefore should not be absorbed within the NHS.[66] However, Bunting's death was registered by his son, Frederick, at that time living in St Helens, Lancashire, so that this might be taken, not as how Bunting described himself at this time, but his son's perception of the nature of his father's occupation.

Born on 11 July 1873, Bunting originated from relatively humble circumstances, growing up in a two-room tenement at 21 Rodney Street, close to the Glasgow branch of the Forth & Clyde Canal, a little over a mile from East Park.[67] His father's occupation was that of 'ship's carpenter', with the likelihood that the ships in question were the vessels that plied the canal.[68] He had two older brothers, John and Archibald, and a younger sister, Elizabeth.[69] Their mother, Mary McDougall, died on 26 June 1879 from phthisis a few days before William's sixth birthday, and nine months later John Bunting embarked on his second marriage, to cotton mill worker Isabella Pomphrey.[70] Like his father, William Bunting also encountered misfortune in the first of his two marriages. He was twenty-two when, in 1896, he married Lizzie Short, daughter of an aerated water salesman, and they had one son, John, a year later, but Lizzie died from lymph sarcoma of the neck in 1904.[71] William was almost

Obviously unaware of the world turmoil that was to occur a few months later, four lads, some in the East Park school uniform, cooperate to repair a steam locomotive.

as swift as his father in taking a new wife, marrying Evelyn Mary Harrison on 23 June 1905.[72] William's second marriage resulted in two children, Frederick William Bunting born in 1908, and Dorothy Evelyn Bunting following in 1912.[73]

While Bunting did not seem to seek adulation during his long service to East Park, his journey from being a carpenter's son to his long tenure as East Park's secretary and treasurer represents noticeable upward social mobility over the course of his life. He was on holiday when the census was taken in 1911, guest of a boarding house in Biggar, and also in 1921, when it was the Hydro Hotel in Pitlochry where he and Evelyn were taking their ease – boarding house to upmarket hotel being one small indicator of William's advancing status.[74] While his personal life was not without trauma, he was able to quickly move on in rebuilding his domestic surroundings. It is perhaps appropriate to consider this chapter, at least in part, as the William Bunting chapter. However, the chapter has not attempted to summarise 'everything' that happened at East Park between the end of the Mitchell/Bowser era and the onset of the Second World War. Rather, it has showcased some key themes and events only. The critical roles of East Park as a place of healthcare and education in the time of William Bunting, and his predecessor, are given separate attention in the next two chapters.

CHAPTER 6

The Healthcare Professionals, 1874–1939

The usual plan of the Scottish [tenement close] … has been all along
essentially bad – a receptacle for foul air, usually closed in at the top and
receiving the effluvia from all the houses on the stair …

William T Gairdner, Medical Officer of Health, c.1870/1[1]

I do not despair of Glasgow's becoming a health resort, provided every family
has a decent habitation and steady income.

Patrick Dollan, Lord Provost of Glasgow, 1939[2]

At different times in its history, the directorate was challenged on the topic of East Park's function. Its name for one hundred and forty years classed it as a 'home', but by 2015 it was operating as East Park School, proclaiming education as its primary purpose in the twenty-first century.[3] However, therapeutic treatment, in various forms, was long a key activity, to the extent that East Park was fortunate to 'escape' absorption by the embryonic National Health Service (NHS) in 1948. Chapter 9 explains East Home's evacuation from Maryhill to the Country Branch at Largs from 1939 to 1945/6, while chapters 9 and 11 explore the often tense negotiations that ultimately resulted in East Park's independence being maintained when other healthcare arrangements were absorbed into the NHS. This chapter therefore explores the nature of therapeutic care at East Park from its 1874 foundation to its 1939 evacuation.

Visiting doctors

Given that the poor health condition ascribed to children by school attendance officers in the 1870s brought about the creation of East Park Home, it should be no surprise that medical intervention and nursing care were part of the regime in the decades before universal healthcare, free at the point of delivery, became a reality in 1948.

Before the era of the NHS, doctors' livelihoods came from private practice through fees from those people who could afford to pay for their services, which was to the obvious disadvantage of the poor, who would only call for a medical practitioner in extreme desperation. Glasgow's main hospitals were charitable institutions, which notable physicians and surgeons attended as their own acts of benevolence to society. Their hospital visits consisted of relatively brief patient examinations during ward rounds, while longer clinical care came from junior doctors at the early stages of learning their craft. The people who provided the real, round-the-clock care were nurses, many of whom were still working towards qualification as probationers.

Given that disability and poor health among children living in Glasgow's most impoverished localities were what spurred the Association to acquire East Park and convert it into a Home, it was inevitable that the medical care of these young inmates needed to be catered for. This resulted in the appointment at the outset of Wilson Bruce as visiting physician. Likewise, alongside 'victualling and clothing', an arrangement for the supply of medicines was concluded with a druggist in October 1874, all recognised as essential for improving the health chances of children discovered and identified as 'infirm'.[4] When East Park Home opened, Bruce entered into a routine of almost daily visits. Dedicated as he was, his stipend from East Park was not what sustained the comfortable life expected by a medical professional in Victorian Glasgow – the Home was just one aspect of his wider medical practice.

The written records of Bruce's early visits to East Park are vague about the

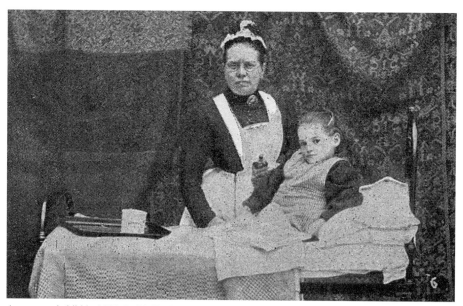

A nurse and child in 1891. Is this Ruth Ann Bowser?

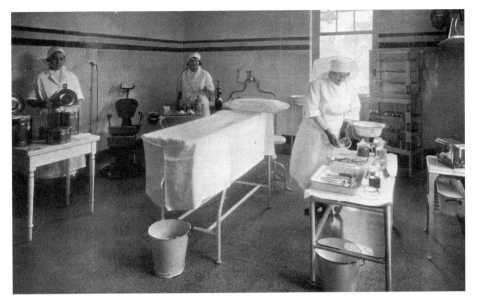

Medical intervention reached its zenith during the interwar period. East Park's operating theatre in 1935.

nature of his ministrations. It might be speculated that he expended much time treating sores and other skin conditions, addressing general infirmity, and directing the nurses on devising diets that would make enfeebled children more robust. In 1890, it became apparent that Bruce's role had now extended beyond the proffered spoon of medicine and the soothing of fevered brows when it was reported that he had recently undertaken a protracted operation on a child to remove a piece of bone.[5] This record does not say that the operation was performed at East Park, but later reports suggest that surgical operations became a regular part of Bruce's regime in the Home. Certainly, by the interwar period, some surgical intervention was carried out at the Royal Hospital for Sick Children (RHSC), which was found to be 'very helpful to the Home in doing all the necessary X-ray work, in fitting children in their splint department with orthopaedic splints, and also promptly admitting to its wards any acute cases that require[d] hospital treatment'.[6] Therefore, by this time, surgical intervention by Bruce at East Park was well established – and demonstrated by a photograph of East Park's operating theatre in the annual report for 1935 – but complemented by specialist paediatric infirmary intervention.[7]

New admissions to East Park were attended by Bruce to assess each child's condition and infirmities, but also as part of a preventative medicine regime aimed at guarding against infections. One report given by Matron Ann Ruth Bowser gives the impression that the resident children reacted with positivity to the glamour they perceived in the grand doctor:

When Doctor arrives he is assailed by a chorus of voices shouting. 'Here is a new patient for you.' Some little girls had arranged a tray of miniature bandages beside a doll carefully wrapped up, and Doctor was told this doll is very ill, her temperature is 102.8. Next day he was told dolly is better, her temperature is down.[8]

By the end of the nineteenth century, a reference to dressings suggests that surgery was indeed being performed on what might be termed an industrial scale, it being noted that two-thirds of the children were 'under surgical treatment', generating a need for 8,000 yards of cotton bandages.[9] Amputations mentioned by William Mitchell may have been performed in the likes of the RHSC, but at East Park Bruce also reported nine children being provided with plaster of Paris jackets, a procedure of intervention in cases of spinal deformity.[10]

In 1919, Bruce had been East Park's medical officer for forty-five years, at which point the Board felt that 'with advancing years he could not be expected to give that personal attention which the duties of the office demanded, or cope with the many new problems affecting tubercular children which would arise in the near future'.[11] How Bruce felt about his retiral is open to speculation, but in a generous recognition of his long service, and to soften the blow that the directors might have perceived, the Board undertook to continue to pay him his then salary of £100 per annum for the rest of his life.[12] That Bruce's task had become increasingly demanding is illustrated

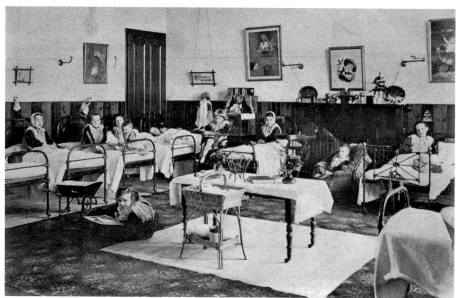

Children in the 1890s. The multipurpose role of an East Park ward.

by a potential successor who decided to turn down the offer of appointment after visiting East Park to evaluate what the post involved, concluding that he would be unable to devote the time required by the scope of the work.[13] Ultimately, the task went to Dr A Bankier Sloan at a salary of £200 annually, double that paid to his predecessor, which, undoubtedly beyond his knowledge, could have been £250 if he had pressed the issue.[14]

Nine months into his tenure, Bankier Sloan reported fifteen operations having been undertaken in the year to September 1920; there were thirty-nine during the year that followed, and fifty-five in the Home's 'operation theatre' in the year to December 1924.[15] Such on-site surgery continued to rise – sixty-four in the calendar year 1925, eighty-one in 1931 and ninety-eight in 1935.[16] While the intrusion of the Second World War, and evacuation from Maryhill to Largs, reduced surgical undertakings, they nonetheless continued. And they resumed at Maryhill when it reopened at the end of 1945, continuing until East Park's later agreement with the NHS brought them to a phased conclusion.

The surgical work at Largs was also constrained by wartime restrictions, the Country Branch visiting surgeon, Dr Herbert Paul, finding that visits from his practice in Millport on the Isle of Cumbrae became virtually impossible because of travel embargoes, so that there were children who had to be sent from Largs to the RHSC in Glasgow for treatment.[17] Matthew White, paediatric surgeon at the RHSC, appointed to East Park as visiting surgeon in 1943, made regular trips to Largs where, of course, evacuees from Maryhill were part of the number.[18] Sloan's role as physician surgeon continued at Maryhill until his retirement in 1948 after twenty-eight years of service to East Park. Declining health was cited by Sloan, but many older doctors, who were used to the freedom that came with independent doctoring and to the often lucrative nature of private practice, also decided not to continue under the new NHS.[19] Even so, it is noteworthy that general medical and surgical care came primarily from the commitment of two men over a period in excess of seven decades – Dr R Wilson Bruce from 1874 to 1919 and Dr A Bankier Sloan from 1920 to 1948.

Nursing round the clock

Clinical guidance and intervention, backed up with medicines and bandages, was not in itself enough. Accordingly, two nurses were appointed to care for the eleven children initially admitted in 1874, soon to be increased to three in anticipation of there shortly being twenty children in the Home. Their annual wage was £15, just £3 more than that accorded the kitchen maid who was also recruited.[20] As will be seen later in this chapter, one 'nurse' at East Park during the interwar period felt that the Home's nurses were afforded such a title to feed their egos, but were untrained.

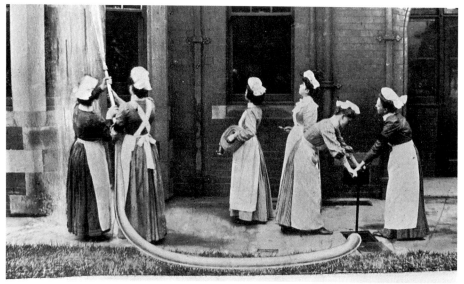

The glamour of nursing. In 1907, nurses participate in a fire drill.

Therefore, it is worth noting the comparison, in 1874, of nurses on £15 per annum, while the part-time teacher received £24 per annum for three hours of work daily.[21]

By taking the 1874 example of Maggie McGill mentioned in chapter 2, paralysed on one half of her body and bed-bound, the duty of care placed on these first nurses cannot be underestimated.[22] Indeed, the improved mobility with which children were being credited after a few months in East Park was reported with enthusiastic positivity in the Annual Reports directed at the Home's subscribers, who were told that '... some of the little children are now able to stand or walk about who have not done so for many months before'.[23] These modestly paid nurses, it seems, were miracle workers.

Following an increase in East Park's capacity from fifty to eighty cots by 1889, Bruce, no doubt wishing to emphasise prudent financial management of the largesse provided by the Association's subscribers, boasted the 'ease and efficiency' that had resulted from the new building, and declared that the increased capacity had only necessitated 'one addition ... to the staff of responsible nurses'.[24] He was generous in his praise of the nurses during the preceding year of upheaval:

> I feel it my duty in submitting my report to state that [the nurses'] work has been performed most ungrudgingly, and often evidently with a true and deep and affectionate interest in the little folk committed to their care. They appear to like their work, which is often more trying than suggests itself even to one familiar with the wards. Just the other day a little fellow

was admitted from a household where there were one or two others quite as ill as he, whose sores were so offensive and numerous that nurse took to summing them up, and was startled to find there were 32 separate wounds that needed daily dressing.[25]

While Bruce's description of this case raises the question of why this child was selected for admission to East Park while his siblings, 'quite as ill as he', were not, it highlights recognition of the dedication of the women who chose, albeit from a limited range of career options in Victorian Scotland, to undertake nursing at the Home. Nonetheless, the enlarged capacity of East Park, as a consequence of the 1888 expansion, would inevitably have placed an increased burden on the nurses and upon Ann Ruth Bowser as matron, or 'lady superintendent' as she was now titled.

The demanding life of nurses was given some focus in 1909 by the granting of a momentous concession – their long hours were now to include an hour being set aside for 'recreation'.[26] However, the directors' magnanimity had its limits. While it might seem wholly appropriate that 'disabled' nursing staff should be willingly embraced and accommodated by an institution that existed to try to restore children with impairments to mainstream life, acceptance of disability within staffing arrangements only went so far. The case of Maria Stroak began with Matron Jean Robertson voicing her concern that Stroak was 'quite unfit for duty owing to deformities due to acute rheumatism', resulting in her dismissal with a 'compensation' payment of £5.[27] Stroak's grade on East Park's salary scale for nurses is not known, but at this time nurses' annual salaries started at £12 so the 'compensation' was the equivalent of five month's salary for junior nurses, less so for nurses of a higher grade.[28] Rejection by East Park, rather than an adjustment to designated duties, may also have been a blow to Stroak that could only be partially softened by the £5 compensatory payment.

Ambiguity surrounds the level of formal training required of East Park's nurses. No evidence has been identified to suggest that Ann Ruth Bowser, matron from 1874 to 1907, had ever trained or practised as a nurse, even though she oversaw with efficiency this aspect of East Park's functions for over three decades. It was perhaps a watershed moment when her successor, Eliza Jane Hendry, upon appointment was directed to make enquiries about securing the services of 'a duly qualified certified nurse as an addition to the staff'.[29] Consequently, Jessie Macnaughton was appointed as a 'Certificated Nurse' from 1 January 1908, her annual salary of £40 perhaps indicating her differentiation as a professional nurse from the girls who, at East Park, were called 'nurses' but were without formal training or credentials.[30] Nurse training, particularly where there might be hospital surgical intervention, had evolved gradually from the time of its introduction from 1860 by Florence Nightingale (1820–

A year before the onset of the Great War, nurses care for some of East Park's youngest residents.

1910) and, by 1900, its importance had become widely recognised.[31] Macnaughton's appointment at East Park was both important and timely yet, during the first two decades of the twentieth century, in terms of required skills and training, the definition of a 'nurse' remained vague and continued until the passage of the Nurses Registration Act of 1919 and the setting up of the General Nursing Council.[32] This legislation, in allowing the process of registration to bed in, laid down that the General Nursing Council should admit to the Register persons who for three years before 1 November 1919 had been 'bona fide engaged in practice' and 'had adequate knowledge and experience of the nursing of the sick'.[33] Therefore, for a transitionary period, some nurses were credited with their years of practical experience as fulfilling the recognition requirements of the General Nursing Council.

There was an indication that a nursing hierarchy at East Park had been in place for some time when, in 1912, it was proposed that nurses' wages be increased. Junior nurses were to receive £12 in their first year, in their second year they would be paid £14 and their third year would be rewarded with £16. Assistant nurses would be paid to a maximum of £18 per annum; and senior nurses to a maximum of £24 per annum. Yet, this is not a reliable guide to any formal teaching and training that might have concluded with an examination and professional recognition.[34] In 1915, when Catherine Thom was recruited, her selection was noted with the observation that she was a 'certificated nurse', perhaps suggesting that she had a qualification that was considered to be a bonus rather than a requirement.[35] What this meant in practice at East Park is difficult to gauge, but as surgical intervention in an operating room within East Park increased during the interwar period, nursing expertise was, by necessity, important.

When a further wages review took place in 1916, a service structure for junior nurses and senior nurses was laid out so that the former were paid from £12 to £20 per annum, and the latter £20 to £30 per annum, both grades receiving increments of £2 over a five-year span.[36] To provide further perspective to nurse wages, in the previous chapter it was noted that the secretary of the Ladies Auxiliary was paid £110 annually, a notable difference that perhaps reflected the directors' notions of her social superiority over nurses, many of whom arrived from working-class or lower middle-class homes.[37]

In 1929, it was stipulated that 'the Assistant Matrons shall be fully qualified Nurses, reside in the Homes [Maryhill and Largs], and wear the distinctive uniform which is provided', perhaps the first formal demand of a qualification rather than nurses arriving with a certification that was seen as a benefit but not stipulated.[38] In reality, availability of qualified nurses during the interwar period, to East Park and beyond, was a problem with which the Ministry of Health was grappling, namely:

> The shortage of trained nurses throughout the 1920s and 1930s had created a situation in which a large part of the nursing workforce was now composed of assistant nurses who had no formal training or registration. The Nursing Registration Acts in 1919 had made no provision for a second grade of nurse.[39]

As the foreboding signs of war increased at the beginning of 1939, Dr J Hunter Kay, physician superintendent, sought permission to conduct Voluntary Aid Detachment (VAD) classes at the Country Branch where he served. This request was granted by the directors, no doubt spurred by sentiments of patriotism, but additional persuasion probably resulted from their knowledge that 'several of the [VAD] members … were Probationers in the Home'.[40] Nursing at East Park was broad in its range by the interwar period, increasingly demanding in its scope, and therefore placed pressure on those 'nurses' who were not 'qualified', or were working as what might be termed auxiliaries.

The qualifications required of matrons and assistant matrons certainly became increasingly important at East Park from early in the twentieth century, but it was the donation of an ultraviolet radiation lamp to the Country Branch in 1926 that highlighted instances of need for nursing expertise. The innovation of this equipment was acknowledged with recognition that 'a special room would need to be set aside … and that the services of a nurse specially trained in this department of work [ultraviolet radiation] would be necessary'.[41] This particular equipment served as a valuable asset for Largs over many years. Its introduction showed that training and qualification of East Park nurses was of increasing importance, but still it remained variable. Elizabeth Hunter, serving as a 'nurse' at Maryhill from the age of nineteen, between 1937 and 1938, believed that only a couple of her colleagues had received formal training: 'They were calling you nurses, but you were actually in as helpers, that's really what you were.'[42] Hunter left East Park to take up a new position where she would receive the training to which she aspired.

Key to the nursing role at East Park was that of the matron and her second in command, the assistant matron. These positions were, by their nature, posts that required dedication and commitment, and as will be seen in chapter 7, ones that were not particularly well rewarded compared to the conditions offered to the senior teaching staff. On more than one occasion, the announcement of her forthcoming marriage by a matron entailed her resignation. This was in keeping with the gendered function of work typical of the times, but also recognised that married life was not compatible with the round-the-clock obligations placed upon East Park's matrons. When Jean Robertson's marriage approached, she resigned her post as matron, but a nice touch occurred in the directors' accession to her request that her wedding take place within East Park Home.[43]

The increased professionalisation of the senior nursing staff by the early twentieth century meant that, unlike in the 1870s, qualifications were expected of job applicants. Some consternation arose in 1917, when Matron Kathleen Jamieson recommended that Madge Kier, working for the Red Cross at Springburn Hospital, should become her Assistant. Kier had nursing experience that included three years at Belvidere fever hospital, but she had not completed formal nurse training. This did not satisfy East Park's directors, but they agreed to employ Kier on a temporary basis as 'chief assistant' to Jamieson at an annual salary of £40.[44] In addition to wartime pressures, this was also the time of transition in the formal introduction and recognition of nurse qualifications. Kier received a salary increase nine months later, but not promotion to 'assistant matron'. However, she assuaged any concerns about her skills because when she resigned in January 1919 she was indeed recorded as 'assistant matron', while her new employers, a new children's home at Mount Vernon, were sufficiently impressed to appoint her as their matron.[45]

An assistant matron had been in post from the earliest days of East Park, Jane Bowser, sister to Ann Ruth Bowser, performing this role in 1881.[46] In 1915, the appointment of a second in command to the matron inaugurated a process of competitive recruitment. The vacant post was advertised in the *Glasgow Herald*, *Evening Citizen* and *Scotsman* newspapers, from which eight applications resulted. Three candidates were invited for interview, all ladies in their late thirties and who had variously trained at the Victoria Infirmary and Stobhill Hospital and whose current employments were at Woodilee Asylum, GRI and in private nursing. The successful candidate, from Woodilee, was Nurse Catherine Thom.[47]

In 1930, thirty-two-year-old Peggy Ligertwood, who had trained at the Northern Infirmary in Inverness, was recruited as a nursing assistant. Most recently, she had nursed at Craigleith Hospital in Edinburgh.[48] Moved to the Country Branch following wartime requisition of East Park's Maryhill home, Ligertwood resigned as 'her association with the Medical Superintendent and the Matron had not been of a harmonious character'.[49] Described more fully in chapter 10, her resignation was accepted, yet later records show that she remained with East Park in Largs and progressed rapidly to be proposed as matron there in 1945. However, with the sudden death of Mary MacEwen, matron at Maryhill, Ligertwood was appointed as her successor.[50] Awarded the MBE in the 1953 New Year Honours, Peggy Ligertwood was matron at Maryhill from 1945 until she retired in 1960.[51]

Outbreaks

The impairments presented by East Park's children have been detailed in chapters 2 and 4, and it was a recurring theme of East Park's annual reports that hospitals and infirmaries wanted to commit beds and treatment to curable cases only and not be burdened with long-stay patients. Consequently, the Home emphasised that many of its admissions were 'children discharged from the Infirmary, hopeless of recovery …'.[52] Additionally, it was not unusual for institutions and hospitals of various descriptions to periodically be faced with an outbreak of some form of contagious disease.[53] While disabling conditions such as tubercular diseases, rickets and polio represented a consistent pattern of infirmities requiring medical attention at East Park, it was the periodic outbreaks of the infectious diseases that invaded Glasgow's wynds and tenements, with devastating effects on children in particular, that were also a challenge to the smooth running of the Home.

East Park had its first such encounter in April and May 1879. Cases of scarlet fever resulted in five girls and two boys being admitted to Maryhill Joint Hospital.[54] By June, it was reported that the girls and one boy were convalescing in the hospital, but the directors were anxious for them to be discharged, seemingly because of uncertainty over what fees might be levied on the Association for their care and treatment. The children's ongoing recovery was pursued by the Association by sending them 'in the first instance, to their own dwellings'.[55] Given that the children had originally been removed from their family homes because of their infirm health and the Association's belief that those homes were unsuited to their well-being, this instruction is surprising. The impression is given that the decision surrounding these six children amounted to the cessation of their residence at East Park, although there was the caveat that 'where the circumstances required it, some of the children would be taken back to the Cottage within a reasonable time'.[56] Freeing up space at East Park would have been expedient because of the Home's waiting list of twenty-five children, Bruce and Bowser being requested by the Board to liaise on '[taking] in the most pressing cases first'.[57]

The source of the fever outbreak, which resulted in the death of the other boy, was, in the view of Dr Bruce, 'traceable to some visitors who had been to the Cottage from infected families and neighbourhoods'.[58] Bruce's view was speculative, the subsequent Annual General Meeting being told as much.[59] Bruce's assumption may have been formed by class prejudice. At the time of the scarlet fever outbreak, the necessity of improving the drainage at East Park was agreed when, 'upon examination, it was found to be in a very defective condition', and £40 was expended on a plumber for rectification work to be undertaken.[60] This remedial labour was, it might be noted, equivalent to the annual salary of at least two East Park nurses, suggesting that it was a significant piece of work.

The incidence of outbreaks of infectious diseases was regularly commented upon in East Park's annual reports, and they carried summaries of the different illnesses that had arisen each year and their consequences. These summaries detailed circumstances which required hospitalisation of infected children and measures taken to contain spread of infection, including quarantining the premises so that no visiting would be allowed while the emergency prevailed. In addition to the outbreak of scarlet fever in 1879, there were other instances such as in 1891, when twenty-two cases of whooping cough had to be quarantined in the Home.[61] If a year passed without serious infectious disease occurring, it was the cause of some self-congratulation. Such outbreaks were a city-wide problem, especially in neighbourhoods with homes that were overcrowded and with poor, or no, sanitation and ventilation. Dr A K Chalmers, Glasgow's energetic and proactive Medical Officer of Health from 1892 to 1925, emphasised the action needed in facilities such as East Park.[62] In 1916, he prompted the directors to devise a new rule which required that 'Any Patient, who after admission to the Institution suffers from any infectious disease, may be removed by the Managers to such other Hospital or other Place of treatment as may be most suitable for the Patient'.[63]

As described in the previous chapter, East Park did not escape the 1918–20 global influenza pandemic.[64] In the twelve months to September 1919, 'several' children were reported to have died from influenza and pneumonia and twelve East Park staff contracted influenza, including Matron Kathleen Jamieson.[65] And, as noted, one nurse, nineteen-year-old Margaret Foster, did not recover.[66] The following year was a trying period for infectious diseases – twenty-two cases of measles, seven of chickenpox, five of diphtheria, four of German measles and three of scarlet fever – with over fifty children confined to bed and the Home quarantined for five months.[67]

Tuberculosis was one of the great scourges of urban populations, such as in Glasgow, during the late nineteenth and early twentieth centuries, and the Corporation of Glasgow had become increasingly proactive in combating tubercular diseases following the discovery of the bacillus of tubercle by Robert Koch (1843–1910) in 1882.[68] Aware of the proactive stance of the Corporation, East Park was optimistically hoping that it would no longer need to admit children with tubercular conditions.[69] However, there was no instant release from caring for tubercular children, and such cases were still a consideration when creation of a Country Branch was being contemplated in 1913.[70] The Home did benefit from various grants, the first coming from the Glasgow branch of the National Association for the Prevention of Consumption in 1916 to the tune of £240.[71] This was followed by a £100 grant from the Corporation in 1917.[72] In 1927, the National Association again provided a grant, this time being a laudable £3,000.[73] Two generations after Koch's discovery, tuberculosis nonetheless remained of concern to East Park and in 1939 six cases of tuberculosis of the spine were recorded for the previous year, along with two of the hip and one of the leg, while a further seven cases of tubercular conditions at the Country Branch were listed.[74]

Six decades after the discoveries by Joseph Lister (1827–1912) that heralded changes in hospital surgical procedures to vastly reduce the spread of infection between patients and from the clinical surroundings in which they were treated, East Park implemented some essential measures to impede the spread of infection. This occurred in 1923 when tiling of walls, to a height of five feet nine inches, was undertaken. The description of this work conveys the extent of East Park's medical intervention during the interwar period because, in addition to work on wards 1, 2, 3, 7 and 9, the operating theatre floor 'was to be re-laid with terrazzo, walls to be tiled 5′ 9″ high and remaining portions of walls to be painted and enamelled'.[75]

Healthcare diversification

From the founding of East Park Home, Wilson Bruce had been an enduring and dedicated presence as visiting surgeon. Following nearly four decades in post, in 1912 he advised that teeth extractions and other dental treatment had been a feature of his work and recommended that the time had come for the appointment of a qualified

Matron and her nurses lead the children in Ring a Ring o' Roses, a children's game that dates back to the Great Plague of 1665–6.

dentist.[76] This proposal resulted in the recruitment, in 1912, of Adams McVey as the Home's first dentist, a role he fulfilled until 1945, with his last five years at the Country Branch due to the evacuation of Maryhill.[77] A flavour of his work was noted in 1913, when the directors were informed that 'the teeth of all the children had been periodically examined and Chloroform had been administered in every case of extraction'.[78] Dental decay, whether caused by the nature of the diet of impoverished children or by poor dental hygiene, was a problem that was to prevail. At the end of 1915, McVey volunteered for military service, but in 1918 he had returned to his visits at East Park and was lobbying for a small dental surgery to be established in the Home, this being agreed to on the proviso that the annual cost did not exceed £70.[79] A few months later, the dental surgery had been completed at a very precise outlay of £59 13s 5d.[80]

While Bankier Sloan perhaps did not wish to be unduly critical of his elderly predecessor, within his first month in post he had made a thorough appraisal of 130 children in East Park. He concluded that forty needed minor surgical intervention, for which he proposed the services of a junior surgeon; he highlighted seventeen instances of ringworm, of which some were long term; to aid infection control he solicited instalment of a steriliser for dressings; and he mooted the services of a dermatologist, all of these requests being acceded to by East Park's Committee of Management.[81] Dr James Mill Renton was recruited as visiting surgeon.[82]

The suggestion of a further area of specialist care had been proposed by director Henry Steele in 1915. This was the appointment of an ophthalmic surgeon. However, this was laid aside until the challenge of creating a Country Branch was resolved, although how the two were connected was not explained.[83] Steele bided his time through the war years, and to his credit again raised the issue in 1919. Dr John Rowan, who had been proposed for the role in 1915, was interviewed, but a decision was again put off by East Park's management committee in order 'to consider the whole question of Medical and Surgical arrangements of the Home'.[84] The subject seems then to have been quietly dropped, and an ophthalmic surgeon was not appointed. In the nineteenth century there had been a rivalry between generalists and the rise of specialists in medical provision. Had Wilson Bruce, in his senior years as physician superintendent, seen this proposal as an assault upon his all-embracing medical expertise, and why it was not taken up by Bankier Sloan from 1920?

In 1922, Sloan, in reporting the 'considerable number' of operations conducted during the year, notably on children affected by paralysis, remarked on the additional benefit that they now experienced through 'skilled massage'. While this physiotherapy appears to have been a new innovation, there were no fewer than five masseuses, Misses Barrie, Cowan, Lodge, Wilson and Allan, providing this treatment on a voluntary basis.[85] Physiotherapy was regarded as a female role in the early twentieth century, masseuses at, for example, the RHSC being appointed and overseen by its Ladies' Committee, and they would not have been regarded as an intrusion upon the physician's work as may have been the case with the arrival of an ophthalmic surgeon.[86]

Conclusion

Sixty-five years after the founding of East Park, the outbreak of war in 1939 saw the vacating of the Maryhill home and evacuation to the Country Branch in Largs. During those decades, the matrix of impairing ailments had undergone some change, but some conditions had also shown considerable resistance to control and eradication.

Living conditions were perhaps not as bad as those described by William Gairdner around 1870, but they had certainly not advanced to being anything near the utopian ideals aspired to by Patrick Dollan. During the period up to 1939, East Park in Maryhill had not only been supported by two dedicated visiting physicians, but had seen medical intervention taking on an increasing surgical nature. Specialist treatment, in the form of dental surgery and physiotherapy, had been brought in to complement general medical care, though specialist eye care had been resisted. But key to medical care had been the role of Maryhill's nurses working round the clock and whose nurse training was variable. The nursing role was, arguably, given inadequate recognition or reward, not least because of the high level of loyalty and devotion shown by East Park's nurses.

Healthcare primarily surrounded the needs of the impairing conditions that brought children to East Park in the first place. But, as seen all too readily in perusal of the Registers of Deaths for Glasgow and nearby communities, life remained fragile for much of the pre-1939 period and before the benefits of antibiotics had become available. That vulnerability to disease was particularly high among poorly nourished, infirm children, and even the walls of East Park Home did not form an impenetrable barrier against periodic outbreaks of infectious diseases such as scarlet fever, diphtheria and influenza.

CHAPTER 7
Teachers and Scholars:
Education at East Park, 1874–1939

It is not without regret that John Ferris, the blind boy, was parted with.
When it is remembered that he came to the Home five years ago, a poor, blind,
ignorant boy, and left it in February last, able to read fluently from raised type,
well-informed and intelligent, it will be admitted that for him the Home has been
one of unspeakable blessing.

William Mitchell, 1880[1]

Work has been adapted to the conditions now met with.
The usual scholastic subjects have their due place in the curriculum.
Handicrafts have had to be simplified, as owing to the increase in the number of
classes, there is a lack of storage accommodation. All handicrafts which involve the
use of various materials and bright colours are essential in the education of paralytic
children. Music is also very necessary and all classes have a piano or a radio.
Broadcast lessons are greatly enjoyed by the older children.

J Maud Fletcher, head teacher, 1940[2]

Caring for children's general health, supported by instances of focused medical intervention, was only one of what was a three-pronged approach to childcare at East Park. In addition to delivering 'home' comforts to deprived children, there were also endeavours to deliver schooling and the basics of education. Given that the founding of the Association and the opening of East Park in 1874 had been prompted by the introduction of compulsory education in 1872, and even as the Home began as a purely temporary expediency, it was natural that schooling should form part of the directors' agenda from the outset.

The opening quotations to this chapter, written six decades apart, give insight to educational challenges encountered at East Park and how efforts to address schooling needs and difficulties were approached. Mitchell's depiction of the journey of John Ferris, a boy whose character left an indelible mark on those who encountered him when the Home was a cottage of modest size, tell us several things. The 1880 statement highlights the early aspirations to accommodate children with a range of impairments before the decision was made to redirect children with mental or sensory impairments to already-existing institutions for those areas of specialisation. It shows how children like Ferris might be totally lacking in education before schooling was made compulsory, and it demonstrates how absence of education did not necessarily equate to lack of talent, intelligence, aptitude, drive and aspiration. The reference to Ferris learning raised type illuminates efforts to offer appropriate specialist aids to the boy, and also his ability to apply himself to learning tactile print to facilitate this process.[3]

Delivering schooling to the children living in East Park had to be flexible, not just delivery of teaching to accommodate children with no, or minimal, earlier outside school attendance, but to allow for different abilities and a cross-section of ages on top of the diverse physiological circumstances surrounding each of East Park's young pupils. While the Home strived to create a school classroom environment in which to deliver education, it also endeavoured to teach children whose impairments inhibited them from joining their friends in a dedicated room with 'blackboard' and desks. The schoolteacher's work was therefore supported by The Ladies (chapter 8), voluntary supporters of East Park who sat with bed-bound children, reading to them, aiding them with the alphabet and spelling, encouraging them to sing, and guiding them to work with their hands in arts and crafts. Education was therefore an activity, both specific and diverse, delivered from the earliest days of the Home.

The origins of East Park as a school

How long the first teacher at East Park, Miss Thomson, remained in post following her appointment in the autumn of 1874 is not known.[4] But, by 1878, it is apparent that Clara Anne Bowser, youngest sister of Matron Ann Ruth Bowser, was firmly established in performing the teaching role, the Association, for example, expressing its satisfaction by approving an increase in her annual salary from £24 to £30. In proposing this salary enhancement, schooling was shown to be falling within the sphere of East Park's 'ladies' as a gendered activity because the raise was subject to the concurrence of the Ladies' Committee.[5] So, while the duties of the matron, nurses and domestic staff were overseen by the directors, provision of education, in the early years, followed a different trajectory in its supervision. The 1881 census, enumerated on Sunday 3 April, lists thirty-one children resident, ranging from five to eleven years of age. While each child is listed as 'patient' under the responsibility of

Matron Ann Ruth Bowser and her assistant, who was her younger sister, Jane Emily Bowser, each and every one is also recorded as a 'scholar', i.e. receiving schooling.[6] Ann Ruth Bowser was the eldest of nine sisters, Jane Emily was the fifth and Clara Anne was the ninth and youngest.

Clara Anne Bowser was born at 30 Monteith Row, a seven-room dwelling in a middle-class tenement overlooking Glasgow Green in the Calton district of Glasgow.[7] Her father, William Bowser, when he registered her birth in 1857, described himself as a 'practical engineer', but the 1861 census gives greater insight to his profession when it describes him as an engineer employing fifty-three men and five boys.[8] William and his wife, Jane, had just one son, while in 1861 nine daughters were recorded; Ann Ruth was the eldest at the age of twenty-two, while Clara Anne was the youngest at age three.[9] It seems that Ann Ruth undertook a special duty of care for her younger sisters. Having grown up under the protective wing of Ann Ruth, Clara Anne perhaps also undertook her teaching duties under the mentoring of her eldest sister as well as directly reporting to the Ladies.

Although recording the children as 'scholars' in October 1881, how well East Park's children were able to participate in even rudimentary learning is unclear. Clara Anne Bowser, referred to, not by name, but just as 'the teacher', was certainly given credit for the task that she embraced. It was a task that was challenged by 'many interruptions through sickness … which speaks well for [her] patience and zeal'.[10] Of thirty-three children listed (an increase of two from the census in April), all but two, eight-year-old Jeanie Morrison who was 'too ill to learn' and five-year-old Elizabeth Duncan, were attributed with some kind of educational progress.[11] Both Jeanie and Elizabeth had hip joint disease, Elizabeth's condition being compounded by spine disease. Yet the extent of schooling prowess overall seems to have been limited, commendation of reading ability among a few of the children perhaps providing some solace and reward to Clara Anne for her efforts, while ability among both girls and boys to engage in some sewing or knitting was often the best that could be aspired to. Indeed, in appraising the children's talents, it was noted that 'nearly all learn to use their hands more quickly than they learn to read'.[12]

In 1882, there were forty-seven children resident at East Park; a decade later there were eighty. While authority to make 'minor' increases in salary to the nurses and servants, 'as seemed fair and reasonable, up to the maximum limit', lay with Matron Ann Ruth Bowser, by 1892 it was the directors who had to authorise increases for the matron, her assistant Eliza Jane Hendry, visiting physician Dr Wilson Bruce and teacher Clara Anne Bowser, therefore affirming the three-pronged hierarchal structure of East Park as residential care, medical care and education. In this instance, each was to receive a salary increase of £10 annually, a decision that firmly places Clara

A crowded schoolroom in 1904 where map reading and world awareness are part of the curriculum.

on record as being not only East Park's teacher, but acknowledges her role as having a status in keeping with that of the matron and her deputy and of the visiting clinician.[13]

The formal style of East Park's early annual reports and minute books, particularly in rarely according women their forenames, has presented challenges to this history. This is not a new phenomenon, it also, in past times, having caused confusion, such as to the compilers of East Park historical booklets published in 1974 and 1988, which credited Matron Ann Ruth Bowser as having teaching within her sphere of responsibilities.[14] This was not the case, but was a consequence of East Park having three Misses Bowser during its formational years. Clara Anne's service was considerable and, when her pending retirement was recorded in 1928, it was noted that she had by then given fifty years of service. For much of that time, it seemed unimportant that she did not have a formal teaching qualification, just as her elder sister did not have a nursing qualification. But because Clara was not a certificated teacher, her retirement after five decades of service did not come with a Scottish Education Department (SED) pension under its Superannuation Scheme for Certificated Teachers. Consequently, East Park proposed that Clara be granted a 'retiring allowance' of £80 annually, this being negotiated with the SED for approval so that it could be accommodated within the 'school account', a budgeting category that enabled an SED subvention to be claimed.[15] Clara Bowser was already seventy when she retired and she died in 1941 at the age of eighty-three.[16]

Delivery of 'education'

Early annual reports had little to say about education at East Park other than commenting briefly on individual attainment against each child's name on the lists of residents published until 1909. These comments ranged from 'no education' through to laudatory entries such as 'good scholar'. Training in needlework and woodcarving were periodically mentioned, but it was Matron Ann Ruth Bowser, not teacher Clara Anne Bowser, who was given the privilege of reporting on both craft training and scholastic aspects of activity, such as in 1893 when she informed subscribers that:

> As regards those who are able to attend the class-room, the work progressed favourably. Some children learn quickly, and are interested in their lessons; but others are very backward, owing chiefly to their physical infirmities.[17]

Aside from variations in aptitude attributed to the impact of 'physical infirmities', it has to be recognised that some children had never received any previous schooling, a situation that harks back to the impetus for the founding of East Park Home in 1874 – to receive children too infirm to attend school following the introduction of compulsory education across Scotland. What teaching took place by the 1890s appears to have been largely informal in respect of those children too infirm to attend Clara Bowser's classroom, and consequently twenty-four 'ladies' were thanked by the directors in 1895 for having 'taught and read to the children in the dormitories', so giving an indication of the scale of their voluntary input.[18]

For more than three decades, delivery of education followed a familiar pattern, one under which reward and frustration were regular companions for Clara Bowser, such as reported by her elder sister in 1903:

> School work is generally slow work with us – owing to the infirmity and weakness of the children, and the age they reach before they begin lessons – so that results are often disappointing, some children after two years of teaching scarcely know their letters. Yet it is a satisfaction to know that by the aid of lady visitors many of the children, although quite bed-ridden, learn to read and can thus while away many weary hours. These latter are fond of doing a little knitting or sewing, and although not rapid workers are very neat and precise.[19]

Some changes had already taken place through Glasgow Corporation setting up 'cripple' classes so that some physically disabled remained in their own communities, explained by Wilson Bruce, reporting in 1903, that 'children suffering from simpler ailments, whom we used to admit, are now sent to the cripple classes under the care

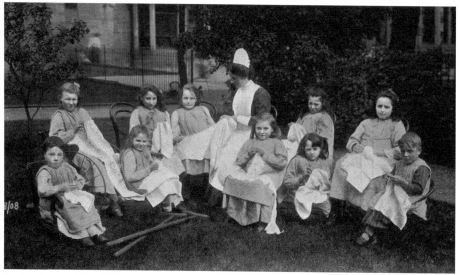

Sewing for the girls in 1908 ...

of the School Board, which are found very helpful'.[20]

However, winds of change were blowing in 1908 when East Park director James Graham proposed that Glasgow School Board should be approached 'with a view to the school being recognised by the Scotch Education Department [SED] as a School for Defective Children'.[21] Dialogue between the Home and the education authorities slowly moved forward over the next four years as requirements, such as additional school rooms and teachers, were considered by the directors, as were the costs involved. Yet, in 1907, Clara Bowser had already been 'granted leave of absence for one month ... in order that she might attend one of the special classes for Cripple Children under the Glasgow School Board so as to obtain a more intimate knowledge of the character of the work performed there'.[22] Nonetheless, this induction did not amount to Clara having a formal teaching qualification and, until this time, East Park had been operating outwith formal and statutory education parameters, fulfilling what it saw as both a need and a responsibility, but detached from outside guidance and regulation.

A benefit of SED recognition was that East Park could access certain grants, but it was apparent that this was accompanied by a requirement to invest in employing certificated teachers, setting up formal classrooms and to conforming with the needs of what the SED termed a 'cripple school'; East Park's previous independence had to give way to compromise, cooperation and compliance.[23] Therefore, in 1912, East Park actively sought the help of the School Board in upgrading its teaching staff. The Board recommended Anna Irving to take charge and she was appointed as head teacher at an annual salary of £105, rising to £120 over the next three years, while Clara Bowser continued as a teacher.[24] Money was an ever-present facet of East Park's educational role and, while recognition required additional outlay and investment in schooling, from 1 November 1912 East Park was able to avail itself of an annual grant under the Day Schools Code.[25] This grant provided £160 at the end of the first year but, with operating costs totalling £301, negotiations resulted in the shortfall being made up by the school boards of Glasgow, Cathcart, Govan and Shettleston, there being children then in residence at East Park from across these areas.[26] The financial equation had, however, changed markedly by 1915 when, with the SED having approved a substantial increase under the annual Parliamentary Grant, by the year-end East Park found itself in the happy situation of having received £543 while its outlays came to £331.[27] After enquiry, East Park established that such surpluses did not have to be returned, but could be spent on maintaining children who were on the school role.[28] Furthermore, a report from H M Inspector of Schools concluded that 'the children are treated with real sympathy and tact and that [their] very satisfactory progress … is admirable'.[29]

While the transition from 'independence' to SED 'grant-supported' schooling appears to have been progressively successful and fruitful, the educational needs of East Park's children remained apart from wider developments in the city for children with disabilities. This was commented upon by James Graham, now vice-president of the Association, at the annual meeting held in the Home on 13 October 1915.

… while the boys are engaged in wood carving.

His conclusions about prevailing education needs and provision were summed up in the reporting of his remarks to East Park's subscribers and supporters:

> Alluding to the cripple schools which had been started by the School Board, Mr Graham stated that there is no overlapping, as the majority of the children in the Home were not sufficiently well to send to the schools. They were taught woodwork and metal-work, in which many had become very proficient, and the Inspector, who had paid a visit to the Home that week, had expressed satisfaction with the progress the children had made.[30]

Graham's statement probably states in succinct form the reality surrounding the diversity to be found in the children's abilities to learn and the challenges arising in delivery of both teaching and skills training. There were, however, children who might be described as success stories, both in terms of scholastic achievement and improved physique. One of these was Mamie, who, unusually, was named as well as photographed (perhaps reluctantly going by her expression) for the 1909 annual report. Mamie was described as arriving at the Home when she was five years old. Weighing seventeen pounds, eight ounces, there were tubercular sores on her hands and feet, and she was described as being in a fragile condition. As far as can be discerned, this child was Mary Hughes, who was admitted in October 1907. Mary was also annotated as being unable to speak, but by 1909 she was attending the infant class and, much improved, was now able to run about. It is a singular instance during this period when we are able to put both a face and a name to one of East Park's children.[31]

In the earliest days of East Park, it had been noted that 'the children generally are fond of singing and learn quickly, especially the girls', but that 'nearly all learn to use their hands more quickly than they learn to read'.[32] While some children were benefiting from being taught writing, reading and arithmetic, such as those admitted because of mobility challenges from the likes of polio or accidents, it is apparent that nurturing in practical handicraft skills held a dominant place in East Park's ambitions to equip children as they grew towards adolescence and adulthood. In 1890, Ann Ruth Bowser reported that some school-age children were 'as helpless as infants', but that others were developing skills in woodworking. She explained how interested 'ladies' had helped this come about:

> Mrs Wilson and her friends presented us with a set of tools, and Miss Henderson of the Kyrle Society taught a small class at the Home, with the result that two of our former patients have been admitted as apprentices to

wood-carving in a large manufactory in the city. Some boys, owing to their infirmities, have not strength to use the tools. Others have been at work, and have carved a number of articles which we offer for sale, and we hope this will lead to profitable employment for them.[33]

This brief report illustrates philanthropy at work by East Park's ladies, it shows how effective training in a craft skill could be, but also highlights how diverse physiological circumstances could deny participation to some children and therefore how schooling and training generally had to accommodate a diverse range of needs.

Two decades later, data was provided on sixty-eight children who had left the Home during 1914/15.[34] Forty-six departing children were listed as progressing to mainstream school attendance, but included two to 'cripple class'; their levels of education ranged from 'Infant 1' to three children who were 'Senior 1', namely ten-year-old William, eleven-year-old Gracie and thirteen-year-old Annie.[35]

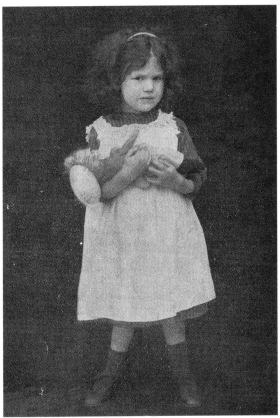

Mamie represents a rare instance in the history of East Park
where it is possible to link a child to a photographic image.

The vast majority of the children on the list had arrived at East Park with no education, suggestive that Anna Irving and Clara Bowser had a significant impact upon children able to participate in the Home's schooling provision, despite their periodic admission of the challenges encountered, and while recognising that annual reports liked to regale subscribers with a narrative of positivity and optimism.

East Park's early records often boasted successful outcomes of departed children who, it claimed, were now making their way in the world. It is probable that children singled out for special mention were carefully selected as glowing examples from an inevitably varied range. However, a warming remark, in 1915, gave instances that come with some substance. This concerned two young women who were still at East Park well after their terms as child 'scholars' were over, but who were, arguably, indeed 'making their way in the world'. That year, the management committee of East Park recorded its recommendation that:

> Nellie Branigan and Sarah Lochhead, who were formerly inmates of the Home, but who for some years had been employed on the Staff – the former as a ward teacher and the latter as ward teacher and clerkess and had given every satisfaction, should in future be recognised as members of the permanent staff. Nellie Branigan was meantime in receipt of a wage of £10 per annum and Sarah Lochhead £6, but the Committee agreed that, as from the 1st [March 1915], the former should receive £12 10s and the latter £10 per annum.[36]

Nellie Branagan, Branigan or Brannagan was seven years old when she was admitted to East Park in November 1890 with general struma (spine disease) and sores, and with no education.[37] Nine years later, she was recorded as 'health improved, sores healed, [yet] still delicate' but a 'fair scholar'.[38] Sarah Ann Lochhead was admitted in November 1896 at the age of five, the victim of an accident, having been 'run over, legs amputated', but 'beginning lessons'.[39] In 1905, she was the longest resident child of East Park, acknowledged as a 'bright, intelligent scholar' in good health; the observation that, by 1906, she had 'disappeared' from listings without being recorded as leaving suggests that she transitioned directly from being an 'inmate' to being a staff member.[40] Both young women were, in 1915, examples where the directors felt genuine pride in reporting that they had overcome challenging physiological childhood circumstances to successfully absorb the 'benefits of the institution', progressing from being beneficiaries of, to being benefits *to* East Park. Their role as 'ward teachers' suggests a move from sole reliance upon Lady Visitors to deliver education to bed-bound children.

Practical skills with a view to adult self-sufficiency. Here, boys are taught cobbling in 1934.

More than just 'education'

Education of young children, in simplistic terms, is thought of as the 'three Rs', reading, writing and [a]rithmetic. Other institutions for children with impairments, such as the SNI, began their educational aspiration with this in mind, but through experience learned that education had to be adapted to include training.[41] Nurse Mairi Smyth, speaking about education at the Country Branch in the 1980s, argued that teaching its children to read and write needed to be balanced with training in other basic tasks that could be of immediate value to them, such as learning how to tie their shoelaces and instructing the boys how to pull their trousers up.[42] It has therefore been a perennial challenge to deliver 'education' to children whose abilities are not only diverse, but whose needs in the present as well as for the future have to be considered on an individual basis.

This was realised from East Park's early years. Where this history has benefited from oral testimony from those who spent several of their childhood years at East Park, at the forefront have been people who were admitted because, in past times, it was considered an appropriate strategy for children who had had their mobility impeded by the effects of polio. These respondents were intelligent and articulate in childhood and often felt that schooling at East Park did not fulfil their needs because their abilities were not being sufficiently stretched.[43] By contrast, there were other children, a significant proportion never having had any previous form of schooling before their admission to East Park, who struggled to learn the alphabet and to pick up the most basic rudiments of reading and writing. In 1934, two certified teachers were appointed specifically to teach bed-bound children in the wards, marking a greater inclusion of all the children in some form of scholastic training and also observed as aiding the mental well-being of immobile children.[44]

Children were also showcased in the likes of annual reports as learning various craft skills to a high level. Specific success stories provided good copy for annual reports and in the 1930s, which seems to have been a decade of several innovative teaching strategies, two instances were highlighted. Cobbling, a craft that was also popular in teaching children resident in deaf schools to prepare them with a trade to earn them a living, was well established as a part of East Park's broad education. One unnamed boy was reported in 1933 as 'making from fifteen to twenty-five shillings a week' following his discharge and return to a similarly unnamed 'country town'.[45] And in 1937, Willie MacLean was held out as an 'ambassador' for East Park when he attained a bursary that enabled him to attend Glasgow School of Art to take classes in commercial art.[46] These glowing examples aside, there was a broader showcasing of craft work in October 1938 when the output of East Park children was displayed at an 'Industrial Exhibition of Cripples' Work' in Glasgow, this including 'examples of embroidery, wood-carving, brass-work, leather-work, glass, china and pottery painting'.[47]

Additionally, broader forms of personal development were pursued. For example, a widening of education for East Park's girls came in 1924 with the formation of a company of Girl Guides to assist 'in training the girls to habits of loyalty and obedience'.[48] This was followed by the forming of a Boy Scout troop in 1925.[49] In 1933, a percussion band was inaugurated, consisting of cymbals, tambourines, triangles, castanets, drums and bells 'so that all can take part', and lauded by Maud Fletcher 'as an added help in training independence of spirit despite the handicap of crippled bodies'.[50] In 1937, a dancing class was introduced and, besides creating interest among the children, physician superintendent Bankier Sloan declared that it had had 'a definite value in medical treatment', suggestive of the combined benefit of home care, of teaching and skills training, and of healthcare.[51]

Each East Park annual report to 1939/40 began with a listing of the key players in governing and running the Home and the Association, a list that included the Patron, President and Vice-president, the directors and the members of the Ladies' Committees, the Honorary Secretary and Treasurer (William Mitchell and William Bunting in the period of this chapter), the matrons, physician surgeons and dental surgeons at Maryhill and, from 1927, at Largs.[52] The list concluded by acknowledging East Park's solicitors, auditors and bankers. Absent is recognition of the head teachers. The roles of Clara Anne Bowser and Anna Irving have been described in this chapter, but tribute should also be paid to Jessie Maud Fletcher, who was responsible for many of the innovations witnessed through the 1930s. When Maud Fletcher died, aged sixty-six, in 1957, she had been in charge of East Park's school for thirty-six years, having arrived at Maryhill in 1921.[53]

Conclusion

East Park's three-fold role – as a Home, as a place of care and medical support of children with physical infirmities, and as the location of supportive education and training – presented dilemmas for bureaucratic officialdom upon the founding of the NHS in 1948, and presented the conundrum that brought about East Park's subsequent survival as an independent entity outwith the NHS. Education provision did not, of course, operate within a vacuum, although it had perhaps operated with some informality and autonomy until 1912. These were strategies that encouraged young people, among other things, to be physically active, and innovations at East Park might be gauged as commendable efforts to encourage children with physical impairments to reject popular perceptions that their circumstances automatically place limitations to their abilities and on their aspirations.[54]

CHAPTER 8

The Unsung Role of The Ladies, 1874–1956

There are few cant phrases to be learned by heart, a few tricks of the trade to be acquired; but this is easy. Scarcely is the mock philanthropist launched when he discovers that he has the women with him, and then he knows he is secure.

The Bailie, 31 March 1875

When the 'Association for Visiting and Aiding the Permanently Infirm and Imbecile Children brought under the Notice of the School Board Educational Inquiry' set out its 'Statement of the Object and Purpose of the Association' in 1874, the deliberations were presided over by Alexander Whitelaw, mentioned in chapters 2 and 3.[1] Next listed was the Ladies' Committee consisting of twenty names, but brought up to twenty-two with the addition of Miss Moir and Mrs Smith as 'Joint Secretaries and Conveners'.[2] Finally, five names were listed as constituting a Consulting Committee of Gentlemen, two of which, William Mitchell and Edward Collins, were designated as 'Joint Conveners and Interim Treasurer'.[3]

While it may be seen as middle-class etiquette for the ladies to be listed first, it should be borne in mind that the initial objective of the Association was not to establish a residential Home, but for these Ladies to visit disabled children in their own dwellings. The initial higher profile of the Ladies in the embryo organisation was totally logical since it was they who were to fulfil the Association's aims and aspirations. Women as the queens of the domestic sphere of household management, and of nurturers of babies, infants and children, were, certainly in male eyes, the natural means of delivery of this mission. This was a common theme in many voluntary bodies, especially in the areas of healthcare and family support. The men saw themselves as providing business acumen in the charitable endeavour and of making weighty decisions after their analysis of complex financial and managerial conundrums. Without detracting from the genuine hard work and commitment of the men who guided the Association in its quest to make a positive difference to the lives of disabled children from Glasgow's poorest districts, *The Bailie* was astute in highlighting that, without having the women with them, their achievements would have been greatly diminished.[4]

In Victorian Scotland, there were also women who refused to be relegated to the shadows. These included Beatrice Clugston, the independent and strong character who has already been highlighted in chapter 4. There were also members of the aristocracy, the landed upper-class strata who held considerable power and adopted high profiles in the decades before the Great War; characters such as the Duchess of Buccleuch, who performed prominent roles in a multitude of charitable outlets. The Association did not initially benefit from aristocratic patronage, but it did recruit, attract and engage a considerable number of upper middle-class ladies, ladies who came from comfortable residences where domestic chores were taken care of by servants, and sometimes butlers, cooks, nursemaids and governesses, and so leaving them with time on their hands. Charitable work was a welcome outlet for their energies and talents in a world where the conventions of 'separate spheres' limited their options – male worlds of work and business, female worlds of idle domesticity.

At the inaugural meeting of the planned Association on 10 February 1874, thirty-one ladies were listed who were to be tasked with visiting poor homes to assess circumstances and needs, notably the particular needs of 'permanently infirm and imbecile' children.[5] The listing of this initial group of Lady Visitors demonstrates that networks of social circles played a dominant role. Almost all of these volunteers resided in the West End of Glasgow, and predominantly in, or in the vicinity of, Kew Terrace where William Mitchell lived. As might be expected, Mitchell's wife was one of their number, and so too were wives and daughters of members of the Gentlemen's Committee.[6] There were twenty married women and eleven unmarried women covering a broad age spectrum. This was merely a start and, indeed, at a meeting two weeks later a further eight Ladies joined their ranks.[7]

A frustration in researching the early years of the Association, and East Park Home, is the tendency, certainly during the decades between 1874 and the Great War, of the failure of the records to give these Ladies full identity. They are almost always referred to only by their surnames – Mrs Brownlie, Miss Macarthur, Mrs Hetherington and so on. And even worse in twenty-first-century eyes, the submerging of their identities by those of their husbands – Mrs James Smith, Mrs Marcus Dods, Mrs George S Buchanan, etc.[8] To varying degrees, this 'anonymity' hampers research of the Ladies and their wider life trajectories. Not only is this frustrating from a research perspective, but it potentially diminishes the credit due for the efforts they made within their constrained worlds bound by conventions of social status. This chapter aims to focus illumination on the largely unheralded efforts of 'the Ladies'.

Lady Visitors

From the outset, the task of the Ladies who volunteered their services was, in certain aspects, a formidable one. School Attendance Officers, in pursuing children found absent from classes under the new requirements of compulsory education, identified households with disabled children. Under the Association's mission, these children became the focus of the Lady Visitors as they set out to assess their full circumstances and needs. While wide-ranging 'improvement' literature of the day portrayed impoverished lower working-class families as willingly inhabiting an environment of squalor, sloth and inebriation, this image did not honestly depict all life within poor communities, there being many families striving to attain rational behavioural patterns in adversity – trying to pursue godliness and cleanliness, sobriety and 'decency' within the constraints imposed by poverty, as indeed the Lady Visitors found in the course of their investigations and enquiries.

Yet the Ladies were entering a world that was in total contrast to their home environments of comfort and prosperity, of good nutrition and high standards of hygiene. They were exposing themselves to conditions that harboured infectious diseases. They were also venturing into places of potential physical danger, alleys subjected to semi-darkness even in the middle of the day where risk of robbery, assault or molestation must surely have lurked. Yet the Association, in its deliberations over the progress of its work, at no point expressed concern about the safety of the Lady Visitors, or discussed any forms of protection being put at their disposal.

Within a month, the Ladies' work had progressed apace, it being recorded on 10 March 1874 that, so far, 'there were 115 children reported as Infirm and Imbecile [and], of this number, 81 had been visited'.[9] There were also children known to the Association who had yet to be visited, but an organisational structure was in place with a Ladies' subcommittee operating to provide written instructions to its Lady Visitors. Did these instructions beseech them to only enter passageways of slums in pairs? Were they given guidance on what to do if they found themselves in situations that might compromise their safety? If they were left to carry out their work while surviving purely on their initiative, their diligence and bravado must surely be admired.

In April 1874, after listing the diversity of cases already encountered, Mitchell gave an indication of what the Ladies' visiting work was already entailing, namely '… a large amount of good has already been done by the ladies without coming to the Association for aid, in seeing children and ministering to their wants and

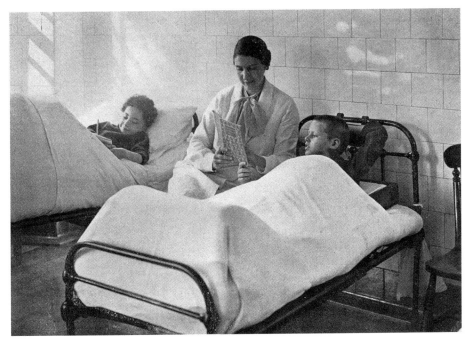

The Ladies played an invaluable role in teaching children the rudiments of reading in instances where they were too infirm to attend the schoolroom.

necessities'.[10] The inference here is that the Lady Visitors were not only identifying what help may best assist the different children discovered, but they were happily calling upon their own resources and initiatives to quickly address situations as they encountered them. It was the accumulative effect of their findings that highlighted the extremities of need and brought about the creation of East Park Home.

With the inauguration of East Park Home, a role was added to the repertoire of the Lady Visitors – visiting the children in the home where they gave lessons, notably to those children who were 'constantly in bed'.[11] Education on the Bible was not neglected, while such craft skills as sewing and knitting were taught to children who 'although not rapid workers are very neat and precise'.[12] Two generations after the opening of East Park Home, in 1913, activities of the Ladies, in addition to raising and collecting donations, were listed. Sixteen were named as visiting the dormitories, including one who travelled from Tullibody in Clackmannanshire. Twelve were recorded as 'sewing meeting participants' where voluntary work on clothing items for the children was undertaken in an environment of conviviality at East Park, while further ladies did sewing at home. The bustle of activity surrounding the work parties is apparent, but such gatherings also provided social circles while serving a laudable cause.[13]

The Grand Bazaar of 1895

When East Park Cottage was acquired in 1874, a grand bazaar was spearheaded by Beatrice Clugston to generate the necessary funds to underwrite the building and its day-to-day functioning. However, in 1882, when the adjacent cottage was purchased by the Association, such a grand event was rejected as a proposition for raising the finance, the preferred strategy of employing subscription cards instead being selected. This operated as a kind of pyramid, with an organising Ladies' Committee at the top, and localities in Glasgow and beyond being identified and allocated to Lady Collectors, who in turn networked with ladies in their designated zones. The Ladies were to revisit the idea of a grand bazaar a decade later.

East Park, in 1893, secured a £3,000 loan in connection with the purchase of land adjoining the original cottage. Raising money to repay this loan was promptly placed on the shoulders of the Ladies, the male directors calling a meeting on 30 November 1894 that 'about One Hundred lady friends and collectors' attended.[14] Mitchell explained the debt and proposed 'the propriety of going on with the Bazaar and Sales of Work which had been indicated in the Annual Report'.[15] The event was to take place in December 1895, but with the tsarina of grand bazaars, Beatrice Clugston, having died seven years previously, how did the 'lady friends' react to such dubious empowerment from the Board? Within the spirit of the age, 'the whole of the ladies expressed themselves as favourable to the … resolution without a dissenting voice'.[16]

During the ensuing months, Mitchell 'made certain arrangements with several firms in London, Japan, etc., to supply goods on very favourable terms' and, in perhaps the first flirtation with the aristocracy by East Park Home, it was announced that the event, to be held in Glasgow's Fine Art Institute, would be opened by the Duchess of Montrose.[17] The thirty-two-page bazaar catalogue gives a flavour of this grand affair at which 'ladies' conducted a range of stalls named after the affluent localities they represented, such as Balgray, Bearsden, Dowanhill, Kelvin, Kew and West Stirlingshire, while commodities on sale included Indian antimacassars, Japanese silk goods, Moorish slippers, Ginkonshiki vases and Wakasa tables. More 'localised' fare ranged from hares, pheasants and rabbits, and deerheads [sic] and skins, to plaids, knickerbocker stockings, embroidered opera jackets and railway rugs, all of which give a flavour of the luxuries enjoyed by the wealthy – and the discomforts of, for example, Victorian travel by train. Supporting advertisements in the brochure add further insight, such as the North British Rubber Company's Buchanan Street shop that offered hot-water bottles, snow boots and shoes, gaiters and leggings, and driving aprons and knee-rugs (for use in open carriages), while Thompson's chemists in Gordon Street offered ladies 'Nervetonine', a 'positive cure',

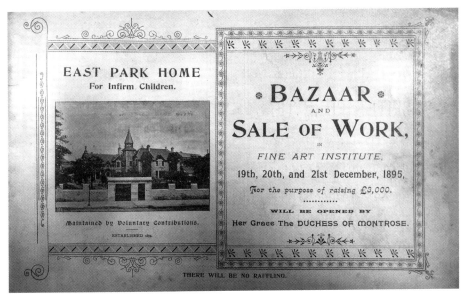

The Duchess of Montrose opened the Grand Bazaar of 1895.

it claimed, for 'all nervous afflictions, exhaustion, debility, depression, hysteria, loss of memory, sleeplessness, paralysis, indigestion, headache, loss of blood, appetite, neuralgia, toothache, rheumatism, lumbago, gout, sciatica, etc.' Was this magic cure-all any good? Don't take Mr Thompson's word for it because he quotes 'A Lady' who assured the chemist that she 'cannot speak too highly of your Nervetonine. It has done me a great deal of good. I bless the day I saw your advertisement: It is not like most advertisements; it tells the truth.'

The bazaar also offered various polite musical entertainments. For those wishing something upon return home, they could buy a copy of William Mitchell's latest book, *House and Home: The Value and Virtue of Domestic Life*, price 1s 6d.[18] The twenty-first-century reader might not be attracted by some of the bazaar's offerings, but its success over the three days was down to 'The Ladies'. As well as paying off all East Park's debt, it was credited with financing the erection of a 'commodious' wash house and laundry.[19]

The Ladies as collectors

By the end of the nineteenth century, the Association had Lady Collectors operating in 146 localities of varying size and bringing in annual sums ranging from a couple of pounds to the £36 realised from a zone encompassing Great Western Terrace, Lancaster Terrace, Westbourne Gardens and Terrace, Crossloan Road and Montgomerie Quadrant, Montgomerie Crescent and Montgomerie Drive.[20]

Miss J R Fairley, the collector for this area, must have burned a fair amount of shoe leather – and undoubtedly consumed many cups of proffered tea – in the course of her rounds.[21] Typically, each donation was shillings rather than pounds, but the publication of each donation in the annual reports probably spurred some donors to, say, increase their contribution from 2s 6d to 5s, and so on, in the knowledge that the reports listed their largesse (or tight-fistedness) for public consumption, such being the nature of human vanity.[22]

Contributors within these collecting networks might be seen as small-scale donors, but it was a case of 'monie a mickle maks a muckle' and, in tandem with other donor categories – notably those involving contributions from commercial companies, employee schemes and sabbath schools – all added up to a vital form of funding. The annually published lists of contributions provide fascinating insights to the composition of Glasgow society and industry in the Victorian city, and give a flavour of the kind of organisations that were popular at the time. The children of two 'day industrial schools', located in Rottenrow and Rose Street, each gathered one guinea, it being noted that the collections from these working-class areas were chiefly farthings.[23] By involving children from the likes of Sunday schools, the female role was significant because it would have been heavily reliant on mothers, school teachers and Sunday school teachers.

Lady networks canvassing West End crescents and terraces remained in full flow in the aftermath of the Great War, 1919/20 being annotated as their most successful year with £1,236 collected.[24] While the roles of the legions of women might have been rewarded by their feelings of doing good works for unfortunate children, their coordination was under the superintendence of a Ladies' Auxiliary Secretary. In 1913, when Susanna Clugston was appointed, she was provided with a salary of £90 annually plus '£10 per annum towards the cost of telephone and office rent', and in 1917 her salary had reached £120 per annum.[25] It is a figure that conveys a sense of the value placed on the fundraising effort and upon what was appropriate reward for a member of middle-class society. It was on a par with East Park's teachers – Anna Irving salaried at £140 per annum and Clara Bowser £100 – while Matron Kathleen Jamieson was paid £110 per annum.[26] It might therefore seem that Clugston was rather generously rewarded, especially in comparison with Jamieson who held such significant responsibility for running the Home and ensuring dedicated care for around 150 children at any one time, but also recognises the importance placed on promoting charitable giving to East Park.

An aspect of collecting by way of household subscriptions is that this money came from the Lady Collectors' middle-class 'sisters' – well over 90 per cent of contributions were recorded in the names of women. They came from comfortable households where women were in charge of the domestic sphere and of domestic budgets. In zone number fifty-six, one of several collection districts in Dowanhill, twenty-nine households made contributions of half a crown during 1928 and in every case it was a woman's name listed as the donor.[27]

In some ways, the grim Great War reality of bloody conflict had been remote from Scottish towns and cities, except, of course, when new recruits paraded through their communities before setting off to the Front – and when the broken bodies of soldiers arrived at Glasgow Central station as a consequence of military bombardment and mustard gas. As epitomised by the 1941 Clydebank Blitz, the realities of war came closer to home in the Second World War and impacted the gathering of silver coinage, one of East Park's 'War Issue' annual reports noting that 'many ladies have found it impossible to continue their good work in District Collecting'.[28] The Second World War blackout was one of the inhibitors that thwarted the Lady Collectors, in a way that had not deterred their predecessors who had, daily, entered the gloom of claustrophobic Victorian alleyways.

With the end of the Second World War, East Park faced the challenge of possibly being absorbed into the new NHS, discussed in chapter 9. One of the concerns of East Park's Board was the effect it might have on the volunteering ethos and the ladies who had long committed themselves to such effort. This was expressed by its president, James Mackenzie:

> The support that was given to the Home by people who took an interest out of regard for the good work that was being done, was greater than could possibly be expected under Nationalisation, and he hoped that East Park Home would be permitted in the future to continue the good work it was doing under its present auspices.[29]

Income from 'ladies' collecting cards' was however in its death throes and by 1956 income had plummeted to £1,773, a modest sum given the impact of inflation since the early days and, tellingly, occupying less than four pages of that year's report while the £833 collected in 1913 came from lists of individuals and localities that ran to sixty pages.[30] Arguably, the key statistic across this span of fifty-three years is not the amount of money collected, but the levels of energy and effort generated by the Ladies.

At the directors' meeting on 3 February 1956, a letter from Mrs Craik, convener of the Ladies' Committee, was read in which she announced the end of the organisation, explaining that 'Its members had gradually resigned until she was the sole member.'[31] The finality of the moment was affirmed by the passing of the Ladies' Committee funds towards furnishing the new physiotherapy wing that was under construction at East Park.[32] It was the end of an eight-decade journey of commitment on the part of the Ladies.

Cautious emancipation?

For East Park's first half-century, the weighty decisions were taken, no doubt in offices of dark panels and in a fog of tobacco smoke, by directors who were exclusively male. At their meeting of 27 March 1917, the directors floated an idea surrounding 'the desirability of appointing a lady member to the Directorate', but 'it was agreed to delay consideration of the matter till a future meeting'.[33] Expectation of a broadening of the electoral franchise when the Great War had come to an end may have been a factor in considering such a change, the 1918 Representation of the People Act granting the parliamentary vote to women over thirty years of age provided that they fulfilled a minimum property qualification.[34] Two and a half years after the proposition had first been suggested, a vacancy on the Board opened the door to such a revolutionary move and the Ladies' Committee was invited 'to recommend one of their number for election'.[35] On 28 January 1920, Mrs Foster Erskine was welcomed to her first Board meeting. Helen Erskine resided at 66 Kelvingrove Street, Hillhead, with her husband, Foster Erskine, proprietor of a printing press. However, her tenure was relatively short, brought about by her death, at the age of sixty-four, on 5 April 1922.[36]

The presence of a woman Board member over the next three decades tended to be intermittent, but in 1950, Dr Mary Stevenson became vice-president, remaining in this role for eighteen years.[37] It was perhaps ironic that an early issue Stevenson had to confront was a threat of resignation by the Ladies' Committee in 1952 'as the services they were willing to render were not being utilised' – a situation that seemed to be addressed by a Board proposal for the Ladies to visit the homes of discharged children, of having a structured programme of ward visiting, and of schemes where the Ladies might 'provide additional comforts' for the children.[38] Indeed, the Ladies' Committee had also exercised its collective muscle in 1948 when it argued for its inclusion in the Constitution, a proposal the directors declined.[39] There is some irony here when it is borne in mind that, as outlined in chapter 1, the original 1874 plan was for the organisation to be a *Ladies* Association for Visiting and Aiding Permanently Infirm and Imbecile Children.[40]

From its foundation in 1874, the position of secretary and treasurer vested in William Mitchell for over three decades was a pivotal responsibility, so the appointment of Mary McLean to this role in 1949, still operating from Mitchell's old office at 134 Wellington Street, was perhaps the signifier that women were gradually assuming their rightful place at the decision-making and financial helm of East Park.[41] More than three decades had passed since a female role in East Park's governance had first been considered. It had been a slow journey for a woman's appointment to high office. What had at last been advanced for women was however still very much within the confines of the status accorded the middle classes. The men and women overseeing the administration of East Park remained people of substance, of status within society, of comfortable means and from professional, educated backgrounds.

However, one earlier female role had been inaugurated, and again status was key. Royal patronage seemingly came about with little fanfare, the 1910/11 annual report merely recording that 'A signal honour has this year [1911] been conferred upon the Home by Her Majesty Queen Alexandra, who has graciously bestowed her Royal Patronage upon the Institution'.[42] Due condolences were expressed upon her death in 1925 and, again with little fanfare, royal endorsement continued under Queen Mary, it being made clear by her private secretary, Harry Veruey, who wrote that because of 'the heavy claims on her time and interest, it will be impossible for Her Majesty to do more for the Home than the granting of her name as Patroness'.[43] And so it continued until Mary's death in 1953, after which the Duchess of Gloucester assumed the role.[44] There seems to have been no impetus to emulate the likes of Glasgow's Royal Infirmary, Glasgow's Royal Hospital for Sick Children or Gartnavel Royal Asylum and become Royal East Park Home. However, royal patronage by Alexandra and Mary conformed to the tradition of child nurturing as being a feminine calling, and so it was in their regal patronage of East Park.

Conclusion

This chapter argues that, during East Park's early decades, the female role was greatly underacknowledged, reflecting the gendered spheres of the times. It might well be wondered why women accepted this marginalisation when the grand plans of the male directors were highly dependent upon wives, sisters, mothers and daughters taking on the hard graft of raising money, aiding destitute families in the most impoverished Glasgow localities and nurturing East Park's children within the Home. It was an imbalanced gender relationship in their support of East Park that was extremely slow to change, and it was the outside forces of world wars and the shift from people being pauperised through dependence on the Poor Law, to a welfare system open to everyone without their means being questioned, that were perhaps the impetuses for East Park to be more gender-inclusive. However, social levelling within East Park's governance was a slower process.

CHAPTER 9

Conflict and Challenge, 1939–48

… This was the year
extremely far rooftops and lit windows
seen from a plane flying its late night mission
had their glow zapped by pinball fire.

Pippa Little[1]

At 11.15am on 3 September 1939, British Prime Minister Neville Chamberlain declared that, as Hitler had not responded to his ultimatum demanding the withdrawal of German troops from Poland, the country was now at war with Germany. Legislation for wartime emergencies gave considerable control over all of Scotland's hospitals to the Department of Health for Scotland as part of its Emergency Hospitals Scheme.[2] The Scheme was set up in anticipation of hospital care being needed for large numbers of military personnel in light of the experiences of the Great War (1914–18). This resulted in the construction of hospitals in rural locations, such as Killearn in Stirlingshire, and the requisitioning of local authority hospitals, charitable hospitals, and other facilities such as convalescent homes.[3] In the Glasgow area, for example, a number of psychiatric patients were evacuated from Gartloch Hospital, allowing the building to be used as an emergency hospital for civilians injured during air raids.[4] A similar strategy was adopted at Mearnskirk Hospital, which was used in peacetime primarily to treat children with tuberculosis, but during the Second World War was utilised for treating military personnel of both Allied and non-Allied forces.[5]

At the monthly meeting of the managers at Glasgow Royal Infirmary (GRI), on 4 September 1939, the chairman reported that, since the Royal Infirmary was located in one of Glasgow's 'danger spots', it was intended to use it as a clearing station for local casualties, and that many regular patients in a condition to be moved had already been evacuated.[6] At a subsequent Medical Committee meeting,

A happy assembly of children and staff at Maryhill, but war clouds were already gathering. (Courtesy of Elizabeth Hunter)

the interim superintendent revealed that patients had been evacuated to East Park Home, Lenzie Convalescent Home and Schaw Convalescent Home where the staff of GRI had undertaken responsibility for their medical and surgical treatment since these institutions were now under the control of the Department of Health.[7]

In East Park's annual report for 1939, the physician superintendent, Dr Bankier Sloan, noted that:

> On August 31st the work of the Home was abruptly terminated by orders from the Minister of Health to evacuate the children that afternoon – starting two hours after receipt of the order.[8]

As a result of this instruction, within twenty-four hours the children were moved by staff with the assistance of volunteer helpers. Sixty-five children left Maryhill to go to the Country Branch in Largs. Of the remainder, thirty-one were returned to their family homes, but with four going to 'other institutions'.[9]

At Largs, care and education of the children continued, while the building in Maryhill was initially used as an Emergency Hospital. Dr Sloan reported that, two days after the evacuation of the children, the Ministry of Health had sent fifty patients from the GRI, 'all bed cases', to continue their treatment and convalescence in East Park Home in Maryhill.[10] The GRI patients occupied the Home until 8 November

1939, the nursing staff at East Park being assisted by senior nurses from the Royal Infirmary. Patients were also attended by members of the Royal Infirmary medical and surgical staff.[11]

To fully appreciate the wartime and immediate post-war experience of both East Park, Maryhill, and the Country Branch in Largs, it is helpful to consider the wider impact of war on Glasgow and Clydeside. An area renowned for heavy engineering, it is not surprising that Glasgow and the Clyde were attractive targets for Luftwaffe bombing raids. During the height of what became known as the Clydebank Blitz, overnight on 13–14 and 14–15 March 1941, there were many casualties in Clydebank and surrounding areas such as Glasgow and Greenock.[12] On 14 March, the West End of Glasgow, including Queen Margaret Drive, less than a mile from East Park, was also hit. Three people were killed and five hundred homes in the area were damaged.[13] At midnight, the bombers struck again, further north and west, hitting St Mary's School and Kilmun Street, Maryhill. The second blast was in the back courts of the sandstone tenements in Kilmun Street. Numbers 32 to 36 were

The artist Ian Fleming RSA RSW RWA was a lecturer at Glasgow School of Art and was also a Special Police Constable based at Maryhill. He was on duty at the scene of the Kilmun Street bombing and witnessed at first hand the rescue operations on the night and during the following days. He was deeply affected by this incident and produced several artworks depicting it. (© The Fleming Family)

destroyed, as were houses in Shiskine Street, Kilmun Lane and Kirn Street, with several others being set on fire.[14] Eighty-three people died in the bombing of Kilmun Street and a further 180 were injured. In total, over a hundred homes were destroyed, a further 250 rendered uninhabitable and 100 shops damaged in the Maryhill area. With East Park's disabled children now safely evacuated to Largs, some Maryhill residents were able to take refuge in East Park Home in the days that followed.[15] The Home was also used as a casualty station. Over forty children who experienced minor injuries and shock were accommodated there, remaining until their parents, whose homes had been destroyed, were able to secure other accommodation.[16]

East Park continued to be designated an Emergency Hospital until early 1942. At that time, the Secretary of State for Scotland considered that the evacuation scheme should continue for the duration of the War. However, at a meeting of the directors of East Park on 18 March 1942, it was recorded that:

> The Medical Officer of Health, Sir Alexander MacGregor had intimated, through the Secretary, that the Home at Maryhill had now ceased to be recognised by the Department of Health as an Emergency Hospital and had asked that a deputation of the Health Committee of the Corporation [of Glasgow] might visit the Home and explore its possibilities as a Wartime Nursery. The Chairman stated that he, along with Dr Sloan and the Secretary, had met with the Convenor of the Health Committee, Baillie Stewart and Dr Wattie and that they had made a favourable report to the Corporation for the taking over of the Home as a Wartime Nursery.[17]

East Park was used as a nursery by the Public Health Department of Glasgow Corporation until the cessation of hostilities in 1945.[18]

One of the consequences of the Second World War was the further development of health and welfare services. From 1939, a number of women and children were evacuated from generally poor, urban areas, sometimes to more prosperous environments, in anticipation of German bombing. This brought about a wider awareness of the deprivation experienced by many working-class families living in urban communities.[19] This process had in fact begun some years previously with Liberal welfare reforms before the Great War as well as recognition of the extent of deprivation during the interwar years.[20] Concerns such as those outlined in the Cathcart Report of 1936 in respect of the poor state of health of the citizens of Scotland and the patchwork of services intended to remedy this were also addressed.[21] On 10 June 1941, Arthur Greenwood, Minister without Portfolio, announced to the House of Commons that he had arranged with all appropriate departments for a comprehensive survey of existing schemes of social insurance and allied services which would be considered in due course by his Committee on Reconstruction Problems. Sir William Beveridge (1879–1963) became chair of the interdepartmental committee which would conduct the survey. The Social Insurance and Allied Services Report, which became known as 'The Beveridge Report', was presented to Parliament in November 1942. In this, Beveridge identified what he referred to as 'five giant evils', namely, Physical Want, Disease (which Beveridge acknowledged often caused Physical Want), Ignorance, Squalor and Idleness.[22] Beveridge proposed that:

> In seeking security not merely against physical want, but against all these evils in all their forms, and in showing that security can be combined with freedom and enterprise and responsibility of the individual for his own life, the British community, and those who in other lands have inherited the British tradition, have a vital service to render to human progress.[23]

Subsequent legislation included the Education (Scotland) Acts of 1945 and 1946. These Acts consolidated legislation that had come into force in the years since the Education (Scotland) Act 1872 and ensured universal secondary education to the age of fifteen and required county councils to appoint Directors of Education.[24] The Family Allowance Act 1945 established a universal benefit that did not carry stigmatising means testing for each second and subsequent child, while the National Assistance Act 1948 abolished the remnants of the Poor Law system and introduced the modern welfare state by '[making] further provision for the welfare of disabled, sick, aged and other persons and for regulating homes for disabled and aged persons and charities for disabled persons'.[25]

The Clyde Report in Scotland and the Curtis Report in England and Wales brought about the Children's Act 1948. This placed a duty on local authorities to create committees and Children's Departments to focus on children's welfare. Possibly the initiatives having most immediate impact on East Park, however, were the Nurses (Scotland) Act 1943 and the National Health Service (Scotland) Act 1947. The Nurses (Scotland) Act 1943 made provision for the enrolment of assistant nurses and for their training, creating the designation of State Enrolled Nurse. The National Health Service (Scotland) Act 1947, the National Health Service Act 1946 for England and Wales and the Health Services Act (Northern Ireland) 1948 brought about the creation of the NHS. The implementation of the National Health Service (Scotland) Act 1947 was to change the future course of East Park.

Post-Second World War

The post-war period has often been described as a period of optimism. There was belief that, as well as developments in health and child welfare, different approaches to working with families would relieve some of the challenges faced by parents and mark a move away from the ethos of the Poor Law.[26] While such positivity was evident in East Park, there were difficulties in the Homes in both Maryhill and Largs, and nationwide, as Britain entered a period of post-war austerity, recovery and reconstruction. Glasgow faced particular post-war challenges. It has been suggested that the social problems evident at the end of the nineteenth century had shown little improvement by 1939. Overcrowding persisted, with nearly half of the inhabitants of Glasgow living in one- or two-roomed dwellings. Only half of Glasgow households had a bathroom while a third had to share toilets with their neighbours. This was despite a Glasgow Corporation programme to construct social housing, reaching its target of 57,000 houses for lower-income families by 1939, and subsidised by central grants from government from the programme's origin in the Addison Act of 1919.[27] Glasgow Corporation and central government were aware of the need for improvement and planning began during the Second World War for post-war reconstruction.

Two primary solutions were applied to the housing situation. The first, based on the Clyde Valley Plan of 1946, written by Sir Patrick Abercrombie and Sir Robert H Matthew, proposed the creation of new towns to which a significant proportion of the population of Glasgow would be decanted.[28] These were initially planned to be located at East Kilbride, Cumbernauld, Condorrat, Bishopton and Houston, although the locations changed over time. The second approach involved the building of new council house estates on the periphery of Glasgow. These became Drumchapel in the west, Easterhouse and Cranhill in the east and Castlemilk, Nitshill and Pollok in the south, retaining these rehoused populations within the Glasgow city boundary.[29] They were policies that have had long-term consequences for life in Glasgow and the surrounding area.

In 1945, at East Park, plans were formulated for resuming services. Having been used as an Emergency Hospital in 1939, then as a refuge for families rendered homeless due to bombing in 1941, from 1942 to 1945 the Home was operated by the Public Health Department of Glasgow Corporation as a wartime nursery.[30] With the end of hostilities in sight, the Town Clerk of Glasgow Corporation announced that the Maryhill home would be returned to the East Park directors at the end of June 1945.[31]

In some respects, despite the cessation of hostilities, life had carried on as normal for the children in the Country Branch at Largs. Teacher Maud Fletcher described children's education as having progressed and with good results. Several children passed the 'Qualifying' examinations, including 'a girl so incapacitated with rheumatoid arthritis that she has received her education in bed', and while there was a shortage of materials, classes in sewing, knitting, rug- and basket-making, weaving, leatherwork and boot-making had been maintained 'with a most successful sale of the children's work in June'.[32] Various music activities continued for all children, and a special feature of infant classes was speech training, action songs and plays. Lessons broadcast over the radio were reported as being enjoyed by all and were described as 'a very valuable means of keeping children in touch with the outside world'.[33]

The Maryhill Home having been returned to the East Park directors, work began in preparation for resuming 'normal' services.[34] A large number of children were awaiting admission while a number also had to be returned to Glasgow from Largs, so plans were made to reopen the Home in Maryhill in September 1945. Matron Mary MacEwen was to resume duties at Maryhill from 1 July 1945 and was tasked with overseeing the domestic staff in preparing the Home in readiness. Margaret Anna Ligertwood, known as Peggy, the Country Branch assistant matron, was promoted to matron at Largs from 1 July 1945. There were, however, a number of setbacks.

Having agreed to return as matron at Maryhill, Mary MacEwen died suddenly on 10 June 1945 at the age of sixty-four.[35] She had been appointed assistant matron in 1920, assuming 'matronship' in 1926. Furthermore, Major William Ritchie, president of the Board, died four weeks later.[36] These were very significant losses, particularly at such a critical point of transition. In order to fill the vacancies, Peggy Ligertwood was transferred from Largs to take up the post of matron at Maryhill, while Janet Torrie, assistant matron in the Country Branch, was recalled from war service, having served in both France and North Africa.[37] At this point she was attached to the 131 General Hospital of the Mediterranean Expeditionary Force, but her war service had been 'at the pleasure of the Directors' and a month's notice to the military authorities was all that was required to release her. Following her return, she took up post as matron in the Country Branch on 1 November 1945.

However, further setbacks emerged. While the children had been removed from East Park in 1939 with two hours' notice, it took considerably longer for the home in Maryhill to be made suitable for their care and for education to resume. The new accommodation for the nurses and the new schoolroom, on which work had begun before the war, had been seriously curtailed because of shortages of labour and construction materials. Furthermore, having then been used for a variety of purposes during the war, East Park needed considerable refurbishment, including alterations, redecoration and renewal of equipment and furniture, at a time when there was still a shortage of labour. Eventually, on 17 December 1945, the first children and young people who had been on a long waiting list, were admitted to Maryhill. The Country Branch in Largs continued in its convalescence role with medical oversight by surgeon Mr Matthew White and physician Dr George T Ross, with what were described as 'progressive and good results'.[38]

During 1946, the building programme to provide eleven additional bedrooms, a new recreation room for nursing staff and a new schoolroom for the children resumed at Maryhill. These developments included installation of central heating and electric lighting, repainting of the buildings and relaying of paving and pathways.[39] Additionally, there was ongoing uncertainty due to requirements arising from the national reorganisation of hospitals and the need to comply with nursing reforms and government controls. Various changes occurring in nursing were attributed to the difficulty in recruiting and retaining suitable nurses, all of which hindered East Park's return to full capacity. Despite these challenges, by the end of 1946, the renovation was almost complete with the number of children in Maryhill increasing from thirteen in January to forty-three by December.[40]

Despite the delays to the resumption of normal service, enthusiasm for developing the Home's facilities remained high. Dr Sloan recommended three new visiting appointments to the Board – an anaesthetist, a dental surgeon and an ear, nose and throat specialist. Reflecting continued uncertainties, the Board's initial response was an invitation for him to investigate his proposals further and to report to future meetings when the work of the Home was in full operation.[41] In April 1946, Dr Sloan returned with nominations and it was consequently agreed to recommend the appointment of Dr J J Fulton Christie as consultant surgeon for ear, nose and throat, and Dr W Allan as anaesthetist.[42] Surgery continued at East Park until 1954, when it was noted that a tonsil operation had been carried out, 'it being impossible to have the child admitted to hospital at that time. It was not a usual occurrence.'[43] Meanwhile, post-war reforms in the health service were to have a significant impact on East Park's future.

Looking back on 1946, Matron Peggy Ligertwood summarised the first full year of the return of peacetime in her annual report:

> The re-establishing the Home at Maryhill presented many difficulties. Much has been accomplished, but owing to the national re-organisation of hospitals, nursing reforms, existing government controls, etc., there has been considerable delay in respect of structural alterations, complying with modern requirements for staff accommodation, and the supply of up-to-date equipment. Uncertainty of the future limits activity to a certain extent and necessitates deferment of approved recommendations.[44]

On closer examination of 'the many difficulties' referred to by Peggy Ligertwood, with the imminent creation of the National Health Service, decisions were required as to whether East Park, both Maryhill and the Country Branch, came within the scope of Section 80 of the National Health Service (Scotland) Act 1947. If deemed to come within the bounds of this legislation, East Park would lose its independent, voluntary status and become part of the new National Health Service.

East Park and the National Health Service

While the NHS in the twenty-first century is regarded by many as a 'national treasure', at the time of its planning in the 1940s there was considerable resistance in some quarters, in particular in respect of the administrative and financial arrangements, and doctors saw it as a challenge to their autonomy.[45] For example, criticism expressed by Andrew Templeton, honorary treasurer of the Royal Hospital for Sick Children at Yorkhill, at its AGM on 13 May 1946, expressed his fears surrounding:

1. The proposed expropriation of all of the buildings and equipment of the voluntary hospitals, which buildings and equipment have been provided as the result of years of voluntary charitable effort;
2. The proposed confiscation of all of the funds, investments and endowments of such voluntary hospitals all of which were donated and are held in trust for particular hospitals, and in many cases for special purposes;
3. The proposed replacement of the existing Boards of Management of voluntary hospitals (who are democratically elected by subscribers and are representative of all interests and classes with their accumulated knowledge of local requirements and local resources, and have been responsible for many years for the successful carrying on of these hospitals) by Regional Boards appointed by a Cabinet Minister.[46]

Similar views were expressed in respect of East Park. At the Annual Meeting of Subscribers reporting on the year ending 31 December 1947, deacon-convenor Douglas McNaughton paid a warm tribute to the work that had been carried out in the Home for so many years and observed that:

> The support which was given to the Home by people who took an interest in it out of regard for the good work which was being done was greater than could possibly be expected under Nationalisation, and he hoped that East-Park Home would be permitted in the future to continue the good work it was doing under its present auspices.[47]

If East Park was deemed to come within Section 80 of the legislation, it is likely that there would have been significant changes affecting the governance of the Home in Maryhill and the Country Branch. The decision-making process as to whether it came within the terms of the National Health Service (Scotland) Act 1947 was somewhat protracted. During the previous year, a Special Board Meeting had been convened on 16 April to consider a memorandum prepared by the medical superintendent and matron, 'regarding the present position of the nursing staff at both homes under the Nurses (Scotland) Act 1943'. Minutes of the meeting reported:

> The position [the chairman] said, was such that the future of the Homes must be considered and a definite decision made at an early date. The following points had to be considered now.
>
> The category in which the Home is to be placed. The number of nursing staff required and the scheme of training the nurses. [Should] application [be made] to the Dept of Health that the Home be allowed to function as an independent Institution?[48]

Counterproposals suggested that East Park assume a role as a Training School for Assistant Nurses, seek an Affiliation with the General Training School (for nursing) or remain an Institution not incorporated with the present hospitals scheme.[49]

After full consideration, the directors agreed to make application to the Department of Health for Scotland on the lines laid down by the memorandum for recognition of East Park as a useful, functioning and necessary Institution *not* incorporated in the present hospital scheme, but functioning with the approval of, and under the direction of, the Department of Health for Scotland in conjunction with the Scottish Education Department, whose approval it had held for the past thirty years.[50]

The Board also decided to provide a certificate of proficiency for trainees, with a carefully planned scheme of training using for study a syllabus similar to that prescribed by the General Nursing Council for Education and Training of Nurses for Sick Children (elementary) to operate two courses for girls aged sixteen to eighteen years. It claimed that 'This does not interfere with recruitment of nurses for General Hospitals but would prove beneficial and advantageous to the potential nurse', and added, 'If the Department [of Health for Scotland] so desired, a representative of the Directorate and medical staff would meet with the officials of the Department and give any further information'.[51]

East Park's aspiration to maintain its independent status was, however, opposed by the Department of Health for Scotland. One area of ambiguity surrounding

East Park's role was in respect of its proposal regarding nurse training. Was this a healthcare function or an educational function? Dr Sloan and Matron Peggy Ligertwood wrote to the Director of Education regarding the employment of girls aged between sixteen and eighteen in a junior nursing capacity, 'which scheme might be incorporated into the pre-nursing course of the education committee', but the Education Department replied that they were unable to support this at present due to current and prospective commitments.[52] Dr Sloan and Peggy Ligertwood suggested an appeal to the General Nursing Council to seek its support for East Park's proposal that a Certificate of Service of two years, issued by the medical superintendent and matron, be recognised in the case of girls completing East Park's nursing courses.[53] While the outcome of these negotiations is not recorded, it was noted subsequently that, at the Country Branch, 'lectures in Anatomy and Physiology were given and ... several nurses, after scoring well in the examinations, have gone on to their General Nursing Training'.[54]

In respect of East Park's status under Section 80 of the National Health Service (Scotland) Act 1947, at a Board meeting on 8 December 1947 it was reported that a letter had been received from the Department of Health for Scotland. It advised that, as East Park Home and the Country Branch came within the scope of Section 80 of the Act, 'the Department would be glad to have a perusal of the documents relating to its heritable securities held by the Directors affecting said Homes'.[55] It was agreed to forward the letter to East Park's solicitors, Messrs Baird, Smith, Barclay and Muirhead, requesting them to communicate with the Department of Health and express the views of the directors that both Homes should continue as at present on a voluntary basis, as some doubt existed as to whether the Homes came within Section 80 of the Act.[56]

The reply from the Department of Health for Scotland was considered at a meeting on 3 February 1948. Dated 23 December 1947, the Department's response read:

> I am directed by the Secretary of State to refer to your letter of 18th November and subsequent correspondence and to say that the position of the above named Homes under the Act has now been considered in the light of the information available in the Constitution and the Seventy-third Annual Report on the Homes. He is advised that this information establishes that the Homes are institutions for the reception and treatment of persons suffering from illness and, therefore, come within the definition of 'hospital' in Section 80 of the Act.
>
> I am accordingly to say that the Department will be glad if you will

arrange to submit at the earliest possible date the returns of premises and endowments and titles to heritable properties as requested in the circular letter enclosed with the Department's letter of 16th October. That circular letter contains references to the various sections of the Act which cover heritable properties and endowments.[57]

East Park's solicitors acknowledged the letter, informing the Department of Health for Scotland that 'they were advising their clients accordingly' and would communicate back with the Department, as it was anticipated that the directors may wish to make representation that the Home did not in fact fall within this definition.[58]

The fightback

The Board did not accept the Department of Health's judgement and a Special Meeting to discuss this was convened on Tuesday 17 February 1948, attended by Richard Barclay, one of the partners of East Park's appointed solicitors.[59] A draft response was discussed:

> The members of the Institution are unanimously of the opinion that the Institution is not a Hospital within the meaning of the National Health Service (Scotland) Act, 1947, and that consequently it should not be taken over in terms thereof, but should continue to exist as a special domestic establishment for the benefit of the children of the community, in which respect it has done an immense amount of useful work in the past and earned appreciation and gratitude all over Scotland, providing a service entirely different from any contemplated in or to be carried on under said Act. They accordingly respectfully submit that a notice should be served on the Institution in terms of Section 6(3) of the Act.[60]

After certain minor alterations, the directors instructed Barclay to forward the letter to the Department of Health.[61]

Special Meetings of subscribers were held on Tuesday 2 March and Monday 15 March, and a Special Meeting of directors was called on Thursday 25 March, where a letter received from the Department of Health for Scotland, and dated one week earlier, was considered.[62]

> I am directed by the Secretary of State to inform you that he has considered the position of East Park Home for Infirm Children, Glasgow (including the Country Branch at Largs) in relation to the provisions of the National

Health Service Act, 1947 and he has decided that the transfer of the Home will not be required for the purpose of providing hospital and specialist services. This letter being a notice of that decision under Section 6(3) of the Act, the relative provisions of the Act have the effect that the Home will not transfer to the Secretary of State on the appointed day unless the governing body serve a notice on him in terms of the proviso to that subsection within one month from the date of receipt of this letter.

The decision has not been reached without some difficulty as the Home undoubtedly undertakes treatment in some cases that would be appropriate to a hospital.

When Sir George Henderson visited the Home recently, however, he gathered that your Directors would be willing to consider with the Department and with the Regional Hospital Board what treatment facilities should be provided within the Home in future, having regard to the implications to exempt the Home from transfer. I should be glad if you would let me know what date would suit your Directors for a conference on the subject.[63]

After some careful consideration, the directors agreed to advise the Secretary of State for Scotland that they deeply appreciated the decision taken by him that the Home should not be transferred under provisions of the National Health Service (Scotland) Act 1947.[64]

There were further Special Meetings of the directors during 1948 to consider the implications of this decision that Maryhill and the Country Branch maintain their independent status; that the use of the premises for children requiring hospital treatment should be gradually reduced; and, when alternative arrangements were made, the premises should be entirely devoted to the provision of a Home for infirm children who do not require active medical and nursing treatment. This requirement applied to both East Park in Maryhill and the Country Branch in Largs. There were consequences, such as a requirement that staff now be recruited on the 'open market' and the possibility that the directors would have to inaugurate a pension scheme.[65]

There were also implications in respect of medical treatments which could be carried out. A Special Meeting was convened on 6 August 1948 to discuss this.[66] After discussion with Mr White, Dr Johnstone and Dr Stevenson, it was agreed that children with certain medical conditions should not be cared for in East Park Home, namely those deemed 'Ineducable from mental defectiveness; [or requiring treatment for] Diabetes and Tuberculosis of the lung', although it was decided that 'certain cases of surgical tuberculosis' could be admitted at the discretion of the medical superintendents. Children with chronic rheumatic heart disease should only be admitted if they had a reasonable expectation of life, 'say two to three years'. There was discussion about the number of children 'suffering from incontinence' and so requiring a great deal of care. It was felt that such children should not exceed 10 per cent of those in the Homes at any one time. Incontinence of bladder and bowel may be caused by a variety of physical and emotional factors.[67] For children and young people in East Park and the Country Branch who had a variety of physical health conditions such as polio, cerebral palsy and coeliac disease as well as the emotional impact of living away from home, it is not surprising that a number experienced incontinence.

Overall, 'the types of cases to be admitted' was considered a matter for the medical superintendents. It was reaffirmed, however, that 'the Home was to deal with long term cases which would not be considered hospital cases', which was the original ethos when East Park was founded in 1874, and it was suggested that minimum residence should be six months. It was noted that admission of children from hospital who were not fit to be discharged directly to their own homes should continue. It was also acknowledged that the Home would still admit children referred by education and welfare authorities, but not those under the 1948 Children Act.[68]

Change in admission criteria had implications for staffing and remuneration. Matron Peggy Ligertwood at Maryhill was of the view that each Home required a matron, two sisters, two staff nurses and a number of assistant and student nurses, and the directors agreed. In respect of remuneration, there was discussion as to whether this should be in accordance with the Wheatley Report for Children's Homes, or if there should be different scales between children's homes and children's hospitals that recognised the additional healthcare needs of the children in East Park and the Country Branch.[69] This was to be explored further with the auditor, as was matron's remuneration. In future, only in isolated instances would East Park continue to supply artificial limbs and other surgical and orthopaedic appliances free, as it was recognised that the children would be in hospital or their own homes when these were required and they would have them supplied through the NHS.[70]

From 1945, Family Allowance legislation was in place. It was recognised that some parents passed their Family Allowance to the matrons at Maryhill or Largs. Because this was occurring in some instances only, the Board felt that, in future, parents should be encouraged upon their child's admission to agree to transfer their Family Allowance, granted in respect of that child, to East Park.[71]

Debate surrounding the decision that East Park would not come under the NHS continued for some time while the Home consolidated its position in respect of its staffing and future role in the care and education of disabled children with healthcare needs. Consequently, at their meeting on 12 October 1948, the directors considered it desirable to put a notice in the press to inform the public that the Home had not been taken over by the government.[72] It was important that supporters were aware of this and that their support by way of donations, subscriptions and bequests continued.

Afternote

The period 1939–48 was arguably one of the most challenging and tumultuous in East Park's history. As well as the changes over time in respect of the children and staff of any care establishment, world events and subsequent development in social policy had a strong influence on life at Maryhill and the Country Branch, and as East Park planned for the future. One can only speculate what may have happened to East Park had it not resisted joining the NHS in 1948.

The treatment, care and education of disabled children has changed considerably since the early post-war years, as the incidence and impact of conditions which brought children into East Park historically, such as polio, tuberculosis and rickets, have been reduced or eradicated in Scotland through programmes of immunisation and other public health initiatives. While developments such as the use of insulin have transformed the lives of children with childhood diabetes, medical advances which improve the life chances of extremely preterm babies have, for some, brought a risk of adverse health and development outcomes.[73] Meanwhile, changes in social policy mean that children with complex healthcare needs, who may previously have lived in East Park, can receive nursing care in their family homes, while increased understanding of neurodiversity and autism have brought children with different health and developmental needs into East Park. These are children who might previously have remained in long-term hospital environments. Although there have been many changes in East Park since the late 1940s, arguably the meetings in 1947/48 discussed in this chapter set the foundation for East Park as we know it today.

CHAPTER 10

A Place by the Seaside:
The Country Branch at Largs, 1927–87

For the lives of little Children, Made dark by suffering,
Small prisoners in the house of pain, Caged birds with broken wing;
To help to bring the sunlight, Across their shadowed way,
And give them gleams of happiness, We ask your aid to-day.

Bessie Dill, *Sunshine & Shadow* (1921)

Bessie Dill's appeal for funds for the creation of East Park Home Country Branch, in the form of a small booklet with an idyllic scene on the cover that depicted carefree girls and young women clutching bouquets and wearing colourful gowns, was produced at a critical time in the aftermath of the Great War. Young men who had survived the horrors of trench warfare had made their way home, and had discarded their khaki uniforms to take up their civilian lives. Men who had served in the military, and the civilian society that welcomed them back, were also cautiously welcoming the end of the worldwide influenza pandemic that had ravaged the globe as it ebbed and flowed through three phases between 1918 and 1920.

In the false dawn of peace, described as 'the war to end all wars', and as society mourned the loss of their sons and daughters to conflict and of their young people to the pandemic, some found consolation by trying to embrace an optimistic outlook on life, such as relieving their pent-up demand for consumer goods that they had been unable to access during these combined catastrophes of war and disease.[1] It was in this atmosphere of hope, and in the absence of awareness of the economic depression that was about to unfold, that East Park embarked upon plans to open a country branch in Largs, Ayrshire.

In doing so, East Park was following a well-trodden path. Convalescent homes, set in rural locations but within easy reach of Glasgow, had been established by philanthropists, charitable bodies and church organisations during the late nineteenth century. Ranging in size from houses that accommodated a dozen people with two or three staff providing domestic service and some basic nursing care, to larger dwellings that might have formerly been the mansions of country gentry, their aims were the creation of healthy rural environments that offered fresh air and a good, wholesome diet. Hospitals made use of these convalescent homes to aid recuperating patients' return to health and vitality after surgical and medical treatment and before discharging them to their own homes, homes that, in the city, were often overcrowded, poorly ventilated and had to share sanitary arrangements with neighbouring households. Families surviving on low incomes made a healthy, restorative diet almost impossible for a child whose body was still weak even weeks after surgery. It was because of the combined effects of poverty that made a restorative diet almost impossible, and overcrowded homes lacking basic amenities, that charity-funded convalescent homes were brought about by concerned patrons. In some instances, hospitals had gone a step further by opening their own country branches under their direct control, which benefited from the attendance of trained nursing staff and periodic visits by hospital doctors.

Five decades after the first children arrived at East Park Home in Maryhill, the charity's accommodation of additional children in a new country branch was a natural extension to the facilities of its now considerably enlarged 'cottage' in the city. William Quarrier had pursued the country concept more than four decades earlier when he moved his orphan homes from the overcrowded and industry-polluted centre of Glasgow in 1878 and began building his 'village' in an idyllic valley near Bridge of Weir in Renfrewshire.[2] During its first three decades, expansion at East Park Home had been relentless. The Maryhill location clearly had its limits and the Association's directors began exploring possibilities for a country branch in 1902. However, not only were they deterred by the necessary adaption work that would entail substantial additional outlays to the purchase price of various rural dwellings investigated, they also faced 'objections raised by neighbours and feuars where suggested premises seemed suitable'.[3]

While these hurdles continued to delay decisive action, East Park periodically sent children to the Homes of other charities in such locations as Dunoon. Such action eased pressure at Maryhill in instances when the number of children admitted exceeded the official capacity. The noticeable benefits accruing to children sent to rural facilities during their 'escape' from the polluted atmosphere of industrial and overcrowded Glasgow were clear.[4] While it was not the first occasion upon which the idea of a country branch had been aired, it was in 1910, at the first Annual General Meeting following the death of William Mitchell, that a vigorous proposal for creating a country branch was mooted. The credit for this initiative goes to Mrs

Rosie Shaw, wife of incumbent Lord Provost, Sir Archibald McInnes Shaw,[5] when she explained her presence at the meeting:

> [It was] to ask for co-operation and help in getting up a well-equipped and well-organised Bazaar for the purpose of establishing a country or seaside branch, and she read a letter sent to the Lord Provost by Mr George Morton, [with a] covering … cheque for £100 as a contribution from his wife and himself towards the new scheme. Mrs McInnes Shaw said the promoters desired to begin building at once, either a country or seaside home, where the little patients from East-Park might go and be permanently benefited.[6]

Supported by former Lord Provost, Sir William Bilsland (1847–1921), her proposal gained the warm approval of the gathering. However, Rosie Shaw's aspirations 'to begin building at once' were, of course, an expression of unbounded enthusiasm that would require to be tempered by the exercise of considerable patience.

Yet the steps were set in motion, William Bunting, Mitchell's successor as secretary and treasurer of East Park, outlining an appraisal in which he noted how the Maryhill home's once-rural location had been transformed by unremitting urban expansion. He explained the plan by highlighting the existence of 'a small hospital' in Aberfoyle that had been established 'mainly through the effort of Miss Penelope Ker'. He noted that the Aberfoyle home required to vacate its 'cottages' in May 1911 and that its management committee was searching for a location in which to construct a permanent building. This turn of events was seen as both a threat and an opportunity; a threat because the Aberfoyle home encroached upon activities that East Park considered to be its preserve, and an opportunity because East Park contemplated advantage by promoting a joint scheme that might initially accommodate thirty to thirty-five children 'whose ailments require more prolonged treatment than is afforded by the Royal Hospital for Sick Children or similar institutions'.[7]

The interlude years

From 1910, the aspiration for a country branch and the raising of funds for such a venture found a regular place on the agendas of Board meetings. The acquisition, or creation, of suitable premises was frequently deliberated over and, for example, in 1913, Dr James H Nicoll's views were sought on 'whether the Coast or Country would be the more suitable for the Treatment of Tubercular Diseases of the bone, etc'.[8] At this time, Nicoll was a noted surgeon attending Glasgow's Western Infirmary and the Royal Hospital for Sick Children's outpatients department in Scott Street where he performed day surgery. His counsel to the East Park Board was formulated by his judgement on the medical conditions that would benefit. He stated that these were '… mainly (a) Rickets, (b) Surgical Tuberculosis (bones, spine, hip and other joints) and (c) Paralysis' and declared that 'there can be little doubt that, for the first two named classes, a Branch out of town would be of great advantage'.[9]

Nicoll then elaborated on his ideas. A country Home should be near a 'township' with a railway station to facilitate recruitment of domestic, nursing and teaching staff. It would be best to build a facility that might be designed to maximise light, air, efficient use of space and incorporate a glass-enclosed veranda. It should be planned for 'care and cure of tubercular cases' with 'a full staff of nurses' supplemented by 'visits of a Medical Man accustomed to Surgical Work'. Nicoll envisaged a location that aspired to 'the great reputation' of Margate, but wrote that he would be happy with 'a well sheltered spot with a Southern Exposure [that] would, in our Scotch climate, be the more beneficial on the whole'.[10]

The directors agreed wholeheartedly with Nicoll's suggestions, concluding that they should be vigilant in their search for just such a property.[11] Periodically, potential sites for a country branch were investigated, plans drawn up and negotiations instigated, such as one at Carmunnock in 1914.[12] However, the onset of the Great War was not only to considerably delay the progress of East Park's aspirations for a country branch, but also in raising the finance to bring it about. Following the Great War, optimism about raising the necessary capital remained in certain quarters. Glasgow's Lord Provost, Sir Matthew Montgomery, in moving the adoption of East Park's annual report for 1924, commented that, 'If you appeal in Glasgow for any good and generous objects, believe me – for I know a good deal about it – you will never appeal in vain'.[13] This confidence was not expressed at the most auspicious time, but rather than constructing a purpose-built facility as proposed by Nicoll, East Park was to be an indirect beneficiary of the Great War, East Park having, in 1923, already concluded an agreement for the purchase of a large house and grounds in the Ayrshire coastal town of Largs.[14]

What became the nucleus of the Country Branch of East Park in Largs had been built as 'Warren Park' mansion for Otto Ernst Philippi (1846–1917), director of foreign sales for thread manufacturers, J & P Coats of Paisley, in 1891.[15] Philippi was born in Prussia, but became a patriotic naturalised British citizen who propelled the famous thread makers, and himself, to seemingly boundless success.[16] Occupying a six-acre site, when the Philippi family moved into their new home, Warren Park, it had eighteen rooms, but a decade later the family had increased its size to thirty-one rooms.[17] However, with indifferent health, Philippi later relocated himself and his family to England, where he died in 1917, aged seventy.

Largs provided fresh air and sunshine.

In the aftermath of the Great War, and having had further extensions added, Warren Park was a Red Cross convalescent home for wounded soldiers.[18] East Park completed its purchase of Warren Park from the Red Cross in 1924 and some of its attributes certainly conformed to Nicoll's earlier guidance:

> The situation of Warren Park for a hospital is ideal. It lies at the south end of Broomfields at Largs with a southern and western exposure and the hills behind give shelter from the east and north winds. In front, the property extends to the sea, the boundary wall abutting on the seaside path leading to the Bowen Craig where the Monument to commemorate the Battle of Largs is erected.[19]

It was February 1927 when the first admissions to the Country Branch took place, followed by a formal opening ceremony by the Duchess of Montrose on 4 June.[20] This achievement, nearly two decades in the making, did however leave East Park financially overstretched. The generosity of the people of Glasgow boasted about by the city's provost was about to be put to the test with the launch of an appeal for £50,000.[21]

War and conflict

From 1927 until the outbreak of the Second World War, the Country Branch performed its intended function, delivering bracing fresh sea air to rachitic and

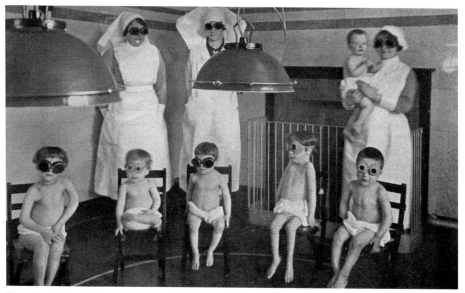

The gift of ultraviolet equipment provided innovative therapy.

tubercular children, in a largely harmonious atmosphere. The curative powers of the seaside did not, of course, always work. The first recorded death was eight-year-old Charles McLellan from nephritis on 6 February 1928.[22] While parents generally made funeral arrangements, in due course East Park had to purchase a triple lair in Haylie Bank Cemetery, located in a verdant setting on a hillside a short distance from the town.[23] A simple headstone, which does not record names, was erected and the last recorded burial was in 1974.[24] There were several interments here during the years of the Second World War that, with the evacuation of children from the Maryhill Home, signalled a fraught time in the running of the Country Branch.

Jessie McKittrick had been appointed as the Country Branch's first matron, but she was moved from her post there on 15 September 1941 and relocated to Maryhill where, while remaining 'matron' in name, she had no real function to perform.[25] In April 1942, following commencement of an arrangement with Glasgow Corporation for it to use East Park's buildings in Maryhill as a 'Wartime Nursery', the directors discontinued McKittrick's employment since the Maryhill home 'has no function to perform … and ceases to exist for the time being'.[26] In recording the period from 1939 to 1942, the East Park minutes of its Board meetings give what appear to be a very condensed summary of events, simply stating that Matron Mary MacEwen at Maryhill had seniority over McKittrick and so had greater entitlement to be matron at the sole Home to continue operating during the war – that at Largs.[27]

More than two decades before the research project to create this history of East Park was launched, in oral testimony Amy (pseud.) described her experiences as a child resident at East Park in Maryhill from 1934 to 1939, and then in the Country Branch from 1939 to 1945.[28] A bright, articulate woman in her late sixties when interviewed, Amy narrated occasional adverse experiences while in Maryhill. But it was following evacuation to Largs that she described going through a particularly unpleasant time.[29] Her description of her time at Largs between September 1939 and 1941 made for disturbing listening, such as 'sour food that had gone off, … a real cruel manner in which they dealt with you, … pushed in my wheelchair, naked, into the classroom', etc. Jessie McKittrick was undoubtedly under extreme pressure at this time, Amy noting that 'some [children] were over the age … so Matron McKittrick … had to get rid of all these older patients. … [to] accommodate the younger ones that were coming in'.[30]

There were clearly serious problems at the Country Branch until control was placed in the hands of Matron Mary MacEwen and Sister Peggy Ligertwood, both described by Amy as 'kind … good … [who] didn't go out to harm you in any way'.[31] Ligertwood had transferred to Largs on 15 January 1940, but had resigned soon afterwards because 'her association with the Medical Superintendent and the Matron had not been of a harmonious character', and she had stated that her decision was because 'there were certain conditions and responsibilities which … she cannot conscientiously accept'.[32] The visiting doctor refuted Ligertwood's complaints, and her resignation, scheduled for 6 May 1940, was accepted. The Board minutes are silent on subsequent events surrounding Peggy Ligertwood. However, she did *not* depart for pastures new, but continued on a long career with East Park and, uniquely, was honoured for her work when, in 1953, she was awarded an MBE.[33]

Although Jessie McKittrick was Country Branch matron for fifteen years, perhaps there had always been a tension between her and the directors of the Association. When appointed, her selection from a total of eight applicants had been unanimous, and she was credited with being 'a fully certificated trained Sister with a large and varied experience of hospital work and was familiar with all the requirements for the equipping and furnishing a Home of this kind'.[34] Yet she drew early criticism for failing to respond to the Committee's correspondence, for appointing an 'uncertified nurse as her Chief Assistant' and for an apparent atmosphere of unhappiness among children transferred from Maryhill.[35] Religious sectarianism again surfaced when the Committee raised its concern that she had appointed 'several members of the nursing and domestic staff of the Roman Catholic persuasion'.[36] However, she received direction from the medical superintendents, and Dr Bankier Sloan assured the directors that he would explain to her 'that arrangements should be made to

The first regular air services in Scotland took off in the 1930s, generating excitement that was not lost on children in the Largs home.

appoint a Certified Assistant and dispense with the services of the RC members of the staff'.[37]

Religious prejudice blighted the west of Scotland during the interwar period, something that McKittrick had either failed to consider or, to her credit, she had tried to counter, but which was subsequently spelt out in no uncertain terms by Dr Sloan in a letter that reiterated several points raised in their meeting and which included the assertion that 'it has been a Principle at East Park to have a wholly Protestant Staff'.[38] This was the year following the short-lived General Strike and prolonged coal miners' strike of 1926, a time which historian Callum Brown observes to be 'noteworthy [for] the largest single fall in presbyterian communion in the inter-war period'.[39] If the directors felt that, in 1926/7, their religious convictions were part of a wider societal crisis of confidence and under threat, this could well have added to their disquiet about McKittrick's recruiting approach when she assembled her initial team. In 1928, continued disquiet about McKittrick's management style remained and the directors might have chosen to demand her departure had it not been for economic considerations. McKittrick was organising a grand fundraising fete for the Country Branch, her role being considered so crucial to its success that, if she had been dismissed, the implications could have been harmful to the financing of the new venture.[40] Although 'certain members of the Committee thought she had not "fitted in" with East Park and was not likely to do so', running of the Country

Branch subsequently settled into a regular operating pattern and functioned relatively smoothly until it was hit by the impact of the mass evacuation of children from Maryhill in 1939, narrated in chapters 9 and 11.[41]

The post-war years

Following the end of the Second World War, the return of children to Maryhill must have provided a welcome relief to the staff at Largs, even though there was the initial impact of Matron Mary MacEwen's sudden death in 1945. The Country Branch was now able to resume full focus on directing effort, and sunshine, towards the restoration of good health to children with the likes of rickets and tuberculosis.

Michael McCreadie (b. 1946) arrived at Largs from his home in Glasgow in 1950 and, apart from some months receiving orthopaedic treatment for his poliomyelitis in Mearnskirk Hospital, remained in Largs until 1961.[42] From this early post-war, post-evacuation era, Michael's memories of his eleven years in the Country Branch at Warren Park were overwhelmingly positive, even though he was mostly estranged from his family whose absence left its mark, especially during weekends and school summer recess: 'Whatever circumstances my parents had thirty-five miles away in Glasgow, I've never blamed them. They had to do what they had to do. And so be it … I was actually quite happy and contented at Largs.' He loved learning in the school, idolised his teacher, Miss Maxwell, saw his involvement with the Boy Scouts as a direct extension of his education, played in goal when the boys played football, and was in an environment where the toxicity of sectarian football rivalry held no meaning for him.

While Michael felt that the Largs children were not shielded or kept apart from the wider Largs community, the big house occupying Warren Park was his normality until it was shattered by a rare visit home. Until then, he had assumed that all dwellings were like that, but in his family's Glasgow tenement he was confronted with sharing a bed with two brothers, using an outside toilet, and seeing neighbouring tenement walls all around when he had been used to looking through his dormitory window to a view of the Isle of Cumbrae across the Firth of Clyde.[43] When interviewed in 2022, Michael reflected on the emotional aspects of his childhood. He did not experience treatment negatively – in contrast to Amy's personal memories of the early 1940s – but he also commented that he had no recollection of ever receiving a hug, something that he would have appreciated upon occasion. In addition to his admiration for Miss Maxwell, an innovation was education via the radio that, to quote Michael, 'brought the outside world into the school' and expanded his knowledge and horizons. Including the nurses and teachers, Michael saw Largs as 'family … a family of many people', and he remained in contact with two childhood friends, Jack

Borland and Ian Rae, throughout their lives. While child mortality was not as high as in the pre-Second World War days, there were still deaths. A poignant memory for Michael was his friend, Frank McCann, telling him during the night that he was dying. Next day, Michael went to school and when he came back, Frank's bed was empty.[44] Michael, however, flourished, and returned home in 1961.

Following his discharge, Michael felt unable to settle comfortably with his family, from which he had been apart throughout most of his childhood, life back in Glasgow all being quite strange to him. The opportunity to attend a 'disabled' workshop in Devon was his break from this uneasy domestic relationship. In adulthood, Michael went on to have a prominent sporting career as a Para-Olympian, one that took him to forty countries. But Michael no doubt speaks for many children who were in his situation, especially where family bonds were severely affected at a young age, when he flags up the importance of telling and listening: 'See telling you the story that I'm telling you now. I couldn't have done that fifteen years ago. It would have hurt me. It's quite healing.'[45]

Michael, and Amy, in their later years, had a multitude of emotions when reflecting upon childhoods spent in a children's home. They were largely denied the experience of growing up in a domestic setting with parents and with brothers and sisters, so a feeling of alienation from their families could set in. Michael had almost totally positive memories of growing up at East Park's Country Branch in the 1950s. Amy had relatively positive memories of Maryhill in the latter 1930s, but negative recollections of Largs in the early 1940s. They also felt confusion about why they had been sent to a Home as a consequence of their paralysis arising from contracting polio in infancy. Their testimonies reveal that emotional scars arising from childhood residential care can be long and enduring. Need of 'a hug' fleetingly symbolises the deficiencies of such an upbringing while, simultaneously, the potential implications of such 'familiar' engagement with children is treated with extreme caution in the twenty-first century.

When the tide goes out …

In 1951, children receiving schooling within the Country Branch had medical challenges that included heart conditions, polio, asthma and nephrosis, and diseases such as coeliac, Perthes' and Still's.[46] By the 1980s, the school register was less expansive on the children's medical circumstances than had been the case three decades earlier, but where listed, there were instances of profound mental 'handicap', Down's Syndrome, blindness, epilepsy, of being 'spastic' and of having spinal injury; additionally, some children were placed in Largs for a 'holiday', i.e. for respite purposes.[47]

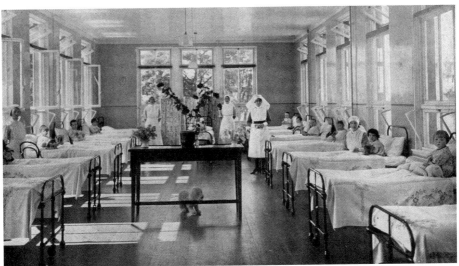

Wards in the Country Branch were at full capacity following the evacuation of East Park at Maryhill.

When the Country Branch might have been gearing up to celebrate its diamond jubilee, it was instead dispersing its staff and children in readiness to leave Warren Park. Closure had been announced at the annual meeting held in Maryhill on 28 February 1986, when Alfred Shaw, the Association's president, put this decision down to 'the drop in the normal birth rate, closer screening of expectant mothers and fostering, all resulting in fewer applications for admission to the Home'.[48] The number of children in both Homes had indeed declined through the post-Second World War years, although the reasons were probably more complex than those listed by Shaw. By the early 1980s, Nurse Elizabeth (pseud.) recalled there being about thirty-three children resident, all having intellectual disabilities, but some of them also having physical impairments. She emphasised that it was a 'home' rather than a hospital, even though children occupied 'wards' rather than dormitories.[49] Nonetheless, she noted a general enthusiasm for returning children to their families or to 'independent' living.

However, Elizabeth recalled children for whom she believed this would not have worked, such as a girl in her early teens with autism who had reduced mobility, but was 'extremely vocal – most of the night too' and who had lived at home until, growing older, her parents had been unable to cope with her needs.[50] Here it needs to be kept in mind that as children grew older, so too were parents ageing and this could constrict their ability to do all that they might wish in order to care for their child. Similar was the case of Charlie, a highly active boy with autism who the nurses had difficulty getting to stay in bed and who had a habit of wandering around the home complex during the night. Elizabeth felt that the children were well cared for and that, while historic malpractice in institutions has been the subject of recent investigations in Scotland, at East Park the good far outweighed the bad. However, she willingly added a caveat:

> There were practices that were acceptable then, that would absolutely not be acceptable now. [Speaking of Charlie] it was common practice to tie his wrists to the frame of the bed as a form of restraint. I hated doing it. The nurses who were on [duty] with me would know that I hated it being done, and that's possibly why he escaped … But it was accepted practice, and there will have been times when I will have done it … These things were not seen as cruelty. They were seen as a health and safety measure.[51]

To place such restraint within the context of the time, despite use of restraint in mental healthcare facilities being advocated against since the 1830s, it has continued to be felt necessary upon occasions for a patient's own protection.[52] And it is worth recalling that physical intervention was accepted practice in other areas of society, such as use of the tawse as a form of punishment in Scottish schools, not banned until 1987.[53] Historic values and practices have to be placed within the ethos of the era in question.

Mairi Smyth agreed to assist a friend, a care worker at East Park, as an escort on a trip that had been organised for the children in the early 1980s. Matron Myra Neil observed how Mairi successfully settled the children down for the night at the end of the outing and asked if she also might like to become one of the Home's care workers. When Mairi explained that she was a qualified nurse, Neil was determined to secure her services and Mairi became one of two trained nurses in the Country Branch in the 1980s. By this period, the number of children in residence having diminished significantly, children tended to develop individual relationships with staff members: 'Everyone adopted one of the staff … had their favourite "aunty".' 'Some children couldn't lift their head from a pillow, couldn't speak, couldn't communicate, just got lifted and fed', while there were also lads, such as Charlie, with boundless energy, 'the wild men' as Smyth called them with a smile. For these boys, Smyth co-opted two unused rooms where they could expend their excess energy. The experiment was transformational, 'the wild men' being seen to change from 'problematic boys who wrecked everything' to youngsters who, for example, were found to love music.[54]

The needs of the Country Branch children were diverse by this period. A couple of children attended mainstream school, while others, who were able, attended the school room in the Home. They were taught the likes of basic arithmetic, while in reality, in Smyth's view, teaching really needed to be tailored to convey practical skills, such as how 'to tie their shoelaces or pull up their trousers'.[55] Outside schooling was emulated in that the children in the Home wore school uniforms, the boys with shirts, ties and grey trousers, the girls in pinafore dresses.

Mairi Smyth described the Country Branch as a happy place.[56] But despondency among staff set in when, in June 1985, it became known, despite initial denials, that it was to be closed.[57] The people of Largs had a close rapport with the Country Branch, Smyth noting that 'before we knew it, there was a fighting committee in Largs, [the community] didn't want it to close down'. Smyth reflected upon the Country Branch facility at this time:

> At Largs, we could take kids through a back gate to a sandy beach. It was a beautiful spot for children. Staff felt that Largs, rather than Maryhill, should stay open, but they were told that they get more money from people in Glasgow. It was about money; it wasn't about children. And the building needed repairs.[58]

The argument that the Country Branch had to close because of the condition of its fabric was subsequently disputed following an inspection instigated by Largs Junior Chamber of Commerce: 'A fireman and an architect examined the Largs building and declared it was sound, there was nothing wrong with it. The notion that it was falling to pieces was rubbish.'[59] Indeed, a register of the Country Branch's children from 1979 suggests that, because of the substantial drop in the number of children with disabilities who were resident, sustainable numbers were having to be maintained by the short-term admission of groups of siblings from families facing various domestic difficulties, but where there was no indication of physiological challenges. The arrival of family groups of children was attributed to 'social problems' in their own homes, which in some instances were identified as being due to 'one parent in hospital', 'mother can't cope with them' and '[on the] waiting list for Lennox Castle', and these represented a sequence of admissions that further suggest, in the Country Branch's final decade, its underutilisation for its primary purpose.[60] When Matron Myra Neil resigned in November 1984, her 'replacements' were senior administrators rather than matrons.[61] As the Largs home was being wound down, a number of children were returned to their parents under the watch of social workers. Transfer of children being relocated to Maryhill was completed in March 1987, drawing to a close the six-decade existence of East Park's Country Branch.[62]

Thomas Johnstone, who served as physician superintendent at Largs from 1946 until his death in 1969, was succeeded by his son, Matthew Johnstone.[63] As the end of the Country Branch approached, Matthew Johnstone voiced a timely reminder of how society should see disabled children and the function of the East Park organisation:

> Nowadays there is a tendency to fit people neatly into categories to make us think that we know who they are. We talk about 'the handicapped' as if they are entirely different from us. This is not true. Each handicapped child is a little person who *happens* to have a disability. Our aim, therefore, at East Park is to provide comfort for all – for the physically handicapped [to nurture] as much independence as possible with a view to *choice* in the way of life he or she will have – [and] for the more severely handicapped, [provide] encouragement in every way possible and the security of a happy home.[64] [original italics]

'A happy home', Johnstone undoubtedly hoped, would be the legacy of the Country Branch despite the challenges that arose during the early years of the Second World War and its fraught demise in the mid-1980s. As for the physical presence of the buildings that had included the late nineteenth-century home of a textile industry baron, they ultimately became Warren Park Care Home, but this closed in 2015.[65] The buildings were demolished in May 2022.[66]

CHAPTER 11

Care and Health, 1946–70

To those who contributed with monetary donations, books, toys, flowers, tinfoil,
clothing, cakes and tea-bread, etc., etc., it is impossible to state in words the debt of
gratitude we owe. We ask one and all to accept our deepest appreciation, sincerest
thanks, and to join in the prayer that the dark clouds of war may soon evaporate,
leaving sunshine on the path we hope to tread in continuing our work of tending
crippled and infirm children, and fitting them for the hazardous battle of life.

Matron Mary MacEwen, January 1940[1]

Post-war optimism and challenge

It took some time for what matron had referred to as 'the dark clouds of war' to
evaporate. Even once peace was restored, considerable adjustment was required. In
the immediate post-war years, children continued to be admitted to East Park for
treatment. For some, as well as illness and infirmity, there was evidence of poverty
and malnourishment. In his Annual Report in January 1946 for the year ending
31 December 1945, Dr George T Ross, physician superintendent of the Country
Branch, reported:

> On the whole it has been gratifying to all concerned to see how poor,
> undernourished, debilitated, and sickly children improved after only a few
> weeks in residence. Good and careful nursing, regular hours, fresh air, and
> sufficient well-cooked food of the right type have all played their part in
> achieving these welcome results.[2]

Although the care and treatment appeared to be effective, there had to be
considerable reorganisation to comply with requirements of the new legislation
discussed in chapter 9. There was also a shortage of nurses and continued difficulty
in obtaining certain materials; indeed, rationing of some food continued nationally
until 1954. In 1946, in Largs the education continued with an average of sixty-two

children on the roll, taught by four teachers, two in classes in school rooms and two in wards for children confined to bed. Three children were presented for, and passed, the Qualifying Examination. As well as the academic component, school work included handwork (what may now be referred to as arts and crafts) and boot-making, and was described as 'adapted to the needs of children at whatever stage they are admitted'.[3] In Maryhill, the school reopened in January 1946 with thirteen pupils, increasing over the year to forty-three with two teachers. Teaching was altogether more challenging, described as difficult due to 'the unsettled conditions'.[4] Although the nature of such 'unsettled conditions' is not recorded, these probably included the ongoing construction of the new school facilities which had recommenced at the end of hostilities.[5] By 1947, however, the difficulties of the immediate post-war years were receding. The new school in Maryhill opened in April 1947. Teacher Maud Fletcher wrote:

> The two bright roomy classrooms have greatly facilitated teaching and made life more interesting for the children. The third classroom, which is used for music, wireless lessons and recreational activities, has been a great joy and proved to be very necessary. In the manual room, which is very well equipped, the children are taught leather-work.[6]

Similarly, Matron Peggy Ligertwood reported:

> The year 1947 can be regarded as satisfactory and progressive. Considerable re-organisation has been necessary to comply with present day requirements and Government Departmental demands. Lack of, and difficulty obtaining materials, incurred delays hindering progress to a certain extent. Much, however, has been accomplished, and it is our earnest hope that in the future the Home will retain the individuality and status of former years.[7]

Having negotiated not to join the NHS, it was agreed that East Park, Maryhill and the Country Branch would provide care and education for children and young people with long-term healthcare needs, but who did not require hospital care. Indeed, children and young people in East Park were living with a wide range of medical and orthopaedic conditions.[8] In January 1948, physician superintendent Dr Bankier Sloan indicated that, during 1947, children and young people in Maryhill were living with the following conditions:[9]

Cardiac disease	11
Coeliac disease	8
Paralysis	10
Perthes' disease	5
Congenital dislocation of hips	3
Asthma	2
Osteomyelitis	3
Talipes	2
Chronic nephritis	2
Spina Bifida	2
Chorea	2
Rheumatoid arthritis	2
Fragilitis ossium	1
Ulcers of Eyes	1
Tuberculosis of spine	1
Tuberculosis of hip	1
Cerebellar ataxia	1
Bronchiectasis	1
Rheumatism	1
Prolapse of bowel	1
Colostomy	1
Epilepsy	1
Hare Lip	1
	Total: 63

Details were not given for the Country Branch in Largs.

Meanwhile, staff training was recognised as important. Younger members of the nursing staff attended weekly lectures on 'the principles and practice of their profession'.[10] These are not specified but staff training in the Country Branch is later described as including anatomy, physiology and practical nursing, with four nurses progressing to General Nurses Training in 1949.[11] Around the same time, East Park also initiated a pension scheme for staff as the directors thought it right that some provision should be made 'for staff who had given loyal service'.[12]

As the NHS became established, Dr Patrick MacArthur, medical superintendent who replaced Dr Sloan in 1948, noted there was severe strain on the accommodation in the general hospitals for acute illness and these hospitals were unable to meet the needs of children who required prolonged care. Consequently, there was increased demand for accommodation in East Park, now operating independently of the NHS.[13] As observed by Lord Inverclyde, Dean of Guild, despite the improvements in housing and hygiene and the care of children generally, there were still many children requiring the special treatment provided at East Park.[14]

Post-war community changes

There had been concerns that the introduction of the NHS may affect voluntary subscriptions and thus funding for East Park, but this proved not to be the case.[15] The Lord Provost of Glasgow, Victor D Warren, suggested that East Park was very close to the heart of the citizens of Glasgow and funds would be forthcoming.[16] Indeed, funds continued to flow in from a wide variety of sources across Scotland and beyond. In January 1951, Matron Peggy Ligertwood recognised the local children in particular, writing:

> A special word of thanks is due to the children who, during school vacations, staged back-green concerts, sales of work, garden parties etc, handing over the proceeds in monetary donations for the provision of outings, parties, comforts and equipment, the knowledge of which gave great joy and pleasure to the children resident in the Home.[17]

Evelyn, who grew up in Maryhill in the 1950s, remembers these concerts. She wrote:

> I was born in Dunard Street, Maryhill, Glasgow and around the early 1950s, as children we used to have concerts in the back courts. I must have been eight or nine years old. There were wash houses in each close back court and we used there as 'dressing rooms' for the performers.
>
> We used to [sing] popular songs of the time and dance 'routines' of the time. … I can remember one of the songs was:
>
> 'You can roll a silver dollar down upon the ground and it will rooooll because its rooooound – a woman never knows what a good man she's got until she turns him dowwwwn, so listen my honey just listen me. I want you to understand a man without a woman is like a fish without a tail or a boat without a sail. There's only one thing worse in the universe and that's a woman without a maaaaaaan!'
>
> We dressed up in our Mum's clothes, trousers, hats, lipstick, etc. and performed all the actions with absolutely no shyness. We charged I think one penny entrance and sold tablet (which I think some mother made) to increase

the funds. The mums all supported us. … What money we made from these 'Concerts' was sent to Pat Roller, a Reporter in the *Daily Record*, for the benefit of Eastpark Home (as it was known then).[18]

Meanwhile, Glasgow and Maryhill were changing, in what has been described as 'nothing less than a housing revolution'.[19] Some 564,000 new homes were built in Scotland in the twenty years after 1945, 86 per cent of these being built in the public sector, an increase of around two-thirds on those constructed between the wars in cities such as Glasgow and towns such as Airdrie, Coatbridge and Motherwell.[20] Plans to build the new towns of East Kilbride and Cumbernauld were approved in 1952 and 1956 respectively, with 'more prosperous Glaswegians' moving outwith the city boundaries to areas such as Newton Mearns and Bearsden where private housing was available.[21] Glasgow Corporation's plans progressed with the construction of the large peripheral housing schemes of Easterhouse and Cranhill, Drumchapel, Castlemilk, Nitshill and Pollok.[22] Vacated properties were demolished and replaced with mainly flats and high-rise buildings. Maryhill, where some tenements lacked lavatories, washing facilities and running water up to the 1980s, was part of these developments.[23] The Wyndford Estate, developed on the grounds of the disused Maryhill army barracks by the Scottish Special Housing Association in close consultation with the Department of Health for Scotland, was billed as 'a flagship attempt to modernise the area's decaying fabric'.[24]

Referred to as 'massage' in earlier years, children undergo physiotherapy in 1957.

Some Reflections of
a Former Patient

The following short narrative was written in 1951 by a former East Park child and appeared in that year's East Park Annual Report, the seventy-eighth such report. The author signed her or his piece off with the initials 'SBH'. While in the years around the Boer War, mentioned in the narrative, children's names are given in full in East Park's annual reports, it has not been possible to pinpoint the identity of SBH.

On visiting East-Park Home recently I was greatly impressed by the way the children were being looked after. The bright appearance of the place, the cheery nurses, and the homeliness of the Matron [Peggy Ligertwood], all brought back to my memory the several years I spent in the Home as a child.

At that time we used to sit at the window on visiting days, watching for Father or Mother, and look down the long narrow passage, thick with trees and hedges, which looked such a long way from the window to the Maryhill Road. There were no such things as wireless or films in those days, but I remember how we used to look forward to the bright painted ships as they sailed along the canal. The boats were called the *Gipsy Queen*, the *Fairy* Queen, and the *May Queen*, and it was great fun to shout for our favourite ship.

Another picture which remains in my memory was the end of the Boer War, when victory celebrations were on. A grand stand was built in front of the Home, and all the children were seated and had a good view of the march past. The soldiers from the Maryhill Barracks marching along the street with their heavy boots, the noise of the band, and the rumbling of the big cannons along the road, coupled with the shouting of the people, and the special cheer the soldiers gave us when passing the Home – that is something I shall always remember.

I thank God that there are still people left in this changing world who can find time to show these children that someone is always thinking about them, for I know from my own experience these children will appreciate this very much.

New direction

Care and education provision for children and young people with long-term health conditions was also changing. As East Park's role was emerging within the new arrangement of health services for children, Dr MacArthur identified a possible function for East Park in the care and education of children and young people with spastic diplegia, a condition we would now recognise as a form of cerebral palsy.[25] This built on existing experiences in the Home. Children with cerebral palsy had been educated in the school for many years, described by teacher Maud Fletcher as 'in an atmosphere of relaxation and encouragement, [they] made good educational progress'.[26] Newer methods of treatment were being developed, however, hence Dr MacArthur's proposal. Having agreed to only admit children requiring longer-term care of over six months, this gave an opportunity to explore and expand treatments.

Because of the focus on cerebral palsy in East Park at the time, it is worth pausing to consider the condition. Cerebral Palsy is an 'umbrella term' given to a group of disorders and functions. It is a lifelong condition whereby people have damage to their brain or their brain has developed atypically. This occurs either before birth or during a child's early development and causes disruption to the development of movement and posture. It is the most common physical impairment in children and at the time of writing, around 1 in 500 births will result in a diagnosis of cerebral palsy. In Scotland, around 150 children are diagnosed each year.[27]

In 1946, the Scottish Council for the Care of Spastics was established in Scotland, changing its name in 1996 to Capability Scotland. The organisation was founded by a group of parents and professionals who came together with the aim of supporting children with cerebral palsy to attend school, obtain employment and 'look forward to a more independent lifestyle'.[28] In 1950, the secretary of the then Scottish Council for the Care of Spastics wrote to the secretary of the Board at East Park requesting that some cooperation be arranged between East Park and 'his Council' regarding spastic children.[29] The Board responded to the effect that 'East Park would be glad to take advantage of experience gained by any organisation in assisting the handicapped child, and at the same time be willing to pass on knowledge gained at East Park during the 75 years of its existence'.[30]

Aware of developments in this field of practice, the proposal to have a focus on care and education of children with cerebral palsy was discussed by the Board on 8 March 1949.[31] As this was going to incur some expense, a small subcommittee was convened.[32] The group met on 31 May 1949, with Dr MacArthur recommending to the directors on 2 June that they proceed with the development.[33] A full-time physiotherapist and speech therapist were proposed as essential to the new initiative.

Already employed part-time as a physiotherapist in East Park, it was agreed that Miss Haldane be offered the full-time post, which she accepted. Miss Haldane coordinated the management and treatment of children with physical impairments. Mr Fraser was appointed master of works and created extensive new equipment, special furniture and remedial aids designed by Miss Haldane to 'aid in the alleviation of the crippling disabilities of individual patients'.[34] As there was no speech therapist in post and only four students due to complete their course that year, this position lay vacant for some time.[35] Dr Anne McAllister and student speech therapists from Jordanhill Training College were involved, sharing their specialist knowledge, skills and experience.[36] Dr McAllister had established the Glasgow School of Speech Therapy in 1935, where she was director until 1964. The East Park post was subsequently offered to one of her students and Miss Donaldson, a full-time speech therapist, was appointed.[37]

Meanwhile, having resisted joining the NHS, a good reciprocal relationship existed between East Park Home and the Royal Hospital for Sick Children (RHSC). The RHSC referred many of its patients to East Park, and staff in the hospital carried out X-ray examinations and provided special splints, admitting to their wards any children requiring clinical treatment.[38] Mr Matthew White, paediatric orthopaedic surgeon and already a regular visitor to East Park, gave advice and assistance in the care and clinical treatment of children with various orthopaedic conditions, also carrying out 'corrective operations' and other treatments.[39] By January 1950, as well as children with a range of other health conditions, ten children with what was referred to at the time as 'spastic paralysis' were receiving care and education at East Park and showing signs of improvement.[40] East Park appeared to have built up an effective multidisciplinary team and support network independent of the NHS, providing care and education for children and young people with a range of long-term healthcare needs.

Meanwhile, the team continued to develop their knowledge and expertise. Miss Haldane spent some weeks visiting hospitals and schools, studying what were described as 'latest ideas on treatment'.[41] It was agreed that Matron Peggy Ligertwood, Miss Fletcher and Miss Haldane attend a Special Schools Conference in Manchester in September 1950,[42] and a series of lecture demonstrations of physiotherapy and speech therapy in cerebral palsy was given in East Park by a visiting expert from London, organised by Dr McAllister.[43] Over time, facilities in East Park for treating children with cerebral palsy were described as having been 'brought right into line with the latest methods in use [in the UK] and in America'.[44] Meanwhile, Miss Gunn, employed in a part-time capacity as physiotherapist in the Country Branch, had her hours extended at the request of Dr Mary Stevenson and Matron, Miss Janet Torrie, at Largs.[45]

A Visitor's Impression included in the Annual Report of January 1950 gives a contemporary description of East Park:

We look first at the ward where a row of little girls are now industriously addressing themselves to sums. Only one is lying quietly idle, detached from the others. 'She only came in this week – we are just letting her get used to things,' Matron nods kindly, and a small answering smile appears on the pale little face.

Across the schoolroom, a class of older children concentrates on sewing, 'for the stall we are arranging next month'. One or two are working with the slow, painstaking effort which marks them as 'spastics': the struggle to co-ordinate arm, hand and fingers so that the needle may be persuaded to go in and out at the right places is immense, but the results are amazingly neat and even.

From the largest schoolroom come the strains of a gramophone. To its rhythm, two more little spastic patients are taking exercise – one on

By 1953, teaching and training was focusing on new skills.

'tram-rails' which keep his feet in the right position as he shuffles forward in time to the music, the other (a small girl) slowly pedalling round on a tricycle …

Next door, a speech therapy teacher slowly takes another child through 'Jack and Jill'. 'He spent several years lying in complete inactivity in a general hospital before he came here,' Matron explains. 'It's taking a little time to wake him up.' Near the fire, a boy is propped on pillows, absorbed in a book.

'He has a chest – this weather isn't good for him.' But he manages a smile and a croaked word of greeting as we pass …[46]

Also in 1950, a child moved into East Park who was to become a well-recognised campaigner for equality and disability rights in Scotland in later years. Jimmy McIntosh was diagnosed with cerebral palsy at birth. He moved into East Park in 1950, aged eleven, having spent several years in Raigmore Hospital, Inverness, after living on his grandfather's farm near Kingussie. Jimmy's recollections of East Park have been published in a biography.[47] He recalled, 'They looked after us very well [at East Park]. My education was very good; the place was good, but not like Raigmore was. There were so many rules.'[48]

Jimmy benefited from a range of professionals working together. Speech therapy had been unavailable at Raigmore but Jimmy recalled, 'It took me a while to talk, but I got there in the end! When I went to East Park Home, I got a speech therapist.'[49] Jimmy was awarded an MBE in the 2006 New Year Honours for Services to Disabled People in Scotland.[50] One can only speculate as to how these early years of speech therapy input at East Park may have contributed to his subsequent achievements.

Until the installation of a lift in 1959, children's movements around East Park were very much restricted. Despite this, some staff adapted their practice to reduce the physical barriers that children faced. Jimmy recalled, 'If there was anything on downstairs for us to go to, they used to get the porter to carry me down on his shoulders.'[51] East Park provided a wheelchair appropriate to his size and needs, 'so he no longer had to crawl across hard floors, grazing himself in the process'.[52] Jimmy recalled:

The school rooms were underneath the nurses' quarter, but the teacher used to come to Scout Ward … I used to sit in an easy chair for my lessons, and I had a table. Then the joiner made me a wooden chair, wheelchair. You ken the old pram wheels? They had that on it and a pram brake. You needed to tip it up to turn it 'cause the wheels only went straight ahead.[53]

In 1953, the Mackenzie Ward is bright and airy, but children working at the beds suggests continuing pressure on space.

Jimmy clearly valued the educational opportunities at East Park. While restricted by the limitations of the building, opportunities were created for him to have relationships beyond the confines of East Park. He recalled, 'I had a pen-pal then too, a boy in America. We used to write to each other a lot, my teacher would print the words and I would write over the top of them.'[54]

Jimmy's memories of East Park were mixed. He enjoyed friendships but he also experienced being bullied by others who, it is suggested, preyed on his vulnerability.[55] He had both new experiences and frustration at an education cut short with no say in future planning of his life when he was moved aged sixteen to Gogarburn Hospital in Edinburgh in 1956.[56] 'I wished they [East Park] could keep me longer, so I could have more education. They said they couldna keep me on because East Park Home only kept you till you were sixteen so the best option they could find was Gogarburn.'[57] Jimmy lived in Gogarburn until 1983, when he married and left to live with his wife in their marital home.[58]

As time went on, East Park was keen to share learning. In addition to the speech therapy students, physiotherapy students visited from Glasgow Royal Infirmary, and student teachers at Jordanhill College of Education, where there was a course for teachers of 'physically handicapped' children, visited and received lectures from Dr MacArthur and Dr Robert A Shanks.[59] Staff at East Park continued to learn from others, drawing on literature from the USA and the World Health Organisation in Geneva, and welcoming visitors from South Africa and Germany as well as the UK.[60] The work of individuals within East Park was recognised, such as Matron Peggy Ligertwood, who was awarded an MBE in the 1953 New Year Honours.[61]

Despite appearing to be well recognised for its work with children with long-term health conditions, there were difficulties in recruiting staff. By 1955, this was impacting on East Park's ability to admit children and young people. Dr Shanks suggested employing 'older girls' and avoiding the term "nurse". The possibility of recruiting 'women interested in the care of children for general duties under the supervision of trained staff' was explored.[62]

Jean trained at East Park in the mid-1950s. She recently shared her experiences with the writer.[63] Personal details are omitted to maintain confidentiality. Jean recalled that Glasgow and the wider community had a tremendous affection for East Park; nothing was too much trouble. She and other young women were known as 'Nurse' and, among colleagues, as 'Nurse [Surname]', although not formally qualified as nurses at the time. She 'lived in' at East Park, sharing a bedroom with another young woman. They were woken at 6.30am and on duty at 7am. The working day was 7am–8pm, with a few hours off during the day. On Sundays, they were on duty 7am–4pm then off for the rest of the day. Others came in at 4pm, so she was able go home for a few hours. Every six months they completed one month of night shifts. They were on night duty for one month at a time, then had one day off for every week worked, known as 'Sleep Days'. Night shift was 8pm–8am. On night shift, there was a 'skeleton staff', a maximum of three on duty with a sister. The duty room was in the front hall and they went up to the wards to check on the children. There were seven or eight children in each ward. They were constantly doing rounds to make sure that the children were comfortable. They received training, much of which was while they were working directly with the children. There were also lectures on child health from Dr Shanks. They then had to take an exam, for which they received a certificate. Jean left after completing her training.

As outlined in chapter 9, during the early 1950s, occasional surgical procedures such as tonsillectomies were still being carried out at East Park. By 1954, however, it was decided that such interventions should cease.[64] The operating theatre should become the sisters' duty room and the sterilising room a treatment room.[65] With this shift in thinking about East Park's role came reflections about the complexity of care. While some of the children and young people living in East Park, both Maryhill and Largs, had health conditions which would improve with time, and some had chronic conditions who, with support, could enjoy a good quality of life, others had progressive life-shortening conditions. It was acknowledged that at times the focus of

In 1955, the schoolroom is less cramped than in former years and has adapted from the traditional regimented rows of desks.

care was 'relief of suffering'[66] and giving the children 'a good happy home life and an efficient education', recognising that in hospital they would be deprived of their education.[67] This was a subject returned to by East Park's directors in subsequent meetings, that the focus was sometimes to 'alleviate distress' as much as to provide specific treatment and cure.[68]

With this increased focus on care and education of children with long-term healthcare needs, it was decided to extend the building in Maryhill to develop a physiotherapy wing, possibly to include a pool.[69] During 1953, fundraising activities were organised, including a coffee morning in Glasgow City Chambers arranged by the Ladies' Committee under the convenership of Lady Warren which raised £807 17s 3d.[70] The physiotherapy wing became known as The Duchess of Gloucester Wing, after East Park's patron. Although there was a reduction in the short term due to ward closures during construction, additional ward accommodation resulted.[71] The Wing was seen as 'heralding a new epoch in the life of East Park'.[72] A few years later, in 1959, a lift was installed in the middle of the Home which enabled children to use the playground more frequently.[73] Recalling Jimmy McIntosh's experience of a few years earlier, the lift was aptly described by Matron Miss Jessie Mackay Ross as having 'provided the children with a sense of freedom, whereby going out to play has now become an accepted part of daily living'.[74]

Never had it so good?

As the 1950s progressed, it has been argued by the historian T M Devine that Scotland 'finally cast off the postwar austerities of rationing and shortage'.[75] In addition to improved housing, there were other developments. Unemployment fell to historically low levels, resulting in the income of the average working-class family rising to 2.5–3 times greater than in 1938.[76] The NHS from 1948 offered free health treatment for all, and the Education (Scotland) Acts of 1945 and 1946 meant that local authorities could insist on the medical inspection of pupils and provide free treatment. Antibiotics were introduced on a major scale in the mid-1940s to treat tuberculosis, and by the early 1960s, Scotland's infant mortality rate was the same as the USA and similar to figures for England and Wales.[77] Prime Minister Harold McMillan famously observed, in 1957, 'Let's be frank about it, most of our people have never had it so good.'[78]

While it is not possible to draw a direct correlation between changes in social policy and child health nationally, staff at East Park and the Country Branch were in a position to notice a change over the years in the well-being of children being referred. As discussed in chapter 9, when reconfiguring the service in 1948 following the creation of the NHS, it had been agreed by the directors that children with certain developmental and health conditions should not be cared for in East Park Home, namely those deemed 'ineducable from mental defectiveness' and those requiring treatment for diabetes and 'tuberculosis of the lung', with the exception of 'certain cases of surgical tuberculosis' admitted at the discretion of the medical superintendents. Children with chronic rheumatic heart disease should only be admitted if they had a reasonable expectation of life and there was discussion about the number of children admitted 'suffering from incontinence'.[79]

As time went on, the profile of children being admitted to East Park changed. In January 1952, there were twenty-one children being treated in East Park and the Country Branch with coeliac. Given a good diet, these children were reported as making good progress.[80] By 1955, it was noted that coeliac was becoming a comparatively rare condition among the children and it was expected that a diminishing number with the condition would be treated in future.[81] By 1957, it was also noted that there was a reduction in the number of children referred with rheumatic heart disease.[82] This was recognised again in 1960, when the 'remarkable fall in numbers of children suffering from rheumatic heart disease' was described as 'a welcome sign in these days of prevention of disease among children'.[83] By 1959, it was noted that the bulk of the children were affected by 'congenital abnormalities', 'spastics' and the more serious results of poliomyelitis, and by 1960 there was recognition that there was now 'an injection against polio' which ultimately influenced referrals.[84] It was also noted, however, that while 'certain ailments [were] in decline', Dr Johnstone described himself as 'mildly alarmed' at the number admitted after accidents on the road as well as in the home.[85] In 1930, rickets was present in some 60 per cent of children resident in East Park, but in 1965 there were no children with this condition.[86] The 'greater problem' was described as being 'congenital deformities' and 'the problem of parental care', with children admitted because of debility or burning accidents in the home. As well as working closely with the RHSC, there was now what was described as 'an excellent relationship' with the Royal Infirmary Burns Unit.[87] Interestingly, it was noted that the physiotherapist could provide help with exercises for children following burning accidents, after which 'children lose their fear so characteristic of such accidents'.[88] Ironically, as more and more children with congenital deficits and paralysing disease survived so the need for their care and treatment had to be met. This was a field of work which was rapidly expanding and becoming better known[89] and has become a subject of research in more recent years.[90] Such was the change in reasons for referral by the mid-1960s that physician superintendent Dr Woolfson noted in his report:

> Major and long-standing physical handicap in childhood is at the present time coming more and more clearly defined by three great diseases. These are Cerebral Palsy, Congenital Cleft Spine and Muscular Dystrophy.
>
> The cause of physical handicap such as Tuberculosis and Poliomyelitis which wrought such havoc among children of former generations have lost their terrible pre-eminence. They are still with us but have been mastered. The hope is this great triad of disease will also suffer a similar fate in the not too distant future.[91]

Over time, some flexibility in referral criteria became apparent. Having decided in 1948 against admitting children with diabetes, in 1955 East Park reversed this decision, it having been realised that their needs could be met within East Park.[92] By 1959, 'a number of diabetic children' had been admitted to the Country Branch, described as a 'valuable innovation' as there was a shortage of residential care for children with this condition.[93]

While it had also been decided, in 1948, not to admit children and young people judged 'ineducable from mental defectiveness', and there was discussion at Board meetings in 1952 about 'the dismissal' of a young resident referred to as a 'mental defective child' thought to be inappropriately placed, this also changed over time.[94] By the early 1960s, some children in the school were assessed to be 'ineducable';[95] indeed, concern was raised that Miss Jane Stewart, the head teacher, 'teaches the ineducable children and this did not seem quite right'.[96] This issue was discussed with representatives of the Scottish Education Department and while it was suggested that, using the criteria of the time, these children should possibly not have been admitted, rather than remove them, it was proposed that the children should have some form of occupational therapy, 'relieving a teacher for more essential duties'.[97] There was further discussion on the longer-term education policy, admissions, teaching staff, 'segregation of low IQ category' of children and control of school hours, with concerns about keeping a balance of children and a suggestion that the Schools Committee in East Park explore this further and report back to the Board.[98] In January 1965, Miss Jane Stewart reported that Mrs Margaret Mallinson SRN, a qualified occupation centre assistant, had joined the school staff in charge of a group of children described as 'ineducable but trainable', observing that 'it is worthy of note that these children whose performance is far below normal standards, have a keen desire to participate in the activities of the school and wherever possible to join in with other school children on special occasions'.[99] It is also worth noting that, by 1973, Dr William R Livingstone, physician, was reflecting that, 'It is too easy at an early age to wrongly classify these children as only suitable for institutions for the mentally deficient.'[100] Shortly after these dilemmas were highlighted, the Education (Mentally Handicapped Children) (Scotland) Act 1974 brought Scotland in line with England and Wales, so that all Scottish children gained a right to education, and children previously classed as 'ineducable' were entitled to education.[101] Some children formerly judged to be 'ineducable' were subsequently shown to be able to read, count and progress to live independently.[102]

Unlike other organisations that had decided to specialise in the care and education of children with specific impairments such as hearing impairment, visual impairment, cerebral palsy or epilepsy, the Board at East Park rejected this singular approach. Physician superintendent Dr Shanks reflected:

Today is the day of specialists, when both men and institutions tend to limit their endeavours to a single problem. Hence we have homes for 'spastics', homes for epileptics, and homes for mentally defectives. We have also specialists in bones, brains, hearts and stomachs, and yet many a child or adult suffers from a disorder affecting more than one of these organs. Moreover a child is often handicapped in more than one system. At East Park we cater for all kinds of physical handicaps. From our consultant surgeon, therefore, we require expert advice not only in orthopaedic surgery but in surgical paediatrics in general. In Mr Matthew White, we are very fortunate in having one who has won distinction in both these fields ...[103]

While he acknowledged some efficiencies in caring for children and young people 'with several handicaps [sic]' together, he also recognised other advantages; reduction in staff stress and opportunities for a nursing experience caring for children and young people with a variety of health conditions, and the ability to respond flexibly to changes in social circumstances such as improved housing conditions, which may lead to fewer disabled children requiring residential care. He also reflected upon the benefits for children that 'they are not in a class by themselves, … that there are all kinds and degrees of physical handicaps, with some of the most severe often appearing the least obvious'.[104] Arguably such flexibility has contributed to East Park's longevity as it adapted over the years to changes in education and social policy and in children's health and development.

Winds of change: into the 1970s

Perhaps changes over the period covered by this chapter are exemplified by the tale of three wheelchairs. Jimmy McIntosh reminisced about the wheelchair made for him in the early 1950s using what he described as old pram wheels and a pram brake 'with wheels that only went straight ahead'.[105] In the Annual Report in February 1967, Dr Harold Woolfson noted:

> Two major technical advances in the design of self-propelling chairs this past year. Both of these are due to the enthusiasm and originality of Mr Noel Blockey, orthopaedic surgeon at the Royal Hospital for Sick Children. From both of these ideas have our children benefited. One design is for the use of paralysed toddlers – paraplegics – a light simply constructed speedy chariot. The other, a most complex electrically powered machine, made for the use of a boy who is so paralysed by poliomyelitis that his only sustained muscular power is effectively the use of his tongue and mouth. By tongue and mouth control he drives this machine.[106]

Changes were not only in respect of children's health, aids and adaptations. Records also indicate changes in childcare practice. Drawing on learning from children's experiences of separation from parents and siblings, particularly through hospital admissions, and evacuation during the Second World War, changes were emerging in established childcare practices.[107] This was particularly marked in the care of children in hospital and parental visiting, culminating in publication of the Platt Report on the welfare of children in hospitals.[108] Although not specified, it seems likely that such ideas influenced practice in East Park. Matron reported in January 1959 that 'an experiment started some three years previously of allowing the children home for various periods during the summer had proved worthwhile'.[109] In 1960, visiting times were extended in line with hospitals from their restrictive two hours on a Saturday afternoon, and physician superintendent Dr Shanks and Matron Jessie Mackay Ross (who replaced Peggy Ligertwood in 1960) would arrange suitable times.[110]

The 1960s were generally seen as a period of rapid social change. They were also a time of significant change in childcare law and policy across the UK. It has been argued by Tom Shaw in the *Historic Abuse Systemic Review* that the framework of laws, rules and regulations between 1950 and 1968 determining how children should be cared for in residential establishments in Scotland was extremely complex.[111] Three significant reports during the 1960s recognised the need for change:[112]

- The McBoyle Committee presented the report 'Prevention of Neglect of Children'.[113]
- The Kilbrandon Committee produced a report making recommendations which included the setting up of Children's Panels in each education authority for young people deemed to be offenders and young people in need of care or protection.[114]
- The government report under the guidance of the Secretary of State for Scotland, which made proposals for change in *Social Work and the Community*, suggesting social work departments should have wider responsibilities than under existing arrangements.[115]

These together led to the introduction of the Social Work (Scotland) Act 1968.[116] The Act brought about the Children's Hearing System, which aimed to ensure the safety and well-being of children and young people through a lay tribunal with decision-making powers called the Children's Panel, regardless of whether the child or young person was perceived to be in need of care and protection or deemed to have committed offences – what has been described as the guiding principle of 'needs not deeds', rooted in the 1964 Kilbrandon Report.[117] To facilitate this ambition, the Act brought together social work professionals from different fields of practice, such as probation, health and welfare and childcare, into one department under one director, with a County Council committee holding responsibility for its oversight.[118] Possibly more immediately relevant to East Park, arguably Kilbrandon presaged the way in which residential care was now perceived, previous legislation being based on the view that, since children were affected by their home environment, the best way to resolve concerns about children whose development was being inhibited or harmed was to remove them from that environment, with an assumption that such removal would be long term.[119] The Kilbrandon Committee was of the view that residential care should not be seen as a permanent solution, but a temporary measure during which intensive training could be given to the child or young person, increasing the chance of a return home. By necessity, this required close contact with the child's family and social work staff.[120] Meanwhile, at the heart of the Social Work (Scotland) Act, through Section 12, was the promotion of social welfare by making available advice, guidance and assistance and, in certain circumstances, the provision of support in cash or kind to individuals in need aged over eighteen, thus providing support to children and their families.[121] It has also been argued by social work specialists and academics Brigid Daniel and Jane Scott that the formation of the Association of Directors of Social Work for senior management and of the British Association of Social Workers for the workforce gave the profession a voice to influence policy and practice.[122]

These changes in policy and legislation are not mentioned in the records at East Park. There were, however, some marked changes appearing in governance and practice. The East Park Constitution was revised and discussed at a special meeting of the Board on 26 November 1963.[123] Decisions to be made included the Name and Objects of East Park. It was decided that the Home continue to be named 'The East Park Home for Infirm Children'. It was also decided that 'the objects of the Home shall be the treatment, gratuitously or for such payment as the Directors may think fit, of physically handicapped children under sixteen years of age whose home circumstances would preclude them from receiving the prolonged care and attention their condition requires'.

There was a marked change from the 1960s onwards in descriptions of what we would now refer to as care planning for children and young people residing in East Park. Early in 1964, there was the possibility of one child being placed in a foster home, although there is no further information on this.[124] Also in the mid-1960s, Matron Jessie Mackay Ross noted that adolescents coming up for discharge were encouraged to have outside contact and spend weekends at home when possible, the aim being independence and social adjustment.[125] She subsequently observed, 'We who are involved with the placing of the young disabled outwith our care are constantly struck by the problems manifested during the rehabilitation period which is so necessary for their acceptance within a sophisticated society.'[126] At the other end of the age spectrum, it was decided to extend East Park's service to include early years activity with the opening of a nursery school and appointment of a trained nursery nurse, Mrs Collard.[127] All of this indicated changes which were to accelerate in the 1970s, the decade of East Park's centenary.

CHAPTER 12

Children's Lives, 1945–1970s

It must be remembered that the care of physically handicapped children involves
not only nursing techniques, but often hard physical work as well.
Moreover if we are to maintain a homelike atmosphere, each nurse must do a
great deal more than merely this; she must stimulate their activities,
supervise their play and above all else, provide affection.

Dr Robert A Shanks, Medical Superintendent, East Park, Maryhill, 1960[1]

While considerable attention was given to the clinical care and education of children and young people in East Park, it is clear that there was also concern about their quality of life; social and emotional relationships, play and new experiences. The early post-war years were decades before aspirations such as those contained in the United Nations Convention on the Rights of the Child (UNCRC), ratified by the United Kingdom on 16 December 1991, Article 23 of which declares:

> State Parties recognise that a mentally and physically disabled child should enjoy a full and decent life, in conditions which ensure dignity, promote self-reliance and facilitate the child's active participation in the community.[2]

Or more recently in *The Promise*, published in 2020, which emanated from the Independent Care Review and states that:

> Scotland must respect, uphold, champion and defend the rights of children and recognise that their rights are most often realised through relationships with loving, attentive caregivers. Scotland must fully incorporate and uphold the UNCRC.[3]

As outlined above in Dr Shanks' statement in the Annual Report of 1960, however, there was still concern about children and young people's experience.[4] This ethos

166

appears to have been aspirational in East Park for some time prior to this statement. Elizabeth stayed in East Park on two occasions in the late 1940s, the first time for about six months and the second time for around ten months or a year. She recalled, 'staff were brilliant, genuinely good folk. Nurses and matron were really good. Staff would go to the picture halls and sing songs from the pictures while making the beds … And the older girls would listen. … They were trying to give us as ordinary a life as possible.'[5] She summarised her experience: 'East Park was amazing. You were secure in it, you were happy in it. There was a lot of joy in it.'[6]

Elizabeth had many good memories of East Park but she is only one voice of the many children over the years who lived in East Park. A few years later there was discussion at a Board meeting about discipline. In the opinion of one senior member of staff, '[smacking] is the only punishment understood by young children, the withholding of privileges being useless'. It was made very clear by the Board that the person in question should be notified that, even if it was entered in the punishment book, which was a requirement of the Administration of Children's Homes (Scotland) Regulations 1959 at the time, 'it was against the rules to do such a thing'.[7]

Going back over the years, there had been efforts to ensure a range of experiences and activities for the children. Some were organised by staff and others were initiated by individuals and organisations outwith East Park and the Country Branch. There was also recognition of the value of peer support and friendships between the children. As discussed in the previous chapter, Dr Shanks had argued against specialising in one form of impairment. One reason for this was, he explained:

> With such a variety of medical conditions in the same home it is easier to maintain an atmosphere of hope and encouragement. It is easier to teach independence as far as this may be possible. Moreover the possibilities of mutual help whereby the children themselves can to some extent make good each other's deficiencies are of incalculable benefit in the cultivation of self reliance.[8]

While the language is very much of its time, Dr Shanks had identified the importance of relationships between the children and young people. The significance of peer relationships in residential care over the years is now recognised and this was apparent among some of those living in East Park at the time. Jimmy McIntosh, whom we met in the previous chapter, used a wheelchair to aid his mobility 'so he no longer had to crawl across hard floors, grazing himself in the process'.[9] He was not alone in this and it led to friendships based on shared experiences.[10] Elizabeth also recalled friendships, particularly with another child, Fiona (pseud.). More generally, she recalled, 'there was a lot of good fun and the children used to take care of each other'.[11] Elizabeth recalled what she described as 'a boss' in each ward, an older girl whom, she explained, 'nurses relied on'. She did not think this was an official arrangement, like a prefect at school, but that the young person would report to the nurse for example if a child was sick.[12] She spoke at length about the relationships between children themselves, describing them as being 'way ahead; weans know everything'. She recalled one incident at night after going to bed when 'the boss' in one of the wards, Clare (pseud.), said:

> 'The wee ones are sleeping.' It was quiet at night time. 'Go and get dressed quickly and go out and get chips.' The watchman left the gate open for the nurses coming home so we got dressed and went out with another girl to get chips. This was 11 o'clock at night. We skipped out to get chips and we were standing in the queue to get chips and the next thing, two nurses [from East Park] came in to the chip shop but they never saw us. They wouldn't recognise us. We got up to the counter; 'three bags of chips', then ran back and sneaked back in. We said, 'Nurses were there, nurses were there.' Clare said, 'Did they see ye?' 'Naw, we don't think they saw us.' Clare had money for chips. She then got a perfume bottle, eau de toilette and sprinkled it on the beds so you didn't smell the chips.[13]

Not all relationships were so harmonious, however, and Jimmy recollected experiences of some peers preying on his vulnerability:[14]

> Sometimes my left leg jumps up. When I was in East Park Home a boy pushed me off the bed. It was 'cause he was angry with one of the staff and I was the only person around. The doctor took a look at it and said it wisna broken but that it would be sore for two or three months. It took six months. I could not straighten it and when I went to bed, I had to keep it on a pillow … Three surgeons had a look at it, but they said there was nothing they could do, I would just have to live with it. They said it would be alright in the summer, but I would have to keep it warm in the winter, so I have to keep it warm otherwise I'm in pain. I can tell how cold it is by my left leg.[15]

Elizabeth also spoke of experiences that she perceived as bullying by a young person, 'the boss' in the other ward in which she had resided. She explained the unwritten understanding that existed between the children:

> It's funny, I didn't tell my dad or my mother anything about what went on in the home. I didn't tell them anything that was nasty. Kids learn rules. Somebody's bullying somebody, if you tell and it comes out in the open, that person's going to get to you. You learn the rules, you don't tell on each other, you don't say anything.[16]

Elizabeth questioned if she and her friend, Fiona, were bullied because they were 'fit' and could move about unaided, unlike many others who were reliant on wheelchairs for mobility and who did not appear to provoke such a response.

Lesley Fox, who wrote the biography of Jimmy McIntosh, observed that Jimmy's perception in hindsight of the social life at East Park Home was undoubtedly coloured by his experiences later in life.[17] While critical of 'the rules' in East Park, in contrast with his previous experience in Raigmore Hospital, on the whole Jimmy spoke fondly of social relationships and leisure activities within East Park and in particular of 'interactions with members of the opposite sex', something which was restricted on his move to Gogarburn Hospital when aged sixteen.[18] Jimmy recollected:

> There was a Scout Ward and a Bunton [Bunting] Ward for older boys, and I was in the Bunton Ward. For the older girls they had a Sunshine Ward and a Maryhill Ward. The girls were down the stairs and the boys were up the stairs … The girls down the stairs, you could talk to 'em and that. And go round wi them, have walks with them and that. And you could mix with them and everything.[19]

Bearing in mind that the lift was not installed until 1959, several years after Jimmy left, it seems that staff went to some effort to facilitate social activities and relationships between children and young people prior to this, carrying them downstairs where necessary.[20] Elizabeth experienced a similar level of freedom to move about the Home and mix with other children. She explained:

> In the Sunshine Ward, there were a lot of children in wheelchairs so they pushed the beds out into the sun. They were bedridden. I remember there was a big rocking horse outside the Sunshine Ward. There were big, big windows at the front of the ward and small windows at the back in the

corridor. I used to ride up on the rocking horse, look in the windows and make faces, then I would be back and up. I used to love that rocking horse; I still laugh, every time.[21]

Activities arranged by staff

Whether due to wartime austerity or other reporting priorities, there is little reference to recreational activities during the Second World War, when the children were evacuated to the Country Branch in Largs, or during the early post-war years. A children's cinema was inaugurated in East Park, Maryhill in October 1948, however, and from then on there is increased reference to children and young people's leisure activities.[22]

Elizabeth does not remember the cinema but she recalls enjoyable routines:

Every Sunday night 6 o'clock, after dinner you sat on your bed and you got a ration of sweets. Matron had a trolley and barrels of sweets. She put her hand in and you got a handful of sweets, and a handful of different sweets and maybe a stalk of rock, quite a lot to keep for the week. You got the sweets and put them in your locker … At Christmas, presents were amazing. You got a pillow slip that was full of toys … There was always something. Certain things stick in your memory. At Easter there were Easter eggs. Everything was celebrated … We used to have shows. People came to perform. There was things happening all the time in that place.[23]

East Park raised funds and as well as film shows, with the sale of crafts made by the older children, a gramophone and records were purchased for class use.[24] Other activities were organised in response to special events.

Coronation and royal patronage

It is possibly not surprising that during the 1950s there was considerable interest in royalty. There were celebrations across the country on the day of the Coronation of Queen Elizabeth II, 2 June 1953. By way of commemorating the Coronation, it was planned that each child (in East Park and the Country Branch) be given a mug or handkerchief, and a Coronation film be shown on 13 July in Maryhill and 14 July in the Country Branch.[25] Trees were planted to mark the occasion at both East Park and the Country Branch, with bronze plaques later fitted.[26] One of the trees regrettably did not survive the winter and was replaced and relocated nearer the home.[27] Following the death on 24 March 1953 of Queen Mary, who had bestowed royal patronage on East Park in 1926, an approach was made to Queen Elizabeth to become patron.[28] She was unable to accept this position but the Duchess of Gloucester was subsequently appointed.[29] The new physiotherapy wing, discussed in the previous chapter, which was functioning from November 1957, became known as the Duchess of Gloucester Wing.[30] Over the years an interest in royalty was maintained. The children saw the Queen and Prince Philip when they visited Largs in 1958,[31] and the Duchess of Gloucester visited East Park on 24 October 1962.[32]

Activities within East Park and the Country Branch

As the 1950s progressed, as well as the cinema, other activities were arranged within East Park and the Country Branch. This list is not exhaustive. Dance teachers and music teachers were recruited.[33] Piano lessons were arranged in both East Park and the Country Branch, including for one pupil with limited use of their left hand.[34] Handicraft classes were arranged on Saturdays costing 25s an hour, a volunteer from the community took the boys swimming, another took children for trips to the country, and two social evenings were arranged 'for good friends who apparently enjoyed the children entertaining them'.[35] There was discussion about developing a scheme whereby members of the community could 'adopt' a child, now known as befriending, taking them on outings, remembering birthdays, etc., and hobbies were encouraged, including gardening, stamp collecting and ornithology, when a school group joined the young ornithologists after a trip to Kelvingrove.[36] Children went on bird-watching excursions, and attended meetings and lectures in the Art Gallery and Kelvingrove Museum, and a discussion group was formed for the older boys.[37] Two concerts were held in East Park, supported by the public; children were described as 'active in providing entertainment'. Matron extended thanks to Claremont Troop of Scouts who helped and taught children to perform.[38] Meanwhile, in the Country Branch a local volunteer visited weekly to teach the boys model-making.[39]

Outings and holidays

A number of outings were arranged over the years for children living in both Maryhill and the Country Branch, as Matron Miss Jessie Mackay Ross explained, 'So as the other side of the gate is no longer a mystery.'[40]

Children visited Kelvingrove Art Gallery and Museum and the Zoo.[41] Theatre trips were arranged and the older girls attended a performance of the ballet *Coppélia*.[42] There was a visit to Midlamington Farm in Ayrshire, and with what was described as 'the support of friends', children went to parties, Christmas shows and the circus.[43] Two boys nearing the age of sixteen attended night school at Allan Glen's School, taken there by the father of one of them, although there is no record of the subject studied.[44]

Similarly, children and young people from the Country Branch took part in outings. There was a bus trip to 'the Three Lochs' and a picnic on Loch Lomondside.[45] The children attended 'the crowning of the Brisbane Queen', a local celebration in Largs, and the Brisbane Queen visited the Home, introduced by the provost and 'accompanied by a large retinue of ladies and gentlemen in mediaeval costume'.[46] Some of the boys visited Prestwick Airport and some of the children visited Glasgow to see the Christmas lights and visit the shops.[47] There was a trip to Millport, and trips to local shops and the cinema.[48] There was a trip to the circus at Kelvin Hall, a visit to an art gallery, outings to Culzean Castle and visits to the Summer Variety Show at Barrfield Pavilion, Largs.[49] The children also had an opportunity to meet the comedian 'Mr Logan', presumably comedian Jimmy Logan.[50]

Local businesses – what would now be regarded as 'corporate supporters' – also took an interest in the Home. One large organisation local to Largs arranged trips to Ayr Gaiety and a Christmas party for the children and their parents, including a gift from Santa.[51] In 1967, employees from another company organised a Christmas party.[52] In January 1968, children and nurses had a trip to a Glasgow theatre where they met The Alexander Brothers, had a meal and saw the Christmas lights.[53]

With a large building adapted for the needs of disabled children and young people on the Ayrshire coast, a popular holiday destination for families from Glasgow during the 1950s and '60s, it is not surprising that the Country Branch welcomed children from Maryhill during summer holidays.[54] On at least one occasion, Maryhill took a holiday cottage in Balmaha.[55]

Brownies, Guides, Cubs and Scouts

Uniformed organisations such as Brownies, Guides, Cubs and Scouts have been part of the landscape of childhood for many in Scotland for over a century. The Scouting movement was initiated in the UK with an experimental camp in August 1907 organised by Robert Baden-Powell.[56] In 1909, a group of girls appeared at a Boy Scout rally, declaring themselves to be Girl Scouts, and Baden-Powell decided that there should be a movement for girls.[57] In 1910, the Girl Guides Association was officially established under the leadership of Agnes Baden-Powell, Robert's sister.[58] Baden-Powell's dream was to bring together all young people, regardless of class, race and social background.

A troop of Scouts was formed in East Park in 1925 under the leadership of Scoutmaster Spencer Breslin. Boys of eleven years of age and upwards were eligible and the corps had a roll of sixteen members. Matron Kathleen Jamieson described a keen interest being exhibited by those 'who have the privilege of membership'.[59] Scouting for 'handicapped' young people in Glasgow was subsequently developed in 1932, by the late Mr Reginald H Levy, who was then the Scout Leader of the

1st Glasgow C Troop. The first troop was established in Mearnskirk Hospital, Newton Mearns, near Glasgow. The Hospital had been established to treat children from Glasgow suffering with tuberculosis.[60] Interestingly, a Scout movement publication describes a Scout troop established in East Park in 1931, registered on 16 April 1932 as the 143rd Glasgow Scout Group.[61] A troop of Cubs was subsequently formed.[62] It may be that the troop formed in 1925, while active, had not formally registered with the Scout movement prior to this.

The first group of Guides (at the time called Girl Scouts), with what are referred to as 'special needs', was formed in 1909 in a hospital in Carshalton, Surrey and thereafter troops for children including those with speech, visual, hearing and other additional support needs/disabilities were set up across the UK, adapting to the needs and abilities of the members.[63] In 1919, this changed with the formation of the 'Extension Branch', a central committee to oversee the companies for children and young people with additional support needs. In 1921, 'Post Guides' were set up, a scheme, linked to the Invalid Children's Aid Association, allowing those confined to their own homes to join the movement.[64] Within Maryhill, in 1924 Matron Kathleen Jamieson reported the formation of a company of Girl Guides, which 'added a new and most interesting feature to the work of the Home and the girls are keen to enjoy the privilege of membership'.[65] The company was in its infancy and matron reported there had not been much

Chief Scout Lord Rowallan meets Cubs at East Park in 1958.

time to develop the group, but a few years later, in 1930, Matron Mary MacEwen described 'a large company of Girl Guides and Brownies' having been set up and extended thanks to Captain Campbell and Brown Owl Anderson for their labour and devotion.[66]

A troop of Scouts was established in the Country Branch in 1954, the East Park Section of the 53rd Ayrshire Group.[67] Mrs Wright, Girl Guide Commissioner from West Kilbride, held the first Guide meeting in the Country Branch in 1962, with the first Brownie meeting held the same year.[68] A special visit was made to the Country Branch troop by the Scout Commissioner for Handicapped Children[69] and a few years later the Chief Scout, Lord Rowallan, visited the Country Branch troop.[70]

Over time, as practice and policy changed, the young people from East Park attended weekly meetings of the 76th Glasgow Scout group outwith East Park. This group had been set up in 1957 by Alan Wild for 'handicapped' young people living in the north and west of the city.[71] Meanwhile, the Country Branch Scouts had monthly meetings with the Largs troop, described as 'greatly enjoyed'.[72]

Once these groups were established, there were regular reports of achievements and social activities. One child was presented with the Brownie Badge of Fortitude by Lady McCance, Girl Guide Commissioner, in 1955, and two members of the troop in the Country Branch were presented with the Cornwell Badge for Bravery in 1959 and 1963 respectively by the Scottish Commissioners for Handicapped Scouts, Mr R R Levy and Dr J C Shiach.[73]

The Scouts and Guides movements gave young people opportunities beyond Maryhill and the Country Branch. In 1954, eight boys from East Park attended the Gang Show together with Sister Briggs, a nurse and two Scout Officers, the tickets having been gifted by the Handicapped Scouts Association.[74] In 1956, Scouts from the Country Branch attended a Scout Rally in Ayr,[75] and in 1967 a patrol leader from Largs was chosen to represent Scottish handicapped Scouts at the National Scout Service at St George's Chapel, Windsor.[76] The tenth anniversary of the formation of the Scout company at the Country Branch was celebrated with a reunion Camp in the grounds in Largs, bringing together twenty-four former members, 'boys who were engaged in interesting jobs, and are still keen scouts'.[77] Eleven members of the East Park troop at the time joined in the Camp.[78] Camping extended beyond the bounds of Scotland, however; in 1965, six boys went to Denmark and in 1968 Scouts from both Maryhill and the Country Branch went with the Handicapped Scouts to Switzerland.[79]

The Scouts, Cubs, Guides and Brownies continued in East Park and the Country Branch for some time. In 1968/69, the lone remaining Guide at East Park transferred to the Rotary Centre (Guide) Company,[80] and over time the young people from

East Park joined with the 76th Glasgow Scout group and attended their weekly meeting outwith East Park.[81] In 1981/82, the Brownie pack was suspended due to a lack of girls in the appropriate age group.[82]

Spirituality and religion

Scotland has a history of faith-based residential care provision.[83] East Park historically was not faith-based and accepted children of all faiths and none; religion is not mentioned in the Articles of Association. There was, however, an underlying Christian ethos to proceedings, with prayers at the start and finish of Board meetings. When the sculptor was designing the children's gravestone for the cemetery in Largs, it was agreed that this should be a cross inscribed with 'If such is the Kingdom of heaven', and when the representative of the Billy Fields Variety Agency contacted the secretary offering to give the Home the proceeds of Sunday evening concerts 'to be organised by [him] next winter', the directors unanimously agreed not to allow the Home's name to be used for such concerts and the secretary was instructed to write accordingly.[84] While not made explicit, one is left wondering if this was on account of the concert being held on a Sunday. In December 1951, it was agreed that Rev. David Hislop of the Church of Scotland be appointed to the Board.[85] He was already involved in East Park Home through the Sunday school established some years previously.[86] The Moderator of the Church of Scotland, Rt Rev Dr Jarvis, was invited to be present at the Christmas Dinner at Maryhill, visiting the children in East Park on Christmas Day. In 1961, Rev Hislop was appointed Chaplain to the Home.[87]

While Sunday school was established in East Park, there is little reference to other faiths. It was agreed that a Roman Catholic clergyman could visit on visiting day and also have one hour each month with Catholic children.[88] The request from Rev Francis Coyle, the parish priest, that two lay teachers visit from St Charles' School to give instruction to children for their First Communion, was not granted, however, nor was the request of some parents to take children to Mass on Sunday mornings.[89] No reason was given for refusal.

There appear to have been differing views on the subject of spirituality, however, and when there was discussion about the decrease in the number of children being referred to East Park and the Country Branch, one Board member was described as 'rather afraid of an overwhelming number of Roman Catholic children being admitted'. No reason was given as to why this should be a matter of concern. Directors Dr Mary Stevenson and Dr Romanes Davidson, however, 'were both of the opinion that the doctors were well aware of the views of Board on this question and disease or infirmity do not attack children of one creed more than another'.[90]

Views changed over time, however, and into the 1970s children from both East Park and the Country Branch made the Pilgrimage to Lourdes.[91] Recognition was given to the Children's Handicap Pilgrimage Trust for their support in making the arrangements and meeting the cost, and special thanks offered to the Catholic Women's League for taking an active interest in the children and supplying pocket money.[92] This was described as 'a highlight of the year' for two of the children, who 'both thoroughly enjoyed and benefited greatly from this trip'. It was noted that the same ladies had already held a concert and raised money once again in aid of two of the children from the Country Branch who hoped to go to Lourdes in 1980.[93]

Activities organised by supporters

East Park and the Country Branch attracted considerable support from other organisations wishing to support both financially in fundraising projects and in kind by providing activities. Some of these were isolated events, for example the art students who painted a mural in East Park.[94] No details were given of the subject of the mural. Some, however, were to develop into regular activities. Horse riding was initially introduced in 1968 by volunteers from St Mary's Cathedral.[95] Over the decades, children and young people have enjoyed riding and continue to do so today.[96]

East Park also has a long history of celebrity interest, either through well-known media personalities visiting the children or raising funds for East Park through concerts; chapter 14 covers this subject. Others visited the Homes and met with the children and young people. Elizabeth remembers one such visit:

> Way back in the 1940s, there was also a singer, Issy Bonn his name was. He was a big star and he came to East Park Home in the late '40s, early '50s. He took me on his knee and sang 'Daddy's Little Girl' to me. Look him up, he was a star in the '40s. Photographers were there taking photographs.[97]

Although located in a small town, the Country Branch enjoyed considerable support from celebrities and the local community. In 1963, Kenneth McKellar entertained the children.[98] Celebrities had been involved in the Country Branch for some years prior to this, however, and in July 1939 Sir Harry Lauder opened a Sale of Work. Such was the interest that the police had difficulty regulating the visitors![99] Sir Harry returned a few years later, this time to open a garden fete held in the grounds of the Home organised by the local branch of a national voluntary organisation. It was estimated that 5,000 people assembled to greet him. The proceeds of £820 were split between the Country Branch and another charity.[100]

The *Caronia* and its crew had a long association with East Park and in 1965 they gathered on the Firth of Forth to present the Home with a minibus.

Ships

Glasgow and the Clyde were well known historically for shipbuilding, shipping and naval activity. Some maritime contacts with East Park were memorable but isolated, such as the visit by young people at the Country Branch to the NATO Fleet in Greenock.[101] Others developed into long-standing relationships, such as with the crews of two ships in particular, Anchor Line's *Caledonia* and Cunard Line's *Caronia*.

Anchor Line entertained the children from 1919 onwards, with the exception of the war years.[102] RMS *Caledonia V* was built at Fairfield S&E Co. Ltd at Glasgow. She was launched and named by the Marchioness of Linlithgow on 12 March 1947 before being towed to her fit-out berth. She sailed a regular service from Liverpool to Bombay until 1965.[103] During the summer months of 1949, East Park's children were described as having enjoyed a very happy day on the *Caledonia*, while the directors had accepted an invitation to lunch.[104] It was here it was suggested that the children might adopt the *Caledonia*, thereby keeping up their interest.[105] This was agreed and the *Caledonia* was formally adopted by East Park in 1949, the adoption being registered with the British Ship Adoption Society.[106] It was suggested that a plaque be given to the ship to state it had been adopted by the children of East Park.[107] It was subsequently agreed there would be correspondence between the children and members of the ship's company.[108]

RMS *Caronia* was launched from John Brown shipyard on 30 October 1947 by HRH Princess Elizabeth. Purpose-built for both regular transatlantic crossings and extended luxury cruises, she served with the Cunard White Star Line until 1967.[109] The children in Maryhill received a visit from members of the crew of the *Caronia*.[110] They were subsequently gifted dolls in national costume representing the different countries visited on a world cruise, an 8mm picture projector and 'a huge cake'.[111] The relationship with the crew was such that it led to the naming of the Caronia Room.[112] It was noted, however, in 1966 that *Caronia* was no longer part of East Park, the ship being decommissioned the following year.[113] Matron reported that 'the crew of this ship for many years gave, with warm affection, much practical support to the Home and were particularly interested in the children'. It was 'hoped that some sister ship will form a social group whereby the link with East Park Home will not be severed',[114] but there is no further reference to links with Cunard.

While the children enjoyed good relationships with both ships, it seems that Anchor Line was described as being 'very annoyed' 'about the *Caronia* connection with the Home and in particular the publicity given by the Press'.[115] It had been previously agreed that the Day Room be named the Caronia Room.[116] The Board agreed to suggest naming a 'Caledonia Room' in an effort to restore 'the former friendly relationship'.[117]

Enduring relationships

Some activities have endured over the years and continue to flourish. Local to Maryhill, Partick Thistle Football Club and Maryhill Charity Football Association were great supporters of East Park, giving donations in their names.[118] Over the years, they have also engaged directly with the children and young people. East Park was described as the birthplace of Jimmy McIntosh's interest in football. He recalled football players representing teams across Scotland visiting East Park arranged by Partick Thistle, who played at the nearby Firhill Stadium.[119] This relationship with Partick Thistle has continued, with players visiting East Park to teach the young people football skills to promote physical activity and community spirit.[120] East Park was also the beneficiary of the Maryhill Charity Cup, which was contested for 107 consecutive seasons by local junior/amateur teams including Ashfield, Glasgow Perthshire, Petershill and Maryhill. The tournament ran uninterrupted from 1887/88 until 1993/94.[121] It is unclear from records as to why the Maryhill Charity Cup became known as the East Park Cup, but one account is that the change occurred in 2014 when Partick

Thistle, who had adopted East Park as their charity that year, organised a football tournament for school teams. It has since been known as the East Park Cup.[122]

Taxi outings

Another relationship which has stood the test of time is the Annual Taxi Drivers' Outing.[123] The first Outing came about in 1945, when three taxi drivers, R McLaren, J Sampson and W Campbell, organised a bus run.[124] This proved successful, leaving them some cash in hand. They decided to use the funds to give some children a trip to the Ayrshire coast, and with the assistance of volunteers, took some children from East Park to Saltcoats in their taxis. Although already located at the seaside, it seems the children in the Country Branch also joined 'the Taximen's outing'. Whether this was the Glasgow Taxi Outing or taxis local to Largs remains unclear.[125] It was, however, noted in 1986 that local taxi drivers took children from the Country Branch to the Irvine Leisure Beach, similar to their colleagues in Glasgow.[126]

Such was the success of the Taxi Outings that they became an annual event and extended to include children with additional support needs from other residential establishments across Glasgow, such as Mearnskirk Hospital, which at the time cared for children with tuberculosis. As rates of tuberculosis in children declined, the organising committee adapted and took children from a variety of schools for

Glasgow taxi owners set off for the seaside in 1972, these outings already having become an enduring feature of the East Park calendar.

children with additional support needs across Glasgow. The annual Outings continue to the present day, when the taxis, decorated with balloons, roll up to East Park with their drivers in fancy dress, ready to collect staff and children for a trip to the seaside. In the early days, children were entertained by Billy McGregor and the Gaybirds from the Barrowland Ballroom, and over the years they have been entertained by clowns, jugglers and musicians.[127] Jimmy McIntosh remembered the Outings, albeit 'in a pallid haze of motion sickness sweeping the blurred scenery past'.[128] Elizabeth also recalls the Taxi Outings with great affection:

> It was brilliant. I went a few times. There was one time I was out of the hospital, I had left the week before and they sent the taxi up for me. I was [at home] at the time. My mother, my grandmother came over to get me and got me dressed. The taxis were done up with balloons on them. The taxis went to places like Saltcoats, Largs I think … They are really amazing. They took baskets of food and drinks. We were playing in the sand. A lot of nurses went with you.[129]

Despite the changes in East Park and the reasons for bringing children and young people within its care, the Glasgow Taxi Outings are still very much enjoyed by all at East Park.

Children's experiences

It is not possible to describe all the activities and experiences of children in East Park and the Country Branch, nor is it possible to recognise all those who have provided support in cash and kind. Elizabeth and Jimmy's memories can only be 'snapshots' of East Park at points in time; others will hold different and equally valid memories. East Park celebrated its Centenary in 1974. This was, however, in a climate of change – in children's health, social values, social policy and legislation; a challenging environment in which to care for some of Scotland's most vulnerable children.

CHAPTER 13
Changing Landscapes, 1970–92

East Park Children have … seen many changes through the years. From horses and later, electric trams, to trolley and internal combustion buses. From gas to electric lighting. The change from making one's own entertainment through to Radio and the opening of a window on the world with Television, firstly Black and White, and now Colour. But the basic needs of a Child, whether handicapped or not, remain the same – Love and Care. These have always been overflowing at East Park and always will be.

A.E.S.P., 1974[1]

During the 1960s there were challenges to established ideas and institutions across Scotland, and within East Park there were signs of change.[2] This was not only in respect of improvements in children's health and innovations in aids and adaptations to support their mobility, communication and participation, but also what would now be referred to as 'care planning', with children being fostered and young people encouraged to have outside contact, spending weekends at home where possible. David formerly worked at East Park and his gran, Anne (pseud.), fostered children from East Park in the 1960s. Over the years she provided temporary care for children under the age of eighteen months when placed. The children had a variety of conditions, such as hip dysplasia, spina bifida, and cleft lip and palate. Some of the children moved on to East Park and some went home. Despite the remarkable care and commitment of people such as Anne, it was difficult finding foster-carers for children from East Park.[3]

Dr William Livingstone became physician superintendent at East Park in 1970. He remembers his introduction to the Home as being a 'ward round' with Dr Robert Shanks, a senior paediatric physician at the RHSC. There was a great commotion as David (pseud.), aged around eight years, was leaping from bed to bed shouting 'expletives', having been banned from going to the swimming pool that night because 'he had been bad'. 'It was a new ball game for me entirely!' mused Dr Livingstone.[4]

He recalled:

> The number of children had been falling dramatically and it looked as though East Park may have to close. There were quite a number of under school age children being referred to me for possible admission but the Board was not keen as they did not get an education grant for these kids so they preferred to limit the numbers of such children. I persuaded them to allow me to admit these, pointing out that they became of school age in due course and it was very difficult for local authorities to find places for them … So we took in quite a few pre-school age kids and so needed a nursery class. That was only achieved by employing a fully trained nursery teacher paid as a nursing auxiliary![5]

In 1970 a playgroup for children under the age of five was established and a nursery school with trained staff opened the following year.[6] A pre-school playgroup was established in 1972 at the Country Branch.[7]

As East Park approached its hundredth anniversary, the pace of change accelerated. It is often not possible to directly correlate social trends and developments in policy and legislation with life in any residential establishment, but these provide the context within which East Park evolved and adapted. It is therefore helpful to pause and reflect on the period from 1970 to the 1990s.

Glasgow's Miles Better – and Maryhill too

Within Glasgow, the changes evident in the post-war years continued during the 1970s and 1980s. The population of the city fell, while unemployment rose. The loss of population between 1971 and 1981 was 22 per cent, while over the same decade, unemployment doubled from 7.5 to 15 per cent.[8] Maryhill experienced similar levels of change, losing much local industry during the 1980s and suffering the associated unemployment.[9] There were, however, initiatives across Glasgow to rectify this trend, and East Park participated in this process. In 1971, children planted bulbs in tubs in the school yard as part of the 'Facelift Glasgow' campaign.[10] In 1983, a national advertising campaign was launched with the slogan 'Glasgow's Miles Better', and in 1988 the city staged the Garden Festival on the site of disused docks on the River Clyde, and again children and staff participated. Head teacher Catherine Leggate (known as Cathie) wrote:

> Each child visited [the Garden Festival] many times using every special ticket available. Money was donated by Britoil specially for our children's

use … On each visit the pupils and staff came back to tell us of some new discovery made or area visited.

We had our own mini-Garden Festival at school with flowers outside, inside and even on walls and ceilings. We started with the story of Jack and the Beanstalk – which started in class 1 and continued to grow and change as it grew right through the school – flowers appearing, giant's boots, giant's hands and a giant's castle until it grew right out of the building. Our summer and autumn terms used many ideas from this as projects and we gained much of our learning from it – language and communication, number work, life skills, movement, concept development, sensory work and all the expressive arts.[11]

Two years later, in 1990, Glasgow was named European City of Culture.[12] East Park hosted a Burns Supper for children, young people and staff, an Easter Party which involved wheelchair dancing, and an exhibition of 'East Park through the Ages'. The Arts Group of Glasgow Council for Voluntary Services also supported the children, young people and staff to dramatise a musical play called *MacJonah*. This was performed firstly at the Scottish Exhibition and Conference Centre as part of 'The Arts is Magic' and later at East Park.[13]

Changing policy, legislation and practice

East Park had seen many changes over what was now approaching a hundred years of its existence. The next fifty years, however, were to see some of the most significant developments, including a threat to its very existence. Sitting as it does at the interface of childcare, education, disability and healthcare services, East Park has been impacted by changes in thinking and practice in each of these fields.

As discussed in chapter 11, during the 1960s there had been significant changes in childcare policy and practice. The Social Work (Scotland) Act 1968 introduced the Children's Hearing System and brought about the creation of Social Work departments. The view of the Kilbrandon Committee, which had informed the Act, was that residential care should only be a temporary solution.[14] This opened the way for what would now be referred to as 'care planning' and interdisciplinary meetings in order to plan effectively for children, young people and their families.

Another factor which arguably impacted children's lives was local government reorganisation following the Local Government (Scotland) Act 1973. This replaced the former structure of councils, burghs and districts in 1975 with a two-tier system of regional and district councils. East Park and the Country Branch fell within

Strathclyde Regional Council.[15] Social work was one of the functions of regional councils. Being such a large local authority and including Glasgow, policy decisions by Strathclyde Regional Council Social Work Department were likely to have a significant impact on East Park and the Country Branch. An example of such a policy was Room to Grow, one conclusion of which was that 'a prime assumption of the Regional Council must be that it is in a child's best interest to remain in the home community. This attitude should be reflected in the increased provision of day-care resources and the tackling of the wider social issues to negate the damaging effects of deprivation.'[16] During the 1970s and 1980s, there was a marked shift in social work practice towards children remaining in their home communities and attending their local school.[17] This was to have a significant impact on East Park and the Country Branch.

The 1970s also brought about changes in the education of children with what is now referred to as additional support needs. The Education (Mentally Handicapped Children) (Scotland) Act 1974 stated that all children had a right to education, including those formerly classed as 'ineducable'.[18] In 1965, Margaret Mallinson, a qualified occupation centre assistant, had been recruited to work with a group of East Park children deemed 'ineducable but trainable'.[19] Under the new legislation, this term was redundant. In 1978, referred to at the time as 'the watershed year', there were further changes with the publication of two reports, the Report of the Committee of Enquiry into the Education of Handicapped Children and Young People, known as 'the Warnock Report', and Her Majesty's Inspectors of Schools (HMI) Report on pupils with learning difficulties.[20] These identified practice in Scottish mainstream schools as a major cause of educational failure for many pupils.[21] The Warnock Report and the HMI Report on pupils with what were referred to at the time as 'learning difficulties', brought about a change in the former model of pupil deficit and handicap to new attitudes and approaches to learning support and providing for special educational needs.[22] There is no mention in the East Park records at the time of the Warnock Report or the new legislation, nor of changes in staffing or practice as a result of these, but it becomes clear over time that these were influencing policy and practice within East Park.

Another significant shift was in perceptions of disability and in legislation which arguably transformed the lives of disabled people. In 1990, the National Health Service and Community Care Act (The Community Care Act) was introduced. This outlined the responsibilities of local authorities towards disabled people as they transitioned from institutions to living in the community. For the first time, mandatory consultation with service users (including residents) was required.[23] Although possibly perceived as more immediately relevant to adults in institutional care, as will become apparent later in this chapter, the Act had a significant impact on East Park.

Attributed to activists in the Union of the Physically Impaired Against Segregation (UPIAS) during the 1970s, what is now referred to as 'the social model of disability' developed. The core definition of the British social model of disability comes from the UPIAS document, *Fundamental Principles of Disability*, an edited version of which is cited by Mike Oliver:

… In our view, it is society which disables physically impaired people. Disability is something imposed on top of our impairments by the way we are unnecessarily isolated and excluded from full participation in society. Disabled people are therefore an oppressed group in society. To understand this it is necessary to grasp the distinction between the physical impairment and the social situation, called 'disability', of people with such impairment. Thus we define impairment as lacking part of or all of a limb, or having a defective limb, organ or mechanism of the body; and disability as the disadvantage or restriction of activity caused by a contemporary social organisation which takes no or little account of people who have physical impairments and thus excludes them from participation in the mainstream of social activities. Physical disability is therefore a particular form of social oppression.[24]

Drawing on this model, Jimmy McIntosh, a resident of East Park from 1950 to 1956, was disabled on arrival at East Park by the lack of both a wheelchair and a lift between floors, rather than by cerebral palsy, which had affected his life since birth. While this position has been challenged by some, the term 'disabled children' is used in Scottish Government policy documents to reflect a social model of disability.[25]

A hundred years of care

In 1973, Matron Sheila Morrison observed that an increasing number of the young people resident in East Park were 'in care' admitted by the Social Work Department. 'These young people are of course not only physically handicapped, but suffer social deprivation as well. Their increasing number and their lack of normal family background could well influence the pattern of the future East Park Home, and the structure of the Child Care Service to be offered within the set-up.'[26] Dr Livingstone recently reflected on the early 1970s:

The Home was more like a hospital than a home. The staff were nursing staff, not care staff. There was a new young enthusiastic matron, Sheila Morrison. We both felt that the institution had to change … Whereas kids would put their feet on a sheet of paper and have the outline drawn round to be taken to the shops to get shoes … now they would be taken to the shops with a member of staff. Some clothes were purchased in bulk but for the older children a staff member would now take them to the shops and they would have some input to the choice of their own clothes. I often took older boys to buy clothes.[27]

Possibly related to these shifting trends, plans were made around this time for a new structure of staffing within the Home. This involved recruiting trained residential care officers, 'housemothers', to cater for the children and young people's care needs, and nurses to supervise clinical aspects of their care. This was a shift away from the previous 'medical model' of care, where nurses had responsibility for all aspects of care. This proved difficult to sustain, however, as Sheila Morrison reported:

Unfortunately a high proportion and turnover of untrained staff tends to be very unsettling for the children and even disruptive in the lives of the children. More trained childcare staff are urgently needed in a Home such as this, and it is gratifying to know that the number of young people (male and female) taking up this type of training is on the increase.[28]

Reflecting on this period, Dr Livingstone concurred that even in the early days of his involvement with East Park, a combination of care staff and nursing staff 'would have been ideal and the head of the Home should have been someone with care qualifications'.[29] It was not until a major restructuring programme during the 1990s, however, that residential care officers became embedded in East Park.[30]

By 1972, there was clear evidence of care planning.[31] One child in the Country Branch had been placed for adoption in 1969, while Dr Livingstone reported that in 1972, one child was 'successfully fostered' and one young person aged thirteen was discharged to a group home for what were described as 'normal children' and was now attending 'normal school'.[32]

Over time, staff within East Park became increasingly involved in interdisciplinary case conferences and reviews of children in their care. Matron Annie Johnston, who took over as matron at Maryhill in 1974, observed that while time-consuming, the time was well spent in these multiagency meetings.[33]

Centenary

East Park's centenary in 1974 was marked by a number of celebrations. The directors reflected:

> Our Centenary year was very hectic but most happy and rewarding. Under the able chairmanship of Mr Prentice a Centenary Committee was formed to organise various functions throughout the year. In May we were indebted to Miss Helen Mackenzie and her colleagues who organised a very successful Coffee Evening at the Grosvenor Hotel. It was opened by [the actor] John Cairney, and as a just reward for a lot of hard work, £1,000 was raised.
>
> Still in May we had a visit by Lady Ballantrae. What was listed as an official visit turned into a happy and informal afternoon.
>
> June was our 'Reunion' month. On the first Saturday we were very proud and happy to welcome approximately 200 ex-'East Parkers' to Maryhill. The gathering included patients, teachers, nurses and all who had in the past helped to build the image of the Home. Many friendships were renewed and we sincerely hope they will continue. The following Saturday a smaller but equally happy reunion took place at our Home in Largs.
>
> We send our greetings and thanks to the children and people of Lochgoilhead who enabled us to spend a very happy day in their beautiful part of the country last June [1974].
>
> The highlight of our year was when our Patroness, HRH Princess Alice, Duchess of Gloucester visited our Maryhill Home on Thursday, 24th October. That same evening HRH attended a Civic Reception kindly given to us by the Corporation of Glasgow in the City Chambers.
>
> On Sunday 27th October, which was the anniversary of the official opening of the Home, a Commemorative Service was held in Ruchill Parish Church and we are indebted to the Rev Muir McLaren, Rev Wm Alston and Father Hendry for making it such a 'family' affair.
>
> In extending our sincere thanks to our many generous friends we will be forgiven if we single out the ladies of Milngavie and Bearsden Circle for their gift of a colour TV for each Home, and to Melody Makers who put a wonderful show on for us in November. To all those not mentioned we offer our sincere thanks and hope you will continue to give us your generous support.[34]

Children participated in many of the events, each speaking with the Duchess of Gloucester and meeting Lady Ballantrae. They attended the Commemorative Service at Ruchill Church in October. Older children met up with former friends during the reunion month while the young children 'entered into the festive spirit'. They made articles for sale at the Coffee Evening and built up a relationship with Lochgoilhead Primary. There was an exchange of letters, information and examples of school work. They then had 'a memorable experience' spending the day at the school at the end of the summer term.[35] A centenary publication was produced, thought to be by Alexander E S Prentice, one of the directors at the time.[36]

Children's lives

Before continuing with this narrative, it is helpful to meet Maura and Tristan. Both were not only resident in East Park – Maura for much of the 1970s and Tristan from the mid-1960s into the 1970s – but both also returned to work in East Park during the 1990s. Their memories help contextualise much of the East Park story during this time.

Maura Morran Kaur

I came to East Park as a child. I only weighed 2 lb 13 ounces when I was born and had chronic asthma. It was very bad and I took attacks on a regular basis. I was often in Yorkhill Hospital and in an oxygen tent. It was very frightening. My parents had difficulty coping with this and it was suggested that I be taken into care; that is why I ended up in East Park. I still have asthma but inhalers have been developed now and I can control it as an adult.

When I came into East Park, I was in the Bunting Ward. Everyone who was in a wheelchair was downstairs and everybody else was upstairs. … In the ward there was sometimes a TV and sometimes there wasn't. We didn't watch much TV to be honest. We didn't have a creative area, there was nothing much, just the bed; it was very basic. There were a lot of us in the ward, about seven of us. Bunting Ward had beds either side and your clothes were laid out on a shelf. Staff would choose the clothes that you were going to wear the next day. It was like a hospital.

I used to enjoy bathing the baby doll in the red and white polka dot dress in a puddle and playing in the Wendy house. Some people would be there for a long time, some would come and go. They all had health conditions, either mental or physical health. You weren't there because you didn't have a family or anything like that, you were there because of your health. I was in the Brownies and then the Guides. There was also a club called Cathie's Club.

The set-up was that on a Friday evening I would go to my family's home and came back to the Home Sunday evening. I had four sisters and three brothers. It wasn't easy going home but I missed my mum and dad and looked forward to seeing them at weekends. They came to collect me and we used to walk home [to the West End of Glasgow].

Staff were nice. You always had your favourites. You looked forward to them coming on a certain night or a certain day. … Matron was very strict; very much 'old school'. One day my friend and I were going out to a function. We had 'function coats'; you used to have 'function coats'. I didn't have a belt, she got onto me about this belt, sent me back upstairs to go and get this belt. I was scared of her. She was a nice lady really and I did respect her. … On the whole it was very strict. You had to have your manners; you didn't get anywhere if you didn't have your manners.

I left the Home when I was aged twelve and went to [secondary school]. I had a social worker before I left the Home. They said to me, 'Do you want to stay in the Home or do you want to go home to your family?' To put that question on a twelve-year-old's shoulders … I thought to myself, what will my family think if I want to stay here? That is what was on my mind so I went home. That was to shape the rest of my life but it was a blessing in disguise. I wouldn't have done what I have done with my life. I have done a lot. … I went to college, where I did my NNEB [nursery nurse training]. I was disadvantaged because I missed so much primary schooling. I did O grades then Highers and have O-grade maths, O-grade arithmetic and Higher English. … Academically I don't have a lot of qualifications but I am very creative. I got Higher Art and enjoy abstract painting, which I did with Project Ability. After achieving my NNEB, I worked in Alberta, Canada and looked after three children. I did that for about eight months then I came back and worked in London. After I worked in London, I went back to Canada, to Toronto to be in charge of a nursery class.

I always wanted to work in East Park so when I came back to Scotland in the 1990s, I worked there for almost two years. I had nowhere to stay so I had to stay in the high-rise flats. It was quite traumatic but Sister Stewart helped me get the job in East Park. I came for an interview with Matron Mrs McCreadie but it was Sister Stewart who helped me get out of the flat, into the nurses' home and back on my feet again. I was truly grateful to Sister Stewart for all the help she gave me.

When I worked in the Home, I was an auxiliary nurse. I wasn't sure how the staff would take it but they said, 'It's OK, you can come back and work here till you are qualified.' You had to do modules; we had in-service days. The rooms were still the same as when I had lived here in the 1970s. The vast majority of the staff were unqualified; the only people that were qualified worked in the duty room, that was the sisters. They didn't directly look after the children; they would tell you what ward you were going to that day, talk about off duty and keep us up to date with what was happening on the wards. There were not a lot of differences from when I was living here in the 1970s and when I was working here apart from a lot of the staff had changed. I then went to work in a bilingual nursery in the Southside.

I am proud of myself. I have achieved a lot and I did it on my own. It means a lot to me, East Park. It was my home; East Park was my family. It was all I knew. I felt protected. I felt looked after. [Even though they were strict] I felt I was in the right place.

I would like to dedicate these memories to Rodderick John Morrison.[37]

Tristan (pseud.)

Tristan's narrative has some similarities to Maura's but there are significant differences, indicating the wide range of circumstances which brought children to East Park and their subsequent experience. Tristan was admitted to East Park in 1965, aged two. Unlike Maura, Tristan is not aware of having had any underlying health or developmental conditions at the time. He had, however, experienced abuse by his mother and stepfather. Tristan explained:

> Some [children] came in; they had asthma, eczema, PKU [phenylketonuria], coeliac diet but usually there were social reasons as well. They also had people with different disabilities, spastic, Down's Syndrome, purple heart. There were children with severe and profound disabilities, a lot of children were non-ambulant, in wheelchairs so it was very mixed.[38]

In the late 1960s, Tristan returned to live with his family but this did not work out and he was readmitted to East Park. He was subsequently fostered with the family of two schoolfriends who lived nearby, but the family moved to England and Tristan returned to East Park. He moved to live with his mother and stepfather when aged around fourteen but he chose to leave the family home at sixteen. He explained:

> I stayed at home for a wee while, was abused again, ran away, was sleeping rough and bumped into an old friend of mine and his mum put me up for a short time, then I had to go back home, then I got a flat of my own. There are points in your life, you think, if that didn't happen, where would I be? And it was like that. What would have happened if I hadn't bumped into my friend that I used to go to school with that day. I got on my feet, and got my own place … East Park is where I thrived. [Miss Johnston, the matron], she had helped me with my flat through contacts with the Salvation Army and different people helped me get furniture. I tried to get help from the Social, but I got nothing.[39]

Tristan worked in clothing factories and clothing shops, but then obtained employment working as a crèche worker with the charity Gingerbread. He began volunteering at East Park and became friends with some of the staff. Matron Annie Johnston offered him a job as an auxiliary. Tristan continued working in East Park for several years, and was one of the first group of staff to move with the children and young people into a house in the community, Robertson House, in 2001. Tristan eventually left East Park and worked with the children's charity Quarriers, supporting adults living in the community. He continues in this work today, albeit working with one young man and his family through Self-directed Support. Reflecting on his childhood, Tristan mused:

> Thinking back, I missed part of my youth; I was institutionalised. I didn't have a proper childhood, having brothers and sisters, going out with mates. You had members of staff going to collect you, having to go to bed or get up and make your bed; you missed having a girlfriend or going to her house. I had a wee bit of foster-care so got a taste of it. I was going to an outside school, but I was not part of it whereas if I had stayed in my own home … East Park was the best thing that happened to me.[40]

We will hear more from Maura and Tristan as we follow the narrative of East Park through to the early 2000s.

Education

While the developmental needs and home circumstances of the children coming to live in East Park were changing, children continued to be offered varied education and leisure experiences. In the early 1970s, head teacher Jane Stewart described endeavouring to create an understanding atmosphere wherein children could develop independence that would serve them in later life.[41] The School was supported by a Speech Reading Unit, Child Guidance and the Speech Therapy Service. Links were established with the Glasgow Schools Library Service and the Schools Museum Service, from which they received books and pictures.[42] An Education Committee was set up in 1975 which met regularly to assess the educational requirements of each child and to ensure that these were fulfilled, 'bringing several minds to bear on difficult individual problems'.[43]

Education took children beyond the confines of East Park, and visits were arranged to the Scottish Farmers' Creamery in Govan, the Marine Biology Station at Millport and the Polmadie Cleansing Unit, where the children were 'fascinated by the various processes employed to combat pollution in our city'.[44] During the

Glasgow 800 Celebrations in 1975, pupils were invited to attend a special display by the armed forces in Bellahouston Park and to spend an afternoon aboard the frigate HMS *Hermione*.[45]

Not all children and young people received their education in East Park, however. Tristan recollects that some children who used wheelchairs went to school in Summerston and others attended a local Catholic school. Tristan attended a local primary school then North Kelvinside Secondary School. Maura initially attended Shakespeare Street Primary School.[46] She was not quite sure why she went out to school:

> Most of the children attended the school [attached to the Home]. I didn't attend there. I attended Shakespeare Street School across the road. I did try going (to the school in East Park) but I think they thought I was a wee bit too advanced for the type of classes they had so that is why I ended up in Shakespeare. Later on, we got moved to Gairbraid.[47]

Dr Livingstone remembers the move towards children attending school outwith East Park:

> I thought youngsters with coeliac and Tristan should really be attending normal school in the community. After negotiating with the inspectorate in Edinburgh, that was allowed without losing the education grant. So these kids went out to school like normal ones, with those with coeliac coming home for their lunch.[48]

Most of the time Maura enjoyed school. There were disadvantages to being educated outwith East Park, however, in that she was unable to see any of her school friends after school. Possibly because of the different timeframe, unlike Maura, Tristan was able to bring friends from school into the Home. He recalled:

> When I started going to outside school, I started to bring friends from outside into the Home. My friends came to visit me. If I had a party, they came here. Quite often … the people I went to school with, their families were working here, their mums or aunties … I went to a class reunion at North Kelvinside. I was only there three years when I left but I still meet up with people from there. I don't see them often but whenever there is a school reunion, I will catch up with them.[49]

By the 1980s, children and young people in East Park and the Country Branch had increasingly complex needs, including significant communication impairments. Staff attended conferences on working with children described at the time as 'profoundly handicapped' and new equipment such as a Possum, an electronic communication aid, was acquired.[50] In writing for the Annual Report for 1982, Cathie Leggate reflected on the diversity of children and young people attending the School. More than 50 per cent were of secondary school age, requiring a curriculum that included the appropriate academic subjects as well as creativity and the arts, while most of the children and young people admitted more recently were what was described at the time as 'physically and severely or profoundly mentally handicapped', necessitating a different approach 'to extend the pupils as far as they are able using whatever innate abilities they have'.[51] Drawing on the work of Mrs (subsequently Baroness) Mary Warnock, she explained, 'We must give much of ourselves to them. We must initiate all of their education – they do not just 'pick up information' and at times we seem to get little back … success for us is not measured only on paper but often just in a smile or a spoken word'.[52]

Individual programmes were designed for each child. These included a combination of physical education, soft-play and therapy using the new Ball Therapy Unit for non-ambulant children, as well as cookery, art, handwork, music, typing and computing. For some children it also included English, mathematics, geography and history; for others it included picture matching, colour recognition, posting shapes, stories and songs while trying to establish eye contact. There was speech therapy input using Bliss symbols, Makaton and Possum. The speech therapist encouraged children to engage in mouth exercise to help eating and swallowing, while the physiotherapist, as well as facilitating motor development and function, encouraged exercises to help children relax.[53] Over time it was recognised that young people over sixteen needed a different educational experience and a separate unit was established for them in 1984/5 where there could be a focus on social, vocational and environmental work with discussions, outings into the community, work experience, integration with other young people and preparation for independence.[54]

East Park continued to embrace technology and in 1986, Cathie Leggate wrote:

Gone are the days of 'talk and chalk'. We do not even have black-boards any more. Instead, we have white boards, magnetic boards, video and tape recorders as aids to communication; all necessary for the education of our pupils in this technological age. We already have a computer for our post-16 group, 'Options', and during 1986 I hope to purchase more computers for the younger children. The Glasgow Council for Voluntary Services has helped to organise this scheme by giving us extra staff to help in the classrooms.[55]

In 1986, East Park School participated in a CALL Centre Project (Communication Aids for Language and Learning Project). The aim was to introduce computer-based technology to a small number of children in the School and to inform and support staff in the use of the technology. This was seen as an asset and it was hoped to continue the relationship with the CALL Centre.[56] The CALL Centre, now known as Call Scotland, is still active in helping children and young people to overcome disability and barriers to learning, and fulfil their potential.[57]

In 1986, the school roll included three 'day pupils', children not resident in East Park, a new trend which has continued to the present day.[58] By this time, it was also a requirement under the Education (Scotland) Act 1980 (updated by Circular 4/96) that local authorities must open a Record of Needs for any child over two years of age with Special Educational Needs (SEN) which are 'pronounced, specific or complex' and 'require continuing review'.[59] This included physiotherapy, speech therapy and occupational therapy, and as only physiotherapy and speech therapy were provided by East Park, the Board authorised the appointment of two part-time occupational therapists.[60]

When the Country Branch closed in 1987, some children and young people were absorbed into the classes at Maryhill. Mrs Meg Breen, the head teacher at Largs, joined the staff at Maryhill. Children and young people attending the School now had very varied needs. There were around fifty-one children and young people in total.[61] Cathie Leggate described the profile of the pupils:
- Three classes of wheelchair-bound children
- One class of 'very active' primary-aged children
- One class of very active secondary school-age children
- One group over the age of sixteen following a different timetable, and
- One group where the focus was mixing with the community, a stepping stone to college.

By now, most children could not communicate verbally and used Makaton, Bliss and 'body language', such as 'smiles, nods, frowns and eye pointing'.[62]

In the 1980s various new methods of learning were explored, such as Conductive Education and Gentle Teaching.[63] The former was not adopted while the latter was taken further.[64] 'Gentle Teaching' was developed in the 1980s for helping people with an intellectual disability and severe behaviour problems. In this approach, it is essential that the caregiver makes authentic contact with the person, based on personal interest and commitment, and with a deep intention to make the person feel well.[65]

In 1992, it was agreed that music therapy be introduced to East Park two afternoons a week.[66] Specialist music facilitator Bryan Tolland was employed by

A musical moment. Singer, songwriter and music specialist Bryan
Tolland has been making music with children and young people
at East Park for three decades. Here, in 1995, Lisa and Bryan are
together in music.

East Park, having worked previously in the Home as part of an Arts project run by
Glasgow Council for the Voluntary Sector (GCVS), which operated in East Park.
Bryan is still in post today. Possibly better known as a co-founder of Del Amitri,
Bryan has also played with Scottish bands The Bluebells and L'Acoustica. A classical
guitarist, singer-songwriter and musician experienced in a wide range of song writing,
recording and performance, Bryan has drawn on all of these skills in his work with
the children and young people. He observed that during the 1990s, it wouldn't be
uncommon to have a class of ten or twelve. Over time, however, almost all of the
young people require 1:1 support. Bryan described the essence of his approach:

> What tended to happen, we had people with more severe challenges,
> more complex needs and so classes got smaller. The starting point is no
> different from my point of view, it is always whoever you are working with,
> so you never start with a conclusion, you always start with the person. The

thing about music is, it has been around longer than language and almost everybody can interact with music at one particular level and it is up to me to have an appropriate index of sensitivity to where that level is, so it doesn't become patronising, but neither does it become overwhelming.[67]

In 1991, work in the School was being recognised and inspectors from the Scottish Office Education Department (SOED) raised the possibility of East Park becoming a national resource and one of Scotland's eight Grant Aided Special Schools (GASS).[68] East Park was helped in this transition by two consultants from the SOED who supported the completion of the East Park Development Plan.[69] East Park's GASS status continues today.

Children's health

While developments in medicine and social policy have improved life expectancy, death and dying remains a reality in the lives of children with complex healthcare needs and of those around them. Maura reflected:

> I think the hardest thing for me in the home was seeing friends die. We always seen it happen. I knew what death was from an early age. I knew I would never see that person again. You knew they had died. The hearse was coming and seeing the coffin. Seeing all that, you knew that person wasn't going to be here anymore.

Staff did not talk about children dying. Maura explained:

> You knew if the person wasn't well and you knew something was going on but it was only when you saw the car with the coffin you knew that person had gone. I just put two and two together. I knew that person was ill. I knew that person had gone. … It has given me a lot of grief and affected me a lot for the rest of my life and I can't cope with grief.[70]

In previous chapters, former residents spoke of the strength of relationships among children and young people, a feature identified by both Tristan and Maura. Maura touched on the difficulties of this, however:

> You see a lot of suffering, seeing those in my ward with their illnesses. It was a lot for a child to take on. I was very, very sensitive as a child. It was pretty traumatic being in the Home sometimes, the suffering … What I

found hard was people used to look at me as if nothing was wrong with me, but when I had asthma, I couldn't breathe; it was hard as I felt a bit of a con. Others were in wheelchairs, when they had physical disabilities. They couldn't see the asthma. It was only when I was ill that people realised and could see the asthma. And I used to think, 'Why am I here? Why do I need to be here?'[71]

Despite a number of health conditions being relegated to history, in many respects children were surviving with more complex healthcare needs. In the Annual Report for 1992, the physician superintendent, Dr Gordon Martin, did not include the table of statistics of health conditions, which had been included in East Park's Annual Report for over a hundred years. He explained that the majority of children and young people had multiple health problems rather than a single problem. Advances in medical science had resulted in fewer children being born with spina bifida and Down's Syndrome but relatively more having 'combined handicaps', mental retardation, deafness and epilepsy, making it difficult and arguably of limited value to categorise.[72]

Medical advances such as new developments in antibiotics and anaesthetics were improving the life experience of children with complex healthcare needs, and by 1991 Dr Martin reported on one medical advance which was significantly improving the quality of life of several children and young people at East Park, the gastrostomy.[73] He described this as:

An operation where a tube is passed into the stomach, allowing nutrition to be passed directly into the stomach via the tube rather than having to be swallowed. Receiving sufficient calories has always been a problem in certain groups of handicapped children, and as a result such children tend to have a less than desirable weight.

By 1991, five children and young people in East Park had had gastrostomies carried out at RHSC and Stobhill Hospital, and this continued over the years. Once early problems were resolved, all were reported as 'doing extremely well, having put on a substantial amount of weight, appearing happier, more alert to date'.[74]

By 1989, the changing profile of children and young people now living in East Park was summed up by Matron Eleanor McCreadie:

We have in our care fifty-four physically and/or mentally handicapped children. Our responsibility 24 hours per day. We must accept the inherent changes. It is easier for new staff to do, who don't have memories of children who ran wild in the corridors, caused chaos in the Units and queued up for pocket money. The children we have resident now at East Park Home are not self-directed or self-motivated, saying 'can I have', 'can I get'. The communication which we enjoy now is much more subtle – sign language taught in School called Makaton, speaking eyes, expressive faces, and when frustration mounts too high – the temper tantrums.[75]

Leisure and activities

As the profile of the children at East Park changed, so did the activities. In 1989, the old playground equipment was demolished and new equipment installed more suited to the children and young people now resident; a double swing, a two-seater swing with tyres, a log ramp for climbing, a double-width slide, a sloping bridge with a slide roundabout and picnic table.[76] A soft-play facility was also developed indoors.[77]

A number of activities discussed in chapter 12 continued. Matron Annie Johnston extolled the joys of 'the Glasgow Taximen's Sick Children's Outings': '[They] always do us proud and the name "Taximen" is synonymous with Friend.'[78]

Uniformed organisations also continued, with a new generation of young people attending camps within the UK and internationally.[79] Tristan was in the Cubs and then the Scouts, and Maura was in the Brownies and Guides.[80] Brownies from the Country Branch went to Brownie camp in West Lothian and Guides from Maryhill travelled by plane to Norway.[81] Scouts from the Country Branch also travelled to Scout Camp in Norway, and eight boys from Maryhill and one from the Country Branch travelled with the Scouts to Denmark.[82] Meanwhile, three young women in the Country Branch were presented with Stars of Merit, a top award in the Guide Movement for outstanding courage and endurance, by Mrs MacCowan, County Commissioner for Ayrshire.[83]

As well as the uniformed organisations, there was a regular 'youth club', referred to by Matron Annie Johnston as 'the Wednesday night gang' and known by the children as 'Cathie's Club', after Cathie who ran it.[84] Matron wrote:

Cathie [Simpson] comes straight from the office in her invalid carriage, has her tea, and then gets started with her Wednesday night club members. Re-organisation within the Home now allows the old theatre to be used as a leisure room and this is the centre of Cathie's activities. Another ex-East Park girl, Ann McAneny, helps Cathie with this activity. The staff are most indebted to Cathie and Ann for giving of their time and enthusiasm on behalf of East Park children who in return love them.[85]

Indeed, children and young people were most enthusiastic about 'Cathie' and her club. Maura remembered:

> She had creative ideas, we played games and toys and lollipops and sweets and we were allowed to do what we wanted to do, to play with what we wanted to play with and we had a good old time. It was on a Wednesday. Everybody who wanted to go went. It was held in one of the rooms near the Inverclyde Ward … both Cathie and Morag [who helped Cathie] were brilliant.[86]

Whether 'Morag' and 'Ann McAneny' were one and the same person or whether Cathie had different assistants over the years is unclear. Cathie's Club ran for some twenty-four years, ending in 1993.[87]

Children continued to participate in activities locally. Some children and young people went horse riding at Kilmardinny Stables in Bearsden and later at the St Mungo Group of the Riding for the Disabled Association.[88] Young people who are interested still have an opportunity to take part in riding today.[89]

During the 1970s, an 'Aunt and Uncle' befriending scheme was established whereby children were taken on outings and for short stays to the Aunt and Uncle's homes.[90] Maura remembered 'Auntie Paddy', whom she understood to be a member of the Board.[91] Maura also remembered a relationship with members of staff Mary and Wendy (pseuds), who were cousins.[92] Tristan met his wife, Jewel (pseud.), when both were working in East Park and they befriended a child from the Home. Tristan recalled with affection, 'My wife and I befriended him through Social Work and his family; we were allowed to take him home. We kept him overnight … He was getting the freedom of being at home and then back to East Park.'[93]

A wide range of activities were organised by staff within East Park. Tristan reflected:

> One of the things you don't realise about East Park, when you are in it as a youngster, you feel deprived, you are not getting the same social outlets your friends at school have … but when you leave East Park, you realise that you are a lot better off than a lot of kids outside. We went to a lot of parties, Christmas you got a big bag of toys, you were well looked after in many ways, apart from when I went home for good.[94]

Sports days took place, and from 1989 the champion was awarded a cup donated by Martin's Jewellers of Maryhill Road, close to East Park.[95] There were excursions to the swimming baths, Burns Suppers, parties, outings, Christmas shows, carol services and trips to the circus, often provided by different groups of 'well-wishers'.[96] There were outings to watch the switching on of the Christmas lights in Glasgow and a trip to a 'Santa Special Day' in Aviemore.[97] Like Elizabeth some twenty years previously, Maura remembered Christmas at East Park:

> We used to watch staff wrapping presents from the bathroom, they didn't know you were watching. I enjoyed that. I enjoyed watching the staff coming and putting the Christmas presents in black bags at the bottom of our beds. I had an umbrella one year and one of my friends took the umbrella off my bed and put it on her own bed. She kept it![98]

Some of the older girls went to the ballet and some to *Peter Pan* at the Theatre Royal.[99] Maura remembered going to a concert of classical music:

> I remember we went to Kelvin Hall and they had an orchestra. … I wasn't sure about going. We got Smarties and crisps and I put on my function clothes and that coat of mine, the one with the belt, and I thought, OK I'll go. They wanted me to go for some reason, I don't know why. … We enjoyed it and that is why I like classical music because of that.[100]

Radio Clyde were supportive of East Park through Cash for Kids, which often launched from East Park, and in 1989 an outing was arranged for children and staff to visit the radio station.[101]

Special events, projects and holidays

Some events were organised by agencies outwith East Park, and staff and children enthusiastically participated. The Variety Club of Great Britain in conjunction with British Caledonian Airways arranged a day trip in May 1979 for fifty 'handicapped children' to Brighton. Six children from the Country Branch travelled with three members of staff, flying Glasgow to Gatwick then by coach to Brighton, where they were welcomed by the Mayor and visited the Dolphinarium.[102] The same year, some of the children went on a day trip to what was described as 'a huge children's party' to mark The Year of the Child in Hyde Park, London. Two years later, the children returned to Hyde Park as part of the celebrations for the International Year of the Disabled to attend the Sunshine Coach Rally. This trip was described by Matron Annie Johnston as an event which 'will long be remembered'. Travelling in April, inclement weather was possibly not anticipated. Annie Johnston described the journey:

Along with our colleagues and children at Largs, we headed south in a convoy as the first snowflakes were falling. After being on Shap for several hours, we decided to give up the thought of reaching London that night. However, thanks to the people of Preston, we were given accommodation for the night in the church hall. The following day we set off for Windsor Barracks. London was full of interest and excitement. We were delighted that the Largs minibus won first prize for its decoration.[103]

Some special events occurred within East Park and the Country Branch, such as visits from East Park's patron, HRH Princess Alice, Duchess of Gloucester, a visit to the Home on 5 September 1985 by Prime Minister Margaret Thatcher and her husband Denis, when they spent an hour touring the building and talking with children and staff, and a visit to the Home by HRH Princess Royal on 22 June 1991, when she was 'well and truly splashed [at the hydrotherapy pool] by one of the children in [an] overenthusiastic pool exercise'.[104]

Some special projects brought artists from outwith East Park to work with the children and young people. Students from the Royal Scottish Academy of Music and Drama and a group from Scottish Opera worked with the children from Maryhill on a *London's Burning* project, and a few years later there were weekly sessions on puppetry and photography provided by the Glasgow Arts Centre.[105] Shirley Hughes, children's author and illustrator, visited and told the children stories, illustrating while she did so.[106]

In Largs, an exchange programme with Whitechapel School near Preston, Lancashire became established.[107] This gave an opportunity to visit the attractions in Blackpool.[108] This was a relationship which developed over the years and sometimes involved children from Maryhill, including Tristan.[109] Possibly the most ambitious of the exchange trips was to Montpellier in France in 1992. Young people from East Park went as guests of the local Franco-Scottish Association and La Cardabelle, a day school for children with motor sensory impairments.[110] When Maura returned to East Park as an auxiliary nurse, she was selected to travel with the children. East Park directors extended the invitation to the French group and in 1993 children and staff from La Cardabelle came to Glasgow, where they enjoyed a varied programme of activities.[111]

Maura explained:

It was a two-week exchange to Montpellier. Madame Flamme was our contact in Montpellier. She gave us a dessert wine to take back to Scotland. She was a very nice lady. All the staff were lovely. The children were a

Maura (centre) at Montpellier, France, on an exchange trip with young people and staff from East Park. (Courtesy of Maura Morran Khan)

delight and we all had a good holiday. They came here. We got into the news in our swimming suits in the sea. It was on ITV Scotland, *Scotland Today*, me in my costume and the children next to me. I have a photo. The French children all had disabilities … There was a French chef who made the meals … It was a good holiday.[112]

Holidays were arranged both within the UK and occasionally abroad. Sometimes children from Maryhill went to the Country Branch in Largs on holiday.[113] Other destinations across the UK included Girvan, Rothesay, Flamingo Land in Yorkshire and a weekend in London, where young people visited the Science Museum and attended the Horse of the Year Show.[114] Tristan remembered holidays in a place called 'the Wilderness', a cottage in rural Galloway where children and staff picked brambles and made jam.[115] An eight-berth caravan was purchased by the Country Branch and subsequently placed in the grounds at Quarriers Homes in Bridge of Weir.[116] In 1990, five children and seven staff went to Majorca, while a group of children and staff enjoyed a long weekend in Benalmádena, Spain, where they

Fun and frolics in Florida when, in 1993, children visited Pluto at Disneyland.

received 'VIP treatment' courtesy of Celtic Football Club, and in 1993 some children and staff went to Disneyland Florida.[117]

Sunday school continued and over time East Park increasingly embraced religious diversity, initially in respect of children and young people from the Catholic faith, and children from Maryhill and the Country Branch began to regularly participate in pilgrimage to Lourdes.[118] As outlined above, Tristan recollected some Catholic children attending a local Catholic school in Maryhill, and in 1982 some of the children from Largs went to Bellahouston Park to see Pope John Paul II.[119]

Glasgow embraces East Park

By the 1990s, on the surface, East Park was thriving. Children and young people were engaged in a range of activities and the School was on its way to becoming a national resource, while teachers were drawing on the latest ideas in the education of children with a wide range of additional support needs. A shop opened on 5 October 1983 in Maryhill Road, run by one full-time member of staff employed to manage the stock, and a group of volunteers.[120] The shop raised additional funds and heightened the profile of East Park.[121] The shop eventually closed in 1998, having contributed £230,000 to East Park's funds.[122] The staff member was re-employed within East Park.[123] Meanwhile, a range of local groups took an interest in the Home, such as the Mercury Motor Cycle Club who visited the children and gave a cheque to East Park, while children and families held fundraising activities such as 'garage sales'.[124] A Fundraising Committee was set up in 1988.[125] A number of initiatives were forthcoming, such as a mini-marathon/fun run, a golf tournament, a Spring Fayre and a Charity Dinner.[126]

Ken McChlery, who became a Board member in 1988, was involved in an innovative fundraising project whereby Billy McIsaac, a Scottish musician who had played with various bands, including Slik, wrote a series of children's songs produced in a book entitled *Songs for Fraser*.[127] A choir made up of children from primary schools in Milngavie recorded the songs.

As discussed in chapter 14, singer-songwriter Paul Simon gave a generous donation as he wished to assist local children in Glasgow and around the same time singer-songwriter and comedian Billy Connolly flew in from Los Angeles to give a performance at the King's Theatre.[128] Billy gave further fundraising concerts, including one in the Winter Gardens in Blackpool, thought to be on 6 March 1995.[129] May Henderson wrote: 'East Park owes much thanks and appreciation to Mr Billy Connolly … East Park has always been close to his heart.'[130]

In September 1990, a Gala Concert organised by the chair of the East Park Children's Trust, Sir Matthew Goodwin, was held at Glasgow's City Halls. The conductor Sir Alexander Gibson, the Scottish National Orchestra and soloist Evelyn Glennie gave their services free. The concert was attended by East Park's patron, HRH The Duchess of Gloucester, and raised in excess of £136,000.[131]

East Park was riding high, close to the heart of Glasgow and Maryhill and embraced by many local groups and celebrities. However, there were growing concerns outwith East Park about its operation – concerns that would threaten its very existence.

CHAPTER 14
The Personality Touch

The Dennistoun Amateur Minstrels, who gave an Entertainment, which realised £52 7s 3d, indicated their willingness to take a continued interest in the Home, and a Cot has accordingly been named 'Dennistoun Amateur Minstrels' Cot'.

Twenty-third East Park Annual Report, 1896/7, p. 4

It was the best surprise ever to be asked to lay the first brick of the [new East Park School]. It was amazing to meet George Bowie and tell him I am his biggest fan. I am really happy that Cassi [Gillespie] remembered me from the last time I met her and gave me a big hug 'hello'. I am looking forward to seeing Greg [Docherty] play for Hamilton against Aberdeen soon.

Liam Cowan, age 16, East Park pupil, 2015[1]

The Dennistoun Amateur Minstrels, a performing group from the East End of Glasgow, may no longer be in vogue, nor their talents proclaimed by bright neon on Broadway, but their contribution to, and recognition by, East Park is an early marker from the last decade of the nineteenth century of the Home's link with public entertainment. Different forms of 'entertainment', embracing music, song, sport, music hall and theatre and, in due course, cinema, radio and television, have played an important role in East Park across the decades. They have brought pleasure, and curiosity, to generations of East Park children, while also providing a feel-good factor, and publicity, to celebrities and aspiring celebrities. East Park has enjoyed enhancement of its profile through these engagements – two-way engagements that have cemented it into the Glasgow community.

While the naming of a cot, an historical practice discussed in chapter 5, was an honour not accorded all visiting entertainers, personalities have continued to beat a path to 1092 Maryhill Road. That procession contains many famous names, some whose celebrity may have been short-lived because of the fickle nature of their professions, while others are personalities whose renown has grown and endured. It would be nice to think that East Park played its part in projecting visiting celebrities to even greater stardom as a consequence of their visits. The list is long and adds colour to the names of city dignitaries and lord provosts who gave profile to East Park in its early years, and to elite ladies, including the long tenures as patron of HM Queen Alexandra (1911–26), HM Queen Mary (1926–53), and HRH Princess Alice, Duchess of Gloucester (1953–2004) who was present at the 1990 Scottish National Orchestra Concert described later in this chapter. Stars of music hall were followed by the gods and goddesses of the silver screen; there were icons of the worlds of music and song; and there were heroes from the sporting world, in which football has long had a special role in raising Glasgow passions.

It is not possible to showcase every star who arrived at East Park. A few were photographed for old Annual Reports. At the time of these portraits, it was felt that the images did not require to be captioned, but with the passage of time, recognition of early personalities may no longer register with later generations, such being the often transient nature of celebrity and public acclaim. Although this chapter cannot pay tribute to all of East Park's star turns from over the years, such is the multitude who have visited or supported East Park, it sets out to record some of the people who have given their time and talents to promote East Park, perhaps to 'give something back' if they had links with Maryhill and Glasgow before achieving fame. For the press, their visit to Maryhill might represent a moving photo opportunity. Such publicity has raised East Park's profile, photo opportunities working in a variety of ways: aiding fundraising efforts, highlighting East Park's role in the community, or encouraging greater understanding of, and empathy towards, children with impairing circumstances.

Our roll call of the 'greats' from cultural and sporting entertainment begins with some of the most enduring names from Glasgow as a place of early mass entertainment.

A procession of celebrity

Harry Lauder (1870–1950) was a music hall and vaudeville entertainer who, over several decades, appeared on stages across the world dressed in excessively accentuated Highland garb. His style might now be considered 'hackneyed', but his repertoire included such songs as *I Love a Lassie, Roamin' in the Gloamin'*, *A Wee Deoch an Dorus* and *The End of the Road* that have stood the test of time.[2] He was already in semi-retirement when he was hailed by Matron Mary MacEwen for his support during the war evacuation from Maryhill to the Country Branch on 29 and 30 August 1939. He was accompanied by his niece, Margaret (Greta) Lauder (1900–66), who served him loyally as secretary and companion following the death of his wife in 1927.[3]

Of greater presence was Aberdonian, Harry Gordon (1893–1957), an entertainer whose style perhaps echoed aspects of Lauder, but whose own personality was established through his use of the Doric dialect in the delivery of his repertoire.[4] The Harry Gordon Gang mounted performances with particular appeal for children – productions such as *Puss in Boots* at Glasgow's Alhambra Theatre in 1938 from which East Park benefited by a collection amounting to £421 15s 11d.[5] Consequently, East Park allocated £100 for the 'naming' of a cot in 1939, 'The Harry Gordon Gang Cot'.[6] The show must go on and, even during the years of the Second World War, the Harry Gordon Gang performed. Following the 1944 performances of *Dick Whittington*, and the presentation of £555 to East Park, 'The Harry Gordon Gang Cot' was 'endowed' at the Country Branch.[7] Although Gordon died in 1957, in the 1963 Annual Report, the last year in which supported cots were listed, there were both 'The Harry Gordon Gang Cot' and the 'Harry Gordon and Will Fyffe Cot', Will Fyffe (1885–1947) being another well-known artiste from the music hall and theatre circuit, and remembered for writing and performing *I belong to Glasgow*.[8]

In the early post-Second World War years, Elizabeth, introduced in chapter 12, recalled sitting on the knee of Issy Bonn (1903–77). Bonn, a Londoner, used his Jewish roots to appeal to popular stereotypical perspectives of Jewish people, *My Yiddishe Momme* being his theme tune, but the acceptability of this type of racially based humour was in decline when he visited East Park and, later, he became a theatrical agent.[9]

As public engagement with the likes of music hall declined, it was not so much the end of an era, but an evolutionary process. In her report for 1953, for example, Matron Peggy Ligertwood reported that 'radio and television remain prime favourites', going on to show that these were not always passive activities – the BBC making a recording at East Park 'under the direction of Mr A P Lee, with Mr Burl Ives, the American Folk-song Singer, Miss Agnes Duncan and the Scottish Junior Singers', but she also suggested that there was an overwhelming procession of offers from concert parties, choirs and dancing schools to engage with East Park's children and that many had to be declined.[10]

The rise of television resulted in a special appeal being broadcast in 1963. This featured Rikki Fulton (1924–2004) and Jack Milroy (1915–2001) appearing as the popular characters, Francie and Josie. The set was a tenement house of almost Victorian depiction with heavily tiled 'hob' fireplace, wallie dugs on the mantelpiece and a brass platter on the wall, and where Francie and Josie held court round the kitchen table.[11] Both actors continued music hall traditions in the likes of pantomime, while Fulton's production of *Scotch and Wry* (1978–92) introduced performers who

Rikki Fulton and Jack Milroy as Francie and Josie.

would later become household names on television. *Last Call* was Fulton's parody of Scottish Television's 'religious thought for the day' transmission, *Late Call* (1960–89), when as the Reverend I M Jolly, he portrayed a rather pessimistic and droll 'man of the cloth' reflecting on society's challenges, clips that have become classic viewing.[12]

How well East Park's children could appreciate entertainers' gags is open to discussion, but many of them certainly would be well aware of further Scottish funny men characters who called by. In the wake of Fulton and Milroy were such multifaceted talents – performers, writers, producers and entrepreneurs – as Jimmy Logan (1928–2001), Cliff Hanley (1922–99) and Johnny Beattie (1926–2020). There were personalities who visited East Park on multiple occasions, unfortunately not always making their way into East Park's Minute Books and Annual Reports, but Logan visited in 1967, Hanley in 1972 and Beattie in 1973. All were characters in different ways and would certainly have entertained both children and staff during their visits. From the 1950s, Jimmy Logan bridged the transition from the music hall of Harry Lauder to television and film, with collaborations ranging from Gordon Jackson in *Floodtide* (1949) to Gregor Fisher's character, Rab C. Nesbitt (1997–9), and Billy Connolly in *The Debt Collector* in 1998.[13] Johnny Beattie moved in circles that were familiar to Logan, and other weel-kent names, for example his participation in Scottish Television's 1974 *A Grand Tour* with Rikki Fulton, Jack Milroy, Billy Connolly, Mark McManus (1935–94) and Stanley Baxter.[14] Cliff Hanley also had a diverse output in his writing and broadcasting, *Dancing in the Streets* being a childhood autobiography, and through his composition of the words to *Scotland the Brave*, making it into an unofficial national anthem.[15]

Popular Scottish song genres were changing by the 1960s and 1970s, and this would have been apparent when folk singer Alastair McDonald came to Largs in 1977.[16] While his repertoire included nostalgic tartanry from battle ballads to Bonnie Prince Charlie, he also had a relaxed style of folk singing that could have an irreverent dig at figures and events of the past. It is easy to imagine his unpretentious singing and lively banjo plucking having an instant appeal to the children of East Park.

Not just music hall and panto

Iceland-born Magnus Magnusson (1929–2007) was a journalist and author, but it was his presenting of the seriously intense quiz programme, *Mastermind*, that made him a household name during his twenty-five-year run as host from 1972 to 1997.[17] However, he was already a busy man when he was scheduled to move the adoption of East Park's ninety-third Annual Report on 21 February 1967, but then had to withdraw at short notice because of a professional engagement.[18] His wife, Mamie Magnusson (née Baird) (1925–2012), an acclaimed journalist and author in her own right, stepped into the breech, and recalled an early visit to East Park as a young reporter. In moving the proceedings, she complimented East Park's 'bright

A summer day at the Country Branch with Alastair McDonald.

atmosphere, lack of carbolic and tiled walls, [and its] feeling of a home with a small "H".[19] From author Hutchison's own experience of Mamie and her mischievous sense of humour, it is not difficult to surmise that, not only would the meeting attendees have been well entertained, but that she would have captivated East Park's children during her visit.[20]

In what Matron Jessie Macdonald described as 'a very happy afternoon', classical tenor Kenneth McKellar (1927–2010) visited the Country Branch in 1963, just one of the celebrities who, in the words of that year's AGM guest at the top table, cinema executive Sir Alexander B King (1888–1973), represented 'the entertainment world [that] has always had a close connection with East Park Home … both at Maryhill and Largs'.[21] The role played by showbiz did find a place in an Annual Report when nearly £600 arising from an appeal on Scottish Television by Rikki Fulton and Jack Milroy in 1963 was acknowledged, and Matron Macdonald's praise of Kenneth McKellar for his impact on the children through a visit to Largs in March of that year.[22] McKellar had many claims to fame, his repertoire over the years including opera, classical, religious, musicals, Scottish, folk and pop, all performed in his own style. He was 'averse to participating in the "tartanry" side of Scottish culture', having abandoned opera early in his career with the words 'I don't need this. All I want to do is sing.'[23] Actor Sean Connery (1930–2020) originated the Scottish International Education Trust to support talented Scots to aspire to success and McKellar, along with the likes of Formula One racing driver Jackie Stewart and orchestral conductor Alexander Gibson (1926–95), was one of its trustees.[24]

Alexander Gibson's name recurred through a massive musical occasion that took place on 6 September 1990 when the Scottish National Orchestra performed a charity concert for East Park. Conducted by Gibson, it featured Mendelssohn's *Hebrides Overture*, Tchaikovsky's Symphony No. 5, and star soloist, the percussionist Evelyn Glennie, in a concerto by Milhaud and a concertino by Creston. Eighty-nine-year-old patron, Princess Alice Duchess of Gloucester, who was to live to 102, oversaw the proceedings of this august occasion.[25] Billed as a 'Gala Concert', the prestigious event raised over £136,000 for East Park.[26]

In the 1960s, children engaged with radio entertainment of their own choice by tuning into distorted transmissions, on basic transistor radios, by Radio Luxembourg, and by the pirate station, Radio Caroline. In the west of Scotland, independent popular radio entered the mainstream with the launch of Radio Clyde on 31 December 1973, and radio hosts such as 'Tiger' Tim Stevens and Dougie Donnelly quickly became popular with young people. Tiger Tim was up early on Christmas morning in 1982 to broadcast an outside transmission from East Park, and also that year, children met American actor Telly Savalas (1922–94) at the Grosvenor Hotel.

Savalas was popular with youngsters as the detective, Kojak, with his catchphrase, 'Who loves ya, baby?'.[27] Dougie Donnelly was a contemporary of Stevens at Radio Clyde, but later became acclaimed as a sports commentator, a genre upon which he had already embarked when he was in the thick of the *Cash for Kids Appeal – Clyde Action* at East Park in 1984.[28]

Now a celebrated international star, in 1990, Billy Connolly donated £20,000 to East Park from a charity concert.[29] Connolly had flown from Los Angeles to perform in the King's Theatre for the benefit of the Home.[30] Knowledge of East Park's role, it seems, was reaching across the Atlantic, because in 1991 £10,000 arrived unexpectedly from Paul Simon of *Sound of Silence* folk duo with Art Garfunkel fame, who had put on three concerts at Glasgow's Scottish Exhibition and Conference Centre that year.[31] Meanwhile, Billy Connolly's support continued, a cheque for £40,789 being the proceeds of another concert, this time at the brand-new Glasgow Concert Hall, an event hailed as 'wonderful' by Matron Eleanor McCreadie.[32] In 1994, it was back to the King's Theatre, when Connolly raised £39,677 at a concert at which supporting performers were folk singers Ralph McTell (*Streets of London*) and Derroll Adams (1925–2000) (*The Rambling Boys*).[33] Connolly's support continued, a 1995 concert in Blackpool raising over £40,000.[34]

Children's choice?

Funny men, famous men, over the years probably had a variety of impacts upon the children at East Park during their visits. However, it was undoubtedly the entertainers, women and men who particularly focused on children, who really brought excitement to East Park's residents. In the 1950s, glamorous cowboy Roy Rogers (1911–98) and his charismatic horse, Trigger, were firm favourites with young television audiences. While entertainers visiting Glasgow benefited from publicity to promote their shows, Rogers with his wife, Dale Evans, was an example where there was much deeper motivation. Their own family lives were touched by disability through their daughter, Robin, who had Down's Syndrome and died before her second birthday. The trio – Rogers, his wife Dale, and Trigger – visited numerous children's homes and orphanages during their Scottish tour in February 1954 and, as a consequence of their visit to an Edinburgh orphanage, they adopted one of its children, thirteen-year-old Marion Fleming. Oddly, Rogers' arrival with Trigger at East Park seems to have been sidelined to myth and folklore – except for the enduring, larger-than-life depiction of Trigger by the towpath wall on display between East Park School and the canal.[35]

Showbusiness people are wise to be cautious about interacting with animals. Fauna of the puppet variety are therefore a more predictable option than real animals. This was undoubtedly the case when Lenny the Lion, popular on television from the mid-1950s, came to East Park in 1965, and equally so when Harry Corbett introduced Sooty and Sweep to the children in 1981. Ventriloquist Terry Hall (1926–2007) is credited with introducing an animal character to the world of ventriloquy entertainment, and Lenny was definitely a lion without a growl, a soft cheery feline with a special rapport with children. Lenny was larger than life, while the glove puppets, Sooty and Sweep, were traditional and diminutive in the safe hands of Harry Corbett (1918–89).[36] Sooty and Sweep were a different style of act; Sweep was mute while Sooty's dialogue of high-pitched squeaks was translated for children's audiences by Harry Corbett. Corbett reduced his appearances after a heart attack in 1975 and his son, Matthew, continued performances for the following twenty-two years. It was therefore likely that it was Matthew who accompanied Sooty and Sweep when they entertained East Park's children in 1981.

National Children's Book Week in 1978 saw library staff bring Shirley Hughes (1927–2022) to East Park. Hughes was well known both as a writer and illustrator. While telling stories to the children, she brought these to life by producing images, on paper, of the scenes and characters from her books. Hughes wrote and illustrated over fifty children's books, but it was the year following publication of her prize-winning publication, *Dogger*, that brought her to East Park.[37]

Also emphasising the influence of art, John Lowrie Morrison, more widely known as Jolomo, was described by Sir John Leighton, director-general of the National Galleries of Scotland, in 2013, as a landscape artist whose 'bold and simple compositions; lonely headlands, empty beaches, wide skies: they rarely feature people but there are often some indications of a human presence with isolated crofts, boats or lighthouses'.[38] However, in 1970, as an art student, Jolomo, for his degree thesis, 'studied art therapy and started working at the East Park Home in Maryhill, where he befriended several young residents'.[39] Images that were described in 2021 as 'vibrant contorted shapes', but also 'sing[ing] with life and cheeky bravado', depicted children David, Jamie and Sandy of half a century ago to provide a thought-provoking exchange between East Park children and the then-aspiring artist, images that still shout out from the walls of Jolomo's Argyllshire studio.[40] These depictions suggest a thought-provoking two-way interplay between East Park children and an art student profoundly influenced by the young people springing from his palette.

Footballing heroes must surely have impressed the children, none more so than the two 'stars', along with the multitalented Cliff Hanley, mentioned earlier, and Gaelic singer Calum Kennedy (1928–2006), when they all appeared round the decorated tree at East Park one Christmas in the early 1970s. The footballers were Davie Wilson (1937–2022) and Davie McParland (1935–2018). Davie Wilson, after a long career

Among those in this East Park supporting cast (from left to right standing) are Cliff Hanley, Davie Wilson, Davie McParland and Alasdair Gillies.

at Rangers, followed by a spell at Dundee United, was then with Dumbarton FC.[41] Davie McParland had chalked up in excess of four hundred appearances at Partick Thistle as a player, but at this point was Partick Thistle's manager. Partick Thistle was notable in its support for East Park extending over several decades. Calum Kennedy's repertoire included *A' Pheigi, a Ghràidh* (Peggy, my love) and *Mo Mhàthair* (My Mother).[42] In 1989, Lisbon Lion, Billy McNeill (1940–2019) and Celtic Football Club, of which he was then the manager, funded a short holiday for eight children and eleven escorts to Benalmádena in Spain.[43]

Matron Annie Johnston seems to have been in some awe when twenty-four-year-old Steve Davis, already an acclaimed snooker champion, came to Maryhill in 1981. 'This was exciting for some of our enthusiasts,' she wrote. 'He related very well with the boys and we are grateful to him for giving up his limited time.'[44] Davis took the snooker world by storm throughout the 1980s and that journey was already underway when he visited East Park, having become World Champion in 1980. His time during his 1981 visit may well have been limited, but a *Glasgow Herald* photo of Davis at a snooker table with some of the East Park boys suggests he was enjoying the occasion every bit as much as his young admirers.[45]

Some celebrities visiting East Park did not get away with just a photo opportunity and having an ice cream with the children. Radio Clyde host George Bowie and travel reporter Cassi Gillespie, along with Hamilton Accies midfielder, Greg Docherty, had to get their hands dirty. Along with pupil Liam Cowan, they appeared among the building works as construction began, in 2015, and when East Park 'cut the turf' for its expansion for the twenty-first century. The Big Lottery Fund had just awarded £500,000 towards the £3 million project to create new school facilities aimed at children with autism. Bowie is not a stranger to East Park and he recalled meeting Liam on a previous trip to the coast: 'Liam's my mate. We met him at the Glasgow Taxi Outing to Troon and we said we'd love to come and lay the first brick of the new building.'[46] Liam's sentiments on the occasion are expressed at the beginning of this chapter.

However, children and staff could also voice their displeasure if celebrity visitors did not, in their opinion, come up to their expectations. It is a long-standing trope in showbusiness that budding careers can die before a demanding and unforgiving Glasgow audience. An oft-quoted example is of comedian Des O'Connor's (1932–2020) performance at the Empire Theatre in 1954 when he 'fainted through fear' as a ploy to escape an unimpressed audience.[47] So it could be too with young people at East Park.

Elizabeth Hunter's vignette of her teenage introduction to nursing at East Park demonstrates how her difficulty settling into her role may have been because of a feeling of fear arising from the unfamiliar impairments she was witnessing: 'I'd never seen a crippled child before. This is why I had difficulty at the beginning.'[48] So too it may have been with some visiting personalities, but children and young people would take strangers at face value. Hunter, still a teenager, was not impressed with Harry Lauder: 'I was so disappointed … because he hardly ever spoke to a single child.'[49] Of course, Lauder's visit may have been choreographed by others and he was already in semi-retirement by 1939. Or perhaps Lauder, like many people who become ill at ease in engaging with the unfamiliar, and as he was now approaching seventy years of age, may have felt intimidated in the presence of East Park's children in a way that he did not experience when performing before audiences of thousands beyond the glare of the footlights.

Vivian Fuchs (1908–99) was an explorer and scientist whose work took him on expeditions to East Africa, the Arctic and the South Atlantic, and who had crossed the

Antarctic in 1957–8.[50] There is no doubting that he was one of the most high-profile of intrepid characters at a time when the world's most inhospitable environments were being challenged by men who were prepared to test themselves to the limits of human endurance.[51] He was the stuff of heroism to boys whose youthful aspiration also had no limit. When he visited East Park at Largs, Michael McCready was in awe of him and asked Fuchs for his autograph. The occasion was one of those distant memories from childhood that remain crisp and clear. The explorer agreed to Michael's request, but for a fee of sixpence. Michael, taken aback, changed his mind. In interview, it was suggested to Michael that Fuchs may have been joking, but Michael believed that Fuchs was deadly serious about charging for his signature.[52] When Fuchs died at the age of ninety-one, one obituary summed him up as 'not a touchy-feely sort of person'.[53]

Aa the airts

Celebrity engagement with East Park's children has long been a part of the Maryhill scene and, in its time, also at the Country Branch. This chapter has showcased some of the personalities who have been involved – celebrities from stage and screen, the arts and the media, and practitioners of a variety of sporting activities. The range of people who tried to brighten lives was diverse. There were also many people in local amateur groups, employee participants from Glasgow's industries, the famous taxi drivers who provided gaily decorated convoys of cabs to the seaside, personnel from the merchant navy, Royal Navy and the police, to name but a few.

Some celebrities made fleeting visits during breaks in busy touring schedules. Others had enduring relationships with East Park and with other worthy causes – successful people who appreciated their own good fortune and so strived to give something back, especially to the young, and even more especially to children who had been dealt a raw deal in the journey of life. For example, Cliff Hanley reflected upon his humble back court childhood and Davie Wilson recalled his start in life in a miners' row with outside toilets in Newton.

Chapter 18 describes the physical evolution of East Park and conveys impressions of it as being shielded from the outside world, but there are many people, famous and not so famous, who have tried to bring their own brand of joy to East Park's young people. And East Park's youthful residents have returned that joy in equal measure. These are important exchanges in the breaking down of barriers and generating greater understanding of the diversity of lived experience.

CHAPTER 15

Gathering Clouds, 1992–7

Historians can validly write 'contrapuntal' history, with parallel story lines that are read horizontally but maintain determinate relation with each other. The independence of voices must be maintained even within a multivocal structure. Too frequent a harmonic coincidence is suspect.

Charles S. Maier, 2003[1]

W hile Glasgow was embracing East Park and celebrities were feting it, there were undertones of concern. These came to a head in the early 1990s.

Dropping numbers

Possibly one of the first signs of difficulties ahead was a drop in the number of children and young people being referred to East Park and the Country Branch. This could have been overlooked as an indicator of concern, as this period saw a significant reduction in the number of children and young people in residential care across Scotland, from 6,304 in 1971 to 2,042 in 1995, for reasons outlined in chapter 11. The number of residential homes and residential schools almost halved around this time.[2] Particularly pertinent, voluntary childcare agencies like East Park were facing closure as the tide turned against residential care for children and Social Work departments found it cheaper and preferable to use their own accommodation.[3]

At a Special Board Meeting on 20 June 1985, it was decided that the Country Branch should close, with the few remaining children transferring to live in East Park, Maryhill. Understandably there were objections to this and letters protesting about the closure were received, including some to the Royal Family. Despite this, plans for the closure went ahead.[4] In order to accommodate the children from the Country Branch, considerable refurbishment was required at Maryhill.[5] A new hall was opened in October 1987 by the patron, HRH The Duchess of Gloucester, and named in memory of the Home's founder, William Mitchell. New buildings on the Maryhill site also included a physiotherapy unit, four classrooms, a store and a heating unit. The hydrotherapy pool was installed around the same time, funded separately by public donation.[6] The Country Branch closed on 31 March 1987.[7]

When discussing the closure of the Country Branch, the subject of increasing the number of residential care officers was resurrected. One Board member expressed concern that the two most senior members of staff in the Home would be trained in residential care when there was so much nursing required. He suggested that the deputy should come from a nursing background. Another Board member disagreed, proposing that nursing staff would be on duty, and that 'the modern system' in homes such as East Park was to have the majority of staff trained in childcare rather than nursing.[8] There does not appear to have been any significant change in the staffing structure at this time, however.

While numbers were dropping, there was also concern about the number of young people now nineteen and twenty years of age still resident.[9] Apart from being inappropriately placed, this blocked places for younger children to be admitted.[10] It was thought that this 'bottleneck' was linked to the introduction of the National Health Service and Community Care Act 1990 (the Community Care Act) and local authorities being faced with finding placements for adults moving on from hospitals such as Lennox Castle and Gogarburn. The significance of the Community Care Act cannot be underestimated in that it gave the opportunity for adults, who had spent their lives in institutions, to live with support in a variety of community settings. When Jimmy McIntosh, former resident of East Park, moved on from Gogarburn, he married and lived with his wife until his death in 2014.[11] Lack of suitable accommodation appears to have been a national problem, however, and in November 1991, East Park was approached by Susie Taylor of the BBC to participate in a *Focal Point* programme about the difficulties experienced in finding suitable placements for young people as they approached adulthood. There was unanimous agreement to participate and this was filmed in December 1991.[12] Soon afterwards, it was suggested by the Social Work Department (thought to be that of Strathclyde Regional Council) that East Park diversify and consider providing a service for older children and young adults.[13] While East Park gave this some consideration, it was several years before it branched out to work with 18–25 year-olds by developing the Workmates Project, still active today.

The Community Care Act not only impacted on the lives of adults; children with complex healthcare needs were increasingly being looked after in their own homes, backed up by additional support not previously available, thus further reducing potential referrals.[14] Possibly related, around this time requests for 'respite care' were increasing markedly.[15] Overall it was difficult to sustain numbers of children in long-term placements.[16] It was clear that there was much discussion at Board meetings as to 'whether East Park [had] a place in the future' and '[were] there enough children to come?'.[17]

Over time it became clear that there were other factors underlying the reduction in referrals. After some 'horizon scanning', it was apparent that some organisations providing a similar service to East Park had waiting lists while East Park had vacancies.[18] All manner of explanations were considered; was it cheaper for local authorities to place children in foster care than in residential care?[19] Having decided against specialising over the years, was this now a deterrent to agencies placing children?[20] Was East Park (still) seen as 'a Protestant organisation', thus deterring local authorities from making referrals?[21] Meetings were convened between East Park, Strathclyde Regional Council and Greater Glasgow Health Board. A number of concerns emerged. Firstly, local authorities were now seeking small units rather than 'institutional care'; East Park's 'vastness' and old building was increasingly out of step with residential care across Scotland, which was moving to smaller 'group home' type provision.[22] Secondly, there was criticism that East Park was 'too much like a hospital', too much controlled by nursing staff and 'had not moved with the times'.[23] Thirdly, there was thought to be a lack of flexibility and integration between the Home and the School.[24] While these concerns reached a peak in the 1990s, it is clear from records that there had been concerns going back decades.

Building

Although critics were very vocal about the building in the 1990s, there had been low-level concerns within East Park about the living accommodation for the children dating back to the 1970s. In 1972, Dr Livingstone reflected:

> It is difficult to envisage house parents in the home as presently structured. The ideal solution would be the establishment of a small group home within East Park but running separately with a different staff structure and making more use of normal educational institutions. This would have to be financed on a different basis.[25]

He returned to this theme in 1974:

> Unfortunately we are in a rather old building which is planned in Wards. This was necessary in the past and is less so now, but for other reasons major structural alterations have been impossible to date. It has been said 'a house

does not make a home' and this is true. Despite what we appear to be at Maryhill, we function very well as a children's home.[26]

Staff within East Park also recollected having had reservations about the building over the years. May Henderson took up post as Administrator in July 1988. She recalled her first encounter with East Park:

> My first impression … was that it was a very forbidding-looking building from the outside and internally was very dated. When I was shown to my office, I recall that everything was brown. Brown carpet, brown desk and dirty brown walls that smelled of stale cigarette smoke, … Although I managed to get my office painted, my impression of East Park did not really change as I settled into my new post.[27]

It is clear talking to staff, former residents and their families that while the 'wards' of Elizabeth and Jimmy's day in the 1940s and 1950s had become the 'dorm' or dormitory when Maura and Tristan were resident in the 1960s and 1970s, they were in effect the same space in which several children lived in the 1990s with no room to play apart from between the beds and no privacy apart from a locker. It does, however, seem to have been inviting. Elena's brother lived in East Park from 1985 to 1997. She remembered visiting him: 'I was quite young but I do remember the dorm where my brother used to be and it seemed very cosy' (lots of children sleeping in the same room together).[28] It was, however, out of step with contemporary thinking on residential children's services. Karen Ferguson has held several posts during her career at East Park where she is currently employed as Care Services Manager. Karen's initial encounter with East Park was in 1997, when she took up a student placement while studying for a Higher National Certificate in Social Care. She remembered at this time 'there were still units that were designed like hospital wards. There was an effort to maintain some privacy and dignity with curtains, etc. However, the idea of a social model of care was definitely not in full flow.'[29]

Medical model of care

As outlined in chapter 13, in 1971, plans were made to restructure the staffing with the appointment of trained residential care officers, 'housemothers', to look after young people's care needs and nurses to look after clinical aspects of their care.[30] This seems to have been difficult to sustain, however, and when Tristan and Maura returned to East Park to work in the 1990s, they were employed as auxiliaries, despite Maura being qualified and very experienced as a nursery nurse.[31]

Pamela Greenhow, who now works as Learning and Development Officer, joined East Park in 1993, initially as a care assistant. She recalled:

> When I started working here, we had to wear a uniform. A blue tunic dress that you were not allowed to wear outside. (If going out with young people we were told to change into our mufti!) The men wore tunic and trousers. The uniforms were laundered on site. This is no longer the case as staff now wear their own clothes. Staff now have ID cards that have name, job role and identify them as East Park staff. Support staff were not permitted to undertake any activities that involved any medical procedures: the trained staff only carried these out but now due to the logistics, staff have been trained to undertake this. A medicine trolley was used to dispense the meds, which was very hospital-like; there was a laundry department on site and the dirty linen was collected every day and clean laundry returned. Now each house has a washer drier.[32]

Maura and Pamela's experience in the early 1990s was very different from the practice in other residential care establishments of the time, where staff wore their own clothing, laundry was carried out in the houses and residential care officers administered medication, albeit following strict procedures.

Absence of flexibility and integration between Home and School

In 1992, Matron Eleanor McCreadie pointed out that East Park was in some ways unique, in that it held a threefold role of Home, School and 'Nursing Home'. This structure brought its challenges, as staff were liaising with education authorities, social work authorities and health-related agencies.[33] Linda Gray, who joined East Park as a teacher in January 1993 and became Head Teacher in 1997, recalled the challenges of operating at the interface of three systems:

> We had Health Board, Social Work and Education all inspecting us and all at different times; they didn't come together. Social Work would come in and say 'why is that shampoo not locked away because it is dangerous' and Education would come and say 'they need to have choice so why is the shampoo not out?' We were trying to make the children as independent as possible, but Health Board were saying 'you can't take him out'.[34]

There was also concern on the part of inspectors about a lack of coordination, particularly between the School and the Home.[35] This may have been compounded by the committee structure within East Park, whereby there were three committees which met monthly. They operated independently of each other, but each reported to the Board; the Finance Committee, the House & Staff Committee and the Education Committee. Each was led by a director.[36] The schism was recognised by the Board and in 1990, May Henderson's role was changed from Administrator to Senior Administrator, having overall charge of the Home in the hope of drawing the Home and School together.[37] Weekly meetings were convened between the management team of Matron Eleanor McCreadie, Head Teacher Cathie Leggate and May Henderson, with the aim of work being coordinated rather than projects running separately.[38] Concerns continued, however, and at a Board meeting on 9 June 1992 it was reported that two inspectors from the SOED were critical that the education programme finished at 3pm. They requested that this continue until the children went to bed; that recreation, including TV, should be part of education (what was subsequently referred to as 'a 24 hour curriculum'); and that there should be one unit, i.e. 'East Park', not East Park Home and School.[39] It was suggested that the School Development Plan required as part of the process of East Park becoming a Grant Aided Special School could become an East Park Development Plan to facilitate cohesion.[40] Concerns continued, however, and as 1993 drew to a close, HMI again recommended that East Park move towards twenty-four-hour care and education, thus providing a more integrated approach involving flexibility and movement between staff which could directly benefit the children. The effect of this, it was noted, would mean maximum use of available 'manpower' and therefore achieve savings on staffing costs.[41]

Matters of governance

Around the same time, there was a period of reflection within the Board as to their role and responsibilities. At this point the Board was meeting monthly. Meetings often started with updates on circumstances of the children and young people resident in East Park. Director Sir Matthew Goodwin suggested that 'efforts should be made by the Directors to take a back seat to allow management to run the Home and only become involved when management required a meeting', a criticism subsequently raised by Strathclyde Regional Council and Greater Glasgow Health Board.[42] There was some discussion, as it seemed the Constitution stated that the directors must be involved in the running of the Home. It was decided that the Constitution needed to be brought in line with current practice, the Board having oversight of policy and financial control rather than directing operations, which should be the responsibility of the Management Team.[43] It was decided that the director who chaired the Admissions Panel should step down and the role was transferred to Senior Administrator May Henderson.[44] During this time there were regular meetings between East Park, Strathclyde Regional Council and Greater Glasgow Health Board.[45] By December 1993, it was agreed to carry out a Review of East Park as a whole, with the appointment of a Review Team comprising representatives from medical, nursing, educational and 'paramedic' (with expertise in physiotherapy) backgrounds.[46]

Following this external Review, it was agreed that May Henderson carry out a Review of Staffing.[47] The Board met to consider implementing this at an Extraordinary Meeting on 17 January 1995.[48] This brought about significant changes to East Park's structure and arguably a shift to embedding a social model of care.[49] May Henderson was offered the post of General Manager and subsequently saw through some of the most significant changes in East Park's history.[50]

Restructuring

The Review used a SWOT Analysis format, identifying Strengths, Weaknesses, Opportunities and Threats in respect of East Park. Many of these points had already been identified by the Board and other stakeholders but the Review brought these together, aligning them and giving an opportunity for systemic change. Priorities were identified which included reviewing the organisation and management structures. The School structure was simplified, with the Depute Head replaced by Senior Teacher and instructors replaced by care/classroom assistants. The most fundamental change was the replacement of Matron, Depute Matron, Sisters and various grades of nurses with Care Manager, Senior Care Leaders, Care Leaders and Care Assistants, both Day and Night.[51] Over time, these have been replaced with Head of Care Services, Care Services Managers, Team Leaders, Depute Team Leaders, Senior Support Workers and Residential Support Workers.[52] In essence, the new structure was less hierarchical than previously, providing an opportunity for greater integration between Home and School, with hospital terminology replaced by care terminology.[53] Redundancies were carried out, which understandably caused some disquiet and media interest.[54] It was agreed that the changeover to the new structure would take place on 1 December 1995. Meetings were held with representatives of Strathclyde Regional Council Social Work Department. They made it clear that they wished to support East Park in the production of a Development Plan.[55] As the new structure was being embedded, concerns continued about the lack of new referrals. It is worth noting that around this time there was a significant change in social work support, in that Strathclyde Regional Council, like all regional councils in Scotland, was abolished on 31 March 1996 by the Local Government etc. (Scotland) Act 1994. In the three years to August 1996, there had been only seven referrals. Apart from one referral for 'respite', there had been none in the eighteen months to August 1996. While the Social Work Department (presumed to be that of Glasgow City Council from 1 April 1996) gave a generally favourable report, there was continued criticism of the old buildings and the communal sleeping arrangements, which were very different to the residential care provision run by the Social Work Department.[56] By 1997, there were major concerns about the number of young people due to leave East Park.[57] Throughout this period, there was discussion about building developments, including a complete rebuild on a different site, but a resistance to 'speculative building', with no clear plan or commitment from the Social Work Department to fill any new spaces.[58]

1997 was a watershed year for East Park. A school inspection was carried out by HMI in January.[59] The overall feedback was that the quality of learning and teaching was variable, ranging from 'unsatisfactory' to 'very good'; several points of action were identified.[60] An inspection was carried out by Greater Glasgow Health Board a few weeks later. Concerns were raised about the temperature of the water and it transpired that a complete overhaul of the hot-water system was required.[61] A few months later, an inspection was carried out by the Social Work Department. Again, this was critical, described as 'very harsh'. The two main areas of concern were the premises and the lack of staff training. It was also noted that there 'was a degree of complacency among staff'. Although details of the report are not available, there was some reference to 'the closure of East Park'.[62] Clearly this was a low point for the Home. Radical intervention was required to ensure that East Park had a future.

The Board and managers fully accepted the recommendations in the inspection reports and took steps to address the issues in a planned and structured way. Due to the extent of work involved, they appointed external consultants Scottish Human Services (SHS) to support them in bringing about change. SHS was well recognised within Scotland at the time as consultants who had expertise in social care, training and management of change. Members of the SHS team worked closely with staff to make improvements in practice and service delivery while helping to develop a vision and strategic plan to ensure East Park's survival.[63]

Before moving on to look at how East Park 'reinvented' itself and became a significant provider of care and education for children with complex additional support needs in Scotland, it is helpful to pause to reflect on why an organisation that had been apparently so successful should come to the verge of closure. A couple of reflections, firstly from Ken McChlery, a Board member at the time:

> We were looking after children but again, Government pressures for example about how to educate children, about 'this should happen, that should happen' and we had to navigate through rules and regulations

without people who were in the decision- making process … We were doing so much for the children but outside forces were making their presence felt. They were going 'East Park should be doing this, East Park should be doing that'. And you are going 'Where do the children fit in …'. Us as lay people were trying to interpret.[64]

Meanwhile, May Henderson, former General Manager, suggested:

East Park was well known and well loved by the local community and engendered much support from businesses across the city. I believe that this good reputation encouraged a complacency within East Park that the organisation could remain untouched by external influences and thus there was a resistance to change. This attitude was clearly the wrong one to have as East Park was on the verge of closure.[65]

Staff and members of the Board at East Park used this experience as a learning opportunity, however, and over the next few years worked together to bring about the changes necessary to ensure East Park's growth and future development to become a significant provider of services for some of Scotland's most vulnerable children and young people.

CHAPTER 16

New Beginnings and Modernisation, 1997–2020s

How can you lead when you don't know where you are going? And that was the hard thing because we didn't know where we were going.

Linda Gray, former Head Teacher, 1997–2014[1]

The adverse inspections of 1997 made their mark on East Park. There were rumours that East Park was closing.[2] Within East Park, work began immediately to address the concerns. In this chapter we will hear from staff who have worked in East Park since the 1990s and through the transformation to the childcare service we know today.

Moving forward

As outlined in chapter 15, East Park recruited the consultancy agency Scottish Human Services (SHS) to help develop a vision and plan for the future, as well as to assist with learning and development.[3] A Report was produced by Pete Ritchie (one of the founders of SHS) which was the basis of discussion by the Board.[4] There was a degree of apprehension on the part of some Board members about this initial plan. A number of concerns were expressed: the ideas were 'quite radical'; SHS was for total integration into the community as well as integration in education; the medical needs of some of the children and young people were not addressed; and while the majority of those currently resident in East Park could settle very satisfactorily in 'ordinary homes', there were others with more significant medical and health needs whom it was felt would be more difficult to look after in this way.[5] Although there was reference to moving to smaller units, the cost had not yet been addressed, and if children were in houses in the community, there was concern that there may be moves to have them placed in local special schools, which would see the demise of East Park.[6] It was thought there was still a need for residential facilities on site and so the possibility of building houses to accommodate the children at Maryhill Road was explored.[7]

Over time, these concerns were addressed. A small pilot study was arranged of five young people in Gloucester Unit, with a view to developing a new model of care whereby staff created individual 'Person Centred Plans' for each of the young people resident.[8] Person Centred Planning is rooted in the belief that disabled people are entitled to the same rights, opportunities and choices as other members of the community. Disability does not justify poor treatment, low standards or injustice or oppression.[9] While these ideas are very much embedded in practice when supporting disabled children, young people and adults today, when introduced in the 1990s, Person Centred Planning was quite different from the more traditional approaches to assessment and individual planning which had gone before. Linda Gray, Head Teacher at the time, remembered its introduction:

> Person Centred Planning became an integral part of the whole organisation, with extensive staff training and development which effected a massive change in direction of East Park from a medical model to a more holistic approach. In the course of this major change we had … reluctance from many staff, some of whom ultimately left. We started sharing support staff between residential and school which took a long time to bed in, and for people to accept.[10]

Some staff, however, were very enthusiastic. Jim McDermott, now a learning support worker in Workmates, remembers the introduction of Person Centred Planning: 'It was very exciting. It was all about the young person, getting their aspirations and their dreams and trying to get as near as possible.'[11] Michelle Devlin, also a learning support worker with Workmates, while completely supportive, recalled the challenges: 'Staff were doing it for young people but it was so time consuming.'[12] Person Centred Planning became embedded in practice within East Park.

Meanwhile, houses in the community for disabled children were being developed by other voluntary agencies within Scotland; arrangements were made for Board members to visit. This eased anxieties.[13] Two workshops were convened with the aim of producing a Development Plan.[14] The first addressed the possibility of a Respite and Family Support Service, and the second explored developments in the School, a post-nineteen service for young people aged 18–25 and residential facilities off site.[15]

Visits continued to residential schools providing care and education for children with similar levels of need. Board members were surprised to find that there were establishments where school and accommodation were on one site, but by this time, they were committed to houses in the community.[16] Several years later, it was recognised that a very small group of young people had marked difficulty with transitions and for them accommodation near to the School was necessary, but at this time the Board was resolved to developing residences off campus.[17]

A Development Plan was produced by May Henderson, agreed by the Board and shared with Glasgow City Council.[18] It was agreed that an abbreviated version would be sent to parents and an open evening was convened.[19] There was a degree of opposition to the plan for moving off the main campus, particularly from some parents 'who were unsure if their children would cope or be properly looked after in that type of setting, away from the relative safety of a large institution'.[20] The plan proceeded, however.

A number of changes were immediately implemented. While looking to develop the new residences, significant improvements were made to the physical environment in East Park through refurbishment and redecoration of residential units and classrooms. Two of the residential units underwent major refurbishment to convert them to four-bedroomed self-contained flats and many of the children now had their own bedroom.[21]

Karen Ferguson, Care Services Manager, recalled returning to East Park in July 1999 to take up post as part-time senior support worker, having been a student on placement in 1997:

> As a student there were still units designed like hospital wards. There was an effort to maintain some privacy and dignity with curtains … When I first started working in East Park, I could see the difference. Units had their space redesigned. Young people had their own rooms.[22]

Around this time, during 1998, Helen Akilade, Head of Care, retired. Mary Wright was seconded from SHS as interim Head of Care until Daniel Davison (known as Danny) took up the post early in 1999.[23] East Park was changing rapidly. Carol Kerr, now a support worker in the Intensive Support Service, recalls this:

> I worked in the kitchen [in the 1990s]. … We had to take supper round all the units, their toast or whatever they were having, then we would go back and collect it, wash the dishes and finish at 8 o'clock. We were instructed not to interact with the young people. The staff in the units were not allowed to push the trolley because that was our job and it's very hard not to speak to the young people when you are in the units … Even though they don't speak, you would talk to them.[24]

While some accepted redundancy, others took the opportunity of a change of role within East Park. Carol enjoyed working in the canteen but she was approached by 'Mary' (thought to be Mary Wright), who asked if she would like to work 'on the care side'. Carol explained that she enjoyed what she was doing. She recollected:

> [Mary] kind of talked me into it. I said 'I'll give it a go.' She said, 'Try it for a few months' and twenty-four years later I am still here.[25]

Carol found some of the changes initially challenging:

> It was Mary. She said, 'Things move on.' She didn't introduce herself as 'I am Mrs …'. 'I am Mary and you are Carol' but it was very difficult to suddenly talk names because it wasn't a formal thing. It was informal, nobody is above anybody else.[26]

With the number of changes underway, it was necessary to amend the Constitution, particularly that in exceptional instances, young people over nineteen could be accommodated.[27] Issues of registration also required addressing. It was established that each individual house did not need to be registered with the Health Board, nor was there going to be a nurse on site permanently.[28] As early as January 1998, the Scottish Office of Education and Industry Department (SOEID) 'were pleased at the way in which East Park was tackling the way forward', a Health Board Inspection was described as 'very good' and in a draft Social Work inspection report in 2000, all standards were met.[29] By 2003, the first joint inspection by HMI and the Care Commission was described as positive, with progress in key areas being recognised.[30]

Meanwhile, a conversation with the Social Work Department indicated that the threat of imminent closure had been lifted while the Development Plan was implemented.[31] A temporary self-imposed hold had been placed on admissions by East Park while changes were underway but this was lifted by August 1999, by which time the short breaks service was operational.[32]

Implementing the Development Plan

Short Breaks

One of the first objectives in the Development Plan was the 'Respite and Family Support Service'. There had been previous reference to East Park providing a 'respite' service as far back as 1973, when Dr Livingstone had explained that 'five of our admissions and discharges during the year were children admitted for a short period only, mainly at the request of Glasgow Social Work Department – to give parents a holiday'.[33] Over the years there were several references to children coming to East Park and the Country Branch for 'respite'. It was made clear by the Social Work Department, however, that they would not accept children on 'respite' placements living with children on permanent placements and on the same site as a school.[34]

By March 1999, Team Leader Lynn Connacher was seconded to develop the service.[35] A Respite and Family Support Service Plan was developed; this necessitated a variation in registration.[36] The new service was operational by August 1999, in what became known as Katrine House. Lynn remained in post managing the service, working with a team of senior support workers and support workers. Nursing input was provided by staff within East Park.[37] Katrine House had four individual bedrooms, a sitting/dining area, a separate kitchen, bathroom and WC, with an additional en-suite bedroom, allowing for four children and young people on short breaks and one admitted as an emergency. This 'emergency placement' often led to a permanent admission to East Park.[38] By April 2002, there were thirty-one children from thirty families using the service. It was noted that, similar to the residential service, the number of children with physical impairments and major health problems was decreasing, while the number with autism and challenging behaviour was increasing, a trend which was to accelerate over the next decade.[39] Lynn Connacher left in 1999 and Helen Gallagher took over as Respite Service Coordinator.[40]

Karen Ferguson initially worked in Katrine House when it opened. She explained that, being a respite service, children visiting had a wider spectrum of impairments than elsewhere in East Park, including conditions such as hearing and visual impairments, autism, Angelman Syndrome, Peters Plus Syndrome, West Syndrome, Down's Syndrome, Fragile X Syndrome and Global Developmental Delay. While most children came for short breaks from their family home, some came from residential schools which closed over the holiday period. Although termed 'Respite and Family Support', the main service was residential with sporadic home support mainly for children and young people who came on an emergency basis.[41]

Around the time the respite service was being established, the use of the term 'respite' was challenged in a publication by The Scottish Executive, *The Same as You*, which stated that 'research on respite care suggests that what is offered is directed more at carers' ends than of people with disabilities. Many families are unhappy with the term "respite", and prefer to use "short breaks", which shows that services should be designed to meet both sets of needs.'[42] This was a view expressed in *The Promise* (2020), one of the final reports of the Independent Care Review: 'Scotland must stop using the word "respite" and rethink the nature and purpose of short breaks.'[43] Over time, 'respite' or short breaks were seen as offering children and young people new experiences and opportunities often not possible at home. Although not explicitly stated, the service in East Park changed to reflect this and children coming for a short break had an activity plan for their stay.

While some staff welcomed the new approach, some appeared reluctant to embrace change. Karen Ferguson, now Care Services Manager, recalled that at the time 'taking them on the journey' proved challenging, for example when they refused to take the children and young people on public transport. She explained:

> Back then, some of these activities were seen as risky and at times I could see the eyebrows being raised by managers! I remember taking three young people [on summer break from residential school] to their very first concert at the Exhibition Centre. They saw Westlife … It was an amazing experience to see their faces light up with the sensory experiences. Everyday activities included swimming, going to the cinema, bowling, shopping, going on public transport, library, parks, going out for dinner, soft play. At the time East Park had a huge garden, so we took full advantage of this … We also took young people to the Carnival and Strathclyde Park. These places were not always wheelchair-accessible so trying to get a young person on a rollercoaster was difficult but we managed!
>
> On one occasion, East Park ran a Christmas decoration competition between the units. Katrine House made a full sensory wall display on the outside of their corridor of a group of young people carol singing. All the children in the display had real clothes on. Katrine House won![44]

From 2012–13 onwards, the respite service experienced a reduction in referrals, thought to be related to the introduction of Self-Directed Support.[45] Young people receiving a short break service were reassessed, leading to some being unable to afford the same level of residential short breaks to which they had become accustomed.[46] Self-Directed Support also gave families more flexibility and autonomy over deciding how to use their personalised budget and as a result, several families chose to use the residential short break service to cover one longer holiday period (e.g. two weeks over the summer) rather than their child attending for a few days on a monthly basis over the course of the year, which had been the previous pattern of usage.[47] Over time, taking into account some new building proposals, it was decided to reduce the service from a four-bed unit to two beds and to call it Transitional House rather than Respite.[48]

Responding to the move away from 'building-based respite', East Park sought to adapt. In 2013, Scottish Government Better Breaks funding enabled an activity scheme during the summer school holidays and an after-school club. The main beneficiaries were to be East Park School day pupils or young people receiving a short breaks service from Katrine House.[49]

By November 2013, Geraldine O'Neill, Head of Care, successor to Danny Davison, reported that East Park had provided a short programme of activities over the summer holidays, known as East Park Active Kids Club, and after-school activities from August 2013.[50] Following a review, it was decided to run school holiday clubs during July 2014, again funded by the Scottish Government's Better Breaks Fund.[51]

Meanwhile, the number of children and young people using the residential short break/respite service continued to drop. It was decided to develop a smaller, more individualised, short- to medium-term service for two children, who may have intensive support needs. The benefit was that this could be used either as a short break service if future demand existed or for emergency placements, supporting children and families through a crisis.[52] The service closed in March 2015 as part of the planned capital project for the intensive support residential service and single-space teaching provision, discussed below.[53]

Workmates

The second strand of the 1998 Development Plan was to develop a service for young people aged 18–25.[54] By December 2000, a plan had been drawn up for what became known as Workmates, still operational today.[55] There had been a precursor to Workmates, known as SCOPE (Social and Community Opportunities Post-Eighteen).[56] It had been recognised by teaching staff that a number of young people leaving school were still resident in East Park; staff were concerned that they would quickly lose skills developed. SCOPE aimed to maintain and develop skills but in a more 'adult setting'. Workmates had similar aims but with the added objective of providing supported work and/or college experience.[57]

Concurrent with these developments, there was a national move towards reimagining day services for adults with learning disabilities. *Make My Day* flowed from the report *The Same as You* (discussed above) and was published in 2006, specifically addressing day services. A number of themes emerged:

1. Users, carers and staff want varied and flexible services offering a mix of opportunities.
2. They want people with learning disabilities to be included in and to make valued contributions to their local communities.
3. People with learning disabilities want to be involved in purposeful activity, leading to employment that suits the individual.
4. A person-centred approach is ideal.

5. Service user and family carer involvement in running services is vital.
6. Partnership working with a broad range of stakeholders is essential.
7. Aspirations are greater than available resources.[58]

Although Workmates developed prior to the publication of *Make My Day*, a number of these features are evident.

Jim McDermott and Michelle Devlin explained about the development of the project. Jim transferred in 2002 from Robertson House, one of the new East Park residences, where he had been working as a support worker. Michelle had transferred with SCOPE, where she had been employed as a learning support worker. She explained:

> The Mission Statement for Workmates is that Workmates offers a one-to-one service for young people in the transition from school to adult services. Young people join the service aged seventeen and leave aged twenty-five as young adults. Since it was established parents are reassured that their young person is going to be supported according to the National Care Standards at minimum, in a person-centred way.[59]

Michelle recalled the transition from SCOPE to Workmates and work experience:

> I was one of the first to go to college with young people, the school link and then work experience … I had a friend who had a hairdresser in Maryhill Road. Lyndsay (pseud.) had left East Park at that point. She came back [to Workmates] and I took her for a work experience in the hairdresser. Lyndsay is a wheelchair user and non-verbal. What we did, we printed off pictures of tea and coffee and I would push her chair up to the person who would be having their hair cut with the picture of tea and coffee and then I'd put the water in the kettle. I would take her over to put the kettle on and put the tea and sugar in the cup … and take the tea to the client. Then I would put the brush in her hand and push her and she would brush up the hair.
>
> Another great one, one of the first ones was in the BBC studios. Lyndsay also worked there, in the office … What we had to do was collect the mail and we would sit at a desk and the people in the office, Moira, John [sorting the mail] then went round the desks with the mail. Emma (pseud.) also worked in the BBC office. She was blind and non-verbal and what I would do was put the mail in front of her, I would tell her what colour it was, she could feel it if it had bubble wrap inside and we would deliver it. I would say, 'You have a light envelope, you have a big envelope

that's a bit bigger', and John would chat with her for all that Emma was non-verbal and blind …[60]

One of the challenges for young people with additional support needs on work experience schemes is that they work for no pay as this can affect their benefits. Through Workmates, some young people carried out paper rounds delivering the *Glaswegian*, a job for which they were paid. Rather than give them a small amount each week, this was saved and distributed between the young people at Christmas as a lump sum.

In previous chapters, the subject of death and dying has been raised. It seems that Emma (the young woman at the BBC) died shortly after leaving East Park. Michelle and Jim acknowledged that quite a few young people had died shortly after moving on from East Park, 'as if with a broken heart', mused Michelle; 'as if it's too much for them', reflected Jim.[61] Clearly death and dying is a feature of the care and support of children and young people with additional support needs, unlike their typically developing peers, a subject that arguably has not received much attention in literature or government policy.

As well as work experience, a range of other activities are open to young people. During the summer, outings include visiting the nearby Children's Woods, where young people and staff enjoy the fire pit, cooking marshmallows and sausages, and community singing. Young people from Workmates attend 'Indepen-dance', an inclusive dance company for disabled and non-disabled people to enjoy, express and fulfil their potential through dance, and Inspire Dance, a performance group.[62] Michelle explained:

> We go [to Inspire Dance] weekly … The last seven years [with the exception of 2020 and 2021 due to Covid] they have performed at the Theatre Royal at the annual Go-Dance event, so it gives the young people an opportunity to be on stage with an audience. It is amazing.

Jim and Michelle explained the opportunities and challenges which performance presents for some young people:

> (Jim) I remember Michael (pseud.) when he joined the group, he used to stand in the corner then gradually joined in. (Michelle) And you've got to walk and stand tall and even getting to put his hands in the air … (Jim) It was a long, long process. It is about understanding verbal instructions and he made progress with different moves every week.[63]

Some young people attend college, where they may do a variety of courses such as drama, music and life skills. Some have worked towards Caledonian Awards, achieved by young people evidencing skills development in an activity such as recycling, litter picking or preparation of food.

In keeping with the ethos of East Park, strong relationships have developed with the local community. When the nearby Viking Bar opened a restaurant for the first time, they invited the young people in for three days to sample the food before they opened to the public.[64] Other activities include working on the allotment, from where vegetables are passed to the local food bank. Workmates also make soup for the local Warm Space in the nearby Mackintosh Halls. Michelle explained:

> We have made this soup for the last year and apparently people wait for it. I make sure the young people help peel, chop, blend; they are involved in every aspect.[65]

As well as making soup for the Warm Space, young people help at the St Gregory's Chapel Food Bank.

The young people won the People Make Maryhill Unsung Heroes Award 2023 for their work in the Warm Space and the Food Bank. Workmates has a long history at East Park and continues to be a much sought-after service.[66]

Move to community

The third strand of the Development Plan to be implemented was that of moving the children and young people to houses in the community. Glasgow City Council demonstrated its commitment to young people living in the community by supporting a small group of young people due to move on from East Park into a flat together with support, rather than them being separated and placed in residential care.[67]

Meanwhile, approaches were made by East Park to other agencies to identify possible sites for new-build accommodation.[68] The Senior Management Team from East Park scoured Glasgow City Council's property register to source vacant sites on which to build the new residences. Over several meetings they negotiated for two sites, in Balornock and Maryhill.[69] It was decided that four houses 'off site' was realistic, with four or five residents in each, and each within 30 minutes' travel of the School on Maryhill Road.[70] Through the good relationship that already existed with Maryhill Housing Association, East Park was able to negotiate two houses in new developments within Ruchill.[71]

The first site was identified in Balornock. This was owned by Glasgow City Council, which was prepared to sell.[72] The house was designed round the needs

Sachin laying bark at the Garscube Allotments, Maryhill, where Workmates have a plot. Vegetables grown here are passed to the local food bank. (Mark Anderson)

Mia is making lentil soup to a secret Workmates recipe for the Warm Space in Mackintosh Hall, Maryhill. Workmates make soup every week for the Warm Space – it's very popular. (Paula McGuire)

specified by East Park, which included individual bedrooms for five young people, two bathrooms equipped with adjustable-height baths, staff sleepover facilities including shower room, office space and a secure room for storage of medication. A sitting room and large dining room where children and staff could eat together, a kitchen, laundry room and garden were also included.[73] The house was opened in 2001. It was agreed that it would be known as Robertson House after the Glasgow-based Trust which made a significant contribution to its funding.[74] Five children moved in in July 2001, along with support staff, and the house was officially opened on 21 September 2001 by the Princess Royal.[75]

Considering the challenges experienced by East Park, the opening of Robertson House was seen as a significant step towards achieving its long-term goals. Tristan, who we met in chapter 13 as a child, had returned to work in East Park. Initially employed as an auxiliary then as a support worker, he was one of the staff to move to Robertson House. He remembered the new care arrangements as being quite challenging. Three of the young people were wheelchair users with significant support needs, and two of the young people were active and very mobile. Staff had to be alert to ensure the safety and well-being of all in what was now a very different care setting.[76]

Around the same time as the official opening of Robertson House, East Park received an unannounced visit by the Glasgow Social Work Inspection and Registration Unit. In contrast to previous inspections, very positive reports were received:

> Robertson House was visited as part of this inspection and time was spent with four of the young people. Staff and the young people have quickly adjusted to their new home and workplace. An excellent standard of accommodation is provided at Robertson House, with its thoughtful and carefully considered design creating a bright, comforting and welcoming home. The young people are observed to get on well together and to enjoy the space and comfort in their new home … Staff are positive about the new house and the greater responsibility they now have for running the unit when the Team Leader is not on shift. Staff say teamwork is effective, the team are clear about and confident in their new role and feel well supported.[77]

Meanwhile, plans were progressing for further residences. East Park had always enjoyed good relations with Maryhill Housing Association. When it was developing new housing in the Ruchill area, East Park was able to have two houses built. The first was initially referred to as 'Ruchill House' and more recently as Harris.[78] The children moved in on 27 September 2002. It was officially opened on 15 November 2002 by Patricia Ferguson MSP.[79]

In January 2003 the first integrated Care Commission and HMI Inspection took place. The Inspectors were particularly impressed with the high quality of accommodation in the new houses, the clear strategic vision, the direction of the Board and senior managers, and the commitment of staff to the welfare of the children and young people.[80]

A third site owned by Glasgow City Council was identified in Maryhill. The young people moved in in early 2004.[81] Lessons were learned from Robertson House: rooms were bigger and had space for turning hoists; all the bathrooms had high/low baths.[82] The house was opened on 23 June 2004 by patron HRH The Duchess of Gloucester and is today known as Arran.[83]

By 2004 the Supported Accommodation Service was almost fully operational, with three out of the four houses established. A fourth (now known as Barra) was developed as part of Maryhill Housing Association's Phase 4 Development. This house had originally been designed for adults moving from Lennox Castle and was built as two semi-detached houses, with each house able to accommodate two young people.[84] The houses shared some facilities, such as the office and sleepover room, but otherwise they were relatively independent of each other.[85] The house was opened on 10 June 2005, the children having moved in on 21 March.[86] The Wooden Spoon Charity had made a significant contribution to the funding, and a stained-glass panel was designed by Impact Arts incorporating the Wooden Spoon logo.[87] The opening was a joint event with Maryhill Housing Association's opening of the Phase 4 development.[88] Former Scottish international rugby players Donnie McFadyen and John Beattie performed the opening ceremony.[89]

Dr Martin declared this the end of an era, as all units except for respite were now off campus.[90] May Henderson reflected on the immediate benefits to the young people of living in an entirely domestic environment 'away from the institution'; this allowed a more natural separation between home and school life, they had their own private gardens, safe and easily accessible, and had an opportunity to get to know their neighbours. Friendships were developing, and non-disabled children and their families had an opportunity to look beyond the young people's disabilities and accept and value them as individuals.[91]

The following year, Danny Davison focused his report for the 132nd Annual Report on the supported accommodation. He wrote:

> The four houses had been designed and purpose built to accommodate 18 young people with disabilities and were fully accessible. The aim of building these houses was to emphasise the ordinariness of community living. This has enabled the young people to live ordinary lives in ordinary neighbourhoods just like everyone else. In the past, young people with disabilities were segregated from the rest of society by living in institutions. The young people in East Park houses can now come to school on the school bus, shop in the local supermarket, help prepare meals and do ordinary things. Accomplishing these events is a major challenge for young people with learning disabilities or autism and requires weeks and months of patience and support on the part of staff. Goals and strategies are developed to ensure these experiences are as positive and as successful as can be. Appropriate strategies are developed to decrease any risks involved. East Park's young people are now able to experience and appreciate the ordinary aspects of day-to-day living in one's own home.[92]

With young people now living in the community and the changing model of care, there was less need for nurses. When Karen Ferguson took over the Gloucester Unit before moving with the young people to Bilsland Drive she was the first non-nursing Team Leader in East Park. Karen reflected, 'It was a huge step for the organisation,

What'll we have for tea tonight? Cooper doing the shopping for Lewis house.

as the medical model and practices were embedded.'[93] Around this time, Danny Davison retired and Geraldine O'Neill was appointed Head of Care.[94]

A school for the future
While the houses were being developed, attention turned to the site on Maryhill Road. A brief was developed for architects to produce proposals on what could be achieved if the children were living in the community, for a new school and a base for SCOPE.[95]

It was also noted around this time that the profile of the children attending East Park School was changing again, the demand for places increasingly being for children and young people on the autistic spectrum.[96] As a result, a considerable amount of work went into creating an autism-friendly environment, while still catering for the care and education of children requiring a significant amount of nursing and general attention.[97]

By 2006, it was clear that the Development Plan drawn up in 1998 and the five-year strategy drawn up by the directors in 2003 were well on the way to being implemented.[98] Attention focused on the final phase of the Development Plan, to redevelop the Maryhill site, as the school building was no longer seen as fit to meet modern special educational requirements.[99] In 2001, while the development of houses in the community was underway, there had been discussions around retaining any of the buildings on the Maryhill site.[100] After some deliberation, partial retention was agreed, with some modification of the existing buildings. Some of the benefits of this decision were only realised many years later when former residents returned to East Park and were able to visit familiar spaces such as 'the Bunting Ward', which is now a conference room.

Work on the new school building began in January 2008.[101] While the planning process was underway, May Henderson and Linda Gray looked for a temporary school.[102] They found a former local authority school in Mamore Street on the South-side of Glasgow and both the School and the administration vacated the site on Maryhill Road. Linda Gray recalls:

> Moving the whole school, contents, staff and pupils into the temporary school was a stressful and time-intensive period. As many of the children by that time were on the autistic spectrum it was important that we prepared them for the changes as thoroughly as possible so as to minimise their anxiety. Credit has to go to all staff involved – the transition there and back was relatively smooth. Everything possible was kept 'the same', including the staff with whom the pupils were familiar.[103]

The new building was completed and handed over on 21 July 2009. All classrooms had new PCs, workstations and smart boards, ready for the start of the new school term on 17 August.[104] The school was visited on 20 August by Adam Ingram, Minister for Children and Young People.[105] The Report of the directors for the period ending 31 March 2010 described the completion of the new school building 'on time and within budget':

> This £4m transformation has created one of the country's most advanced educational facilities for children and young people with a range of additional support needs. The project which was led by Glasgow architects Macpherson & Bell has seen the re-design and construction of an innovative teaching, therapy and life skills facility that is state of the art. The rebuild of our school is the culmination of a 12-year plan which initially

saw the development of four new purpose-built houses in the community. The cutting-edge design of the school has incorporated a number of creative concepts aimed at stimulating the senses aiding identification for the children. These include the creation of eight custom-designed classrooms with easily recognisable coloured doors, each opening directly on to the landscaped playground which incorporates a sensory garden picnic area, planting, grassed area and safety surfaces. As both the classroom and playground are important teaching and learning environments, the design of the school facilitates seamless transition from classroom to playground as the children move from one learning environment to another.

With the safety of the children in mind, the playground has been positioned to the rear of the school, protected by the main building, with all vehicular traffic restricted to the front of the school. Internally all classrooms have built-in storage areas and the finishes are in keeping with the principles of minimalist sensory stimulation, which can be particularly important for young people with autistic spectrum disorders.[106]

On 22 April 2010, Glasgow Warriors rugby stars Chris Cusiter, Al Kellock, Mark McMillan and Johnnie Beattie (son of John Beattie mentioned on page 237) officially opened the new school and joined the young people in the celebration.[107] An artwork was commissioned with the names of all donors, designed by Australian artist Digger Nutter and completed by students at Glasgow School of Art, and this is now in the reception area at East Park.[108] An 'East Park' rose was commissioned from Harkness Roses to be given to every person who attended the opening, and Sir Matthew Goodwin planted the first East Park Rose at the school.[109]

May Henderson retired in 2012, after twenty-three years' service.[110] Judy Cromarty subsequently became Executive Director.[111] East Park had come some way since the adverse reports of the 1990s, and in 2014 Linda Gray retired, having shared leadership during one of the most significant periods of change in East Park's history. Helen Dunlop was appointed as Head of Education.[112]

Learning and development

As work was being carried out on the fabric and buildings of East Park, attention was also focused on staff development. In 1997, the Social Work Department had been critical of staff training, including 'a degree of complacency among staff'.[113] In light of such criticisms, a great deal of effort went into learning and development, initially focusing on disability awareness, communication, challenging behaviour, sexuality awareness and Person Centred Planning.[114] As discussed above, Person

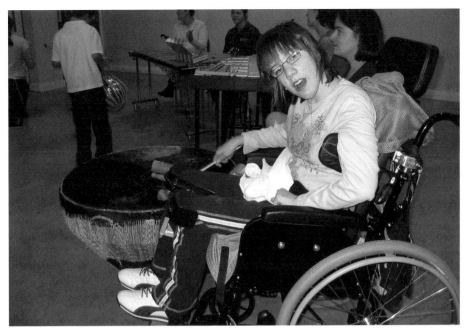

Where words fail, music speaks, wrote Hans Christian Anderson. Ashley and friends jamming together.

Centred Planning was an innovative approach being piloted in the Gloucester Unit.[115] Staff were reorganised into teams, with individual members of staff linked to individual children and their families. May Henderson reported that using a Person Centred Planning approach had encouraged more creative thinking, and as a result, children had developed interests outwith East Park as well as closer links with families, and staff providing support within the family home.[116]

Another focus for training was supporting residential support workers through completion of Scottish Vocational Qualifications (SVQs). Educational staff, meanwhile, received training on children's rights, challenging behaviour and child protection.[117]

While East Park had prioritised training as part of its Development Plan, within Scotland training of residential care officers had been pushed higher up the national agenda. In 2002, under the Regulation of Care (Scotland) Act 2001, the Commission for the Regulation of Care (often referred to as the Care Commission, replaced in 2011 by the Care Inspectorate) was established, replacing the former Health Board and Social Work structures for registration and inspection of services. New National Standards were set up.[118] The Scottish Social Services Council (SSSC) was established, which determined the minimum qualifications for residential care practitioners and managers. Danny Davison, Head of Care, reported:

Three organisations were involved in staff development, the Care Commission, the Scottish Institute for Residential Child Care (SIRCC) and the Scottish Social Services Council, who determined the minimum qualifications for residential child care staff. An audit carried out of East Park's staff working in residential child care showed that 52 care staff (60%) had no appropriate qualifications … In order to increase the number of staff with minimal qualifications, a number of staff attended Langside College over the last 18 months with a further group commencing the course this year [2003]. It is anticipated that it will take 5 years for all East Park staff to achieve minimum qualification standard.[119]

By December 2004, it was recognised in East Park that all residential care workers were required to be registered with the SSSC by summer 2006. Additional resources were required to achieve this and, supported by a grant from the Glasgow North Key Fund, Vicki Ross was appointed as Training Manager.[120] She was joined by Lesley Watson as Training Officer; Lesley remains in post today as Learning and Development Manager. Over time, East Park became an SQA centre approved to offer the full HNC in Social Care, making it one of the first non-college centres to offer traditionally college-based qualifications.[121]

Learning and development has continued. Much is essential in-service training such as child protection, food hygiene, fire safety, moving and assisting, record keeping and report writing, epilepsy awareness and positive behaviour support using CALM (Crisis Aggression Limitation Management), an approach to understanding and preventing behaviour that challenges.[122] Training in communication such as Makaton and intensive interaction, play pedagogy and creativity, are all delivered. Care staff were trained in aspects of care formerly provided by nursing staff, such as administration of medication. The Learning and Development Team continues to provide a wide range of training essential to delivering a high-quality service and meeting staff requirements for registration.

Intensive Support Project

East Park had met the objectives of the Development Plan, having established the Short Break Service, Workmates, the four houses in the community and the new school, and addressed the learning and development needs of staff. Having developed the residences away from the main campus, it was realised, however, that some children and young people had difficulty with this transition, from home to school. A different model of care and education was needed, not because of their physical health, which had been the reason for the original hesitation about moving away from the main East Park campus, but rather because of the complexity of their sensory needs. By 2013, it was realised there was a need for residential facilities and single-space teaching for children who require a high level of individual support. Following a feasibility study, work began on what became known as the Intensive Support Project, subsequently Skye and Lewis, and the Single Space Teaching facilities. The building was completed in July 2016 and opened on 8 November, when Deputy First Minister John Swinney visited.[123] By December, three young people had moved in to the new service. The facility was shown to make the transition to school considerably less traumatic for some. Barbara, originally a support worker in Skye and Lewis and now a Deputy Team Leader, and support worker Carol described the difference for one young person who had previously travelled daily from a nearby residence: 'She had real difficulty coming up here to go to school. It was more dangerous crossing the road. She would sit on the road crying and because the traffic lights take so long to change, she doesn't have any sense of time – so she transferred up here.'[124] Within school, the young people used the individual classrooms but quickly proved able at times to integrate with the class and share space with other young people.[125] Overall, the service appears to reduce anxiety, while supporting young people to build up skills in a gradual way to help them predict and cope when outside.[126]

In October 2016, the First Minister of Scotland, Nicola Sturgeon, made a commitment that Scotland would 'come together and love its most vulnerable children to give them the childhood they deserve'.[127] She announced an independent root-and-branch review of care (The Care Review), driven by those with experience of care. In the introduction to *The Promise*, which followed from The Care Review, Fiona Duncan, Chair of the Review, wrote of Scotland's ambition 'to be the best place in the world to grow up' so that children and young people feel 'loved, safe and respected and realise their full potential'.[128] *The Promise* (2020) subsequently states: 'All caregivers, wherever children live, must know that their primary purpose is to develop nurturing, patient, kind, compassionate, trusting relationships so that children in their care feel loved and safe.'[129] At Skye and Lewis, this ambition is manifest and integral to practice.

Skye and Lewis are home to two and four young people respectively. All the young people have significant neurodevelopmental needs and sensory processing difficulties. Some have also experienced trauma. There is therefore a need for careful matching of young people in the group, thinking of sensory overload and impact on each other. Each young person is supported by one or two staff members indoors and two when out in the community. Each has their own studio apartment with bedroom, shower room and living room. There is a communal sitting area and kitchen. Rooms are personalised, designed around young people's interests, sensory needs and preferences. Some of the young people have a 'safe space' into which they can retreat when they feel a need to withdraw.[130] Staff remain with the young person at all times and can still engage, either if they are invited in by the young person or by sitting by the 'window' to the safe space.

Young people are supported to pursue their interests and engage in activities. While Skye and Lewis were designed with the sensory needs of children and young people in mind, the Care Services Managers had ideas for improvements. With support from corporate sponsors, as part of the process of developing 'sensory diets' for each of the young people, the garden to which young people have easy access was upgraded with a view to each finding at least one enjoyable sensory experience. A swing, climbing frame, outdoor musical instruments and a hot tub were installed. A sensory garden was created, offering tactile, auditory and olfactory experiences through fragrant herbs and plants, a butterfly garden, water feature, wind chimes and a 'mud kitchen'. Another corporate donor contributed towards the development of a sensory room.[131]

As a highly specialised service, there are significant training implications. For staff applying to work in the houses, training is provided in subjects such as love and nurture, children's rights, play pedagogy and creativity, transforming psychological trauma, sensory-based behaviour, autism and approaches to communication such as Makaton and Intensive Interaction as well as core training such as child protection, recording and report writing.[132]

The Care Services Managers identify areas for future study within East Park, such as changing the narrative about autism, recognising the difference between autism and pathological demand avoidance, and that autism manifests in different ways, in particular between male and female, as a result of which females are left under-recognised and often unsupported.

East Park had come a long way from being on the point of closure, and a remarkable number of staff stayed the course. Over the years, amid this transformation, children continued to have new experiences, explored in the next chapter.

CHAPTER 17

Children's Lives, 1997 onwards

Mrs Henderson concluded by intimating that many changes would be taking place inside East Park over the next few months with staff reorganising themselves around the needs and preferences of the young people, as well as developing expertise and building a reputation and a track record over the next year … She could not finish without mentioning the enthusiasm and willingness of the staff who were the gold dust of the organisation and it was through them and their commitment to the children that change would be realised.

East Park, 124th Annual Report, 1998[1]

While East Park was undergoing radical transformation, care and education of the children and young people continued. Within class, children were now grouped chronologically, moving from a single all-age school into separate primary and secondary departments, in line with the way in which local authority special schools were organised. The children could now enjoy the same 'rites of passage' and opportunities as their peers in mainstream school.[2] A curriculum audit was carried out involving new timetabling arrangements and a revised format for Individualised Educational Programmes was introduced. A wrap-around model of care was developed, with personal organisers provided for each child and young person. These were important documents, containing a profile of the young person; their preferences, care plans, behaviour support plans (where appropriate) and Personal Learning Plan. This provided a comprehensive picture of the young person and how they should be supported, which in turn facilitated joint planning. Such an approach ensured consistency and continuity between disciplines and departments, 'promoting a holistic and individualised approach to each child and young person'.[3] Links were established with mainstream schools and some children were able to spend meaningful time in these settings, while children from the local Wyndford School attended the Harvest Festival at East Park.[4] In 1999, in contrast with the previous year, excellent inspection reports were received from HMI.[5]

New methods of SMART target setting and evaluation were put in place, which involved all disciplines, including the therapies, residential support and parents. Within the context of East Park, SMART targets are Specific, Measurable, Achievable, Relevant and Timebound.[6] Striving to achieve an integrated approach between school and care staff had been an objective within East Park over the years and addressed concerns referred to in inspection reports.[7] Over time, some children and young people completed Caledonian Awards, which provided an opportunity for young people and adults with special support needs to participate in an educational programme to help them achieve their full potential.[8] Projects were personal to the individual, such as Andrew who enjoyed CDs and DVDs. His brother David Traynor, now a Team Leader at East Park, takes over the story:

> Andrew's main area of interest at home was watching VHS tapes which eventually progressed to DVDs as they began to replace the old tapes. He had accumulated a massive collection over the years with several duplicate copies of his favourite movies just in case they got scratched. I can remember growing up that although he loved these DVDs he didn't have the organisation skills to manage this collection and at times his room was quite chaotic. He would rummage through case to case, mixing DVDs up or leaving them all lying around, meaning they often got lost, scratched or broken. This ultimately led to him often being frustrated with disorder and uncertainty of 'where his favourite DVD was' and the panic my mum used to feel if his DVDs no longer worked due to how they had been stored.[9]

Andrew completed a project on listening to story CDs, sitting at a table, choosing, sorting, selecting, listening to stories and using earphones. Photographs and an explanation were submitted as evidence of his achievements. David explained the value of this method of skills development and assessment:

> In hindsight, after reading what the Caledonian Awards focused on I believe this had a really positive impact on his ability to focus on looking for whatever DVD he wanted as well as safely replacing and storing DVDs after use. In the workbooks Andrew is looking through music CDs but it had the same effect. This may seem like a skill that most people would take for granted but it had real significance for Andrew; not only did it help him focus but it improved his skills in matching and placing things in order, it increased his sense of responsibility, and in turn, lowered the anxiety that came with uncertainty – but ultimately he was able to enjoy and sustain the thing that

made him happiest. In other words, this wasn't seen by me as a basic life skill, this was a life-changing skill relative to Andrew and his needs.[10]

Caledonian Awards have more recently been replaced within the School by JASS (Junior Awards Scheme for Scotland) Awards and SQA National 1 and National 2.[11]

With the profile of the children changing, there was a focus in staff learning and development on the needs of children and young people with autism, that 'staff could develop a better understanding of all things "autism" and treat pupils accordingly'.[12] In January 2007, this was highlighted when East Park became one of the first schools in Scotland to achieve accreditation with the National Autistic Society.[13] East Park was recognised as having in place a number of 'autism friendly' strategies and techniques, which enabled staff to provide effective support for young people whose difficulties were diverse and challenging.[14] Linda Gray, Head of Education at the time, led the Autism Working Group, training East Park staff on the needs of young people with autism and seeking to embed good practice.[15]

When Curriculum for Excellence was rolled out in schools across Scotland, replacing the former national curriculum guidance, this was adapted in East Park to what Linda Gray described as an 'elaborated curriculum'. Within Curriculum for Excellence, there was one framework for those aged 3–18 years, which was advantageous for young people in East Park as it focused on capacity building rather than individual subjects. It was therefore easier for staff to tailor teaching and learning to the strengths and development needs of individual pupils.[16] Over time the staff familiarised themselves with the Curriculum for Excellence, with the aim over the next few years of developing the East Park curriculum to fit the guidelines.[17]

Education at East Park continued to draw on a wide range of activities, some of which have evolved in response to the changing profile of the children and young people, such as music with music specialist Bryan Tolland. Whereas formerly classes might have had ten or twelve students, this reduced over time, with most requiring 1:1 support. During the School move to Mamore Street and while the new School was being built, education continued, taking cognisance of world events, such as a whole-school theme of China inspired by the Olympic Games in Beijing.[18] New projects were initiated such as a circus theme, making costumes, and using technology to make a 'super-storm'.[19] 'The Great East Park Cook off' was hosted, the aim of which was to explore and heighten awareness of healthy eating. Following in the footsteps of Mary Berry, each teaching area planned, shopped for and made a meal to incorporate their learning. The meals were presented to a panel who judged on the content of the four healthy food groups, portion size, and presentation and taste.[20] Other initiatives included working towards becoming an ECO-school, which involved young people in collecting litter, recycling, growing vegetables and promoting energy efficiency, a project for which they were awarded a Green Flag.[21] East Park was awarded the Church of Scotland Stevenson Prize for encouraging excellence in the fields of religious observance and religious education for 'the Joseph Project'. The school had made Joseph the whole-school theme. Joseph's coat was sent round the East Park residences and out to young people's homes, and a photo album was made showing 'the adventures of the coat'. The project was thought to have made great use of the school community, and the values in the Joseph story such as friendship, respect and family had been explored.[22]

An initiative that reached beyond the School was the East Park iPad Project, carried out in conjunction with Edinburgh University during 2013/14. Researcher Sinead O'Brien, an Educational Research Masters Student from Moray House School of Education, worked alongside staff to evaluate the use of iPads, particularly in respect of communication.[23] East Park obtained funding for all young people to have access to an iPad.[24] Key findings included increased student engagement, responsibility and enjoyment of independent work and homework. Teachers also benefited, using the iPad as an organisational tool, for collating evidence of academic work and student progress, for quick internet searches, playing music in the classroom, and taking photos and videos of students.[25] Angela Constance, Cabinet Minister for Education and Lifelong Learning, was 'happy to read about innovative practice in Scottish Schools and was enthused to read the report'.[26] East Park was invited to present the findings at the National Digital Learning Forum.[27] Now all children in East Park have access to a tablet of some sort. Those who require access to a talker or a range of digital symbols use iPads, with others using a Kindle or tablet. There is no doubt that iPads and tablets are a valuable resource for children and young people with complex additional support needs.

As the profile of children changed, so did leisure activities. There was no further involvement in organised groups such as Scouts, Guides, Cubs and Brownies, but other activities continued: the Annual Taxi Outing to the Ayrshire coast, holidays to a variety of destinations, and invitations from community groups and corporate sponsors to participate in special events.[28] With the move to houses in the community, however, what may be regarded as everyday experiences became significant activities. Support worker Carol Kerr explained:

> In Robertson House, Rhona [Team Leader] preferred us to use public transport … We maybe went to the park, cinema, bowling … we went swimming …going to the carnival; you would work out their interest and try to go with that. It was a massive thing to go on a bus to the city centre.[29]

While iPads have been found to be a valuable resource for supporting education and communication, young people also enjoy them for relaxation. Thomas chilling with his iPad. (Pete Copeland)

Celebrities maintained their interest and Radio Clyde brought *X Factor* star Matt Cardle to visit East Park. Radio Clyde's *Cash for Kids* also helped East Park purchase an in-house broadcasting system, which was found to be of great value to the children and young people in developing communication and social skills.[30] During 2006, the School became involved in Operation Christmas Child, helping Eastern European people by filling shoeboxes with gifts.[31]

East Park is always looking for opportunities for education and leisure outdoors. A small group of young people created a sensory garden within East Park supported by the Newlands Scout Group. In 2019, the School took delivery of ten eggs which were placed in an incubator.[32] Two days later, there were nine newly hatched hens. Two chicks, Ginger and Moondust, remained at East Park and the others were re-homed. The young people tended and cared for Ginger and Moondust until Moondust died and, knowing that hens are unhappy living alone, Ginger was re-homed to a farm.[33]

Ever keen to use resources in the local community, as discussed in chapter 16, in 2013 the School and Workmates curriculum was significantly enhanced with the participation in an outdoor learning initiative using woodland and meadows in North Kelvinside, known as the Children's Woods.[34] The main purpose of the initiative was to build knowledge and appreciation of greenspace and environmental issues,

Esther enjoying time in the Art Room. (Pete Copeland)

through exploring and looking after the environment. There were sensory stories, storytelling, cooking outdoors, arts and crafts. Head Teacher Linda Gray reported this initiative as improving young people's concentration, awareness of surroundings and overall well-being and calm.[35] In 2021, a group of young people met Queen Elizabeth II when she visited the Children's Woods.[36] Jay, who attended East Park on a daily basis from 2017 to 2022, enthused:

> Meeting the Queen was such an inspiration for me because my mum said not many people meet the Queen. I am disappointed that all people can't meet the Queen. I asked if she wanted to cook marshmallows with us and the Queen said, 'No thank you.' I said, 'OK' … And I said, 'What brings you to Glasgow your Majesty?' She said, 'To see the Children's Woods.' She said something along the lines of, 'I'm really excited to be here because I can see what you are doing.'[37]

Two other initiatives demonstrate the willingness of staff at East Park to give young people the opportunity of new experiences while showcasing their talent. During 2012–13, the Centre of Excellence for Looked After Children in Scotland (CELCIS) at the University of Strathclyde ran a seminar series in partnership with the universities of Edinburgh and Glasgow and the children's charity Action for Children through the Scottish University Insight Institute based at the University of Strathclyde. Under the overall title 'Getting it Right for Looked After Disabled Children', the seminars explored the themes of Being Counted, Being Heard, Being

Included and Being Valued.[38] During the planning process, it was thought the project would be enhanced if the voices of disabled children and young people could be heard. Between August and December 2012, six resident young people from East Park participated in a drama project led by Active Enquiry Forum Theatre in conjunction with CELCIS which culminated in a performance of a play they had created entitled *Alisha's Surprise* at The Lighthouse in Glasgow as part of the seminar, Being Heard: Listening to and Learning from Looked After Disabled Children and Young People in Residential Care. The project was an outstanding success and CELCIS requested East Park's young people continue to be involved in another project, working with Glasgow School of Art to consider looked-after young people's input into designing their service.[39] In addition to the live performance, a second filmed version of *Alisha's Surprise* took place at an event to which more local authority staff and academics were invited.[40] East Park hosted an 'Oscar Awards ceremony' for the young people involved:

> 'Bling' and best outfits were obligatory and the Mitchell Hall [in East Park] was appropriately decorated Hollywood style with red carpet and glitter ball. Tension was high as the golden envelopes were opened and winners announced. Oscar statuettes and Shooting Star awards were presented to all who participated.[41]

Toasting marshmallows, telling stories, climbing trees, making dens, enjoying the dogs, meeting the Queen – the Children's Woods is treasured by young people at East Park and the wider Maryhill community. (Amy Little)

Aiden enjoying leisure time in his studio apartment. (Pete Copeland)

Staff and the young people also received a Reaching Higher Award from the Scottish Institute for Residential Child Care at the 2013 SIRCC Annual Conference.[42]

In 2014, the Commonwealth Games took place and, as with previous significant events in Glasgow, children and young people were supported to take part. In January 2014, a small group was involved in a music project on the theme of Travelling Birds. This project was run by the community music charity Hear My Music and musicians Emily Carr-Martin and Noel Bridgeman.[43] The music created was performed by the young people at the SIRCC Annual Conference in Edinburgh on 10 June 2014.[44] The project aimed to 'celebrate hidden voices' and showcase the talents of young people who can face challenges both in self-expression and being heard.[45]

Meanwhile, within the School, as the Commonwealth Games approached, each class chose a Commonwealth country to focus on. This fitted with the Curriculum for Excellence, which the School embraced. Where possible, the young people learned about and experienced some of the Commonwealth Games sports. The School also worked with a specialist theatre maker to create an individualised 'Commonwealth adventure' using sensory theatre techniques and simple role play. Led by the art teacher, East Park took part in an art competition to create posters for display in the athletes' village, and possibly most exciting for one young man, his family and East Park, pupil Malcolm Hollamby was chosen to represent the School in the Queen's Baton Relay.[46]

2014 was also the 140th anniversary of East Park opening its doors to provide care and education for infirm children and young people, and a number of activities took place to mark the event. One of these was a knockout football tournament organised for local primary schools by Partick Thistle Football Club. The winning school was presented with the Maryhill Charity Cup at East Park's Annual Awards Ceremony.[47] It appears that from this point the Maryhill Charity Cup became known as the East Park Cup.[48] The trophy remains in the hands of East Park today.

East Park had travelled a long way since the negative feedback of the 1997 inspections. In April 2014, the School was graded overall Excellent in an inspection by the Care Commission, and received the Advanced Autism Accreditation with the National Autistic Society in 2020. The penultimate chapter – chapter 19 – in this story of East Park so far, explores its achievements and challenges as it celebrates 150 years of caring for some of Scotland's most vulnerable children and young people.

CHAPTER 18

Looking Out, Looking In:
A Physical Presence in Space and Time

The Home was being very much encroached upon by new tenements of houses rising
on both sides and threatening to injure its amenity, and accordingly the Directors
secured the large field which stands as a kitchen garden to the west of the Home, and
at the same time bought up the feus and ground annuals, built a boundary wall, and
also a wash-house and laundry at a cost of about £4,500.

William Mitchell, 1898[1]

Fifteen decades after East-Park Cottage, as it was known in 1874, first opened its doors to receive infirm children 'rescued' from dwellings with poverty and deprivation as their hallmarks, East Park School in 2024 is entered through modern buildings. Its protective boundary is marked out with colourful panels that proclaim to the passing world East Park's role in the early twenty-first century – supporting autism; education and training; providing an intensive support service; and supported accommodation. It is imagery that proclaims East Park is a centre of 'special' education serving the needs of children and young people in a place that sees itself as a *part* of the local community rather than being perceived as apart from it.

The modest cottage that marked East Park's beginning has gone, but other features from the late nineteenth century remain. Mitchell's words of 1898, in appraisal of East-Park Home's first twenty-five years, give a sound insight to how much, during that time span, its surroundings had changed, but they also reflect how the Home itself was evolving. The original cottage was already dwarfed by the addition of the buildings erected during those first twenty-five years while remaining at the heart of the complex. However, with the erection of 'The Tower' in 1889, its spire became, and has remained, not only a central feature, but has come to symbolise East Park's presence in the Maryhill community.[2]

The evolving nature of the city and of Maryhill

An 1890 depiction of East Park Home shows the original cottage, its entrance door now transformed into a bay window, while adjoining it to the right is the imposing new structure with the distinctive tower, at the bottom of which is the main door. The buildings are enclosed within a high wall of sandstone masonry blocks and the wooden entrance gates to the grounds are of apparent solid construction. Outside the enclosure, a horse-drawn buggy is parked on Gairbraid Street. The horseman, who is in a standing position on his buggy, would be hard pressed to manage a glimpse over the wall. At this time, East Park was a community that was well-shielded from the outside world.[3]

The nature of the outside world in the late nineteenth century can be gleaned from Ward & Lock's *Popular History of and Illustrated Guide to Glasgow and the Clyde* of 1880.[4] On the northern edge of the compilers' 'Plan of Glasgow and Suburbs' is Maryhill, but it is an area largely unencumbered by development – with the exception of the Glasgow Branch of the Forth & Clyde Canal running to the loading berths at Port Dundas and then continuing eastwards as the Monkland Canal. The Glasgow Branch of the canal, rather than being an industrial encroachment on East Park's initial rural environment, arguably provided a shielding and protective boundary to the northern side of the Home and one which was already well established when the Association acquired the original East-Park Cottage. The Guide format suggests that Maryhill was of insufficient significance to warrant mention, and reasons for this are conveyed by Ward & Lock in their etchings of city vistas. The busy Broomielaw is the domain of pedestrians and horse-drawn traffic, while the River Clyde's marine bustle is a mixture of sailing masts, funnels and steam-driven paddles – the latter providing an indicator of the change arising through modernising developments. Similarly, road scenes are presented of the days before trams and motor vehicles in the etchings of Buchanan Street, Jamaica Bridge and Trongate where, from a modern perspective, pedestrians and horse-drawn vehicles appear to seek routes to their destinations with anarchic abandon. The city's predominant buildings were grand and noble, shipping was becoming increasingly sophisticated, but road transport still relied on the muscle power of man and beast and had yet to benefit from technological advancements that were to come from the combustion engine and from electrical propulsion of trams.[5]

Perhaps the most revealing reminders of the 1880s are conveyed by the advertisements carried by the Guide. Readers are regaled by the benefits of Dr Collis Browne's 'original and only genuine chlorodyne', a remedy that treated coughs, colds, asthma, bronchitis, cholera, dysentery, diarrhoea, epilepsy, spasms, colic, palpitation, hysteria, neuralgia, gout, cancer, toothache, and rheumatism; by 'Orchard's Cure for Deafness';[6] by 'Sylvia's Home Help Series of Useful Handbooks for Ladies', which may well have been a source of reference by some of the East Park Ladies' Committee members and supporters discussed in chapter 8; and by competing railway companies offering the likes of the 'Pullman Drawing Room Cars' that were offered by the Midland Railway. And travellers were being further tempted by a gamut of hotels proclaiming hydropathic facilities, conducive temperance environments, and livery stables that were a prerequisite for the long-distance road traveller.[7] Ward & Lock, in effect, through their guides of Glasgow and elsewhere, reflect the lives of the wealthy male members of society who might have been found directing East Park Home in the course of their committee meetings, and the lives of their wives and adult daughters who formed the legions of lady helpers who laboured tirelessly in the background.

While Ward & Lock convey an impression of Glasgow in the early years of East Park when Maryhill was outwith the city, the Home's directors, in their discussions surrounding developments beyond the walls of their institution, deliberated on the changes taking place and how these gave periodic cause for concern. In addition to the directors' wish to accept more children, expansion was also spurred by worries that nearby developments would deny them of the opportunity for future growth if

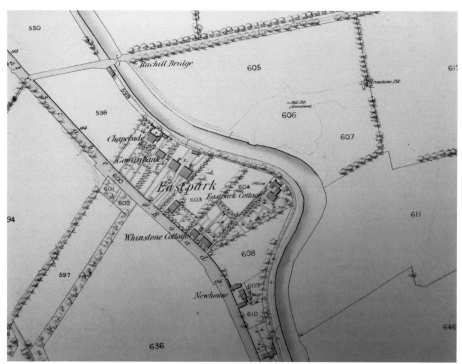

In 1861, 'Eastpark' was a small gathering of cottages bordered by the canal but surrounded by a rural hinterland in all directions. (OS © Crown copyright 1861)

they did not protect their interests. In this respect, this chapter uses four Ordnance Survey maps to reflect the changes occurring in Maryhill before the Second World War. These maps of 1861, 1896, 1913 and 1935 illustrate how East Park's immediate environment transformed from its initial situation as an idyllic backwater to a prominent location in a rapidly expanding urban and industrial conurbation.

When East-Park Cottage was purchased in 1874, it was one of a small cluster of countryside dwellings off Gairbraid Street, a road that ran from Cowcaddens to Maryhill. The rural ambiance of the area was apparent, pastoral land criss-crossed by hedgerows stretching out from the likes of Ruchill House beyond the canal to the east and Garrioch House to the west. While the collective of dwellings recorded as 'Eastpark' was on what had been built as a prominent turnpike road in the eighteenth century, the house that was to become East-Park Cottage occupied a notably rural setting, which of course was an attraction when it was acquired by the Association.[8]

Two decades later, in the survey of 1896, the immediate surroundings of East Park still had some semblance of a countryside environment, but on the north side of the canal were a large rubber works, an iron foundry and a chemical works, while on the opposite side of Gairbraid Street, a brickworks and its associated excavation sites

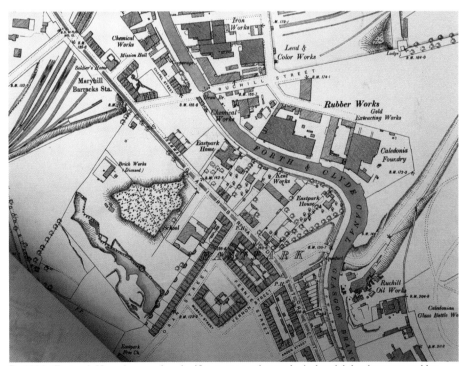

By 1896, 'Eastpark Home' was seeing significant encroachment by industrial development and by residential tenements. (OS © Crown copyright 1896)

for sand and clay had already made an environmental impact and subsequently fallen into disuse, tenement housing having risen nearby.[9] The 1896 map has innocuous lines running along Gairbraid Street, a portent of the urbanisation that was already making its mark, these indicating the arrival of tram services.[10]

As the Great War approached, the urbanisation occurring outside East Park's front gate was complete. On the opposite side of Gairbraid Street was the line of tenements with their street-level shops that still stands today, while further tenements stood shoulder to shoulder with the grounds of East Park, Sandfield Street to the south, and Ruchill Street to the north that, in addition to tenements, contained the United Free Church (now Maryhill Ruchill Parish Church). Beyond the junction of Ruchill Street with Gairbraid Street was Maryhill railway terminus complete with passenger station, goods shed and cranes, the site now occupied by the Tesco *extra* supermarket.[11] Glasgow was well known for its air pollution in the early decades of the twentieth century and, East Park's idyllic rural setting now gone, the Home must have been conscious of the effects of the activities of the Glasgow Rubber Works, the Caledonian Foundry, the Glasgow Lead and Colour Works, the Ruchill Iron Works, the Ruchill Oil Works, the Caledonian Glass Bottle Works and the Cassel Cyanide

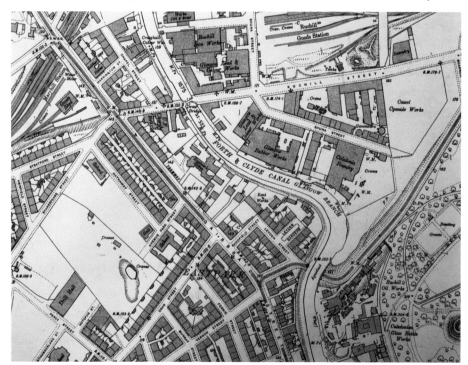

By the dawn of the Great War, East Park was in a truly urban setting – tram services had arrived. (OS © Crown copyright 1913)

Works on the opposite side of the Forth & Clyde Canal.[12]

The year 1921 was the last in which East Park gave its address as 382 Gairbraid Street. Without moving an inch, its location became 1092 Maryhill Road.[13] New street names aside, by the interwar period there was little change to the locality and its manufacturing operations along the canal. The tenement housing lining Maryhill Road in proximity to the Home had already matured with little scope for further additions, although need for entertainment had been satisfied by the erection of a 'picture house', this cinema having been built virtually next door to East Park Home.[14]

In the decades that followed the Second World War, the area continued to evolve. Old tenements have been demolished and new homes have built been built, a process that was noticeable from the 1960s and that has continued into the twenty-first century. While the tenements built immediately opposite East Park remain, such diverse offerings as shop premises providing 'fake bake' spray tanning, Greek cuisine, African food provisions and vaping accessories are symbols of a modern age that William Mitchell could not have imagined in the Maryhill of more than a century ago. His view on what was acceptable at that time is demonstrated by his vigorous

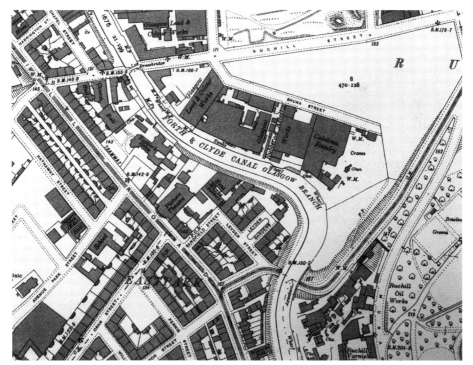

By 1935, East Park (left of centre in this map) was surrounded by tenements, and by factories producing a range of toxic materials. (OS © Crown copyright 1935)

disapproval, in 1909, of a licence application for the opening of a public house at 458 Gairbraid Street.[15]

East Park – from Cottage to Community

When the Association purchased East-Park Cottage in 1874, its surroundings echoed the strategy adopted by many other institutions that aimed to give their residents a therapeutic living space that offered rural calm, greenery and fresh air. East Park, as a locality, lay to the northwest of Glasgow, on the way to Maryhill. The road that passed East Park was labelled on maps as Gairbraid Street and East Park Home was number 382. When the area was surveyed in 1861, a mere thirteen years before the Cottage's acquisition by the Association, the landscape charted was one that is largely unrecognisable today, an exception being the continued presence of the Glasgow Branch of the Forth & Clyde Canal, completed in the last decade of the eighteenth century.[16]

The role of the canal in defining East Park was multifaceted. On the one hand, East-Park Cottage might almost have felt hemmed in by Glasgow's eighteenth-century watery highway. But the canal also formed a defensive barrier at East Park's north boundary, preventing the Home being encroached upon, while the canal also ensured that until the end of the nineteenth century, it restrained the growth of urban and industrial sprawl. East Park therefore had 'only' to contend with what development was occurring outside its front gate and, as shown by Mitchell's comment in 1898, what might happen on each side of the Cottage. Indeed, when the Country Branch opened in 1927, it was recalled that 'when the Cottage [in Maryhill] was purchased [in 1874] it stood practically in country surroundings, but the City was rapidly growing and the district … was [by 1903] covered by tenement dwellings and industrial works'.[17] Maryhill burgh had been absorbed into the city of Glasgow in 1891.

Just as the years from 1874 through to the beginning of the twentieth century represented a period of rapid change for Maryhill, this was also a period during which the original concept of East-Park Cottage as a small, temporary refuge for infirm children was the subject of frequent review and action. The Home's increase in scope over the following three decades was driven by need and expediency. On the one hand there was, it seemed, a never-ending waiting list of children who fitted East Park's mission of aiding infirm children unable to achieve improved health in a city environment where their lot and that of their families was poverty and deprivation. On the other hand, the directors of East Park's governing Association felt obliged to acquire adjoining land as it became available for purchase to prevent the Home being hemmed in by the erection of new tenements, and which they then put to use in aiding ever-expanding numbers of physically disabled children.

In October 1880, the directors' press release detailing the proceedings of the sixth annual meeting noted that 'this was the first meeting held in the Cottage since they were free from debt'.[18] This was not to last, Ann Ruth Bowser proposing to the Board in May of the following year 'that the playroom might be used as a dormitory for a few months for the admission of some very pressing cases'.[19] This heralded East Park's first expansion, when William Mitchell announced the purchase of the adjoining cottage so that 'the Directors will now be able to extend the benefits of the Institution to 20 additional children, or *50* in all' [original italics].[20] This necessitated negotiation of a bank loan and this new capital debt also required acknowledgement that there would be increased running costs, inevitably resulting in the directors calling a meeting with the Ladies' Committee 'to consider how to raise the money required'.[21]

Five years later, in 1887, there was a further capacity crisis when it was reported that fifty-eight children were resident and that this had only been made possible by using the dining room as a dormitory.[22] No reference is made as to where the fifty-eight children were taking their meals during this arrangement, but summer weather might have served as a short-term practical consideration. However, the approach of colder weather in September 1887 resulted in 'the surplus number [being] sent away, restoring the Home to its usual condition'.[23] Recalling the home conditions from which many of the children had been 'rescued', it seems strange that their home conditions in the cooling weather of the autumn were considered more suited to their comfort and well-being than the temporary accommodation in East Park's dining room.

In the late 1880s, Glasgow's rapid growth was accompanied by construction of new tenement houses. In 1887, the first intimation of the effect that this might have on East Park's previously rural surroundings arose. A notice sent to Mitchell perhaps caused a little alarm because 'a proposed land of houses [was] to be built on the East Boundary of the Home and [he] suggested the propriety of getting a suitable wall built either jointly with the neighbouring properties or, if necessary, at the expense of the Association'.[24] It was also mooted that a piece of land to the west of East Park should be investigated, the Association again looking to its future needs and wishing to ensure prudent forward planning.[25] It is probable that the directors' concern about encroaching tenement construction is the explanation for the high wall depicted in the 1890 image mentioned earlier.

The 1888 expansion was a key moment in the evolution of East Park into a large institution within this rapidly urbanising environment. Ann Ruth Bowser's personal esteem in the eyes of the directors had perhaps risen by 1888 because, along with

Dr Bruce, her opinion was actively solicited, and rightly so. Mitchell then proposed wider consultation, namely with the Lady Collectors and Lady Visitors. This, of course, was no mere courtesy. There was a rub – the Ladies, he said, might consider 'the propriety of having a sale of Ladies' work in the Autumn of this year [1888] in which they might all be interested and also state the necessity that would exist for additional revenue'.[26] In other words, again, it fell on the Ladies' shoulders to raise most of the money for this expansion.[27] In launching the appeal, Mitchell explained to the 'friends of this benevolent institution' that 'in addition to the 50 children at present in the Home there was a list of 40 infirm children waiting for admission, all in very distressing circumstances, and certified by Dr Bruce as eminently suitable for the Home'.[28] He stated that there were three possible options for addressing what he depicted as a situation now assuming crisis proportions. 'Poor suffering children [could be] left to pine in unwholesome dwellings', i.e. be totally ignored; children could continue in their present circumstances until spaces became available through discharge or death; or, supporters and donors could reach into their pockets 'to extend the accommodation of the present Home'.[29]

Pledges were immediately forthcoming and the inevitable third course of action was embarked upon. And so, further funds were to be pursued, Ladies were to be spurred into action to collect items that would be sold at a sale of work, and the Lady Collectors and Lady Visitors were to be increased in number, a task that was to be coordinated by Ann Ruth Bowser.[30] Within a matter of weeks, £1,032 had been raised, a worthy sum but ultimately inadequate to complete the expansion debt-free so that, again, a bank loan of £500 was to be arranged that would be underwritten by the trustees of the Association.[31] However, six months later, in part because of the anticipated proceeds of the imminent sale of work, it was concluded that resort to the bank would prove unnecessary – ladies' efforts and philanthropic enthusiasm remained high, not only to sustain East Park Home, but to enable its capacity to be almost doubled.[32] The sale of work raised £1,700, less expenses of £100, surely a great success, although Mitchell's mind was also focused, as before, on the increased running costs that would result from outlay on furnishing and catering costs for a larger number of children.[33]

By the time of publication of the 1889 annual report in October of that year, the enlargement of East Park had been completed. East Park now had accommodation for eighty children. Acknowledgement was made of Bowser and her colleagues, who had endured 'a very trying year' in consequence of the building operations, coupled with alterations within the old premises, while at the same time 'the varied interests of [the] children … had to be closely looked after'.[34] However, Ann Ruth Bowser was quite matter-of-fact about the expansion, despite the increased burden that it must have placed on her shoulders. She wrote:

> Almost monotonous regularity of work makes it difficult to infuse freshness
> into our record of services for another year. It has, however, been a period
> of internal changes such as a protracted 'flitting' usually entails. The
> consequent excitement has been shared by the children and given them
> considerable enjoyment.[35]

Matron Bowser had therefore taken challenges and tribulations in her stride and the
children saw any disruption as welcome distraction and adventure that created an
exciting interlude to the predictability of a world with otherwise limited horizons.

Besides the ever-present demand for places for children for whom admission was
being sought, increasing urban encroachment also became a growing impetus for
East Park's growth. This was voiced by Mitchell in 1892 when he argued:

> … the desirability of acquiring a portion of the vacant field on the north
> west of the Home on which tenements were in course of erection. He
> explained the circumstances making this desirable and was authorised to
> make an offer of 15/- per yard for 1,000 yards being a piece of ground
> immediately adjoining the Home and extending from Maryhill Road to
> the Canal.[36]

The adjoining land consisted of 2,919 square yards in total and East Park's interest
lay in a one-third portion, but this was not of interest to Pearson, the landowner.
Pearson's offer was to sell the full area for £2,200, or there would be no deal. Some
bargaining then ensued, the result being an arrangement where East Park purchased
the full area for £2,000, for which a loan had to be negotiated.[37] The loan, a bond
at 3½ per cent interest, was for £3,000 over five years and was provided by a trust
which sought a guarantee 'as the subjects produce no rent', as would have been
the case in respect of the burgeoning construction of nearby tenement housing.[38]
The loan negotiated was more than the land cost, but the surplus was to be used
for constructing a boundary wall and installing drainage.[39] Mitchell and his fellow
directors had then to focus on how the sum secured by the loan arrangement was to
be repaid. As described in chapter 8, this task was again delegated to 'the ladies'.[40]

With the passing of another decade, the pressure for additional places continued
so that, in 1901, subscribers to East Park were told that one hundred children
were resident, but with an explanation that this had been made possible by twenty
places being offered through the winter months at a Fresh Air Fortnight home of

the United Evangelistic Association.[41] This being a short-term expediency only, in 1902 the decision to build a new wing at Maryhill, one that would bring East Park's capacity to 120 cots, was made.[42] When, on 24 April 1903, Glasgow Provost, Sir John Ure Primrose (1847–1924), presided over the formal opening of the new building, performed by the Duchess of Montrose, Violet Hermione Graham (1854–1940), well-known in Glasgow philanthropic circles at the time, the gathering was informed that 'the institution is now supplied with 130 cots [not 120], and is very complete in all its arrangements – including baths, lavatories, and suitable accommodation for nurses and servants'.[43]

It was the erection of the new '1903' wing that prompted the directors to first engage with the idea of electric lighting whereas, until this time, they had relied solely upon gas for internal illumination. However, this was to be a gradual change, the gentlemen agreeing only to 'installation of the [electric] light into a certain portion of the new wing'.[44] So, while the first electric lights were switched on in 1903, it was not until 1920 that Matron Kathleen Jamieson was able to report 'the electric light recently installed throughout the Home has been found a great boon'.[45] Indeed, internal amenities for both children and staff had been improved gradually over time, but, as described in chapter 10, further physical expansion now moved to the creation of a Country Branch, although this goal was not reached until 1927.

The eventual achievement of the Country Branch prompted journalist and writer Neil Munro (1863–1930) to reflect on his personal observations of change at East Park over a period of nearly four decades.[46] Penned when the momentous opening of the Country Branch at Largs was being heralded, he wrote:

For nearly forty years I have known the East-Park Home in Maryhill, and the good work it has been doing there. I recall it first as little more than a suburban villa, from which, at the Annual Meetings, the children were put out in to a little space of garden while the meeting talked to them. On these occasions I had an uneasy feeling that we were intruders on a home (without a capital H), and that in some former incarnation I might have been known as 'Mr Bumble'.

If it had been a good big garden of several acres, with hills around it, and a glimpse of the sea, and these had been rampageous children fit to make the best use of their liberty out of doors, our usurpation of their dwelling for a little would have seemed less hard.

The old East-Park Home is grown almost out of my recognition in a photograph. I fear I could not find my way to it in a Maryhill that seems further away than ever from hill and sea and expansive gardens. But I am

By 1927, the year the Country Branch opened, in Maryhill the original Eastpark Cottage was dwarfed by decades of expansion of the Home.

glad to think that though these old physicians of nature cannot be brought to Maryhill, the little folk of East-Park Home can be taken to them.

The new country branch at Largs is a great idea! Half the impetus to recovery from ailment and infirmity may come from seeing from a sick-room window or a garden cot that the world outside and around is wide, and beautiful, and alluring.[47]

Munro's memories of East Park stretching back 'nearly forty years' recalled an association with the Home commencing around 1890, his reminiscences very much reflecting the time when the Home was expanding to accept ever more children and of the period, described earlier, when the immediate surroundings were becoming increasingly urban.

The full maturing of East Park's urban setting can be seen in the memories of Amy (1931–2017), admitted to the Home in 1934. Amy liked to stand at the iron gates of 1930s East Park to watch the trams rattle past. Observed by girls working in Ross's Dairy on the opposite side of the road, Amy ended up in hot water with matron, Mary MacEwen.

The lassies used to come over and hand me these caramelised biscuits … I wasn't sweet toothed and wasn't interested in biscuits, but the matron thought I was standing there for this purpose, but I wasn't. What I did was, I counted all the different tram cars, different colours, and that's what I was interested in. But then you weren't even allowed to go to the gate.[48]

The scene outside was very different from that of 1874, the year in which East-Park

Cottage was acquired and received its very first children. Maryhill Road was now a busy thoroughfare and Amy was indignant at being scolded for appearing to be encouraging the biscuit gifts.

The modern era

As described in chapter 9, East Park Home was closed to children in 1939 upon the outbreak of the Second World War, and their evacuation to the Country Branch. It resumed its role at the end of 1945, but was almost immediately faced with the battle to retain its independence under the proposals for the creation of the NHS. However, the Maryhill facilities having been returned to the Association in July 1945, work on the new Nurses' Home and new school rooms, delayed by war, was resumed and reached completion in 1946.[49] Reflecting changed needs and the facilities offered, in the early post-war years the number of children resident settled at around sixty or fewer at any one time.[50] Consequently, the post-Second World War period at Maryhill might be regarded as one of consolidation, a time when any structural changes focused upon improvement of amenity, especially with the Country Branch well established and offering generous space and facilities in a conducive environment by the sea.

By the late 1950s, the number of children at Maryhill was still in overall decline, and this influenced accommodation needs. However, building work continued in some form or another, with attendant 'noise and dust', but modernisation of facilities was the primary focus, physician superintendent Robert Shanks remarking on the installation of a lift 'to fulfil our obligations to the severely handicapped child … to bring children down from the upper floor'.[51] A substantive project was the building of the Duchess of Gloucester Wing. Although it had ward accommodation 'in the upper flat', its main function was therapeutic, fitting in with the changes from the 1940s that moved from quantity (of children accommodated) to quality of amenity provided to children and staff, in this instance the expansion of physiotherapy facilities.[52]

Disruption necessarily occurred during modernisation projects, such as in 1968 when Ward 7 could not be used for accommodation of children while a new bathroom was built, or in 1975 when adaptions had to be made that complied with new fire regulations.[53] With the closure of the Country Branch in 1987, it was inevitable that, after a long consolidatory period at Maryhill, some building work had to be embarked upon to accommodate children arriving from Largs as well as new facilities for the likes of hydrotherapy, physiotherapy and schooling, (only) half of the financial outlay coming from the sale of the Ayrshire facility.[54] By the end of 1988, there were fifty-three children resident at Maryhill, compared with twenty-one two years earlier.[55] In 1994, 120 years after East Park Home opened, there had been upgrading of one

East Park School: 150 years and facing the twenty-first century with optimism. (Iain Hutchison)

of the children's units, a conservatory extension to the physiotherapy department, installation of a new hot-water system in the school, upgrading of a lift, and roof repairs, while on the 'wish list' for the coming year were a new telephone system, upgrading of corridors, classroom alterations – and roof repairs.[56]

The arrival of the twenty-first century heralded structural changes, not just in terms of bricks and mortar, but in the provision of supported care for young people. In 2002, five children transferred from what had been East Park Home for Infirm Children, but was now 'East Park Home for Children and Young People with disabilities', to 'a new purpose-built house in Balornock', while a second house for four young people was nearing completion in Ruchill.[57] General Manager May Henderson welcomed these developments as they complemented Katrine House, which had opened as a respite and family support unit in 1999, and she was looking forward to an eventual four 'supported accommodation' houses aiding the integration of East Park children and young people into local communities.[58] As such developments were progressing, Henderson explained to subscribers on 10 May 2004 that plans had been considered to 'demolish all the buildings on the [Maryhill] site and build a new school', but that later thinking favoured 'a combination of both demolition and new build'.[59] What resulted was a £3million project for a school building – including, despite East Park's once rural location, ground stabilisation work because of the presence of old mine workings.[60] Once the grounds had been made secure, Henderson reported the children having temporarily been transferred to another part of the city and work having commenced in January 2008. Ruchill Parish Church Hall was the venue for the 2008 subscribers' meeting, where she reported that 'the site had been cleared and ground consolidation works had been completed' and that 'construction work was due to start during the month of July with an expected completion date of June 2009'.[61]

The dawn of the East Park of the twenty-first century was heralded by May Henderson as 'a very exciting time as the organisation looks forward and plans for the future', while cautioning that 'a number of challenges lay ahead, but with focus, teamwork and sustained effort from every member of the workforce, East Park looks forward to these challenges'.[62]

CHAPTER 19

East Park Today

We are on a continuing journey in understanding ordinary love that will, hopefully organically, develop a cultural norm with the extra-ordinary end result that all children who leave East Park Services can reflect on their lived experience in the knowledge that they were loved by those who supported them.

Liam Feeney, *Scottish Journal of Residential Child Care*, 2020[1]

Arrive at East Park at the start of a new school day and you will be struck by the energy, the fun, the care and compassion which abound.[2] Taxis, family cars and minibuses roll up as children and young people arrive from home or the East Park residences, supported by a parent, an escort or a support worker. Each is greeted personally by their designated learning support workers who are waiting for them, easing the process of transition from home to school. Friendships between parents have developed here at the school door, through the shared experience of supporting a young person with complex additional support needs. Receptionist Peter McLanachan welcomes each young person by name, with a smile and their preferred method of communication – a simple wave, a Makaton greeting or a 'high five' – as he has been doing since joining East Park in 1995.[3] The reception area is bright and airy, festooned with young people's artwork from their latest project.

Young people go to their class. Some are in their individual space with a 2:1 ratio of staff to young person. Some are in very small groups. Each has an individual plan, identifying communication preferences and what motivates them to interact. Each also has a personal 'timetable', which involves a wide range of activities suited to their preferences and developmental needs: number work or exploring books in 'the Book Nook', art or Fischy Music, sensory circuits, horse riding, cycling, completing 'the daily mile' (walking round the playground with their designated learning support team), music or dance, in a group or individually. Some young people enjoy canoeing in the canal at the rear of East Park; the opportunities are rich and varied. Staff meet children and young people where they are comfortable. David (pseud.) feels more comfortable outdoors so dance specialist Ruth joins him, dancing in the gentle autumn rain. When able to manage the complexity of the task, each takes their turn as 'Snack Captain', wheeling the snack trolley round the classes, greeting staff and young people as they choose refreshments. Communication is part of every activity as teachers and learning support workers use body language, objects, symbols, Makaton, social stories and words of encouragement to communicate with young people. While some children and young people will have lessons in literacy and numeracy, most are working at Early Level on the Curriculum for Excellence. Head of Education Catriona Campbell explains:

> Shifting our approach to embrace Play Pedagogy, and underpinning our curricular development with an understanding of the impact of trauma and the value of nurture has made a big difference. We need to meet our learners at their developmental stage, but still ensure we are preparing them for life beyond school … We have benefited from groundbreaking work in the Early Years sector in Scotland in recent years. Froebelian practice has inspired us to empower children through play and to ensure that they are active participants in our wider community. We were invited to take

Ewan as Snack Captain. What a choice! (Pete Copeland)

part in Play Scotland's Play Pedagogy Award pilot and the structure of this initiative helped us develop a cohesive plan for play at East Park. As part of the pilot, we were able to help shape the awards process, and the organisers were keen to work with us to create an award that would be valuable for Additional Support Needs provision across Scotland. In January 2023, we were awarded the Gold Level Award, one of only two schools in Scotland.[4]

East Park also achieved Advanced Autism Accreditation with the National Autistic Society in 2020, renewed in 2023. Catriona is not complacent, however:

Education in Scotland is going through significant change, with Education Scotland, the General Teaching Council for Scotland and qualification framework all evolving in ways that are not yet fully clear. It has been critical for school leaders to ensure that the needs of their learners are recognised and not overlooked during these processes, so I need to be constantly scanning for new developments and consultation arrangements. We cannot afford to be left behind.[5]

As Catriona outlines, qualifications frameworks evolve and whereas students formerly completed Caledonian Awards as outlined in chapter 17, at present, classes S1–S3 complete the JASS Awards (Junior Awards Scheme for Scotland) and S3–S6 complete SQA National 1 and National 2 Awards.[6] These provide opportunities to

Josh enjoying sensory play in the School Garden. (Pete Copeland)

assess a wide range of skills and competencies. For some young people, these may be core 'academic' skills such as using money, whereas for others, it will be life skills such as developing communication, emotional regulation and accessing resources in the community.[7]

Awards and achievements are celebrated in East Park. One way of recognising these is at the weekly Assembly on Friday, attended by young people from the School and Workmates. Music Specialist Bryan Tolland explains:

> The development of the Assembly Project went really well because it made everyone aware they were part of a community and they look forward to it … We gather together to celebrate the achievements of the youngsters that week and to recognise each other and recognise their peers and applaud their peers' achievements and there is an element of performance … The Assembly Project structure is important to most of our young learners, so it has a structure where you have the same song at the beginning and at the end. We reflect on topics that Workmates and classes have been doing that week and they will sing or perform one of the songs and we will help them do it.[8]

While all children and young people have complex additional support needs, there is a wide range of ability and talent. Jay attended East Park on a daily basis from 2017 to 2022. When attending East Park, he sometimes led Assembly. He wrote songs with Bryan, and Bryan recorded some of these. A highlight for Jay was singing at Glasgow's George Square supported by Bryan at the switching on of the Christmas Lights. Jay explains:

> I remember one time I was in the Christmas Show. I had to stand on the actual stage. I sang *Santa Claus is Coming to Town* with Bryan playing the guitar. It was really, really good. And that thing that I learned from Bryan is that I have to be more myself and all that … There were a lot of people listening to me and when the song finished everyone was just clapping me and I thought to myself, this is the most challenging thing I have ever done in my life.[9]

Bryan says later:

> For me it's exciting if I can get youngsters close to the mainstream of artistic activity, close to the mainstream of the music world, on the radio, on telly, that kind of thing … We arranged a fee for Jay to sing in George Square when the lights were switched on.[10]

And so education at East Park is creative and imaginative, drawing on a wide variety of approaches, meeting the learners at their developmental stage and capitalising on their abilities.

At the end of the day, there is a gentle wind-down; for some there may be a 'story massage' where staff tell them a story or talk about their day using a range of symbolic massage strokes. Some children and young people return to their family home, others to the East Park residences to relax and unwind. There has been criticism of the poor relationship between education and care services in the past but various strategies have been employed to address this. Some support staff from residences will be working in the school setting, plans are shared across education and care services, and each day, rather than a verbal exchange in front of the young person which can be difficult, an online recording system is in place whereby care and education staff can exchange details of a young person's activities and well-being, involving them as appropriate.

The residences are homely, comfortable spaces which blend into the community. Long gone are the days of communal sewing, laundry and cooking. All of these tasks are carried out by support staff in the houses with participation from the young people where possible, in preparation for when they move on from East Park. Since the houses opened, the numbers of young people in each have been reduced. With more young people requiring a 2:1 ratio of staff support, residences had become busy, high-stimulus places, not the relaxing home environment which the young people needed. A former bedroom is now used as a quiet space or a sensory room. Bedrooms are personalised; some are low-stimulus, relaxing personal spaces, others are adorned with pictures and favourite toys, and while there is a television in the communal space, each young person also has a television in their room.

Like others up and down the country after school, young people relax with their favourite activities, watching videos on their iPads, playing with toys or on the trampoline in the garden. Each has a picture schedule to remind them what is happening over the course of each day and across the week. They may help shop for and cook a meal for themselves and their support staff. Some eat communally, while others prefer to eat alone with their support workers. A wide range of activities is on offer; swimming, cinema and bowling are popular. One young person loves his scooter and travels round the community with a support worker, while another recently acquired a bicycle which he is learning to ride. Relationships have developed across the residences and sometimes a young person from another house will join an activity. Barbecues are organised and birthdays celebrated. Group and individual outings are arranged, taking account of the young people's interests, such as trains, music, hillwalking or dance. Recently a group from different houses went on holiday to Blackpool. Some went for several days, while some who were less confident went for a couple of nights with a view to building on this on future trips. Due to her personal circumstances, one young person who previously had difficulties leaving the house now has her own car under the Motability Scheme and is able to enjoy outings with support staff. Contact is maintained with families, with some young people spending weekends at home. For others, family are welcome to visit whenever it suits. Care Services Manager Karen Ferguson explains:

> The team supporting the young person in the residences strive to be an extension of their family, working in partnership with families they hold in high regard, knowing the knowledge and experience a family can bring to enhance the young person's life is invaluable. Residential houses strive to be seen as a home away from home, with a family atmosphere, loving and nurturing.[11]

Meetings are convened regularly to ensure continuity in care planning and building on successes. Gradually, young people are able to enjoy a wider range of opportunities. One parent, Lesley, wrote of her son's experience at East Park:

> Our son Stuart arrived at East Park residence in April 2014 and stayed in Harris House. He left last year [2022] after leaving school. I will always have very precious memories of his time in East Park, how everyone knew and loved him so well and allowed him to meet his potential. Amazing committed staff who put him first even through a global pandemic. He had so many opportunities and I will always be grateful. He went canoeing, camping, fairgrounds, seaside trips and enjoyed many a buffet meal. Never forget the Troon annual taxi outings! … He was one happy boy and we were very blessed parents.[12]

Behind the scenes

To keep a complex resource like East Park delivering such a personalised, quality service, a number of people work hard behind the scenes: the Learning and Development Team, Human Resources, Finance, Fundraising, Administration, Maintenance and Domestic Teams and Catering.

As outlined above, support services in East Park have changed considerably over the years. In the kitchen, Lauren Black prepares lunches single-handedly. The menu steers towards 'healthy eating', with chips only two days a week. The aim is that all meal servings should look similar, rather than a young person being singled out as having a 'special diet'. Some young people eat in The Hive with support staff and classmates, while others who would find the sensory experience too difficult eat in their classrooms.[13]

In chapter 11, we were introduced to the Master of Work and joiners, who designed furniture and made remedial aids for the children in the 1940s and 1950s.[14] This role has changed over the years and is now held by Keith Greene, Assets and Facilities Manager. While they no longer design aids for the young people, the members of the Maintenance Team play an invaluable role. All drive the school buses and carry out a wide range of maintenance tasks. The maintenance service is on call twenty-four hours for emergencies. Meanwhile, the full-time Domestic Team clean the school daily, then visit the residences when the young people are in school, supporting staff to keep the houses homely, clean and fresh.[15]

Another group previously at the forefront of East Park but now working 'behind the scenes' are health professionals, doctors, psychologists, psychiatrists, speech and language therapists, physiotherapsts and occupational therapists. Community nurses from the Specialist Children Services for Additional Support for Learning (ASL) Schools visit annually in respect of children with particular conditions, and community child health nurses carry out vaccinations, as might be expected in any school. East Park, however, no longer has a physician superintendent or a link medical practitioner. Instead, the children and young people attend the local health centre as required. Several are registered with the NHS Greater Glasgow and Clyde Child and Adolescent Mental Health Service (CAMHS), which provides mainly psychological and psychiatric services to young people in East Park. Rather than working directly with the individual young person, practitioners work with the 'team around the child', thus ensuring that everyday interactions with children and young people reinforce developmental objectives. The role of the speech and language therapist, for example, changed around 15 to 20 years ago to focusing on creating a Total Communication Environment, embedding the use of objects, pictures, symbols and Makaton signs throughout East Park.[16] The therapist joins in activities, and observes young people's preferred communication and the support staff who have everyday contact with them. They meet regularly with relevant staff, participate in review meetings and discuss tools and strategies such as individualised and alternative communication methods and Communication Passports, which are shared across East Park.[17]

One group in East Park which has changed considerably over the last thirty years is the Board of Trustees. Unlike boards of yesteryear, the Board in East Park's 150th year comes from diverse backgrounds and includes those with experience in education, social work and/or social policy, risk management, finance, charity law, fundraising, estate management and business. Personal and/or family experience of children and young people with complex additional support needs is a hugely valued additional asset and the Board retains one trustee position for the parent or carer of a child receiving a service at East Park.

As with all registered charitable organisations, the Board's operating framework is the charity's Constitution, described by the recent Chair, Gerry Wells, as 'an unglamorous legalistic document that has gone through various revisions over the years, the most recent in 2021'.[18] The 'objects' of the organisation have been subtly nuanced to reflect the current needs. Trustees' lengths of service are now restricted and archaic Articles have been brought up to date to comply with equality matters.[19] As discussed in chapter 15, the Board was criticised historically for being too involved in direct practice. While the Board has responsibility for the strategic direction of the organisation and ensuring high standards of governance, it has to operate to governance standards set by many regulatory bodies and statute, influenced by continually rising societal expectations. Gerry Wells reminds us, however, that ultimately the Board delegates to the Senior Management Team, 'the critical backbone and public face of the organisation, setting its culture through their leadership'.[20]

Expecting the unexpected

Over the years, East Park has regularly had to respond to the unexpected, such as evacuation at very short notice to Largs and the threat of takeover by the new NHS, to name but two. More recently, there have been challenges which arguably caught the residential care sector in Scotland unawares. During the 2000s there was an increasing awareness of Scotland's legacy of historical institutional abuse as survivors came forward sharing narratives of a wide range of abuse in residential and foster care in Scotland.[21] This resulted in a range of initiatives, such as the Scottish Child Abuse Inquiry established in October 2015, and, following passage of the Redress for Survivors (Historical Child Abuse in Care) (Scotland) Act in 2021, Scotland's Redress Scheme, which was launched on 8 December 2021.[22] This was open to adults abused while in care as children before 1 December 2004 and some next of kin.[23] Chief Executive Kieron O'Brien and the Board decided to embrace the Redress Scheme. By doing so, they were agreeing to East Park contributing to the Scheme financially and to certain requirements: 'acting consistently with its spirit and ethos, and acknowledging the harms of the past'.[24]

Reflecting on this, Kieron writes:

> When I was deliberating on [East Park's] participation to join the Redress
> Scheme, it brought to light disturbing abusive practices across the sector

that impacted very negatively not only on survivors but on their families too. Having spent six years in the ministry in southern Africa, I was only too aware of how such abuse could not only destroy the individual but communities too.

Considering the shameful cases brought to light in the sector between 1934 and 2004, it was not a difficult decision to make that East Park would participate in the Redress Scheme to send a strong message of support to the survivors of such abuse and acknowledging that there may have been times that some aspects of practice during those years may not have been always perceived as in the best interests of the individual.[25]

East Park acknowledges 'that there may have been times during the period covered by the Redress Scheme when practice at East Park fell short of the high standards and lacked the scrutiny we would expect today'.[26] In its 2022 Annual Report to the Scottish Government, a requirement of all contributors to the Scheme, East Park outlined various redress activities being implemented. These included access to historical records, promoting visits from former residents and the proposed renovation of gravestones marking where East Park had taken responsibility for interments.

A few years ago, East Park was made aware of a gravestone in the Glasgow Necropolis commemorating children who had died while in the care of East Park Cottage Home (as it was known between 1875 and 1885). Twenty-nine children and one nurse are named on the stone. East Park also learned of some children buried there subsequent to the stone being erected, but their names had not been added; this is being rectified. At the end of chapter 3, an attempt has been made to trace the lives of three children who were buried at the Glasgow Necropolis. Further graves have been traced elsewhere in the Glasgow Necropolis, at the city's Western Necropolis, and at Largs. Children here will be similarly remembered.[27]

Another significant challenge in recent years was the Covid-19 pandemic beginning in 2020. As outlined above, Stuart's mother commended 'committed staff who put him first even through a global pandemic'.[28] However, it would be inaccurate to suggest that the pandemic was unprecedented in the history of East Park. As outlined in chapter 5, there had been the global influenza pandemic of 1918 to 1920, and during this time some children and a member of staff had died. For many reasons, although requiring very sensitive management, the Covid-19 pandemic was not so devastating in its impact and indeed had some unexpected consequences. Chief Executive Kieron O'Brien, who took over from Judy Cromarty in November 2017, reflected:

The Covid-19 pandemic had the potential to bring the organisation to a standstill and put it into a staffing crisis and financial uncertainty. However, the embedded culture saw staff from all services work together. Not only did the staffing complement increase by 20 per cent during this time, but the services continued, with home schooling and support in place. Staff improvised and even when they were unable to use buses for trips into the city, the staff with the children built their own scaled-down model of buses with chairs and cardboard boxes in the residential houses for the children and staff to play bus trips. This received media coverage and inspired others to work through the pandemic, showing that there were ways to continue the education and care of the children.[29]

During the Covid-19 pandemic, unemployment increased significantly.[30] Some of those made redundant applied for posts with East Park. They were described as coming 'from all walks of life' and bringing a range of experience and skills.[31] While some moved on after restrictions eased, several stayed, receiving training relevant to the post.[32]

Evolving and adapting

East Park has changed considerably since the late 1990s, Kieron O'Brien describing it as 'evolving, making adjustments and enduring the ever-increasing legislative changes in care and education for looked after children in Scotland'.[33]

In 2015, in order to allow a more detailed scrutiny of governance and practice, the Board formed two subcommittees: the General Purposes Committee to support issues of quality, property and finance, and the Inclusion and Achievement Committee to support the practical delivery of services.[34] In 2016, however, a school inspection by Education Scotland was critical, with one issue being a lack of cohesive collegial and professional support between the care and education services. The Board responded immediately, creating a new School Quality Assurance Group to drive further change. This was led by trustee Helen Glenn, an educationalist, offering support to the Senior Management Team, that came to include new Head of Education, Catriona Campbell, appointed in 2018.[35] By 2019, positive reports were again being received from Education Scotland; and the short-term Group to drive change soon morphed with the Inclusion and Achievement Committee to become the current Services Quality Assurance and Development Committee:

> This was no easy task but with staff motivated to put the children and young people first, East Park has shown over the last five years that it is possible to get a cohesive and collegial connect between Care and Education staff …

John makes lemon drizzle cake in Workmates – because it's yummy! (Pete Copeland)

Since 2017, significant changes have ensured East Park has become a national resource, and one of the sector leaders in education and care for children and young people with profound autism and complex additional support needs. Representation on national committees, papers delivered at conferences and workshops, sustained placement requests, fully subscribed services and ever-increasing demand for the Workmates young adults service … are evidence of the successful transition from an institutionalised medical model to the complex additional support and autism model it is today.[36]

Reflecting on the task of the Chief Executive, Kieron emphasises the importance of scanning the horizon, looking outward and being aware of factors which may impact on the way forward:

East Park continues to face challenges that potentially could bring closure to many independent additional support organisations as local authorities increasingly find it challenging to meet the required annual fee uplifts so necessary to sustain the organisation, recruit and retain professional skilled staff, continually upgrade resources and ensure that children and young people only experience the highest standard of care and education.[37]

While this might explain the management perspective, how is this experienced by young people and staff?

'Embracing Love in our Care Environment'

As well as providing high-quality care and education for children and young people with complex additional support needs, East Park aspires to create a learning environment for staff, and to become a beacon, sharing knowledge, skills and experience across the care sector, and helping to change the narrative of neurodiversity and trauma.[38]

In October 2016, Scotland's First Minister, Nicola Sturgeon, made a commitment that Scotland would 'come together and love its most vulnerable children to give them the childhood they deserve'. She announced an independent root-and-branch review of care, driven by those with experience of care.[39] From that came *The Promise*, which states that 'Scotland has an ambition "to be the best place in the world to grow up" so that children are loved, safe, and respected and achieve their full potential'.[40]

East Park is explicit about the role of love in the care and education of its young people, and 'Embracing Love in our Care Environment' beams out from the cover of the *East Park Patter*.[41] At the opening of this chapter, Liam Feeney, Care Services Manager, writes of the staff at East Park 'loving' the children and young people whom they support. Indeed, Stuart's mother reflected that 'everyone knew and loved [Stuart] so well and allowed him to meet his potential'.[42] The sense of love is palpable in the School and houses at East Park. Gone are the days when children were 'banned' from swimming because they had been 'bad', as witnessed by Dr Livingstone in 1970, discussed in chapter 13.[43] Rather, strategies are in place to ensure that young people have fun, enjoy rich rewarding experiences to achieve their potential, and critically, that they feel loved while their sensory preferences are respected. Stephen (pseud.) comes in from school and tells staff about a worry he has, something he might do when he is out. He is gently reassured by staff that they will make a plan with him to ensure this does not happen and he goes on his way, seeming happy, to continue his day. In another house, Sophie (pseud.) is not attending school today, feeling unwell, and is snuggled on the sofa watching TV, with staff nearby making sure she is cosy and comfortable. In a third house, Ashley, who has experienced significant trauma in her life as well as having complex additional support needs, invites a member of staff to join her in the 'safe space' in her room. The member of staff gently makes sure that she is welcome before entering and engaging in an activity of Ashley's choosing.[44]

In writing of love, Liam draws on Liddell and Scott, who refer to *agape*, described by the ancient Greeks as 'the highest form of love, charity'.[45] Liam reminds us that this is different to the kind of love we might feel for a partner, our own children, friends, family or colleagues: 'We used agape as an explanation of how we can feel love that is selfless and without condition for people who require our support.'[46] Liam describes ways of developing team systems in order to maintain 'a golden thread of understanding how to demonstrate love in practice'. Embedding the principles of love is included in the recruitment and induction processes at East Park.[47] Once in post, staff are encouraged to have loving, trusting and meaningful relationships with young people and to identify what love means to each young person. This means assessing, planning and practising in a way cognisant of each young person's interpretation of love. Staff are supported in this by mandatory training which, as well as the areas outlined in chapter 16, includes Transforming Psychological Trauma and Love and Nurture in the context of children's rights. Each young person has a Trauma Profile and an Autism Profile, to ensure that staff differentiate and follow a 'trauma response' or an 'autism response' as required in the circumstances. Love is on the agenda for staff supervision, peer assessment and coaching, and is an agenda item at every team meeting. Liam initially piloted this model of working in the Intensive Support Service but over time the approach has been extended across East Park's residential services. There are found to have been fewer seclusions, fewer physical interventions and more loving engagements.[48]

Reflecting on this approach, Geraldine O'Neill, Head of Care Services, writes:

When we first introduced the residential staff to the concept of 'love in the care setting' around 2018, many expressed discomfort about using the word 'love' in relation to the children we support. This was understandable, given how risk-averse care had become due to the various high-profile scandals which had been reported in previous years. Exploring with staff the various types of love that we all experience with friends, family, colleagues, etc., and how this varies according to the relationship, but can still be validly expressed as 'love', supported them to develop the confidence to acknowledge and express those emotions appropriately. Staff now routinely talk about 'love' and consciously consider and discuss at Key Team Meetings, 'Does Mary (pseud.) feel loved?', 'How does John (pseud.) know that we love him?'. Many young people also have now learned the language of 'love' and are able to express it, in their own way, to parents, siblings and staff. The message we want to give to young people is, 'However distressed you are today, whatever you've done as a result of that distress, we will continue to love you unconditionally.'[49]

Craig enjoys sharing a book. (Pete Copeland)

Moving forward

Looking back over the 150 years since East Park opened its doors to provide care and education for infirm children, it is clear that it is has become not only a much sought-after resource providing high-quality care and education for children and young people with complex additional support needs, but also remains part of the fabric of Glasgow and Maryhill, held in affection by many. In completing this 'East Park Story', childhood memories of East Park over the decades flowed in from across Scotland; recollections of waving at the children from the top of the bus travelling down Maryhill Road, Sunday school collections, back court concerts and 'garage sales' to raise funds for the Home, donating toys and gifts, helping out as part of the Duke of Edinburgh's Award scheme, all for the children of East Park. One marked feature of East Park is its capacity to adapt to change, be it in response to children's health needs as scourges of the past such as rickets, polio and tuberculosis have been virtually eliminated from the UK, or responding to changes in childcare policy whereby children with complex additional support needs are no longer kept in institutions away from their home community. As East Park faces the challenges of the future, prepared for the unexpected, Kieron O'Brien reminds us of the acronym for the School's values: CARING – Collaborative, Ambitious, Respectful, Inclusive, Nurturing and Growth.[50] However, we should leave the final word to Jay, a young person who recently left East Park:

I was going to say what school meant to me. It was an absolute privilege to learn stuff for the past five years that I have been here because I have made loads of friends, done all the work, met new friends and all that and I just want to thank all the people at East Park for everything, looking after me, and showing me who I really am, so I just want to say a big, big, big thank you to everyone who has been by my side.[51]

CHAPTER 20

Conclusions

F
ifteen decades have passed since implementation of the 1872 Education (Scotland) Act prompted the formation, in February 1874, of the 'Association for Aiding and Visiting Permanently Infirm and Imbecile Children …' in their own homes. Only a few months later, East-Park Cottage was acquired as a temporary expediency to provide for the care of up to thirty children for whom, it was felt, home environments could not possibly ensure their survival.

However, rather than early reversion to home visiting as the means of supporting children with complex physical impairments, as the Association had always intended, East Park 'cottage' was absorbed into an increasingly significant institution through the construction of larger, adjoining buildings. The Home responded to the need of, and demand for, places for large numbers of children for many years after the Second World War and the creation of the National Health Service – including the facility of a second Home in the form of a Country Branch, opened in Largs, in 1927.

The story of East Park Home, now East Park School, has been one of survival, adaption and innovation. As East Park Home evolved from being a temporary support into a much-needed, 'permanent' facility fuelled by never-diminishing demand through the Victorian and Edwardian eras, it took on a three-pronged role that, at different times, presented demanding challenges, but proved also to be its salvation. It served as a place of long-term residence for children with impairments with often extensive support needs; as a place of education for children impeded from accessing mainstream schooling; and as a place of healthcare, therapy and medical intervention. Until well into the post-Second World War era, demand for places in the Homes at Maryhill and Largs continued to exceed availability of beds.

The resources for this provision initially came from philanthropically motivated members of the comfortable classes in Glasgow and beyond. Especially in the years before the Great War, state intervention to aid needy members of society was minimal. The economic void between rich and poor had become a chasm as Glasgow grew exponentially and the different social classes, who had once lived in close proximity within the old city radiating from Glasgow Cross, became separated physically and ideologically through the relentless process of urban expansion. They were also separated by religiosity, and by sectarian prejudices from which East Park was not immune through its early decades and that this story has recognised on several occasions.

East Park has not been cut off from wider societal trends and emotions through the course of its 150-year history. Its history shows the influence of the jingoism that surrounded the Boer War and the Great War, and has reflected the hardship experienced when the Poor Law was often the only support available to families facing destitution – even after the additional support legislated for during the Edwardian era – but which was inadequate to relieve the deprivation that confronted society during the depression years of the interwar period.

The creation of East Park was prompted by the passage of a law to address deficiencies in Scotland's education, school attendance being voluntary until 1872. Scotland's often-made claims to have long had superior education were not borne out by the consequences of non-mandatory education provision, and significant levels of illiteracy prevailed in the late nineteenth century. Schooling at East Park was therefore a feature from the outset, in initial years largely provided by a sole, untrained but highly dedicated teacher, becoming the bedrock of East Park's twenty-first-century role in society.

Until the immediate post-Second World War period in particular, East Park also increasingly engaged in medical and surgical intervention, often in association with the Royal Hospital for Sick Children. In the early decades, physically impairing conditions such as tuberculosis of the bones and joints, rickets and the effects of polio had a prominent prevalence among East Park's children. The Home, from the outset, had enduring support from the medical profession, and surgical intervention was increasingly performed in East Park itself, notably during the interwar period. This was the medical model of disability at its most strident, as efforts were made to 'fix' 'broken' children rather than accommodate individual needs by making adaptions to their living environment. An image of a boy negotiating an East Park internal staircase on his crutches dramatically highlights the philosophy of that period.

East Park often had to develop through the changing circumstances encountered between 1874 and 1939. However, the decade following the onset of the Second World War was a crisis period for the Home's survival. East Park's story demonstrates the challenges that were faced by the temporary closure of the Home in Maryhill when its children were evacuated to Largs for the duration of the conflict. During that time, it had to counter plans for the creation of a National Health Service that involved forceful attempts to 'nationalise' East Park. This was where East Park's three-pronged role was its salvation, enabling its continuation as an independent entity. In the 1940s, East Park, with its significant level of medical intervention, seemed ill-placed to argue that it should not come under the NHS, but its other roles as Home and education provider were key to saving the day, the new NHS perhaps realising that its founding tasks were sufficiently complex for it to want to avoid involvement in residential care and specialised schooling.

It was not only the nature of healthcare provision that changed from 1948; the disabling conditions encountered by the original Association had also been changing. While by no means eradicated, rickets, polio and tubercular conditions were in decline. Some other impairments, such as congenital conditions and the consequences of accidents that necessitated amputation, naturally prevailed. Additionally, the development of community care and increased support to families led to changes in the ways that children and young people were being referred to East Park. During the late twentieth century, East Park therefore had to adapt and seek a new niche within changing circumstances. This is seen in its now predominant role in working with children and young people with complex additional support needs, including autism. Care of its young people has also included rehabilitating them from their experiences of trauma, such as that precipitated by abuse or family breakdown.

Therefore, as East Park evolved, it not only addressed children's and young people's physical needs. Staff became tasked beyond conventional nursing techniques, tending to emotional well-being, arranging activities, supervising play and, above all else, providing affection. Corporal punishment by the tawse continued as the norm in mainstream schools in post-Second World War Scotland, but was not permitted in East Park; indeed, it was against the rules to smack children. This has continued to be a part of the ethos of East Park, which is now a beacon in ensuring that staff love children and young people unconditionally.

It is noteworthy how the twenty-first-century age profile of care provision embraces young people of an age group who would not appreciate being referred to as 'children'. Indeed, childhood itself has been constantly redefined. Since 1872, legislation to regulate the ages to which young people should be required to receive a minimum of education, and to determine entry to full-time employment, have been revised.

Relationships and hierarchies have also changed since the time when sombre, bearded middle-class gentlemen convened in a Wellington Street office to pontificate over the fecklessness of the lower orders, the squalor in which they lived, and the ill health they experienced as a direct consequence. In 1874, such men made bold decisions about action to be taken to right various ills, but it was women, the loyal, unquestioning wives and daughters of the West End's columned villas and imposing terraces, who undertook much of the painstaking chores of supporting East Park, ranging from collecting donations to reading to bedbound children. Likewise, the salaried staff, the nurses, helpers, domestics and teachers were women. It was a slow evolution before women were accorded places on the Board of Directors and involved in senior managerial direction, while men eventually became actively involved in direct care and teaching, as is apparent within this history.

Gender equality, as with the removal of religious sectarianism, was a long time coming, as was the transition to increased child-centred care – adult/child relationships having fundamentally changed in modern Scotland since East Park's foundational years. Today's East Park young people no longer occupy communal dormitories. Indeed, East Park is no longer a Home, residents now largely occupying supported off-site units in which they are encouraged to exercise independence and agency. Some only attend East Park for schooling, while others are residents but attend school elsewhere. Specialist support staff operate in a variety of fields, in contrast to the voluntary help of the early decades from Lady Visitors and from teaching and nursing staff who were not all formally trained and professionally qualified.

The National Health Service celebrated seventy-five years of universal healthcare provision in 2023. During that time, the NHS has faced its challenges, such as in the arena of funding to keep up with medical developments and the costs surrounding ever-increasing sophistication of clinical intervention. East Park, continuing as an independent charity through those seventy-five years, has also had to adapt, such as in the acquisition of new specialisations to enable it to confront twenty-first-century health challenges, to provide independence to a broadening age range that now encompasses young people as well as children, to supply off-campus homes that give young people dignity and freedom, and to deliver tailor-made education geared to the needs of the individual.

One hundred and fifty years after William Mitchell inspired the creation of East Park and energetically steered it to the dawn of the twentieth century, his 'temporary' home is still in the same location in Maryhill and is still supporting children according to their needs. The original cottage has gone, but the 1889 tower that has come to symbolise East Park's presence in the local community remains as an iconic landmark on Maryhill Road, while surrounding school buildings represent an East Park that is performing a progressive role in the post-modern world. There are undoubtedly many things about the twenty-first century that would not gain Mitchell's approbation, but he would surely feel pride and satisfaction that East Park still provides the joy, optimism and compassion that motivated him, his colleagues and the East Park staff when they began their work 150 years ago.

References

Introduction

1. East Park (EP), Minute Book 1874–92, EP/2/1, 7 Apr 1874, p. 19. Mentally impaired children had been received for several years by Baldovan Institution, near Dundee, and by the Scottish National Institution for the Education of Imbecile Children at Larbert.
2. Michel Foucault, *Folie et déraison: Histoire de la folie à l'âge classique* (1961), translated as *Madness and Civilization* (London: Routledge Classics, 2001), pp. 35–60, 229–64.
3. www.eastpark.org.uk/school/ [accessed 28 Oct 2023].
4. Paul K Longmore and Lauri Umansky (eds), *The New Disability History: American Perspectives* (New York: New York University Press, 2001), p. 8.
5. Ibid., p. 19.
6. Michael Oliver, *Understanding Disability: From Theory to Practice* (Basingstoke: Palgrave Macmillan, Second Edition, 2009), pp. 42–3.
7. Scottish Government, *National Guidance for Child Protection in Scotland, Part 4: Specific Support Needs and Concerns, Protection of disabled children* (2021, updated 2023), p. 6; Scottish Government, *A Fairer Scotland for Disabled People: Our Delivery Plan to 2021 for the United Nations Convention on the Rights of Persons with Disabilities* (Edinburgh: Scottish Government, 2016, updated Jan 2017), p. 7.
8. Hanna Björg Sigurjónsdóttir and James G Rice, *Understanding Disability Throughout History: Interdisciplinary Perspectives in Iceland from Settlement to 1936* (London: Routledge, 2022), p. 181.
9. Haraldur Thor Hammer Haraldsson, 'Fictive Osteobiographical Narrative – The Missing Puzzle Pieces', in Hanna Björg Sigurjónsdóttir and James G Rice, *Understanding Disability Throughout History*, p. 163.

Chapter 1

1. Heatherbank Museum of Social Work (HMSW), 'To the School Children of Glasgow', letter of appeal from William Mitchell on behalf of East Park Home, 1891.
2. Charles Withers, 'The demographic history of the city, 1831–1911' in W Hamish Fraser and Irene Maver (eds), *Glasgow, Volume II: 1830–1912* (Manchester: Manchester University Press, 1996), p. 142.
3. Glasgow City Archives (GCA), Schoolmaster's Log 1866–1901, Parish of Inchinnan, CO2/5/6/40B/2/1, 23 Mar 1866.
4. Ibid., 30 May 1866.
5. Ibid., 1 Oct 1866.
6. Ibid., 11 Jun 1867.
7. Ibid., 1 Oct 1867.
8. Ibid., 23 Mar 1868.
9. Ibid., 12 Jul 1869.
10. Richard Winters, '"The Empire of Learning": The School Board of Glasgow and elementary education, 1872–1885, with particular reference to the work of William Mitchell', PhD Thesis, University of Glasgow (1997), pp. 189–90.
11. Iain Hutchison, 'Institutionalization of mentally impaired children in Scotland, c.1855–1914', *History of Psychiatry*, 2011, 22:4.
12. Shadow [Alexander Brown], *Midnight Scenes and Social Photographs: Being Sketches of Life in the Streets, Wynds, and Dens of Glasgow* (Glasgow: Thomas Murray, 1858), second edition, published as *Glasgow, 1858: Shadow's Midnight Scenes and Social Photographs* (Glasgow: University of Glasgow Press, 1976), p. 7.
13. J M West Watson, *Report upon the Vital, Social, and Economic Statistics of Glasgow for 1877* (Glasgow: James MacNab, 1878), p. 108.
14. Ibid.
15. East Park (EP), Minute Book 1874–92, EP/2/1, 6 Nov 1874, p. 37. Report of a meeting of the committee of East Park Home on 22 Oct 1874, reported in the *Glasgow News*.
16. National Records of Scotland (NRS), 1871 Decennial Census, Parish of Govan.

17. See Chris Philo and Jonathan Andrews, 'Introduction: histories of asylums, insanity and psychiatry in Scotland', *History of Psychiatry*, 28:1 (2009).
18. The inaugural meeting was held in the Religious Institution Rooms, Glasgow, on 10 Feb 1874. EP, Minute Book 1874–92, EP2/1/1, pp. 1–8.
19. Ibid., pp. 2–4.
20. Ibid., p. 2.
21. Ibid.
22. EP, Minute Book 1874–92, 10 Feb 1874, p. 1, and 27 Feb 1874, p. 9.
23. EP, Minute Book 1874–92/ EP2/1/1, 7 Apr 1874, p. 19.
24. EP, Minute Book 1874–92, EP2/1/1, 10 Feb 1874, pp. 2–5.
25. EP, Minute Book 1874–92, EP2/1/1, 2 Apr 1874, p. 16.
26. EP, Minute Book 1874–92/ EP2/1/1, 7 Apr 1874, p. 19.
27. Ibid., pp. 20–1.
28. EP, Minute Book 1874–92, EP2/1/1, 10 Mar 1874, p. 11.
29. EP, Minute Book 1874–92, EP2/1/1, 7 Apr 1874, pp. 18–20.
30. Ibid., p. 22. For more on rural and coastal convalescent homes in late nineteenth- and early twentieth-century Scotland, see Jenny Cronin, 'The Origins and Development of Scottish Convalescence Homes, 1860–1939', PhD thesis, University of Glasgow (2003).
31. EP, Minute Book 1874–92, EP2/1/1, 7 Apr 1874, p. 22.
32. Ibid.
33. Ibid., pp. 23–4.
34. Ibid., p. 23; NRS, 1881 Decennial Census, Barony Parish.
35. EP, Minute Book 1874–92, EP2/1/1, 17 Aug 1874, p. 25a.
36. Ibid.
37. Ibid.
38. Ibid., p. 25b.

Chapter 2

1. EP, Minute Book 1874–92, EP2/1/1, 27 Oct 1874, p. 33.
2. Jacqueline Jenkinson, Michael S Moss and Iain Russell, *The Royal: the history of the Glasgow Royal Infirmary, 1794–1994* (Glasgow: Glasgow Royal Infirmary NHS Trust, 1994).
3. Hutchison, Iain, Malcolm Nicolson and Lawrence Weaver, *Child Health in Scotland: A History of Glasgow's Royal Hospital for Sick Children* (Erskine: Scottish History Press, 2016).
4. Loudon MacQueen and Archibald B Kerr*, The Western Infirmary 1874–1974: a century of service to Glasgow* (Glasgow: John Horn, 1974).
5. Charles Duguid, *Macewen of Glasgow: a recollection of the chief* (Edinburgh: Oliver & Boyd, 1957).
6. GGCHBA, Hospital for Sick Children, First Annual Report, 1883, HB2/3/1.
7. Callum G Brown, 'Religion, Class and Church Growth', in W Hamish Fraser and R J Morris (eds), *People and Society in Scotland, Volume II, 1830–1914* (Edinburgh: John Donald, 1990), p. 329.
8. Esme Cleall, *Colonising Disability: impairment and otherness across Britain and its Empire, c.1800–1914* (Cambridge: Cambridge University Press, 2022), p. 58.
9. EP, Minute Book 1874–92, EP2/1/1, 9 Oct 1874, p. 26.
10. Ibid., pp. 9–10.
11. Ibid., p. 10.
12. Ibid.
13. Ibid.
14. Ibid.
15. EP, Minute Book 1874–92, EP2/1/1, 13 Oct 1874, p. 28.
16. Ibid.
17. EP, Minute Book 1874–92, EP2/1/1, 27 Oct 1874, pp. 31–2.
18. EP, Minute Book 1874–92, EP2/1/1, 20 Oct 1874, p. 28.
19. Ibid., pp. 28–9.
20. EP, Minute Book 1874–92, EP2/1/1, 27 Oct 1874, pp. 29–31.

21. Ibid., pp. 31–4.
22. Ibid., p. 37.
23. EP, Minute Book 1874–92, EP2/1/1, 2 Feb 1875, p. 45.
24. Ibid.
25. EP, Minute Book 1874–92, EP2/1/1, 27 Oct 1874, p. 32.
26. Ibid.
27. Ibid.
28. Ibid., p. 33.
29. EP, Minute Book 1874–92, EP2/1/1, 7 Apr 1874, p. 21; 27 Oct 1874, p. 40.
30. EP, Minute Book 1874–92, EP2/1/1, 20 Oct 1874, p. 28; 27 Oct 1874, p. 33.
31. EP, Minute Book 1874–92, EP2/1/1, 27 Oct 1874, p. 33.
32. Ibid., pp. 33–4.
33. Ibid., pp. 34–6.
34. Ibid., p. 34.
35. Ibid., pp. 37–8.
36. Alexander Gammie, *William Quarrier and the Story of the Orphan Homes of Scotland* (Glasgow: Pickering & Inglis, 1937), p. 108.
37. EP, Minute Book 1874–92, EP2/1/1, 27 Oct 1874, p. 38.
38. EP, Minute Book 1874–92, EP2/1/1, 22 Dec 1874, p. 41.
39. EP, Minute Book 1874–92, EP2/1/1, 27 Oct 1874, p. 40.
40. EP, Minute Book 1874–92, EP2/1/1, 22 Dec 1874, p. 42.
41. Ibid.
42. EP, Minute Book 1874–92, EP2/1/1, 6 Dec 1875, p. 58.
43. EP, Minute Book 1874–92, EP2/1/1, 2 Feb 1875, p. 44.
44. EP, Minute Book 1874–92, EP2/1/1, 20 Apr 1875, p. 48.
45. Iain Hutchison, 'Institutionalization of mentally impaired children in Scotland, c.1855–1914', *History of Psychiatry*, 22:4 (2011).
46. EP, Minute Book 1874–92, EP2/1/1, 2 Feb 1875, p. 45.
47. EP, Minute Book 1874–92, EP2/1/1, 20 Apr 1875, p. 49.
48. Ibid.
49. Ibid.
50. Ibid., p. 50.
51. Christine Kelly, 'Reforming Juvenile Justice in Nineteenth-Century Scotland: the subversion of the Scottish Day Industrial School Movement', *Crime, Histoire & Sociétés/Crime, History and Societies*, 20:2 (2016), p. 56.
52. EP, Minute Book 1874–92, EP2/1/1, 20 Apr 1875, pp. 49, 51.
53. EP, Minute Book 1874–92, EP2/1/1, 12 Oct 1875, p. 52.
54. EP, Minute Book 1874–92, EP2/1/1, 25 Oct 1875, p. 53; NRS, Registration of Death, District of Kelvin, 23 Oct 1875.

Chapter 3

1. EP, Minute Book 1874–92, EP2/1/1/1, 25 Oct 1875, p. 53.
2. Ibid.
3. NRS, Decennial census 1871, Parish of St David, Glasgow; Death registration, District of Kelvin, Glasgow, 23 Oct 1875.
4. EP, Minute Book 1874–92, EP2/1/1/1, p. 38.
5. At the time of the 1861 census, held on 7 April 1861, Ann Ruth Bowser was recorded as aged twenty-two, and in the 1871 census, held on 2 April 1871, she was shown as thirty-three. That of 1881 was held on 3 April, and the 1891 census was on 5 April, when she was listed as forty-two and fifty-two respectively. Her age on the 1871 census may therefore be inaccurate.
6. EP, Minute Book 1874–92, EP2/1/1/1, 6 Nov 1875, p. 56.
7. EP, Minute Book 1874–92, EP2/1/1/1, 18 Oct 1876, p. 73.

8. EP, Minute Book 1874–92, EP2/1/1/1, 12 Oct 1878, p. 88.
9. EP, Minute Book 1874–92, EP2/1/1/1, 20 Feb 1877, p. 78.
10. EP Thirteenth Annual Report (AR), 1887, pp. 4–5.
11. Iain Hutchison, 'Institutionalization of mentally impaired children in Scotland, c.1855–1914', *History of Psychiatry*, 22:4 (2011).
12. EP, Minute Book 1874–92, EP2/1/1/1, 7 Feb 1876, p. 63.
13. Ibid., p. 64.
14. EP, Minute Book 1874–92, EP2/1/1/1, 7 Feb 1876, p. 64; 6 Mar 1876, pp. 67 and 71.
15. University of Dundee Archives (UDA), Baldovan Asylum, Minute Book No. 3, 31 Dec 1874, pp. 34–5.
16. Ibid., 31 Dec 1875, p. 59.
17. Ibid., p. 60.
18. Ibid., 24 Apr 1878, p. 93.
19. Ibid., p. 94.
20. While searches have proven inconclusive, Alexander McGilvery may have been the son of Mary McGilvery, a twenty-eight-year-old married woman living in a single-room tenement dwelling in Barony Parish in 1871 with her four-year-old son, John, three-year-old daughter, Ann, and eight-month-old son Alexander. NRS, Decennial Census, 1871, Barony Parish.
21. EP, Minute Book 1874–92, EP2/1/1/1, 6 Mar 1876, pp. 70–1.
22. EP, Minute Book 1874–92, EP2/1/1/1, 7 Feb 1876, p. 65.
23. On 14 September 1908, when removal of blind and deaf children from Smyllum to a new Blind and Deaf Mute Home at Tollcross was being discussed, Sister Teresa wrote in despair to her Archbishop that 'many ignorant parents have sent their children to Langside and to the protestant Blind Asylum to the loss of their faith' (Archdiocese of Glasgow Archives).
24. EP, Minute Book 1874–92, EP2/1/1/1, 7 Feb 1876, pp. 65–6. Research of the outcome of this case is inhibited because the child is not named in the report, nor further reported upon at a subsequent meeting.
25. EP, Minute Book 1874–92, EP2/1/1/1, 6 Mar 1876, p. 67.
26. EP, Minute Book 1874–92, EP2/1/1/1, 30 Oct 1876, pp. 74–5.
27. Ibid., p. 73.
28. Helen J MacDonald, 'Boarding-Out and the Scottish Poor Law, 1845–1914', *Scottish Historical Review*, LXXV, 2: 200 (Oct 1996), pp. 197–220.
29. EP, Minute Book 1874–92, MB2/1, 26 Mar 1877, p. 81. See also Harriet Sturdy and William Parry-Jones, 'Boarding out insane patients: the significance of the Scottish system 1857–1913', in Peter Bartlett and David Wright (eds), *Outside the Walls of the Asylum: The History of Care in the Community 1750–2000* (London: Bloomsbury, 1999), pp. 86–114.
30. EP, Minute Book 1874–92, EP2/1/1/1, 14 Aug 1877, pp. 83–4.
31. EP, Minute Book 1874–92, EP2/1/1/1, 17 Oct 1879, p. 96.
32. Ronnie Scott, *Death by Design: The True Story of the Glasgow Necropolis* (Edinburgh: Black & White Publishing, 2005).
33. Registration of Death, Renfrew Parish, 4 Jun 1879.
34. EP, Minute Book 1874–92, EP2/1/1/1, 5 May 1881, p. 105.
35. EP, Minute Book 1874–92, EP2/1/1/1, 9 Dec 1881, p. 109; 14 Apr 1882, p. 110.
36. EP, Fifteenth AR, 1889, p. 3.
37. Ibid., p. 5.
38. Ibid.
39. Ibid., p. 3.
40. Ibid.
41. EP, Nineteenth AR, 1893, p. 4.
42. EP, Thirty-fourth AR, 1908, p. 6.
43. GML, EP Sixth AP, 1880, pp. 12–13.

44. EP, Thirty-fourth AR, 1908, p. 3.
45. EP, Twenty-fourth AR, 1898, p. 7.
46. EP, Twenty-ninth AR, 1903, pp. 14–15.
47. GML, EP Sixth AR, 1880, pp. 8–9.
48. Ibid., p. 8.
49. ML, EP Sixth AR, p. 8. Certainty of the exact year is inhibited by annual reports preserved in archival resources having a tendency of being placed in bound volumes, a process which frequently involved the removal of the cover pages of the original reports.
50. EP, Twenty-ninth AR, 1903.
51. EP, Minute Book 1874–92, EP2/1/1/1, 12 Jun 1879, p. 93.
52. EP, Thirty-fourth AR, 1908, p. 6.
53. Ibid.
54. NRS, Register of Deaths, District of Maryhill, 7 Aug 1907.
55. Decennial censuses, 1861 Parish of St James, Glasgow, and 1871 Parish of Govan.
56. EP, Thirty-third AR, 1907, p. 4.
57. Ibid., p. 5.
58. Two days after Ann Ruth Bowser's death, on 9 August 1907, a funeral service was held at East Park Home. EP, Minute Book 1893–1908, EP2/1/1/1/2, 8 Aug 1907, p. 207.
59. EP, Minute Book 1893–1908, EP2/1/1/1/2, 4 Feb 1908, p. 220.
60. EP, Minute Book 1874–92, EP2/1/1, 2 Mar 1889, p. 138.
61. NRS, Registration of Birth, Govan Parish, 19 Mar 1865; EP, Minute Book 1874–92, EP2/1/1, 2 Mar 1889, p. 138.
62. EP, Thirty-fourth AP, 1908, pp. 4–5.
63. NRS, Registration of Deaths, District of Maryhill, 14 May 1908.
64. Registration of Death, Partick, Jane Mitchell, 22 Dec 1903.
65. Registration of Death, Moffat, William Mitchell, 12 Aug 1910.

Chapter 4

1. EP, Minute Book 1874–92, EP2/1/1, 10 Apr 1874, p. 25.
2. Olive Checkland, *Philanthropy in Victorian Scotland: Social Welfare and the Voluntary Principle* (Edinburgh: John Donald, 1980), p. 5.
3. *The Bailie*, 'Men you know, No. 737', on William Mitchell, 1 Dec 1886.
4. Ibid., p. 1.
5. Ibid., p. 2.
6. Ibid.
7. 'The Kyrle Society', *Charity Organisation Review*, 15 Dec 1885, p. 506.
8. Ibid.
9. *The Bailie*, 'Men you know, No. 737', on William Mitchell, 1 Dec 1886, p. 2.
10. Ibid.
11. William Mitchell, *Rescue the Children (or Twelve Years of Dealing with Neglected Girls and Boys)* (London: William Isbister, 1885), p. 16.
12. 'Death of Mr William Mitchell LLD', *Glasgow Herald*, 13 Aug 1910, p. 6.
13. GCA, East Park Free Church of Scotland, Session Minute Book 1878–1909, CH3/1669/1/1; Deacon's Court Minute Book 1879–97, CH3/1669/2/2/1.
14. GCA, East Park Free Church of Scotland, Session Minute Book 1878–1909, CH3/1669/1/1, 16 Oct 1896, pp. 178–9.
15. Ibid., 24 Apr 1896, pp. 169–70.
16. Ibid., 'United Free Church of Scotland, Uniting Act, Dated 31st October 1990'. Printed statement inserted between minute book pages 231 and 232.
17. Richard Winters, '"The Empire of Learning": The School Board of Glasgow and elementary education, 1872–1885, with particular reference to the work of William Mitchell', PhD thesis, University of Glasgow (1997), p. iv.

18. NRS, Old Parish Register, Glasgow.
19. NRS, Decennial Census, Barony, 1841.
20. NRS, Decennial Census, Bonhill, 1851.
21. NRS, Decennial Census, Bonhill, 1851.
22. NRS, Old Parish Records, Bonhill, 1850; Old Parish Records, Govan, 1850.
23. NRS, Old Parish Records, Glasgow, 1829.
24. Ibid.
25. NRS, Decennial Census, Govan, 1861.
26. Ibid.
27. NRS, Decennial Census, Govan, 1871.
28. NRS, Decennial Censuses, Govan, 1881, 1891 and 1901.
29. EP, Minute Book 1874–92, EP2/1/1, 6 Feb 1886, pp. 124–5.
30. Ibid.
31. NRS, Decennial Census, Hillhead, 1891 and 1901.
32. GCA, Education Endowments (Scotland) Commission – Marshall Trust, MP13.137.
33. Ibid.
34. Trades House of Glasgow Archive (THGA), Minutes of the Trades House of Glasgow and Committees (MTHGC) 1888–97, Report for 1889–90, p. 3.
35. THGA, MTHGC 1888–97, Report for 1896–7, p. 4.
36. James Nicol, *Glasgow 1881–1885: Vital, Social, and Economic Statistics of the City* (Glasgow: Town Council of the City of Glasgow, 1885), p. 231.
37. THGA, MTHGC 1888–97, Report for 1895–6, p. 3.
38. Ibid., MTHGC 1901–5, Report for 1903–4, p. 4; MTHGC 1905-05, Report for 1907–08, p. 5.
39. 'Death of Mr William Mitchell LLD', *Glasgow Herald*, 13 Aug 1910, p. 6.
40. Report from the Departmental Committee on Habitual Offenders, Vagrants, Beggars, Inebriates, and Juvenile Delinquents [for Scotland], Edinburgh: HMSO, 1895.
41. Ibid.
42. In 2022, the Scottish Government was formulating a National Action Plan intended to address inequalities still being experienced by Scottish Gypsy/Travellers, scottishgypsytraveller_agenda_20220325.pdf (parliament.scot) [accessed 14 Jul 2022].
43. Robert Fell, '"It happened at the berry-time when Travellers came to Blair": Traveller Voices in *Tobar an Dualchais/Kist o Riches*', *Scottish Archives*, 28 (2022), pp. 16–33.
44. Report from the Departmental Committee on Habitual Offenders, p. 9, question 201.
45. NRS, Registration of Death, Partick, 1903.
46. NRS, Registration of Death, Moffat, 1910.
47. NRS, OPR, Barony Parish, 1827.
48. University College London (UCL), Centre for the Study of the Legacies of British Slavery, database listing for Duncan McKenzie.
49. NRS, Registration of Death, Larkhall, 27 Mar 1855.
50. NRS, Will of John Clugston, compeared at Glasgow, 8 Apr 1856.
51. NRS, Will of Mary Clugston, presented at Dumbarton, 25 Nov 1881.
52. NRS, Registration of Death, Milton, 18 Mar 1859.
53. Jenny Cronin, 'Beatrice Clugston', in Elizabeth Ewan, Sue Innes and Siân Reynolds (eds), *Biographical Dictionary of Scottish Women* (Edinburgh: Edinburgh University Press, 2007), p. 77.
54. Obituary, 'Death of Miss Beatrice Clugston', *Glasgow Herald*, 5 Jun 1888.
55. See Douglas G Lockhart, 'The Queen of all Bazaars', *Scottish Local History*, No. 111, Spring 2022.
56. EP, Minute Book 1874–92, EP2/1/1, 20 Apr 1875, p. 47.
57. Beatrice Clugston, *Missing Links in Scotland's Charities and how the chain may be repaired* (Glasgow: David Bryce, 1880).
58. EP, Minute Book 1874–92, EP2/1/1, 23 Sep 1887, pp. 128–9.
59. NRS, Decennial Census, Kirkintilloch, 1881.

60. Olive Checkland, 'Clugston, Beatrice (1827–1888)', in H C G Matthew and Brian Harrison (eds), *The Oxford Dictionary of National Biography*, Vol. 12 (Oxford: Oxford University Press, 2004), pp. 224–5.

61. www.mycityglasgow.co.uk/index_files/ckugston.htm [accessed 2 Feb 2023].

62. NRS, Register of Deaths, Kirkintilloch, 1881; Decennial Census, Kirkintilloch, 1881.

63. A D Morrison, *The Story of Free St David's* (1926), p. 83; NRS, Decennial Census, Kirkintilloch, 1881.

64. Database by the Centre for the Study of the Legacies of Slavery, UCL.

65. Scott Crawford, *The History of Broomhill and Lanfine Homes* (Kirkintilloch: Scott Crawford, 2018), p. 24.

66. Anon., *Helping the Helpless* (n.d.), p. 31; Scott Crawford, *The History of Broomhill and Lanfine Homes*, p. 75. Jenny Burgon and Don Martin, 'An Appreciation of Beatrice Clugston, 1827–1888', a presentation at a joint meeting of the Kirkintilloch Soroptimists and the Kirkintilloch & District Society of Antiquaries, 16 Mar 2022, youtube.com/watch?v=oSD7_duaink [accessed 11 Jul 2022]. The painting was stolen from Broomhill Home in 1994, but was later recovered in a damaged condition from The Barras market in Glasgow and acquired by East Dunbartonshire Museums in 2011. I am grateful to Jennifer Binnie for this information.

67. David Alston, *Slaves and Highlanders: Silenced Histories of Scotland and the Caribbean* (Edinburgh, Edinburgh University Press, 2021), p. 164. The legacy of slavery was poignantly highlighted in a modern context in the 2004 episode of *Who do You Think You Are?* featuring the broadcaster, Moira Stuart (b. 1949), who when tracing her descendancy from slaves was confronted with the sobering realisation that she was also descended from slaveholders. BBC, *Who do You Think You Are?*, Series 1, Episode 6.

68. Alston, *Slaves and Highlanders*, pp. 284–5.

69. Daniel Livesay, *Children of Uncertain Fortune: mixed race Jamaicans in Britain and the Atlantic Family, 1733–1833* (Williamsburg: Omohundro Institute of Early American History and Culture/Chapel Hill: University of North Carolina Press, 2018), p. 401.

70. Morrison, *The Story of Free St David's* (1926), p. 85, does note that £800 from the bazaar in the Kibble Palace aided the purchase of East Park Home.

71. William Hunter, 'Outposts of the benign empire of a local heroine', *The Herald*, 21 Mar 1995, p. 14.

72. Examples include William Quarrier, *A Narrative of Facts relative to Work done for Christ in connection with the Orphan and Destitute Children's Emigration Homes, Glasgow* (Glasgow, 1872); John Urquhart, *The Life Story of William Quarrier* (London: S W Partridge, 1900); J Climie, *William Quarrier, the Orphan's Friend* (Glasgow: Pickering & Inglis, c.1905); Alexander Gammie, *William Quarrier* (Glasgow: Pickering & Inglis, 1937); Eva May Sawyer, *William Quarrier and his Homes* (Glasgow: Pickering & Inglis, 1962); James Ross, *The Power I Pledge* (Glasgow: Glasgow University Press for Quarrier's Homes, 1971).

73. Anna Magnusson, *The Village* (Bridge of Weir: Quarriers Homes, 1984); Anna Magnusson, *The Quarriers Story* (Edinburgh: Birlinn, 2006).

74. Anna Magnusson, *The Village*, p. 91.

75. Anna Magnusson, *The Quarriers Story*, p. 193.

76. Hutchison et al., *Child Health in Scotland*, p. 220.

77. Brian Talbot, 'William Quarrier: Philanthropist and Social Reformer', *Records of the Scottish Church History Society*, 39 (2009), pp. 89–129.

78. Talbot, 'William Quarrier', p. 91.

79. William Quarrier, *A Narrative of Facts*, p. 3.

80. J Climie, *William Quarrier*, pp. 19–21; Talbot, 'William Quarrier', p. 93.

81. E M Sawyer, *William Quarrier and His Homes*, p. 9; Climie, *William Quarrier*, p. 33.

82. Talbot, 'William Quarrier', pp. 104–7.

83. Quarrier, *Narrative of Facts*, pp. 5–6.

84. Talbot, 'William Quarrier', p. 107.

85. Olive Checkland, *Philanthropy in Victorian Scotland* (Edinburgh: John Donald, 1980), p. 261.

86. Talbot, 'William Quarrier', p. 125.

87. Quarrier, *Narrative of Facts*, p. 27.
88. *The Bailie*, No. 414, 22 Sep 1880.
89. Ibid.
90. Quarrier, *Narrative of Facts*, p. 28.
91. Magnusson, *The Quarriers Story*, pp. 42, 46–7.
92. *Glasgow Herald*, 26 Aug 1878.
93. Ibid., 27 Aug 1878.
94. Frank appears in the 1881 census, aged twelve, but is absent from the 1891 census and has not been found in Scottish death records for the intervening period or later.
95. 'Death of Mr William Mitchell LLD', *Glasgow Herald*, 13 Aug 1910, p. 6; EP, Minute Book 1893–1908, EP2/1/2, 27 Jun 1901, pp. 52–3.

Chapter 5

1. EP, Minute Book 1930–50, 31 Jan 1936, EP2/1/5, p. 84. This would appear to be Robert McNair Wilson (1882–1963), born in Maryhill and who was both a surgeon and a prolific author.
2. EP, Minute Book 1908–12, 12 Nov 1908, EP2/1/3, pp. 6–7.
3. EP, Forty-sixth AR, 1920, p. 7.
4. See T M Devine, *Scotland's shame?: bigotry and sectarianism in modern Scotland* (Edinburgh: Mainstream, 2000).
5. Máirtín Ó Catháin, '"Dying Irish": eulogising the Irish in Scotland in *Glasgow Observer* obituaries', *The Innes Review*, 61:1 (2010), pp. 76–91.
6. EP, Minute Book 1908–12, 22 Jan 1909, EP2/1/3, p. 20.
7. Ibid.
8. EP, Constitution of the East Park Home for Infirm Children, 1912, EP1/1.
9. EP, Minute Book 1908–12, 9 Feb 1912, EP2/1/3, p. 102.
10. EP, Minute Book 1874–92, EP2/1/1, 7 Apr 1874, pp. 18–19. Steve Bruce et al., *Sectarianism in Scotland* (Edinburgh: Edinburgh University Press, 2004), pp. 38–9.
11. Aspects of societal experience during the interwar period can be found in Jon Lawrence, 'The First World War and its Aftermath', pp. 151–68, Dudley Baines, 'The Onset of Depression', pp. 169–87 and 'Recovery from Depression', pp. 188–202, Bernard Harris, 'Unemployment and the Dole in Interwar Britain', pp. 203–20 and Sue Bowden, 'The New Consumerism', pp. 242–62, all in Paul Johnson (ed.), *Twentieth-Century Britain: Economic, Social and Cultural Change* (Harlow: Longman, 1994).
12. For a succinct but insightful overview of the post-Boer War years' rise of targeted state intervention, see J R Hay, *The Origins of the Liberal Welfare Reforms* (Basingstoke: Palgrave, 1983).
13. EP, Thirty-seventh AR, 1911, p. 4.
14. Juggernaut is an Anglicised form for the Hindu god Jagannath, Lord of the Universe.
15. EP, Thirty-seventh AR, 1911, p. 4.
16. For a flavour of this, see Steve Bruce, *No Pope of Rome: Anti-Catholicism in Modern Scotland* (Edinburgh: Mainstream, 1985).
17. Callum G Brown, *Religion and Society in Twentieth-Century Britain* (Harlow: Pearson, 2006), p. 137.
18. Irene Maver, *Glasgow* (Edinburgh: Edinburgh University Press, 2000), p. 234.
19. EP, Thirty-eighth AR, 1912, p. 5; EP Jubilee 1922/23 AR, 1924, p. 8.
20. EP, Thirty-fourth AR, 1908, p. 3; EP Fortieth AR, 1914, p. 7.
21. EP, Minute Book 1912–29, 22 Mar 1915, pp. 71–2.
22. Ibid., 19 May 1915, pp. 73–4.
23. Ibid., 12 Jul 1926, p. 275.
24. See Annmarie Hughes, *Gender and Political Identities in Scotland, 1919–1939* (Edinburgh: Edinburgh University Press, 2010), which besides its focus on female political activism, examines femininity and masculinity in the public and private spheres. For post-Second World War change to marriage/work conventions, see Andrea Thomson's 2014 doctoral thesis, 'Marriage and marriage breakdown in late twentieth-century Scotland'.
25. EP, Fortieth AR, 1914, p. 5.
26. EP, Forty-first AR, 1915, p. 4.

27. For many of the prevailing sentiments held at the time, see Catherine Hall and Sonya O Rose, *At home with the empire: Metropolitan culture and the imperial world* (Cambridge: Cambridge University Press, 2006) and Adrian Gregory, *The Last Great War: British Society and the First World War* (Cambridge: Cambridge University Press, 2008). Portrayal of the Great War in the popular imagination is the subject of continued debate, Tammy Proctor arguing the need for 'a history that aligns more productively with the reality of the conflict as it was experienced': Tammy M Proctor, 'Beyond God, Country, and Empire: The United Kingdom and the Transnational Turn in the First World War', *Britain and the World* (2023), 16:2, p. 129.

28. Ian S Wood, '"Be Strong and of Good Courage": the Royal Scots' Territorial Battalions from 1908 to Gallipoli', in Catriona M M Macdonald and E W McFarland, *Scotland and the Great War* (East Linton: Tuckwell, 1999), pp. 103–24, p. 109.

29. Maver, *Glasgow*, p. 193.

30. EP, Forty-first AR, 1915, pp. 3, 5; EP, Minute Book 1912–29, 10 Oct 1916, p. 106.

31. EP, Forty-second AR, 1916, p. 3.

32. EP, Minute Book 1912–29, EP2/1/4, 27 Dec 1916, pp. 109–10.

33. Niall Johnson, *Britain and the 1918–19 influenza pandemic: a dark epilogue* (London: Routledge, 2006).

34. EP, Forty-fifth AR, 1919, p. 4.

35. Ibid., p. 8. Dr Vera Bruce was the wife of Dr Robert Bruce who, in turn, was the son of Dr Wilson Bruce, East Park's physician superintendent: Decennial Census, Maryhill, 1911 and Kelvinside, 1921.

36. In 1909, fifty-three children were recorded being discharged, their ages were 6 years – 8 children, 7 years – 8, 8 years – 13, 9 years – 7, 10 years – 3, 11 years – 2, 12 years – 5, 13 years – 3, 14 years – 2 and 16 years – 2. Twenty-eight discharged children had been treated for rickets who would have benefited from fresh-air therapy and a nutritious diet. There were ten cases of spine disease, five of polio and four of tubercular diseases. In all but one case, improvement in health while at East Park was claimed. Thirty-two children had commenced mainstream school attendance and ten had been admitted to the rolls of 'cripple' schools. EP, EP Thirty-fifth AR, 1909, pp. 14–15.

37. R D Anderson, *Scottish Education since the Reformation* (Economic & Social History Society of Scotland, 1997), p. 48.

38. EP, Minute Book 1912–29, EP2/1/4, 28 Jan 1920, pp. 156–7.

39. EP, Minute Book 1912–29, EP2/1/4, 21 Jan 1924, pp. 214–15.

40. Registration of Death, Hillhead, 6 Jan 1924.

41. Decennial Census 1921, Maryhill, East Park Home.

42. The classic text on the formation of class identity in rapidly industrialising states is E P Thompson, *The Making of the English Working Class* (London: Penguin, 1963, 1968, 1980). Thompson argues the case for speaking of the 'working class', but other historians argue the complexities of stratification within such broad categories as the working class and also the middle class. The 'working class' ranged from unskilled labour, who in their spare time engaged in such pursuits as gambling and pub culture, to the skilled workers who embraced certain middle-class values such as educational self-improvement, respectability, church attendance and temperance. See, for example, W Knox, 'The Political and Workplace Culture of the Scottish Working Class, 1832–1914', in W Hamish Fraser and R J Morris (eds), *People and Society in Scotland II, 1830–1914* (Edinburgh: John Donald, 1990), pp. 138–66.

43. Anthony Cooke, *A History of Drinking: The Scottish Pub since 1700* (Edinburgh: Edinburgh University Press, 2015), pp. 124–5.

44. EP, Thirty-seventh AR, 1911, pp. 22–3.

45. EP, Fourteenth AR, 1888, p. 47. When William George Teacher was killed during the Great War, his father, distiller and whisky merchant, William C Teacher, commemorated him by endowing a bed at the RHSC for £2,000 and gave £7,000 to the Western Infirmary, but also commissioned a memorial window in Hyndland Parish Church for £5,000: Hutchison et al., *Child Health in Scotland*, pp. 79–80.

46. EP, 'Supplementary to Annual Report [1888?], East Park Home for Infirm Children, Extension of Premises', p. 3.

47. EP, Sixty-sixth AR, Jan 1940, p. 25.
48. 'Voluntary' hospitals were hospitals that were funded by charitable endeavour, such as Glasgow Royal Infirmary (1794) and the Royal Hospital for Sick Children (1883).
49. EP, Forty-fifth AR, 1919, p. 7.
50. EP, Forty-sixth AR, 1920, p. 5.
51. Ibid., pp. 26–7.
52. EP, Sixty-sixth AR, Jan 1940, p. 25.
53. In Section P, Lairs Nos 487, 488, 489 and 490. EP, Minute Book, 1908–12, 17 Dec 1908, p. 16; Western Necropolis Proprietors' Register, Folio 10696; Western Necropolis Register of Interments, Folio 10696, in which twenty-one interments are recorded between 1908 and 1927.
54. EP, Minute Book 1912–29, EP2/1/4, 14 Jun 1923, p. 200.
55. Western Necropolis, Register of Lair Owners 1918–45, D-CEM1.22.2.3.3; Register of Interments, D-CEM1.22.2.7; Register of Lairs, D-CEM1.22.5.2.
56. Registration of Death, District of Kelvin, 6 Jul 1963.
57. Registration of Death, District of Largs, 6 May 1948. Register of Corrected Entries, District of Largs, Vol. 3, p. 209.
58. EP, Minute Book 1930–50, 12 May 1948, p. 241.
59. EP, Seventy-fifth AR, 1949, p. 3.
60. At the time of the death of his first wife, his address was 'Halidon', Cambuslang. When he, in turn, died in 1948, his address was 'The Grange', Grenville Drive, Cambuslang.
61. Registration of Marriage, District of Blythswood, Burgh of Glasgow, 2 Apr 1896.
62. Decennial Census, Maryhill, 1901.
63. Registration of Marriage, District of Blythswood, Burgh of Glasgow, 23 Jun 1905.
64. Decennial Census, Biggar, 1911, where Bunting was in holiday lodgings with his wife, Evelyn, and two-year-old son, Frederick.
65. Decennial Census, Pitlochry, 1921, when, again, Bunting was on holiday at the time of the census enumeration.
66. Registration of Death, District of Largs, 6 May 1948.
67. Registration of Birth, District of Milton, Burgh of Glasgow, 11 Jul 1873. Decennial Census, Parish of Milton, 1871.
68. Decennial Census, Parish of Milton, 1871; City Parish, 1881.
69. Decennial Census, Parish of Milton, 1881.
70. Registration of Death, District of Milton, 26 Jun 1879; Registration of Marriage, District of Dennistoun, 19 Mar 1880.
71. Registration of Marriage, District of Blythswood, 2 Apr 1896; Registration of Birth, Parish of Eastwood, 11 Mar 1897; Registration of Death, Parish of Cambuslang, 23 May 1904.
72. Registration of Marriage, District of Blythswood, 23 Jun 1905.
73. Registration of Births, Parish of Cambuslang, 11 Nov 1908 and 1 Dec 1912.
74. Decennial Census, Parish of Biggar, 1911; Decennial Census, Moulin Parish, Burgh of Pitlochry, 1921.

Chapter 6

1. Quoted in A K Chalmers, *The Health of Glasgow, 1818–1925: An Outline* (Glasgow: Glasgow Corporation, 1930), p. 157. Gairdner was Glasgow's first Medical Officer of Health, serving from 1863 to 1872. See obituary, 'Sir William Tennant Gairdner KCB, MD, FRCP Edin, FRS', *British Medical Journal*, 2 (2427), 6 Jul 1907, pp. 53–9.
2. EP, Sixty-fifth AR, 1939, p. 3.
3. EP, 'East Park School (trading as East Park) (A company limited by guarantee), Report and Financial Statements for the year ended 31 March 2015', EP2/1/39.
4. EP, Minute Book 1874–92, EP2/1/1, 7 Apr 1874, pp. 23–4.
5. EP, Sixteenth AR, 1890, p. 3.
6. EP, Sixty-fifth AR, 1939, p. 7.
7. EP, Sixty-second AR, 1936, front matter.

8. EP, Eighteenth AR, 1892, p. 4.

9. EP, Twenty-fourth AR, 1898, p. 5.

10. Ibid., p. 8.

11. Ibid., 10 Jul 1919, p. 146.

12. Ibid.

13. Ibid., 12 Sep 1919, p. 148.

14. Ibid., 14 Oct 1919, p. 151; 6 Nov 1919, p. 152.

15. EP, Forty-sixth AR, 1920, p. 8; Forty-seventh AR, 1921, p. 10; Forty-ninth AR, 1923/24, p. 13.

16. EP, Fifty-second AR, 1926, p. 9; Fifty-eighth AR, 1932, p. 10; Sixty-second AR, 1936, p. 10.

17. EP, Sixty-seventh AR, 1941, pp. 8–9.

18. EP, Sixty-ninth AR, 1943, p. 9.

19. EP, Seventy-fifth AR, 1949, p. 5.

20. EP, Minute Book 1874–92, EP2/1/1, 9 Oct 1874, p. 27; 6 Nov 1874, p. 32.

21. EP, Minute Book 1874–92, EP2/1/1, 20 Oct 1874, p. 28.

22. EP, Minute Book 1874–92, 6 Nov 1874, p. 33.

23. EP, Minute Book 1874–92, EP2/1/1, 2 Feb 1875, p. 44.

24. EP, Fifteenth AR, 1889, p. 4.

25. Ibid.

26. EP, Minute Book 1908–12, EP2/1/3, 3 Jun 1909, p. 33.

27. Ibid., 20 Dec 1909, p. 44.

28. EP, Minute Book 1912–29, EP2/1/4, 23 Dec 1912, p. 16.

29. EP, Minute Book 1893–1908, EP2/1/2, 13 Mar 1907, p. 202 and 10 Sep 1907, p. 211.

30. Ibid., 24 Sep 1907, p. 215. The 1911 Decennial Census for East Park shows Macnaughton, now assistant matron, as a 'hospital nurse', while the wider cohort of nursing staff, thirteen in total, were each annotated as 'sick nurse' by the enumerator. Jessie Macnaughton died in post on 9 Jan 1912: EP, Minute Book 1908–12, EP2/1/3, 9 Feb 1912, pp. 101–2.

31. Pamela Wood, 'Pus, pedagogy and practice: how "dirt" shaped surgical nurse training and hierarchies of practice, 1900–1935', in Anne Marie Rafferty, Marguerite Dupree and Fay Bound Alberti (eds), *Germs and governance: The past, present and future of hospital infection, prevention and control* (Manchester: Manchester University Press, 2021), pp. 81–4.

32. Brian Abel-Smith, *A History of the Nursing Profession* (London: Heinemann, 1960), pp. 94–8.

33. Ibid., pp. 99–100.

34. EP, Minute Book 1912–29, EP2/1/4, 23 Dec 1912, p. 16.

35. EP, Forty-first AR, 1915, p. 5. Thom left East Park the following year to nurse military personnel: EP, Forty-second AR, 1916, p. 8.

36. EP, Minute Book 1912–29, EP2/1/4, 23 Jun 1916, pp. 103–4.

37. Ibid., p. 104.

38. EP, Fifty-fifth AR, 1929, p. 22.

39. Susan McGann, 'No Wonder Nurses Quit! What the New Health Service meant for Nurses in 1948', in Chris Nottingham (ed.), *The NHS in Scotland: The legacy of the past and the prospect of the future* (Aldershot: Ashgate, 2000), p. 40.

40. EP, Minute Book 1930–50, 24 Jan 1939, pp. 113–14.

41. EP, Minute Book 1912–29, 12 Oct 1926, p. 282.

42. Interview with Elizabeth Hunter (b. 1917), 26 Aug 1999.

43. EP, Minute Book 1912–29, EP2/1/4, 22 Mar 1915, p. 71; 10 Jun 1915, p. 78. Robertson's marriage was held on 26 Jun 1915: Registration of Marriage, District of Maryhill.

44. Ibid., 9 Jan 1917, p. 111.

45. Ibid., 11 Oct 1917, p. 121; 29 Jan 1919, p. 138.

46. Decennial Census, East Park Home, Maryhill, 1881.

47. EP, Minute Book 1912–29, EP2/1/4, 13 Aug 1915, p. 84.

48. EP, Minute Book 1930–50, EP2/1/5, 10 Jun 1930, pp. 9–10.

49. Ibid., 22 Apr 1940, pp. 134–5.

50. Ibid., 26 Jul 1945, pp. 199–202; EP, Seventy-ninth AR, 1953, p. 4.

51. EP, Eighty-seventh AR, 1961, p. 6.

52. EP, Tenth AR, 1884, p. 3.

53. See Anne Marie Rafferty, Marguerite Dupree and Fay Bound Alberti (eds), *Germs and governance: The past, present and future of hospital infection, prevention and control* (Manchester: Manchester University Press, 2021).

54. EP, Minute Book 1874–92, EP2/1/1, 12 Jun 1879, p. 90. Knightswood Hospital was built between 1875 and 1877 as a joint infectious diseases hospital for the burghs of Maryhill, Hillhead and Partick.

55. EP, Minute Book 1874–92, EP2/1/1, 12 Jun 1879, p. 91.

56. Ibid.

57. Ibid.

58. Ibid., p. 90.

59. EP, Minute Book 1874–92, EP2/1/1, 28 Oct 1879, p. 96.

60. EP, Minute Book 1874–92, EP2/1/1, 12 Jun 1879, pp. 91–2.

61. EP, Seventeenth AR, 1891, p. 4.

62. 'A K Chalmers MD LLD', *British Medical Journal*, 7 Feb 1942, p. 202; 'Dr A K Chalmers', *Nature*, 7 Mar 1942, pp. 266–7.

63. EP, Minute Book 1912–29, EP2/1/4, 20 Jun 1916, pp. 101–2.

64. For an historical analysis of the pandemic in Glasgow, see Graham MacSporran, 'Influenza Epidemic in Glasgow, 1918–19: Source, Impact and Response', *Journal of Scottish Historical Studies*, 42:1 (2022), pp. 92–117. For a brief overview of the pandemic in Scotland from a medical perspective, see A R Butler and J L Hogg, 'Exploring Scotland's influenza pandemic of 1918–19: lest we forget', *Journal of the Royal College of Physicians of Edinburgh*, 37:4 (2007), pp. 362–6. For a detailed social historical study that places the influenza pandemic in a wider context, see Ida Milne's *Stacking the Coffins: Influenza, War and Revolution in Ireland* (Manchester: Manchester University Press, 2018).

65. EP, Forty-fifth AR, 1919, p. 8.

66. Ibid., p. 4; Register of Deaths, Maryhill, 22 Feb 1919.

67. EP, Forty-sixth AR, 1920, pp. 4, 6, 8.

68. A K Chalmers, *The Health of Glasgow*, p. 91.

69. EP, Minute Book 1912–29, EP2/1/4, 21 Nov 1913, pp. 39–41.

70. Ibid.

71. Ibid., 20 Jun 1916, p. 101.

72. Ibid., 27 Mar 1917, p. 113.

73. Ibid., 3 Feb 1927, p. 291.

74. EP, Sixty-fifth AR, 1939, pp. 8, 11.

75. EP, Minute Book 1912–29, EP2/1/4, 26 Jun 1923, p. 203.

76. Ibid., 16 Oct 1912, pp. 8–9.

77. Ibid., 19 Dec 1912, p. 13; McVey's retirement during 1945 is indicated by changes to holders of appointments as shown in the 71st and 72nd ARs, but is not otherwise commented upon.

78. EP, Minute Book 1912–29, 12 Dec 1913, p. 43.

79. Ibid., 16 Oct 1918, p. 134; 31 Oct 1918, p. 134.

80. Ibid., 29 Jan 1919, p. 139.

81. Ibid., 28 Jan 1920, p. 153.

82. Ibid., 20 Feb 1920, pp. 157–8.

83. Ibid., 19 May 1915, pp. 73–4; 10 Jun 1915, pp. 78–9.

84. Ibid., 29 Jan 1919, p. 139; 26 Jun 1919, pp. 145–6.

85. EP, Forty-eighth AR, 1922, p. 8.

86. Iain Hutchison et al., *Child Health in Scotland*, pp. 102, 144.

Chapter 7

1. GML, EP, Sixth AR, 1880, p. 7.
2. EP, Sixty-sixth AR, 1940, p. 13.
3. The nature of the tactile print that Ferris could read is not recorded in the East Park records, but in 1870s Glasgow it may have been Alston raised type. See Helen Dunbar, *History of the Society for the Blind in Glasgow and the west of Scotland, 1858–1989* (Glasgow: 1989), and Iain Hutchison, *Feeling our History: The experience of blindness and sight loss in Edwardian Edinburgh, the Lothians and the Scottish Borders* (Edinburgh: RNIB, 2015), pp. 48–9.
4. EP, Minute Book 1874–92, EP2/1/1, 20 Oct 1874, p. 28.
5. EP, Minute Book 1874–92, EP2/1/1, 12 Oct 1878, p. 88.
6. Decennial Census, Maryhill, 1881.
7. Registration of Birth, Calton, Glasgow, 24 Oct 1857.
8. Ibid.; Decennial Census, St James, Glasgow, 1861.
9. Decennial Census, St James, Glasgow, 1861.
10. GML, EP, Seventh AR, 1881, p. 7.
11. Ibid., pp. 12–13.
12. Ibid., p. 13.
13. EP, Minute Book 1874–92, EP2/1/1, 23 Jan 1892, pp. 148–9.
14. *1874 Centenary 1974 East Park Home* (1974) and *East Park Home for Infirm Children* (1988).
15. EP, Minute Book 1912–29, EP2/1/4, 1 May 1928, p. 339.
16. Clara Anne Bowser was born in Glasgow on 24 October 1857. The registration of her death on 29 February 1942 says that she was eighty-four when she died, but she was actually eighty-three: Registration of Death, Kelvingrove, Glasgow.
17. EP, Nineteenth AR, 1893, p. 5.
18. EP, Twenty-first AR, 1895, p. 64.
19. EP, Twenty-ninth AR, 1903, p. 5.
20. Ibid.
21. EP, Minute Book 1908–12, EP2/1/3, 12 Nov 1908, pp. 10–11.
22. EP, Minute Book 1893–1908, EP2/1/2, 4 Feb 1908, p. 221.
23. EP, Minute Book 1908–12, EP2/1/3, 3 Sep 1909, pp. 38–9; 24 Aug 1910, pp. 65–6; 4 Oct 1910, p. 73; 28 Feb 1912, p. 105; 13 Jun 1912, p. 113; 25 Jun 1912, p. 116.
24. EP, Minute Book 1912–29, EP2/1/4, pp. 3–4.
25. Ibid., 19 Dec 1912, p. 12.
26. Ibid., 18 Mar 1914, p. 47.
27. EP, Minute Book 1912–29, EP2/1/4, 15 Feb 1915, p. 67; 3 Dec 1915, pp. 91–2.
28. Ibid., 8 Mar 1916, p. 97.
29. Ibid.
30. EP, Forty-first AR, 1915, p. 2.
31. EP, Thirty-fifth AR, 1909, facing p. 1 and pp. 8, 10–11.
32. GML, EP, Sixth AR, 1880, pp. 12–13.
33. GML, EP, Sixteenth AR, 1890, p. 5.
34. EP, Forty-first AR, p. 7.
35. Ibid., pp. 9–10.
36. EP, Minute Book 1912–29, EP2/1/4, 15 Feb 1915, pp. 67–8.
37. EP, Seventeenth AR, 1891, pp. 6–7.
38. EP, Twenty-fifth AR, 1899, pp. 6–7.
39. EP, Twenty-third AP, 1897, pp. 6–7.
40. EP, Thirty-first AR, 1905, pp. 6–7.
41. See Hutchison, 'Institutionalization of mentally impaired children'.
42. Oral testimony, Mairi Smyth, 14 Apr 2023.
43. Oral testimony, Amy, 13 Sep 1999, and Michael McCready, 15 Dec 2022.
44. EP, Sixty-first AR, 1935, pp. 4, 11.
45. EP, Fifty-ninth AR, 1933, pp. 12–13.

46. EP, Sixty-third AR, 1937, p. 13.
47. EP, Sixty-fourth AR, 1938, p. 13.
48. EP, Fifty-first AR, 1925, p. 10.
49. EP, Fifty-second AR, 1926, p. 10.
50. EP, Fifty-ninth AR, 1933, p. 13.
51. EP, Sixty-third AR, 1937, p. 7.
52. At the Country Branch, schooling of children was a feature from its opening, Margaret Smith being appointed as head teacher in 1927 and assisted by certificated teacher Janet Begg: EP, Minute Book 1912–29, EP2/1/4, 2 Sep 1927, pp. 304–5; EP fifty-fourth AR, 1928, p. 6.
53. EP, Eighty-fourth AR, 1958, pp. 5, 14.
54. The founding ethos of the Boy Scout movement was laid out in Robert Baden-Powell, *Scouting for Boys* (London: Boy Scouts, 1908).

Chapter 8

1. EP, Minute Book 1874–92, EP2/1/1, printed statement affixed to inside front.
2. Ibid.
3. Ibid.
4. *The Bailie*, 31 Mar 1875, No. 128, p. 1.
5. EP, Minute Book 1874–92, EP2/1/1, 10 Feb 1874, pp. 3–4.
6. Ibid.
7. EP, Minute Book 1874–92, EP2/1/1, 24 Feb 1874, p. 7.
8. EP, Minute Book 1874–92, EP2/1/1, 6 Nov 1874, pp. 35–6.
9. EP, Minute Book 1874–92, EP2/1/1, 10 Mar 1874, p. 11.
10. EP, Minute Book 1874–92, EP2/1/1, 7 Apr 1874, p. 23.
11. EP, Twelfth AR, 1886, p. 3.
12. EP, Nineteenth AR, 1893, p. 5; Twenty-ninth AR, 1903, p. 5.
13. EP, Thirty-ninth AR, 1913, p. 87.
14. EP, Minute Book 1893–1908, 30 Nov 1894, p. 9.
15. Ibid.
16. Ibid., p. 10.
17. EP, Minute Book 1893–1903, 14 Sep 1895, p. 12.
18. ML, 'East Park Home for Infirm Children: Bazaar and Sale of Work, 19–21 December 1895', G362-780941435EAS.
19. EP, Twenty-second AR, 1896, p. 3.
20. EP, Twenty-fifth AR, 1899, pp. 28–9.
21. Ibid., p. 28.
22. Ibid., pp. 28–66.
23. Ibid., p. 22.
24. EP, Forty-sixth AR, 1920, p. 6.
25. EP, Minute Book 1912–29, EP2/1/4, pp. 31, 124. There is no apparent family connection between Susanna Clugston and Beatrice Clugston, Susanna coming from Stewarton, Ayrshire, where her father and her grandfather were Free Church ministers, while Beatrice's family were involved with textiles and dyeing in the likes of the Vale of Leven. It is earlier mentioned that when Beatrice died she had no close family relatives. Sources include Registration of Marriage, Stewarton, James and Jemima Clugston, 24 Apr 1860, and Registration of Birth, Susanna Clugston, 31 Aug 1867.
26. EP, Minute Book 1912–29, EP2/1/4, 21 Dec 1917, pp. 123–4.
27. EP, Fifty-fifth AR, 1929, p. 47.
28. EP, Sixty-eighth AR, 1942, p. 6.
29. EP, Seventy-fourth AR, 1948, p. 3.
30. EP, Eighty-third AR, 1957, pp. 16, 47–8, 50–1; EP, Thirty-ninth AR, 1913, pp. 27–86, 90.
31. EP, Minute Book 1954–64, EP2/1/7, 3 Feb 1956, p. 86.
32. EP, Eighty-second AR, 1956, p. 3.

33. EP, Minute Book 1912–29, EP2/1/4, 27 Mar 1917, p. 115.

34. www.parliament.uk/about/living-heritage/transformingsociety/electionsvoting/womenvote/parliamentary-collections/collections-the-vote-and-after/representation-of-the-people-act-1918/ [accessed 6 Dec 2022].

35. Decennial Census, Sandyford, Glasgow, 1911.

36. EP, Forty-eighth AR, 1922, p. 6; Registration of Death, Hillhead, 7 Apr 1922.

37. EP, Seventy-seventh AR, 1951, p. 4; Ninety-fifth AR, 1969, p. 4.

38. EP, Minute Book 1950–53, EP2/1/6, 13 May 1952, pp. 83–4.

39. EP, Minute Book 1930–50, EP2/1/5, 14 Jan 1948, p. 260.

40. EP, Minute Book 1874–92, EP2/1/1, 10 Feb 1874, pp. 2–4.

41. EP, Seventy-sixth AR, 1950, p. 2.

42. EP, Thirty-seventh AR, 1911, p. 5.

43. EP, Fifty-second AR, 1926, pp. 2, 4; letter, 29 Jan 1926, Buckingham Palace to East Park, appended to p. 265, EP Minute Book 1912–29, EP2/1/4.

44. EP, Eightieth AR, 1954, p. 6.

Chapter 9

1. Pippa Little, 'This was the Year', *Overwintering* (Oxford: Carcanet Press, 2012).

2. Iain Hutchison, Malcolm Nicolson and Lawrence Weaver, *Child Health in Scotland: A History of Glasgow's Royal Hospital for Sick Children* (Erskine: Scottish History Press, 2016), p. 113.

3. Ibid.

4. Personal correspondence from Laura Stevens, NHS GGC Archives with Moyra Hawthorn, 28 Sep 2023.

5. Ibid.

6. GRI, Monthly Meeting of Managers, 4 Sep 1939, HB14/1/46, p. 169.

7. GRI Medical Committee, 19 Sep 1939, HB14/1/46, p. 183.

8. EP, Sixty-sixth AR, 1940, p. 7.

9. Ibid., p. 12.

10. EP, Minute Book 1930–50, EP2/1/5, 31 Oct 1939, p. 126; Sixty-sixth AR, 1940, p. 7.

11. EP, Sixty-sixth AR, 1940, p. 7.

12. NRS, The Clydebank Blitz, 13–15 Mar 1941. https://www.nrscotland.gov.uk/research/learning/features/the-clydebank-blitz-13-15-march-1941 [accessed 30 Aug 2022].

13. Scott Hope, The Luftwaffe Bomb, Kilmun Street, Maryhill (1941). https://www.maryhillburghhalls.org.uk/blog/2020/5/8/1941-the-luftwaffe-bomb-kilmun-street-maryhill [accessed 25 Apr 2022].

14. Ibid.

15. Ibid.

16. EP, Sixty-eighth AR, 1942, p. 4.

17. EP, Minute Book 1930–50, EP2/1/5, 8 Mar 1942, p. 163.

18. EP, Sixty-ninth AR, 1943, p. 6.

19. Arthur Marwick, *The Home Front: The British and the Second World War* (London: Thames and Hudson, 1976); Bob Holman, *Champions for Children: The lives of modern childcare pioneers* (Bristol: Policy Press, 2001).

20. George C Peden, *British Economic and Social Policy: Lloyd George to Margaret Thatcher* (London: Philip Allan, 1985).

21. Jacqueline Jenkinson, *Scotland's Health 1919–1948* (Oxford: Peter Lang, 2001).

22. William Beveridge, 'The report on social security and allied services' (Beveridge Report) (London: HMSO, 1942), p. 170.

23. Ibid.

24. James Scotland, 'The Centenary of the Education (Scotland) Act of 1872', *British Journal of Educational Studies* 20:2 (Jun 1972), pp. 121–36.

25. National Assistance Act 1948.

26. David Crimmens and Ian Milligan (eds), *Facing Forward: Residential child care in the 21st century* (Lyme Regis: Russell House Publishing, 2005); Harry Hendrick, *Child Welfare: Historical dimensions,*

contemporary debate (Bristol: The Policy Press, 2003); Bob Holman, *Champions for Children: The lives of modern childcare pioneers* (Bristol: Policy Press, 2001).

27. Michael Boulton-Jones, *Glasgow Works: An account of the economy of the city* (Thatcham: Dolman Scott, 2009).

28. Sir Patrick Abercrombie and Sir Robert Hogg Mathew, 'Clyde valley regional plan: 1946: a report prepared for the Clyde valley regional planning and advisory committee: preliminary edition' (The committee, 1946).

29. Boulton-Jones, Michael, *Glasgow Works: An account of the economy of a city* (Thatcham: Dolman Scott, 2009).

30. EP, Seventy-second AR, 1946, p. 6.

31. EP, Minute Book 1930–50, EP2/1/5, 17 May 1945, p. 197.

32. EP, Seventy-second AR, 1946, p. 13.

33. Ibid.

34. EP, Minute Book 1930–50, EP2/1/5, 17 May 1945, p. 197.

35. Registration of Death, Milton, 10 Jun 1945.

36. Registration of Death, Neilston, 4 Jul 1945.

37. EP, Minute Book 1930–50, EP2/1/5, 26 Jul 1945, p. 199.

38. EP, Seventy-second AR, 1946, p. 12.

39. EP, Minute Book 1930–50, EP/2/1/5, 30 Jan 1946, p. 205.

40. EP, Seventy-third AR, 1947, EP/3/7, p. 13.

41. EP, Minute Book 1930–50, EP/2/1/5, 30 Jan 1946, p. 204.

42. EP, Minute Book 1930–50, EP/2/5, 16 Apr 1946, p. 209.

43. EP, Minute Book 1954–64, EP2/1/7, 11 May 1954, p. 23.

44. EP, Seventy-third AR, 1947, p. 12.

45. Iain Hutchison et al., *Child Health in Scotland*.

46. Ibid., p. 128.

47. EP, Seventy-fourth AR, 1948, p. 4.

48. EP, Minute Book 1930–50, EP2/1/5, 16 Apr 1946, p. 207.

49. Ibid., p. 208.

50. Ibid.

51. Ibid.

52. EP, Minute Book 1930–50, EP2/1/5, 16 Oct 1946, p. 213.

53. Ibid.

54. EP, Seventy-fifth AR, 1950, p. 14.

55. EP, Minute Book 1930–50, EP2/1/5, 8 Dec 1947, p. 227.

56. Ibid.

57. EP, Minute Book 1930–50, EP2/1/5, 3 Feb 1948, pp. 229–30.

58. Ibid., p. 230.

59. EP, Minute Book 1930-1955, EP2/1/5, 17 Feb 1946, pp. 232–4.

60. Ibid., pp. 232–3.

61. Ibid., pp. 232–4.

62. EP, Minute Book 1930–55, EP2/1/5, 2 Mar 1948, 15 Mar 1948, 25 Mar 1948, pp. 235–40.

63. Ibid., pp. 234–5.

64. Ibid., p. 239.

65. EP, Minute Book 1930–55, EP2/1/5, 11 Jun 1948, p. 247.

66. EP, Minute Book 1930–55, EP2/1/5, 6 Aug 1948, pp. 249–52.

67. ERIC, *The Children's Bowel and Bladder Charity*, https://eric.org.uk [accessed 4 Feb 2024].

68. EP, Minute Book 1930–55, EP2/1/5, 6 Aug 1948, p. 250.

69. Ibid., p. 251.

70. Ibid.

71. Ibid., p. 252.

72. EP, Minute Book 1930–55, EP2/1/5, 12 Oct 1948, p. 258.

73. Tamanna Moore, Enid M Hennessy, Jonathan Myles, Samantha J Johnson, Elizabeth S Draper, Kate L Costeloe and Neil Marlow, 'Neurological and developmental outcome in extremely preterm children born in England 1995 and 2006: the EPICure studies', *British Medical Journal* (2012), 345:e7961.

Chapter 10

1. 'The war to end all wars' was the optimistic prediction expressed by author H G Wells (1866–1946) and arose from his 1914 novel *The War That Will End War*.
2. Magnusson, *The Quarriers Story*, p. 47.
3. EP, Twenty-eighth AR, 1902, p. 3.
4. This had been noted, for example, in 1897 by Dr Bruce in his observations of the benefits that had accrued to twenty children who had been sent to Port Bannatyne on the Isle of Bute during construction work at East Park: EP, Twenty-third AR, 1897, pp. 4–5.
5. Archibald had an iron-founding business in Maryhill, while Rosie's father had operated a wine-importing business: Registration of Marriage, Rosie Fraser and Archibald McInnes Shaw, 5 Nov 1891, District of Blythswood.
6. EP, Thirty-sixth AR, 1910, pp. 3–4.
7. EP, 'East Park Home: Suggestion for a Country Branch', memorandum by William Bunting appended to EP, Thirty-sixth AR, 1910, EP3/2.
8. EP, Minute Book 1912–29, EP2/1/4, 25 Jun 1913, p. 28.
9. Ibid., pp. 28–9.
10. Ibid.
11. Ibid., p. 29.
12. Ibid., 9 Oct 1914, p. 62.
13. EP, Fifty-first AR, 1925, p. 4.
14. EP, Jubilee AR, 1923/4, p. 3.
15. https://www.geograph.org.uk/photo/6010359 [accessed 20 Oct 2022].
16. The records of J & P Coats and its associated companies are held by Glasgow University Archives, GB249 UGD 199.
17. Decennial censuses, Largs, 1891 and 1901.
18. EP, Jubilee AR, 1923/4, p. 3.
19. EP, 16-page supplement, p. 7, contained in the Fifty-fourth AR, 1928. The Battle of Largs of 1263 ended Viking ascendancy over large parts of Scotland. In light of East Park's later fight to ward off being incorporated into the NHS after the Second World War, the self-description here of Warren Park being a 'Hospital' is interesting.
20. Ibid., p. 9.
21. Ibid., p. 11.
22. Death Registration, 6 Feb 1928, Largs.
23. North Ayrshire Council, Register of Lairs, Haylie Bank Cemetery, Section Y, lairs 395, 396 and 397.
24. Sculptor's quotation of £58 10s was accepted in 1949 for a 'Creetown granite cross' of five feet in height: EP, Minute Book 1930–50, EP2/1/5, 8 Nov 1949, p. 308.
25. EP, Minute Book 1930–50, EP2/1/5, pp. 153–4.
26. Ibid., pp. 162–4.
27. Ibid., p. 164.
28. Amy (pseud.), oral testimony, 13 Sep 1999.
29. Documentary sources, such as the records of the RHSC where Amy had experienced several admissions to the orthotics department, support a high degree of accuracy in Amy's recollections.
30. Amy, 13 Sep 1999.
31. Ibid.
32. EP, Minute Book 1930–50, 22 Apr 1940, pp. 134–5.
33. EP, Eightieth AR, 1954, p. 3.

34. EP, Minute Book 1912–29, EH2/1/4, 6 Jul 1926, pp. 272–3 and 12 Jul 1926, pp. 274–5.
35. Ibid., 15 Mar 1927, p. 293.
36. Ibid.
37. Ibid., p. 294.
38. Ibid., 22 Apr 1927, p. 298.
39. Callum G Brown, 'Religion and Secularism', in Tony Dickson and James H Treble (eds), *People and Society in Scotland III, 1914–1990* (Edinburgh: John Donald, 1992), p. 52.
40. EP, Minute Book 1912–29, EH2/1/4, 30 Aug 1928, pp. 350–1.
41. Ibid., p. 352.
42. Michael McCready, oral testimony, 15 Dec 2022.
43. Ibid.
44. Frank died at Largs in 1960 at the age of thirteen.
45. Michael McCready, 15 Dec 2022.
46. EP, Country Branch Register of School Pupils 1951–83, EP4/2, admission nos. 1–21.
47. Ibid., admission nos. 855–79.
48. EP, 111th AR, 1985, p. 4.
49. Elizabeth (pseud.), oral testimony, 16 Mar 2023.
50. Ibid.; EP, 112th AR, 1985, p. 11.
51. Elizabeth.
52. W A F Browne, *What asylums were, are and ought to be* (Edinburgh, 1837).
53. 'Remembering the Lochgelly Tawse', *The Scotsman*, 4 Sep 2018.
54. Mairi Smyth, oral testimony, 14 Apr 2023.
55. Ibid.
56. Ibid.
57. EP, Minute Book 1980–92, 20 Jun 1985, p. 319; 13 Aug 1985, p. 323.
58. Ibid.
59. Mairi Smyth, oral testimony, 14 Apr 2023 and telephone conversation 20 Jul 2023. A request to the Board by the Chamber for permission to make a survey was refused, but it made its survey without Board permission: EP, Minute Book 1980–92, 14 Jan 1986, p. 361.
60. EP, 105th AR, 1978, p. 9; Largs Registration Book East Park Home School, EP4/2.
61. EP, 111th AR, 1984, p. 5.
62. EP, 113th AR, 1986, pp. 5, 11, 12, 15; 114th AR, 1987, pp. 4–5.
63. EP, Ninety-fifth AR, 1968, p. 4.
64. EP, 111th AR, 1984, p. 10.
65. https://www.geograph.org.uk/photo/6010359 [accessed 20 Oct 2022].
66. https://www.largsandmillportnews.com/news/20129081.demolition-day-final-pieces-warren-park-torn/ [accessed 20 Oct 2022].

Chapter 11

1. EP, Sixty-sixth AR, 1940, p. 12.
2. EP, Seventy-second AR, 1946, p. 10.
3. EP, Seventy-third AR, 1947, p. 13.
4. Ibid.
5. EP, Seventy-third AR, 1947, p. 13.
6. EP, Seventy-fourth AR, 1948, p. 13.
7. Ibid., p. 11.
8. Dr Livingstone, physician at East Park from 1970, was later to report that a Senior Orthopaedic Surgeon at Yorkhill Hospital said that East Park had children with the greatest variety of medical and orthopaedic problems under one roof in the whole of Scotland. Written testimony, Dr William Livingstone, 6 Oct 2023.
9. EP, Seventy-fourth AR, 1948, pp. 8–10.
10. EP, Seventy-fifth AR, 1949, p. 9.
11. EP, Seventy-sixth AR, 1950, p. 14.

12. EP, Seventy-sixth AR, 1950, p. 3.
13. EP, Seventy-fifth AR, 1949, p. 3.
14. EP, Minute Book 1930–50, EP2/1/5, 14 Dec 1948, p. 262; EP, Seventy-fifth AR, 1949, p. 4.
15. EP, Seventy-sixth AR, 1950, pp. 3–4.
16. Ibid., p. 4.
17. EP, Seventy-seventh AR, 1951, p. 13.
18. Evelyn Mellan, Childhood Memories of Back Court Concerts. Written submission, 19 Jul 2022.
19. T M Devine, 'The Sixties in Scotland: A Historical Context', in Eleanor Bell and Linda Gunn (eds), *The Scottish Sixties. Reading, Rebellion, Revolution?* (Amsterdam and New York: Rodolpi, 2013), pp. 23–46 (p. 31).
20. Ibid.
21. Michael Boulton-Jones, *Glasgow Works An account of the economy of a City* (Thatcham: Dolman Scott, 2009).
22. Ibid.
23. Barry Hazley, Lynn Abrams, Ade Kearns and Valerie Wright, 'Place, memory and the British high rise experience: negotiating social change on the Wyndford Estate, 1962–2015', *Contemporary British History*, 35:1 (2021), pp. 72–99.
24. (SRO) SSHA Minutes of the Council of Management, 1960, p. 70, in Barry Hazley, Lynn Abrams, Ade Kearns and Valerie Wright, 'Place, memory and the British high rise experience: negotiating social change on the Wyndford Estate, 1962–2015', *Contemporary British History*, 35:1 (2021), pp. 72–99.
25. EP, Seventy-fifth AR, 1949, p. 3.
26. Ibid., p. 13.
27. Cerebral Palsy Scotland. 2022. *What is Cerebral Palsy?* https://cerebralpalsyscotland.org.uk/get-information/what-is-cerebral-palsy/ [accessed 25 Jan 2023].
28. Moyra Hawthorn. Personal correspondence, 18 Jan 2023, with Capability Scotland.
29. EP, Minute Book 1939–59, EP2/1/5, 14 Mar 1950, p. 329.
30. Ibid.; EP, Minute Book 1939–59, EP2/1/5, 11 Apr 1950, p. 332.
31. EP, Minute Book 1930–50, EP2/1/5, 12 Apr 1949, p. 280.
32. Ibid.
33. EP, Minute Book 1930–50, EP2/1/5, 2 Jun 1949, pp. 290–1.
34. EP, Seventy-sixth AR, 1950, p. 10.
35. EP, Minute Book 1939–1950, EP2/1/5, 2 Jun 1949, pp. 290–1.
36. EP, Seventy-sixth AR, Jan 1950, p. 10.
37. EP, Minute Book 1939–50, EP2/1/5, 13 Jun 1950, pp. 344–5; EP, Seventy-seventh AR, 1951, p. 10.
38. EP, Seventy-sixth AR, 1950, p. 10.
39. EP, Seventy-fifth AR, 1949, p. 9; Seventy-seventh AR, Jan 1951, p. 10.
40. EP, Seventy-sixth AR, Jan 1950, p. 3.
41. EP, Minute Book 1939–50, EP2/1/5, 11 Apr 1950, p. 333; Seventy-seventh AR, Jan 1951, p. 10.
42. EP, Minute Book 1939–50, EP2/1/5, 12 Sep 1950, p. 361.
43. EP, Seventy-seventh AR, 1951, p. 10.
44. Ibid.
45. EP, Minute Book 1939–50, EP/1/5, 9 May 1950, p. 336; EP, Minute Book.1939–50, EP/1/5, 15 Jun 1950, p. 342.
46. EP, Seventy-sixth AR, 1950, pp. 8–9.
47. Lesley Fox, *As Long as We've Got a Voice: The Life of Jimmy McIntosh* (Edinburgh: Thirsty Books, 2022).
48. Ibid., p. 21.
49. Ibid.
50. Supplement to the *London Gazette*, of Friday, 30 December, 2005, 57855, 1 Jan 2006, p. 19. https://www.thegazette.co.uk/all-notices/notice?service=all-notices&text=James+Alexander+McIntosh [accessed 19 Nov 2023]; Lesley Fox, *As Long as We've Got a Voice: The Life of Jimmy McIntosh.* (Edinburgh: Thirsty Books, 2002), p. 181.

51. Ibid., p. 23.
52. Ibid., p. 24.
53. Ibid., pp. 23–4.
54. Ibid., p. 23.
55. Ibid., p. 24.
56. Ibid.
57. Ibid., p. 27.
58. Lesley Fox, *As Long as We've Got a Voice: The Life of Jimmy McIntosh* (Edinburgh: Thirsty Books, 2022), p. 230.
59. EP, Minute Book 1950–3, EP2/1/6, 13 Oct 1953, pp. 157–8; EP, Minute Book 1954–64, EP2/1/7, 12 Oct 1954, p. 36.
60. EP, Seventy-eighth AR, 1952, p. 9.
61. Supplement to the *London Gazette* of Tuesday, 30 December, 1952, 39732, 1 Jan 1953, p. 18. https://www.thegazette.co.uk/London/issue/39732/data.pdf [accessed 20 Nov 2023]; EP, Eightieth AR, 1954, p. 3.
62. EP, Minute Book 1954–64, EP2/1/7, 11 Oct 1955, p. 1.
63. Oral testimony, Jean, who trained at East Park 1956–8.
64. EP, Minute Book 1954–64, EP2/1/7, 11 May 1954, p. 23.
65. EP, Minute Book 1954–64, EP2/1/7, 12 Oct 1954, p. 36.
66. EP, Eighty-first AR, 1955, p. 9.
67. EP, Seventy-ninth AR, 1953, p. 4.
68. EP, Eighty-first AR, 1955, p. 9.
69. EP, Minute Book 1950–3, EP2/1/6, 11 Mar 1952, p. 76 and 8 Apr 1952, pp. 78–9; EP, Seventy-ninth AR, 1953, p. 3.
70. EP, Eightieth AR, 1954, p. 3.
71. EP, Eighty-third AR, 1957, p. 8.
72. Ibid.
73. EP, Eighty-sixth AR, 1960, p. 3.
74. EP, Eighty-eighth AR, 1962, p. 12.
75. T M Devine, 'The Sixties in Scotland: A Historical Context', in Eleanor Bell and Linda Gunn (eds), *The Scottish Sixties. Reading, Rebellion, Revolution?* (Amsterdam and New York: Rodolpi, 2013), pp. 23–46 (p. 31).
76. Ibid., p. 28.
77. Ibid.
78. Ibid.
79. EP, Minute Book 1930–50, EP2/1/5, 6 Aug 1948, pp. 249–51.
80. EP, Seventy-eighth AR, 1952, p. 4.
81. EP, Eighty-first AR, 1955, pp. 8–9.
82. EP, Eighty-third AR, 1957, p. 11.
83. EP, Eighty-sixth AR, 1960, p. 10.
84. EP, Eighty-sixth AR, 1960, p. 8; EP, Minute Book 1954–64, EP2/1/7, 14 Apr 1959.
85. EP, Eighty-seventh AR, 1961, p. 4.
86. EP, Ninetieth AR, 1964, p. 4.
87. Ibid.
88. EP, Ninety-third AR, 1967, p. 10.
89. EP, Ninety-second AR, 1966, p. 7.
90. Tamanna Moore, Enid M Hennessey, Jonathan Myles, Samantha J Johnson, Elizabeth S Draper, Kate L Costeloe and Neil Marlow. 'Neurological and developmental outcomes in preterm children born in England in 1995 and 2006: the EPICure studies', *BMJ*, 4 Dec 2012.
91. EP, Ninety-first AR, 1965, p. 7.
92. EP, Minute Book 1954–64, EP2/1/7, 11 Oct 1955, p. 73.
93. EP, Eighty-sixth AR, 1960, p. 4.
94. EP, Minute Book 1950–3, EP2/1/6, 13 May 1952, p. 85 and 10 Jun, pp. 88–9.

95. EP, Minute Book 1954–64, EP2/1/7, 8 Oct 1963, p. 345.

96. Ibid.

97. EP, Minute Book 1954–64, EP2/1/7, 12 Nov 1963, p. 347.

98. EP, Minute Book, 1954–64, EP2/1/7, 10 Dec 1963, p. 357.

99. EP, Ninety-second AR, 1966, p. 13.

100. EP, Ninety-ninth AR, 1973, p. 7.

101. Marion McLarty and Moyra Hawthorn, 'Special Educational Needs: Working with Children and Families', in Deborah Baillie, Kathryn Cameron, Lesley-Anne Cull, Jeremy Roche and Janice West (eds), *Social Work and the Law in Scotland*. (Basingstoke: Palgrave Macmillan, 2003), pp. 191–202.

102. Wendy Hewitson, Joyce Hawthorn, Moyra Hawthorn and Carolyn Johnston, 'The Famous Five Adventures', WDSC Conference, Glasgow, 24–27 Jul 2018.

103. EP, Eighty-fourth AR, 1958, p. 9.

104. Ibid.

105. Lesley Fox, *As Long as We've Got a Voice: The Life of Jimmy McIntosh* (Edinburgh: Thirsty Books, 2022), pp. 23–4.

106. EP, Ninety-third AR, 1967, p. 8.

107. Frank C P van der Horst and René van der Veer, 'Changing attitudes towards the care of children in hospital: A new assessment of the influence of the work of Bowlby and Robertson in the UK, 1940–1970', *Attachment & Human Development*, 11(2), pp. 119–42; John Bowlby, 'The Nature of the Child's Tie to his Mother', *International Journal of Psycho-Analysis*, 39 (1958), pp. 350–73; J A Robertson, *A Two Year Old Goes to Hospital* (Film), http://www.robertsonfilms.info/2_year_old.htm [accessed 23 Jan 2023].

108. Ministry of Health, *The welfare of children in hospital. Platt Report*. London: HMSO, 1959.

109. EP, Eighty-fifth AR, 1959, pp. 11–12.

110. EP, Minute Book, EP2/1/7, 11 Oct 1960, p. 217.

111. Tom Shaw, *Historic Abuse Systemic Review: Residential Schools and Children's Homes in Scotland 1950–1995*, The Scottish Government, 2007, p. 65.

112. Ibid., pp. 65–6; Brigid Daniel and Jane Scott, '50th Anniversary: Social Work Scotland Act', *Social Work Scotland*, p. 5, https://socialworkscotland.org/sws-projects/50th-anniversary-of-the-social-work-scotland-act-1968/[accessed 26 Jan 2023].

113. McBoyle Report, *Report of the Committee of the Scottish Advisory Council on Child Care* (1963).

114. Kilbrandon Report, *Report of the Committee on Children and Young Persons, Scotland*. Edinburgh: HMSO, 1964.

115. Social Work and the community: proposals for reorganizing local authority services in Scotland: presented to Parliament by the Secretary of State for Scotland … October, 1966 (Edinburgh: HMSO, 1966).

116. Tom Shaw, *Historic Abuse Systemic Review: Residential Schools and Children's Homes in Scotland 1950–1995*, The Scottish Government, 2007, p. 65.

117. Ibid.; Children and Families Directorate (Dec 2018), *Progressing the Human Rights of Children in Scotland: A Report 2015–2018. Report to the Scottish Parliament under part 1 of The Children and Young Person (Scotland) Act 2014*, p. 116, https://www.gov.scot/binaries/content/documents/govscot/publications/progress-report/2018/12/progressing-human-rights-children-scotland-report-2015-2018/documents/00544569-pdf/00544569-pdf/govscot%3Adocument/00544569.pdf [accessed 26 Jan 2023].

118. Brigid Daniel and Jane Scott, '50th Anniversary: Social Work Scotland Act', *Social Work Scotland*, p. 5, https://socialworkscotland.org/sws-projects/50th-anniversary-of-the-social-work-scotland-act-1968/ [accessed 26 Jan 2023].

119. Kenneth McKenzie Norrie (2017), *Legislative Background to Children Living Apart from their Parents*. https://www.childabuseinquiry.scot/sites/default/files/2023-03/norrie_legislative-background-to-the-treatment-of-childrenyoungpeople-bmd-181017.pdf, p. 69 [accessed 18 Dec 2023].

120. Ibid., p. 70.

121. Brigid Daniel and Jane Scott, '50th Anniversary: Social Work Scotland Act', Social Work Scotland, p. 5, https://socialworkscotland.org/sws-projects/50th-anniversary-of-the-social-work-scotland-act-1968/ [accessed 26 Jan 2023].

122. Ibid.
123. EP, Minute Book, EP/2/7, 26 Nov 1963, pp. 151–2.
124. EP, Minute Book, EP/2/7, 11 Feb 1964, p. 371.
125. EP, Ninety-second AR, 1966, p. 9.
126. EP, Ninety-third AR, 1967, p. 9.
127. EP, Ninety-eighth AR, 1972, p. 8.

Chapter 12

1. EP, Eighty-sixth AR, 1960, p. 8.
2. The Office of the High Commissioner for Human Rights (OHCHR), *Convention on the Rights of the Child*, Adopted and opened for signature, ratification and accession by General Assembly resolution 44/25 of 20 November 1989. Entry into force 2 September 1990, in accordance with article 49. https://www.ohchr.org/sites/default/files/Documents/ProfessionalInterest/crc.pdf
3. Scottish Government, Keeping the Promise Implementation Plan, 30 Mar 2022, https://www.gov.scot/publications/keeping-promise-implementation-plan/pages/2/ [accessed 3 Feb 2023]; The Independent Care Review, *The Promise*, 30 Mar 2022, p. 26, https://www.carereview.scot/wp-content/uploads/2020/02/The-Promise.pdf [accessed 19 Apr 2023].
4. EP, Eighty-sixth AR, 1960, p. 8.
5. Oral testimony, Elizabeth Thompson, 13 Mar 2023.
6. Ibid.
7. Kenneth McKenzie Norrie (2017), *Legislative Background to Children Living Apart from their Parents*. https://www.childabuseinquiry.scot/sites/default/files/2023-03/norrie_legislative-background-to-the-treatment-of-childrenyoungpeople-bmd-181017.pdf, p. 203 [accessed 18 Dec 2023]; EP Minute Book 1954–64, EP2/1/7, 8 Aug 1961, p. 249.
8. EP, Eighty-seventh AR, 1961, p. 9.
9. Ruth Emond, 'An outsider's view of the inside', in David Crimmens and Ian Milligan (eds), *Facing Forward: Residential Child Care in the 21st Century* (Lyme Regis: Russell House Publishing, 2005), pp. 127–36; Moyra Hawthorn, PhD Thesis, 2018, *Looking Back and Moving Forward: An Exploration of Survivors' Narratives of Historical Institutional Child Abuse*; Lesley Fox, *As Long as We've Got a Voice: The Life of Jimmy McIntosh* (Edinburgh: Thirsty Books, 2022), p. 24.
10. Ibid.
11. Oral testimony, Elizabeth Thompson, 13 Mar 2023.
12. Ibid.
13. Ibid.
14. Lesley Fox, *As Long as We've Got a Voice: The Life of Jimmy McIntosh* (Edinburgh: Thirsty Books, 2022), p. 24.
15. Ibid.
16. Ibid.
17. Lesley Fox, *As Long as We've Got a Voice: The Life of Jimmy McIntosh* (Edinburgh: Thirsty Books, 2022), p. 22–3.
18. Ibid., pp. 21, 27.
19. Ibid., pp. 22–3.
20. Ibid., p. 23.
21. Oral testimony, Elizabeth Thompson, 13 Mar 2023.
22. EP, Seventy-fifth AR, 1949, p. 12; EP Minute Book, EP2/1/5, 1930–50, 3 Aug 1950, p. 359; EP, Seventy-eighth AR, 1952, p. 13.
23. Oral testimony, Elizabeth Thompson, 13 Mar 2023.
24. EP, Seventy-fifth AR, 1949, p. 13.
25. EP, Minute Book 1950–3, EP2/1/6, 14 Apr 1953, pp. 134–5; EP, Minute Book 1950–3, EP2/1/6, 9 Jun 1953, p. 151.
26. EP, Minute Book 1950–3, EP/2/1/6, 9 Jun 1953, p. 147; EP, Minute Book, EP/2/1/6, Board Minutes, 1950–3, EP2/1/6, 10 Nov 1953, p. 162.
27. EP, Minute Book 1954–64, EP/2/1/7, 14 May 1957, p. 1.

28. EP Eightieth AR, 1954, p. 3.
29. EP, Eighty-first AR, 1955, p. 3.
30. EP, Eighty-third AR, 1957, p. 3; EP, Eighty-fourth AR, 1958, pp. 3, 5.
31. EP, Board Minutes, 9 Sep 1958, p. 146; Eighty-fifth AR, Jan 1959, p. 12.
32. EP, Eighty-ninth AR, 1963, p. 3.
33. EP, Minute Book 1954–64, EP/2/1/7, 9 Jul 1963; EP, Ninetieth AR, 1964, p. 8; EP, Ninety-first AR, 1965, p. 9.
34. EP, Minute Book 1954–64, EP2/1/7, 11 Oct 1955, p. 74; EP, Minute Book 1954–64, EP/2/1/7, 9 Jul 1963, p. 337; EP, Minute Book 1954–64, EP2/1/7, 12 Mar 1963, p. 324; EP, Minute Book, 1954–64, EP/2/1/7, 12 Oct 1954, p. 36; EP, Eighty-fifth AR, Jan 1959, p. 14.
35. EP, Minute Book 1954–1964, EP2/1/7, 11 Sep 1962, p. 302; EP, Ninetieth AR, Jan 1964, p. 8; EP, Ninety-fifth AR, 1969, p. 9.
36. EP, Minute Book, 1954–64, EP2/1/7, 12 Feb 1963, p. 319; EP, Ninety-second AR, 1966, p. 13.
37. EP, Ninety-second AR, 1966, p. 13; EP, Ninety-third AR, 1967, p. 13; EP, Ninety-first AR, 1965, p. 9.
38. EP, Ninety-fourth AR, 1968, p. 9.
39. EP, Minute Book, 1954–64, EP/2/7, 10 Oct 1961, p. 262.
40. EP, Ninety-first AR, 1965, p. 9.
41. EP, Ninety-first AR, 1965, p. 13; EP, Ninety-first AR, 1965, p. 9.
42. EP, Ninety-third AR, 1967, p. 13.
43. Ibid.; EP, Ninety-sixth AR, 1970, p. 9.
44. EP, Minute Book 1954–64, EP2/1/7, 10 Oct 1961, p. 262.
45. EP, Eighty-first AR, 1955, p. 14.
46. EP, Ninety-third AR, 1967; Ninety-fifth AR, 1969, p. 12; EP, Eight-first AR, Jan 1955, p. 14; EP, Ninety-fifth AR, 1969, p. 12.
47. EP, Eighty-first AR, Jan 1955, p. 14; EP, Ninety-second AR, 1966, p. 12.
48. EP, Ninety-second AR, 1966, p. 12.
49. EP, Ninety-third AR, 1967, p. 12; EP, Ninety-fifth AR, 1969, p. 12.
50. EP, Ninety-third AR, 1967, p. 12.
51. EP, Eighty-ninth AR, 1963, p. 13.
52. EP, Ninety-fourth AR, 1968, p. 12.
53. Ibid.
54. EP, Eighty-eighth AR, 1962, p. 12; EP, Minute Book, 1954–64, EP2/1/7, 11 Jul 1961, p. 247.
55. EP, Ninety-first AR, 1965, p. 9.
56. Scouts, 2023, *How Scouting Grew*. https://www.scouts.org.uk/about-us/our-history/how-scouting-grew/ [accessed 3 Feb 2023].
57. World Association of Girl Guides and Girl Scouts, 2023. https://www.wagggs.org/en/about-us/our-history/ [accessed 14 Apr 2023].
58. Ibid.
59. EP, Fifty-second AR, 1926, p.10.
60. Personal correspondence and *The First Fifty Years* (nd), Scouts Scotland with Moyra Hawthorn, 15 Feb 2023; EP, Fifty-eighth AR, 1932, p. 11.
61. Ibid.
62. EP, Eighty-first AR, 1955, p. 13.
63. Alison Maloney, *Something for the Girls, The Official Guide to the First 100 Years of Guiding* (London: Constable, 2009).
64. Ibid.
65. EP, Fifty-first AR, 1925, p. 10.
66. Ibid.; EP, Fifty-sixth AR, 1930, p. 11.
67. EP, Eighty-first AR, 1955, p. 14; EP, Ninety-first AR, 1965, p. 12.
68. Personal correspondence, Archivist, Girlguiding Ayrshire North with Moyra Hawthorn, 21 Oct 2023; EP, Eighty-ninth AR, 1963, p. 13.
69. EP, Eighty-second AR, 1956, p. 14.
70. EP, Eighty-fifth AR, 1959, p. 12.

71. Personal correspondence and *The First Fifty Years* (nd), Scouts Scotland, with Moyra Hawthorn, 15 Feb 2023.

72. EP, Ninety-second AR, 1966, p. 12.

73. EP, Eighty-second AR, 1956, p. 5; EP, Eighty-sixth AR, 1960, pp. 12–13; EP, Ninetieth AR, 1964, p. 11.

74. EP, Minute Book, 1954–64, EP2/1/7, 11 May 1954, p. 23.

75. EP, Eighty-third AR, 1957, p. 13.

76. EP, Ninety-fourth AR, 1968, p. 12.

77. EP, Ninety-first AR, 1965, pp. 9, 11.

78. Ibid., p. 12.

79. EP, Ninety-second AR, 1966, p. 11; EP, Ninety-fifth AR, 1969 pp. 9–10.

80. Personal correspondence, County Archivist, Girlguiding Glasgow with Moyra Hawthorn, 25 Mar 2023.

81. Personal correspondence and *The First Fifty Years* (nd), Scouts Scotland with Moyra Hawthorn, 25 Mar 2023.

82. Personal correspondence, County Archivist, Girlguiding Glasgow with Moyra Hawthorn, 25 Mar 2023.

83. Lynn Abrams, *The Orphan Country, Children from Scotland's Broken Homes from 1845 to the Present Day* (Glasgow: Bell and Bain, 1998).

84. EP, Minute Book, 1930–50, EP2/1/5, 8 Nov 1949, p. 308; EP, Minute Book, 1930–50, EP2/1/5, 12 Apr 1949, pp. 280–1.

85. EP, Minute Book, 1950–3, EP2/1/6, 11 Dec 1951, p. 62.

86. EP, Seventy-fourth AR, Jan 1948, p. 12; EP, Minutes, 13 Dec 1961, p. 272.

87. EP, Minute Book, 1954–64, EP2/1/7, 14 Dec 1954, p. 45; EP, Eighty-first AR, 1955, p. 3; EP, Minute Book, 1954–64, EP2/1/7, 13 Dec 1961, p. 272.

88. EP, Minute Book, 1950–3, EP2/1/6, 8 Dec 1953, p. 168.

89. Ibid.; EP, Minute Book, 1954–64, EP2/1/7, 13 Mar 1956, p. 90.

90. EP, Minute Book, 1954–64, EP2/1/7, 12 Apr 1960, p. 195.

91. EP, 102nd AR, 1976, p .8; EP, 103rd AR, 1977, p. 9; EP, 105th AR, 1979, p. 10; EP, 106th AR, 1980, p. 11.

92. EP, 104th AR, 1978, p. 9; EP, 106th AR, 1980, p. 11; EP, 107th AR, 1981, p. 12.

93. EP, 106th Annual Report, 1980, p. 11.

94. EP, Minute Book, 1930–50, EP2/1/5, 8 Mar 1949, pp. 275, 278.

95. EP, Ninety-fifth AR, 1969, p. 9.

96. Written testimony, Catriona Campbell, 11 Sep 2023.

97. Oral testimony, Elizabeth Thompson, 13 Mar 2023.

98. EP, Ninetieth AR, 1964, p. 13.

99. EP, Sixty-sixth AR, 1940, pp. 12–13.

100. EP, Seventy-first AR, 1945, p. 10.

101. EP, Eighty-fourth AR, 1958, p. 13.

102. EP, Minute Book, 1950–3, EP2/1/6, 9 Oct 1951, p. 52.

103. Anchorline. RMS *Caledonia V* 1948. http://ssmaritime.com/MS-Circassia-Cilicia-Caledonia.htm [accessed 16 Apr 2023].

104. EP, Minute Book, 1930–50, EP2/1/5, 13 Sep 1949, p. 299.

105. Ibid.

106. EP, Minute Book, 1930–50, EP2/1/5, 11 Oct 1949, p. 303; EP, Minute Book, 1930–50, EP2/1/5, 8 Nov 1949, p. 307; EP, Minute Book, 1950–3, EP2/1/6, 9 Oct 1951, p. 52.

107. EP, Minute Book, 1930–50, EP2/1/5, 8 Nov 1949 p. 307.

108. EP, Minute Book, 1930–50, EP2/1/5, 13 Dec 1949, p. 313.

109. RMS *Caronia* Timeline. https://caronia2.info/home.php_ [accessed 29 Mar 2023].

110. EP, Minute Book, EP2/1/6, 1950-1953, 7 Aug 1951, pp. 38–9.

111. EP, Eighty-third AR, 1957, p. 13.

112. EP, Minute Book, 1950–3, EP2/1/6, 7 Aug 1951, p. 39.

113. EP, Ninety-fourth AR, 1968, p. 9; RMS *Caronia* Timeline. https://www.caronia2.info/yr1967.php [accessed 29 Mar 2023].

114. EP, Ninety-fourth AR, 1969, p. 9.

115. EP, Minute Book, EP2/1/6, 1950–3, 9 Oct 1951, p. 52.

116. Ibid.

117. Ibid., pp. 52–3.

118. Seventy-fifth AR, 1949, p. 7; Seventy-eighth AR, 1952, p. 6; Seventy-ninth AR, 1953, p. 6.

119. Lesley Fox, *As Long as We've Got a Voice: The Life of Jimmy McIntosh* (Edinburgh: Thirsty Books, 2022), p. 25.

120. East Park Patter, *Partick Thistle Training*, Issue 12, Jun 2017, p. 4.

121. Brian Reilly, *Up and Down the Hill, A History of Maryhill Football Club* (Lulu Press, 2009), p. 13, https://www.lulu.com

122. Written testimony, David Pool, 4 Oct 2023.

123. EP, Seventy-seventh AR, 1951, p. 13; EP, Ninety-first AR, 1965, p. 9.

124. Glasgow Taxi Outing Fund. *Goin tae Troon since 1945.* https://gtof.org.uk [accessed 16 Apr 2023].

125. EP, Ninety-second AR, 1966, p. 12; Ninety-eighth AR, 1972, p. 12.

126. EP, 113th AR, 1987, p. 12.

127. Ibid.

128. Lesley Fox, *As Long as We've Got a Voice: The Life of Jimmy McIntosh* (Edinburgh: Thirsty Books, 2022), p. 25.

129. Oral testimony, Elizabeth Thompson, 13 Mar 2023.

Chapter 13

1 . A.E.S.P., *1874 Centenary 1974.* East Park Home.

2. Tom Devine, 'The Sixties in Scotland: A Historical Context', in Eleanor Bell and Linda Gunn (eds), *The Scottish Sixties: Reading, Rebellion, Revolution?* (Amsterdam and New York: Rodolpi, 2013), pp. 23–46 (p. 23).

3. EP, Ninety-second AR, 1966, p. 4; Written testimony, David Pool, 4 Oct 2023.

4. Written testimony, Dr William Livingstone, 6 Oct 2023.

5. Ibid.

6. Oral testimony, Tristan (pseud.), 26 Sep 2023; EP, Ninety-seventh AR, 1971, p. 9; EP, Ninety-eighth AR, 1972, p. 8.

7. EP, Ninety-ninth AR, 1973, p. 5.

8. Michael Boulton-Jones, *Glasgow Works: An account of the economy of a city* (Thatcham: Dolman Scott, 2009), p. 67.

9. Personal communication, Aurora Degnan, Maryhill Burgh Halls Trust, 5 Jun 2023.

10. EP, Ninety-eighth AR, 1972, p. 13.

11. EP, 115th AR, 1989, p. 11.

12. *The Scotsman*, 'What Impact has the City of Culture had on Glasgow – 30 years on', 12 Oct 2020.

13. EP, 117th AR, 1991, p. 13.

14. Kenneth McKenzie Norrie (2017), *Legislative Background to Children Living Apart from their Parents, Part 1: The Statutory Framework.* p. 72. https://www.childabuseinquiry.scot/sites/default/files/2023-03/norrie_legislative-background-to-the-treatment-of-childrenyoungpeople-bmd-181017.pdf

15. David Ross, *Scotland: History of a Nation* (Glasgow: Geddes and Grosset, 2000), pp. 22, 357.

16. Strathclyde Regional Council, *Room to Grow*, 1979, p. 13.

17. Andrew Kendrick, Erin Lux, Sharon McGregor and Richard Withington, *Development of Children's Care Services in Scotland: Report for the Child Abuse Inquiry*, 2021, p. 244. https://pureportal.strath.ac.uk/en/publications/development-of-childrens-care-services-in-scotland-report-for-the [accessed 20 Sep 2023].

18. Marion McLarty and Moyra Hawthorn, 'Special Educational Needs: Working with Children and Families', in Deborah Baillie, Kathryn Cameron, Lesley-Anne Cull, Jeremy Roche and Janice West (eds), *Social Work and the Law in Scotland* (Basingstoke: Palgrave Macmillan in association with The Open University, 2003), pp. 191–202.

19. EP, Ninety-second AR, 1966, p. 13.
20. Committee of Enquiry into the Education of Handicapped Children and Young People, *Special Educational Needs* (Warnock Report) (London: HMSO, 1978); Her Majesty's Inspector of Schools, *The Education of Pupils with Learning Difficulties in Primary and Secondary Schools in Scotland* (Edinburgh: HMSO, 1978).
21. Marion McLarty and Moyra Hawthorn, 'Special Educational Needs: Working with Children and Families', in Deborah Baillie, Kathryn Cameron, Lesley-Anne Cull, Jeremy Roche and Janice West (eds), *Social Work and the Law in Scotland* (Basingstoke: Palgrave Macmillan in association with The Open University, 2003), pp. 191–202.
22. Ibid., p. 201.
23. Lesley Fox, *As Long as We've Got a Voice: The Life of Jimmy McIntosh* (Edinburgh: Thirsty Books, 2022), p. 230.
24. Michael Oliver, *Understanding Disability: From Theory to Practice* (Basingstoke: Palgrave Macmillan, Second Edition, 2009), p. 42.
25. Tom Shakespeare and Nicholas Watson, 'The social model of disability: an outdated ideology?', *Research in Social Science and Disability*, 2 (2002), pp. 2–28; Scottish Government, *National Guidance for Child Protection in Scotland, Part 4: Specific Support Needs and Concerns, Protection of disabled children* (2021, updated 2023), p. 6; Scottish Government, Scottish Government, *A Fairer Scotland for Disabled People: Our Delivery Plan to 2021 for the United Nations Convention on the Rights of Persons with Disabilities* (Edinburgh: Scottish Government, 2016, updated Jan 2017), p. 7.
26. EP, Ninety-ninth AR, 1973, p. 8.
27. Written testimony, Dr William Livingstone, 6 Oct 2023.
28. EP, Ninety-ninth AR, 1973, p. 8.
29. Written testimony, Dr William Livingstone, 11 Oct 2023.
30. East Park Proposed Restructuring, Feb 1995.
31. EP, Ninety-ninth AR, 1973, p. 7.
32. EP, Ninety-sixth AR, 1970, p. 10; EP, Ninety-ninth AR, 1973, p. 7.
33. Oral testimony, Tristan, 26 Sep 2023; EP, 103rd AR, 1977, p. 9.
34. EP, 101st AR, 1975, p. 6.
35. Ibid., p. 15.
36. A.E.S.P., *1874 Centenary 1974*. East Park Home.
37. Oral testimony, Maura Morran Kaur, 12 Jun 2023.
38. Oral testimony, Tristan, 26 Sep 2023.
39. Ibid.
40. Oral testimony, Tristan, 26 Sep 2023.
41. Ninety-sixth AR, 1970, p. 13.
42. EP, Ninety-ninth AR, 1973, p. 14.
43. EP, 102nd AR, 1976, p. 6.
44. EP, Ninety-ninth AR, 1973, p. 14; EP, Ninety-eighth AR, 1972, p. 13.
45. EP, 102nd AR, 1976, p. 12.
46. EP, 104th AR, 1978, p. 9.
47. Oral testimony, Maura Morran Kaur, 12 Jun 2023.
48. Written testimony, Dr William Livingstone, 6 Oct 2023.
49. Oral testimony, Tristan, 26 Sep 2023.
50. EP, 107th AR, 1981, pp. 13–14.
51. EP, 109th AR, 1983, p. 12.
52. Ibid.; Committee of Enquiry into the Education of Handicapped Children and Young People, *Special Educational Needs* (Warnock Report) (London: HMSO, 1978), p. 5.
53. EP, 110th AR, 1984, p. 13.
54. EP, 111th AR, 1985, p. 12.
55. EP, 112th AR, 1986, p. 13.
56. EP, 113th AR, 1987, p. 13.
57. CALL Scotland, https://www.callscotland.org.uk [accessed 27 Jul 2023].

58. EP, 113th AR, 1987, p. 13.
59. Marion McLarty and Moyra Hawthorn, 'Special Educational Needs: Working with Children and Families', in Deborah Baillie, Kathryn Cameron, Lesley-Anne Cull, Jeremy Roche and Janice West (eds), *Social Work and the Law in Scotland* (Basingstoke: Palgrave Macmillan in association with The Open University, 2003), p. 198.
60. EP, Minute Book, 1980–92, EP2/1/8, 14 May 1985, p. 311.
61. EP, 114th AR, 1988, p. 11.
62. Ibid., p. 14.
63. EP, Minute Book, 1980–92, EP2/1/8, 13 Sep 1989, p. 712.
64. EP, Minute Book, 1980–92, EP2/1/8, 6 Mar 1990, p. 769.
65. EP, Minute Book, 1980–92, EP2/1/8, 8 Oct 1991, p. 907; Gentle Teaching – A Summary, https://www.gentleteaching.nl/gentle/en/wat-is-en/sum [accessed 20 Jul 2023].
66. EP, Minute Book, Jan–Dec 1992, EP2/1/9, 4 Mar 1992, p. 83.
67. Ibid.
68. EP, 119th AR, 1993, p. 4; EP, 120th AR, 1994, p. 4.
69. EP, 119th AR, 1993, p. 4; EP, Minute Book, Jan–Dec 1992, EP2/1/9, 1 Dec 1992, Meeting of the Board of Directors with SOED Consultants, pp. 7–11; EP, 120th AR, 1994, p. 14.
70. Oral testimony, Maura Morran Kaur, 12 Jun 2023.
71. Ibid.
72. EP, 119th AR, 1993, p. 10.
73. EP, 113th AR, 1987, pp. 5–6.
74. EP, 118th AR, 1992, p. 10.
75. EP, 116th AR, 1990, p. 10.
76. EP, Minute Book, Jan–Dec 1989, EP2/1/8, 13 Jun 1989, p. 645.
77. EP, Minute Book, 1980–92, EP2/1/8, 14 Mar 1989, p. 624.
78. EP, 103rd AR, 1977, p. 9.
79. EP, 100th AR, 1974, p. 11; EP, 104th AR, 1978, pp. 9–10; EP, 107th AR, 1981, p. 10.
80. Oral testimony, Tristan, 26 Sep 2023; Oral testimony, Maura Morran Kaur, 12 Jun 2023.
81. EP, 107th AR, 1981, p. 10.
82. EP, Ninety-eighth AR, 1972, p. 12; EP, 104th AR, 1978, pp. 9, 12.
83. EP, Ninety-ninth AR, 1973, p. 13.
84. EP, 101st AR, 1975, p. 11.
85. Ibid.
86. Oral testimony, Maura Morran Kaur, 12 Jun 2023.
87. EP, Minute Book, Jan–Dec 1993, EP2/1/10, 9 Mar 1993, p. 6.
88. EP, Ninety-seventh AR, 1971, p.7; EP, 106th AR, 1980, p. 10; EP, 110th AR, 1984, p. 9; EP, 114th AR, 1988, p. 12.
89. Correspondence with Catriona Campbell, Head of Education, East Park, 11 Sep 2023.
90. EP, Ninety-ninth AR, 1973, p. 9; EP, 102nd AR, 1976, p. 8.
91. Oral testimony, Maura Morran Kaur, 12 Jun 2023.
92. Ibid.
93. Oral testimony, Tristan, 26 Sep 2023.
94. Ibid.
95. EP, 116th AR, 1990, p. 11.
96. Oral testimony, Tristan, 26 Sep 2023; EP, 116th AR, 1990, p. 11; EP, Ninety-sixth AR, 1970, p. 9; EP, Minute Book, 1980–92, EP/2/1/8, 11 Dec 1984, p. 276; EP, Minute Book, 1980–92, EP2/1/8, 12 Dec 1989, p. 738.
97. EP, Minute Book, 1980–92, EP2/1/8, 11 Nov 1986, p. 421; EP, 111th AR, 1985, p. 9.
98. Oral testimony, Maura Morran Kaur, 12 Jun 2023.
99. EP, 105th AR, 1979, p. 11; EP, 106th AR, 1980, p. 12.
100. Oral testimony, Maura Morran Kaur, 12 Jun 2023.
101. EP, Minute Book, 1980–92, EP2/1/8, 8 Nov 1988, p. 583; EP, Minute Book, Jan–Dec 1994, EP2/1/11, 8 Nov 1994, p. 6; EP, Minute Book, 1980–92, EP2/1/8, 14 Mar 1989, p. 624.

102. EP, 106th AR, 1980, p. 11.
103. EP, 108th AR, 1982, p. 8.
104. EP, 109th AR, 1983, p. 9; EP, 112th AR, 1986, p. 4; EP, 118th AR, 1992, pp. 4, 8.
105. EP, 104th AR, 1978, p. 13; EP, 105th AR, 1979, p. 11.
106. Ibid.
107. EP, 105th AR, 1979, p. 12; EP, 107th AR, 1981, p. 12.
108. EP, 106th AR, 1980, p. 11.
109. EP, 108th AR, 1982, p. 10; Oral testimony, Tristan, 26 Sep 2023.
110. EP, 119th AR, 1993, p. 12.
111. EP, 120th AR, 1994, p. 4.
112. Oral testimony, Maura Morran Kaur, 12 Jun 2023.
113. EP, 101st AR, 1975, p. 15.
114. EP, 103rd AR, 1977, p. 9; EP, Minute Book, 1980–92, EP2/1/8, 10 Jun 1986, p. 396; EP, 109th AR, 1983, p. 9; EP, 111th AR, 1985, p. 9.
115. Oral testimony, Tristan, 26 Sep 2023.
116. EP, 103rd AR, 1977, p. 10; EP, 104th AR, 1978, p. 12.
117. EP, Minute Book, 1980–92, EP2/1/8, 9 Oct 1990, p. 805; EP, 116th AR, 1990, p. 8; EP, 120th AR, 1994, p. 4.
118. EP, Ninety-seventh AR, 1971, p. 9; EP, 102nd AR, 1976, p. 8; EP, 103rd AR, 1977, p. 9; EP, 105th AR, 1979, p. 10; EP, 109th AR, 1983, p. 9.
119. Oral testimony, Tristan, 26 Sep 2023.
120. Written testimony, Pamela Greenhow, 10 Jul 2023.
121. EP, Minute Book, 1980–92, EP2/1/8, 13 Sep 1983, p. 186.
122. EP, 124th AR, 1998, p. 4.
123. Written testimony, Pamela Greenhow, 10 Jul 2023.
124. EP, Minute Book, 1980–92, EP2/1/8, 1 Nov 1991, p. 1; Oral testimony, Ken McChlery, 9 Feb 2023.
125. EP, Minute Book, 1980–92, EP2/1/8, 11 Oct 1988, p. 580.
126. Written testimony, May Henderson, 7 Jun 2023; EP, Minute Book, 1980–92, EP2/1/8, 12 Jun 1990, p. 790; EP Shop and House Staff Committee, 2 Mar 1993, in EP, Minute Book, Jan–Dec 1993, EP2/1/10, 2 Mar 1993, p. 61; 117th AR, 1991, pp. 5, 8.
127. EP, Minute Book, 1980–92, EP2/1/8, 13 Sep 1988, p. 572.
128. EP, 118th AR, 1991, p. 8; EP, 117th AR, 1990, p. 8.
129. Written testimony, May Henderson, 7 Jun 2023.
130. Ibid.
131. EP, 116th AR, 1990, p. 6; EP, 117th AR, 1991, pp. 4, 8.

Chapter 14

1. Catriona Stewart, 'Stars lay first brick for £3m expansion at school', *Evening Times*, 12 Nov 2015.
2. Harry Lauder, *Roamin' in the Gloamin'* (London: 1928); Gordon Irving, *Great Scot!: the life story of Sir Harry Lauder, legendary laird of the music hall* (London: 1968); William Wallace, *Harry Lauder in the Limelight* (Lewes: 1988).
3. EP, Sixty-sixth AR, 1940, p. 12.
4. Iain Watson, *Harry Gordon: The Laird of Inversnecky* (Aberdeen: Aberdeen District Council, 1993).
5. EP, Sixty-fifth AR, 1939, p. 33.
6. EP, Sixty-sixth AR, 1940, p. 26.
7. ER, Seventieth AR, 1944, p. 7. See chapter 5 for an explanation of 'named' and 'endowed' cots.
8. ER, Ninetieth AR, 1964, p. 21; Albert David Mackie, *The Scotch Comedians: from music hall to television* (Edinburgh: Ramsay Head, 1973).
9. Richard Baker, *Old Time Variety: an illustrated history* (Barnsley: Pen & Sword, 2011), pp. 67–8.
10. EP, Eightieth AR, 1954, p. 13.
11. EP, Ninetieth AR, 1964, following p. 26.
12. Rikki Fulton, *Is It That Time Already?* (Edinburgh: Black and White Publishing, 1999); Kate Fulton, *Rikki & Me* (Edinburgh: Black and White Publishing, 2004).

13. Jimmy Logan, *It's a Funny Life* (Edinburgh: Black and White Publishing, 1998); Stephen Dixon, Jimmy Logan obituary, *The Guardian*, 14 Apr 2001.

14. The Newsroom, 'Obituary: Johnny Beattie, much-loved Scottish Comedian and actor', *The Scotsman*, 14 Jul 2020.

15. Cliff Hanley, *Dancing in the Street: the classic account of a Glasgow upbringing* (London: Hutchinson, 1958).

16. EP, 104th AR, 1978, p. 18.

17. Magnus Magnusson, *I've Started So I'll Finish: The Story of Mastermind* (London: Warner, 1997).

18. EP, Ninety-third AR, 1996, p. 4.

19. Ibid., pp. 4–5.

20. Occasioned by meeting at an anniversary event to mark the longevity of the Icelandair service between Reykjavik and Glasgow. Mamie's story is narrated by her daughter, Sally Magnusson, *Where memories go: why dementia changes everything* (London: Two Roads, 2014).

21. EP, Ninetieth AR, 1964, pp. 4, 13.

22. Ibid., pp. 3, 13.

23. Dave Laing, 'Kenneth McKellar obituary', *The Guardian*. 12 Apr 2010.

24. D. Cameron Peter, *The Kenneth McKellar Story: 'Don't look at the Wallpaper'* (Johnstone: Linn Publishers, 2011), pp. 87–8.

25. Programme, *Scottish National Orchestra Royal Gala Charity Concert in aid of East Park Home for Infirm Children*.

26. EP, 117th AR, 1990, p. 4.

27. EP, 109th AR, 1982, p. 8; Tim Stevens and Brian Beacom, *The Adventures of Tiger Tim: The Authorised Biography of Tim Stevens* (Edinburgh: Black and White Publishing, 2000).

28. EP, 111th AR, 1984, p. 12.

29. EP, 117th AR, 1990, p. 4.

30. Ibid., p. 8.

31. EP, 118th AR, 1991, p. 8; Marc Eliot, *Paul Simon: A Life* (Toronto: John Wiley, 2010).

32. EP, 119th AR, 1992, pp. 5, 8, 12.

33. EP, 120th AR, 1993, p. 4.

34. EP, 122nd AR, 1995, pp. 5; Billy Connolly, *Windswept and Interesting: My Autobiography* (London: Two Roads, 2021); Billy Connolly, *Rambling Man: My Life on the Road* (London: John Murray, 2023).

35. Roy Rogers and Dale Evans, *Happy Trails: Our Life Story* (New York: Simon and Schuster, 1994); Robert W Phillips, *Roy Rogers: A Biography* (Jefferson: McFarland, 1995).

36. Geoff Tibballs, *The Secret Life of Sooty* (Letchworth: Ringpress Books, 1990).

37. Shirley Hughes, *Dogger* (London: Bodley Head, 1977).

38. Jolomo, *A Passion of Colour: Jolomo, The Retrospective* (Tayvallich: Jolomo, 2013), p. 8.

39. Jan Patience, 'Galleries: Scope of Jolomo's work surprises and delights our critic', *The Herald*, 5 Jul 2021.

40. Ibid.; Jolomo, *A Passion for Colour*, pp. 59–63.

41. Davie Wilson, with Alistair Aird, *Wilson on the Wing: the Davie Wilson Story* (Chichester: Pitch Publishing, 2020).

42. Brian Wilson, 'Obituary. Calum Kennedy: Gaelic singer whose career ranged from the Bolshoi to the village hall', *The Guardian*, 22 Apr 2006.

43. EP, 116th AR, 1989, p. 10.

44. EP, 108th AR, 1981, p. 8.

45. Ibid., p. 18.

46. Catriona Stewart, 'Stars lay first brick for £3m expansion at school', *Evening Times*, 12 Nov 2015. Docherty subsequently went on to play for Glasgow Rangers, Shrewsbury Town, Hibernian and Hull City.

47. Andrew Young, 'Empire on which the sun did set', *Glasgow Herald*, 9 Sep 1989.

48. Oral testimony, Elizabeth Hunter, 26 Aug 1999.

49. Ibid.

50. Anthony Tucker, 'Obituary: Sir Vivian Fuchs', *The Guardian*, 12 Nov 1999.

51. Vivian Fuchs, *Of Ice and Men: the story of the British Antarctic Survey, 1943–73* (Oswestry: Anthony Nelson).

52. Oral testimony, Michael McCready, 15 Dec 2022.

53. Anon., 'Obituary: Sir Vivian Fuchs', *The Economist*, 19 Nov 1999.

Chapter 15

1. Charles S Maier, 'Overcoming the Past? Narrative and negotiation, Remembering and Reparation: issues at the Interface of History and the Law', in John Torpey (ed.), *Politics and the Past: On Repairing Historical Injustices* (Oxford: Rowman and Littlefield Publishers, Inc., 2003), pp. 295–304.

2. Andrew Kendrick, Erin Lux, Sharon McGregor and Richard Withington, *Development of Children's Care Services in Scotland: Report for the Scottish Child Abuse Inquiry*, May 2021, p. 243.

3. Viviene E Cree, *From Public Streets to Private Lives: The Changing Task of Social Work* (Avebury: Ashgate Publishing, 1995), p. 147.

4. EP, Minute Book, 1980–92, EP2/1/8, 13 May 1985, p. 323.

5. EP, 113th AR, 1987, p. 13.

6. EP, Minute Book, 1980–92, EP2/1/8, 23 Feb 1988, p. 523.

7. EP, 114th AR, 1988, pp. 4, 8.

8. EP, Minute Book, 1980–92, EP2/1/8, 5 Oct 1985, p. 340.

9. EP, Minute Book, 1980–92, EP2/1/8, 11 Jul 1989, p. 655; EP, 117th AR, 1991, p. 6.

10. EP, Minute Book, 1980–92, EP2/1/8, 12 Dec 1990, p. 737.

11. Lesley Fox, *As Long as We've Got a Voice: The Life of Jimmy McIntosh* (Edinburgh: Thirsty Books, 2022), pp. 107, 207.

12. EP, Minute Book, 1980–92, EP2/1/8, 25 Nov 1991. Special Meeting of the Board to discuss a request from Miss Susie Taylor that the Home participate in a television programme, pp. 923–5.

13. EP Minute Book, Jan–Dec 1994, EP2/1/11, 8 Nov 1994, p. 10; EP Minute Book, Jan–Dec 1994, EP2/1/11, 13 Dec 1994, p. 3.

14. EP Minute Book, Jan–Dec 1993, EP2/1/10, 13 Apr 1993, p. 48.

15. EP, 119th AR, 1993, p. 10.

16. EP Minute Book, Jan–Dec 1992, EP2/1/9, 8 Sep 1992, p. 34.

17. EP Minute Book, Jan–Dec 1992, EP2/1/9, 26 Aug 1992, p. 43.

18. EP, Minute Book, Jan–Dec 1992, EP2/1/9, 8 Dec 1992, p. 2.

19. EP Minute Book, Jan–Dec 1993, EP2/1/10, 19 Jan 1993, p. 74.

20. Ibid., pp. 81–2.

21. EP Minute Book, Jan–Dec 1992, EP2/1/9, 8 Dec 1992, p. 4.

22. EP Minute Book, Jan–Dec 1993, EP2/1/10, 19 Jan 1993, p. 82; EP Minute Book, Jan–Dec 1992, EP2/1/9, 10 Nov 1992, p. 16; EP, Minute Book, Jan–Dec 1996, EP2/1/13, 13 Aug 1996, p. 18; East Park Proposed Re-Structuring, Feb 1995, p. 5.

23. EP Minute Book, Jan–Dec 1992, EP2/1/9, 10 Nov 1992, p. 16; East Park Proposed Re-Structuring, Feb 1995, p. 5.

24. EP, Minute Book, Jan–Dec 1992, EP2/1/9, 9 Jun 1992, p. 55; EP, Minute Book, Jan–Dec 1992, Meeting with SOED, 1 Dec 1992, p. 8; East Park, Proposed Re-structuring, Feb 1995, p. 5.

25. EP, Ninety-eighth AR, 1972, p. 8.

26. EP, 100th AR, 1974, p. 8.

27. Written testimony, May Henderson, 7 Jun 2023.

28. Written testimony, Elena, 16 May 2023; Moyra Hawthorn, correspondence with Elena, 16 and 22 May 2023.

29. Written testimony, Karen Fergusson, 10 Jul 2023.

30. EP, Ninety-eighth AR, 1972, p. 8.

31. Oral testimony, Tristan, 26 Sep 2023; Oral testimony, Maura Morran Kaur, 12 Jun 2023.

32. Written testimony, Pamela Greenhow, 10 Jul 2023.

33. EP, 118th AR, 1992, p. 12.

34. Oral testimony, Linda Gray, 17 Aug 2023.

35. EP, Minute Book, Jan–Dec 1992, EP2/1/9, 9 Jun 1992, p. 55; EP Minute Book, Jan–Dec 1992, EP2/1/9, meeting with SOED, 1 Dec 1992, p. 8.

36. Written testimony, May Henderson, 7 Jun 2023.

37. EP, Minute Book, 1980–92, EP2/1/8, 11 Sep 1990, p. 804.
38. EP, Minute Book, 1980–92, EP2/1/8, 15 Jan 1991, p. 836.
39. EP, Minute Book, Jan–Dec 1992, EP2/1/9, 9 Jun 1992, p. 55; EP, Minute Book, Jan–Dec 1992, EP2/1/9, meeting with SOED, 1 Dec 1992, p. 8; EP Minute Book, Jan–Dec 1992, EP2/1/9, 8 Sep 1992, p. 34.
40. EP, Minute Book, Jan–Dec 1992, EP2/1/9, meeting with SOED, 1 Dec 1992, p. 8.
41. EP, Minute Book, Jan–Dec 1993, EP2/1/10, 14 Dec 1993, p. 3.
42. EP, Minute Book, 1980–92, EP2/1/8, 10 Sep 1991, p. 903; EP, Minute Book, Jan–Dec 1992, EP2/1/9, 14 Jan 1992, p. 938; EP, Minute Book, Jan–Dec 1992, EP2/1/9, 10 Nov 1992, p. 16.
43. Ibid.
44. EP Minute Book, Jan–Dec 1993, EP2/1/10, 9 Mar 1993, p. 59.
45. EP Minute Book, Jan–Dec 1993, EP2/1/10, 9 Mar 1993, p. 59; EP, Minute Book, Jan–Dec 1993, EP2/1/10, 14 Dec 1993, p. 1; EP, Minute Book, Jan–Dec 1994, EP2/1/11, 10 May 1994, p. 31.
46. EP, Minute Book, Jan–Dec 1993, EP2/1/10, 14 Dec 1993, p. 3; Written Testimony, May Henderson, 7 Jun 2023.
47. EP Minute Book, Jan–Dec 1994, EP2/1/11, 10 May 1994, p. 31.
48. EP, Minute Book, Jan–Dec, EP2/1/12, Extraordinary Meeting of the Board, 17 Jan 1995, pp. 49–51.
49. East Park Proposed Re-structuring, Feb 1995.
50. EP, Minute Book, Jan–Dec 1995, EP2/1/12, 14 Feb 1995, p. 43.
51. East Park Proposed Re-structuring, Feb 1995.
52. Oral testimony, Karen Ferguson and Liam Feeney, 11 Oct 2023; written testimony, Karen Ferguson, 1 Dec 2023; oral testimony, Geraldine O'Neill, 7 Dec 2023.
53. EP, Minute Book, Jan–Dec 1995, EP2/1/12, 13 Jun 1995, p. 31.
54. EP, Minute Book, Jan–Dec 1995, EP2/1/12, 7 Jul 1995, p. 25; EP, Minute Book, Jan–Dec 1995, EP2/1/12, 8 Aug 1995, pp. 20, 22.
55. Ibid., p. 22; EP, Minute Book, Jan–Dec 1995, EP2/1/12, 12 Sep 1995, p. 17; EP, Minute Book, Jan–Dec 1995, EP2/1/13, 10 Sep 1996, p. 13; EP, Minute Book, Jan–Dec 1995, EP2/1/12, 12 Dec 1995, p. 2.
56. EP, Minute Book, Jan–Dec 1996, EP2/1/13, 13 Aug 1996, p. 18.
57. EP, Minute Book, Jan–Dec 1997, EP2/1/14, 11 Feb 1997, p. 37.
58. EP, Minute Book, Jan–Dec 1994, EP2/1/11, 11 May 1994, p. 31; EP, Minute Book, Jan–Dec 1996, EP2/1/13, 13 Aug 1996, p. 18; EP, Minute Book, Jan–Dec 1997, EP2/1/14, 3 Jul 1997, pp. 19–20.
59. EP, Minute Book, Jan–Dec 1997, EP2/1/14, 14 Jan 1997, p. 38.
60. EP Minute Book, Jan–Dec 1997, EP2/1/14, 11 Mar 1997, pp. 32–3.
61. EP, Minute Book, Jan–Dec 1997, EP2/1/14, 8 Apr 1997, p. 28; EP, Minute Book, Jan–Dec 1997, EP2/1/14, 13 May 1997, p. 25.
62. EP Minute Book, Jan–Dec 1997, EP2/1/14, 12 Aug 1997, p. 16.
63. EP, 124th AR, 1998, p. 5.
64. Oral testimony, Ken McChlery, 7 Mar 2023.
65. Written testimony, May Henderson, 7 Jun 2023.

Chapter 16

1. Oral testimony, Linda Gray, 17 Aug 2023.
2. EP, Minute Book, 1998, EP2/1/15, 10 Mar 1998, p. 66.
3. EP, Minute Book, 1997, EP2/1/14, 19 Oct 1997, p. 10; EP, Minute Book, 1998, EP2/1/15, 10 Feb 1998, p. 70.
4. EP, Minute Book, 1998, EP2/1/15, 19 May 1998, pp. 52–5.
5. EP, Minute Book, 1998, EP2/1/15, 10 Feb 1998, p. 70; EP, Minute Book, 1998, EP2/1/15, 19 May 1998, p. 52.
6. EP, Minute Book, 1998, EP2/1/15, 19 May 1998, p. 53; EP, Minute Book, 1998, EP2/1/15, 9 Jun 1998, p. 44.
7. EP, Minute Book, 1998, EP2/1/15, 21 Apr 1998, p. 59.

8. EP, Minute Book, 1998, EP2/1/15, 10 Mar 1998, pp. 63–4.
9. Helen Sanderson, Jo Kennedy, Pete Ritchie with Gill Goodwin, *People, Plans and Possibilities: Exploring Person Centred Planning* (Edinburgh: SHS, 1997), p. 16.
10. Written testimony, Linda Gray, 27 Aug 2023.
11. Oral testimony, Jim McDermott, 24 Aug 2023.
12. Oral testimony, Michelle Devlin, 24 Aug 2023.
13. EP, Minute Book, 1998, EP2/1/15, 19 May 1998, p. 55; EP Minute Book, EP/2/1/15, 9 Jun 1998, p. 43.
14. EP, Minute Book, EP2/1/15, meeting held on 7 Sep 1998, pp. 23–6 and 15 Sep 1998, pp. 16–26.
15. EP, Minute Book, EP2/1/15, 7 Sep 1998, pp. 23–6; ibid., pp. 16–22.
16. EP, Minute Book, EP2/1/16, 15 Oct 1999, p. 55.
17. EP, Minute Book, EP2/1/37, Extraordinary Board Meeting, 9 Jul 2013, pp. 6–8.
18. EP, 125th AR, 1998, p. 5.
19. EP, Minute Book, EP2/1/15, 13 Oct 1998, p. 13; EP, Minute Book, EP2/1/15, 26 No 1998, p. 4.
20. Oral testimony, Linda Gray, 17 Aug 2023; EP, Minute Book, EP2/1/20, 13 Feb 2001, p. 6.
21. EP, 125th AR, 1998, p. 5.
22. Written testimony, Karen Ferguson, 19 Jul 2023.
23. EP, 125th AR, 1998, p. 5.
24. Oral testimony, Carol Kerr, 31 Aug 2023.
25. Ibid.
26. Ibid.
27. EP, Minute Book, EP2/1/19, 13 Jun 2000, pp. 34–5; EP, Minute Book, EP2/1/1912, Sep 2000, p. 43; EP, Minute Book, EP2/1/19, 12 Dec 2000, p. 69.
28. EP, Minute Book, EP2/1/19, 10 Oct 2000, p. 52; EP, Minute Book, EP2/1/19, 14 Nov 2000, p. 58.
29. EP, Minute Book, EP2/1/15, 13 Jan 1998, p. 75; EP Minute Book, EP2/1/19, 8 Aug 2000, p. 39; EP, Minute Book, EP2/1/19, 12 Sep 2000, p. 45.
30. EP, 129th AR, 2003, p. 8.
31. EP, Minute Book, EP/1/16, 12 Jan 1999, p. 4. Throughout this chapter there is periodic reference to the Social Work Department. Although not specified, from 31 March 1996, when Strathclyde Regional Council was abolished, this is assumed to be Glasgow City Council Social Work Department.
32. EP, Minute Book, EP/1/16, 16 Mar 1999, p. 15; EP, Minute Book, EP/1/16, 10 Aug 1999, p. 41.
33. EP, Ninety-ninth AR, 1973, p. 7.
34. EP, Minute Book, EP2/1/15, 21 Apr 1998, p. 58; EP, Minute Book, EP2/1/15, 11 Aug 1998, p. 32.
35. EP, Minute Book, EP2/1/16, 16 Mar 1999, p. 16.
36. EP, Minute Book, EP2/1/16, 8 Jun 1999, p. 34.
37. EP, Minute Book, EP2/1/16, 10 Aug 1999, p. 41.
38. Written testimony, Karen Ferguson, 23 Aug 2023.
39. EP, 128th AR, 2002, p. 7; written testimony, Karen Ferguson, 23 Aug 2023.
40. EP, Minute Book, EP2/1/16, 9 Nov 1999, p. 59.
41. Written testimony, Karen Ferguson, 23 Aug 2023.
42. Scottish Executive, *The Same as You* (Edinburgh: Scottish Executive, 2000).
43. The Independent Care Review, *The Promise*, 2020. https://thepromise.scot/what-is-the-promise/independent-care-review [accessed 2 Nov 2023].
44. Written testimony, Karen Ferguson, 17 Aug 2023.
45. EP, Minute Book, EP2/1/36, 13 Nov 2012, p. 3; EP, Minute Book, EP2/1/37, 15 Jan 2013, p. 3; EP, Minute Book, EP2/1/37, 21 May 2013, p. 7.
46. EP, Minute Book, EP2/1/37, 21 May 2013, Care Report 2012–13, p. 7.
47. Written testimony, Geraldine O'Neill, 17 Oct 2023.
48. EP, Minute Book, EP2/1/38, 21 Jan 2014, p. 6.
49. EP, Minute Book, EP2/1/37, 21 May 2013, p. 8, Annual Care Report.

50. EP, Minute Book, EP2/1/37, 22 Oct 2013, p. 6, Interim Care Report 2012–13, May–Nov 2013.
51. EP, Minute Book, EP2/1/38, 18 Mar 2014, pp. 7–8, Annual Care Report 2013–14.
52. Ibid.
53. EP, Minute Book, EP2/1/41, 17 Mar 2015, p. 8, Annual Care Report 2014.
54. EP Minute Book, EP2/1/15, 15 Sep 1998, pp. 16–22.
55. EP, Minute Book, EP2/1/19, 12 Dec 2000, p. 63.
56. EP, Minute Book, EP2/1/16, 14 Sep 1999, p. 51; oral testimony, Michelle Devlin and Jim McDermott, 24 Aug 2023.
57. Written testimony, Linda Gray, 17 Aug 2023.
58. Scottish Executive, *The Same as You* (Edinburgh: Scottish Executive, 2000); Scottish Executive, *Make My Day* (Edinburgh: Scottish Executive, 2006), p. 77.
59. Oral testimony, Michelle Devlin, 24 Aug 2023.
60. Ibid.
61. Oral testimony, Michelle Devlin, 24 Aug 2023; oral testimony, Jim McDermott, 24 Aug 2023.
62. Oral testimony, Michelle Devlin, 24 Aug 2023.
63. Oral testimony, Jim McDermott and Michelle Devlin, 24 Aug 2023.
64. Oral testimony, Michelle Devlin, 24 Aug 2023.
65. Ibid.
66. Oral testimony, Jim McDermott and Michelle Devlin, 24 Aug 2023.
67. EP, Minute Book, EP2/1/16, 12 Jan 1999, pp. 2–3.
68. EP, Minute Book, EP2/1/15, 7 Sep 1998, p. 29.
69. Written testimony, May Henderson, 13 Dec 2023.
70. EP, Minute Book, EP2/1/16, 14 Sep 1999, p. 50; EP, Minute Book, EP2/1/19, 10 Oct 2000, p. 53; EP, Minute Book, EP2/1/19, 8 Feb 2000, p. 10.
71. Written testimony, May Henderson, 13 Dec 2023.
72. EP, Minute Book, EP2/1/19, 11 Apr 2000, p. 23; written testimony, May Henderson, 7 Jun 2023.
73. Written testimony, May Henderson, 7 Jun 2023.
74. EP, Minute Book, EP2/1/19, 12 Dec 2000, pp. 65–8.
75. EP, 128th AR, 2002, p. 6.
76. Oral testimony, Tristan, 26 Sep 2023.
77. Glasgow Social Work Inspection and Registration Unit, Proposed Summary Inspection Report, 27 and 28 August 2001, in EP, Minute Book, EP2/1/20, 9 Jan 2001, pp. 28–32.
78. EP, Minute Book, EP2/1/21, 8 Oct 2002, p. 4.
79. EP, Minute Book, EP2/1/21, 12 Nov 2002, p. 1; EP, Minute Book, EP2/1/21, 10 Dec 2002, p. 4.
80. EP, 129th AR, 2003, p. 6.
81. EP, 130th AR, 2004, p. 4.
82. Oral testimony, Barbara Simpson, 31 Aug 2023.
83. EP Board Meeting, 9 Mar 2004, p. 4; EP Board Meeting 8 Jun 2004, p. 4; EP Board Meeting, 10 Aug 2004, p. 1.
84. Correspondence, May Henderson to Board of Directors, 23 May 2002.
85. EP, 129th Annual Report, 2003, p. 6.
86. EP, Minute Book, EP2/1/25, 10 May 2005, p. 4.
87. Ibid.
88. Ibid.
89. EP, Minute Book, EP2/1/25, 10 May 2005, p. 12; EP, Minute Book, EP2/1/25, 14 Jun 2005, p. 3.
90. EP, 131st AR, 2005, p. 6.
91. EP, 131st AR, 2005, pp. 4–5.
92. EP, 132nd AR, 2006, p. 5.
93. EP, Minute Book, EP2/1/26, 16 Apr 2006, p. 5; written testimony, Karen Ferguson, 10 Jul 2023.
94. EP, 133rd AR, p. 4.
95. EP, Minute Book, EP2/1/16, 14 Sep 1999, p. 51.
96. EP, 128th AR, 2002, p. 8.
97. EP, 128th AR, 2002, p. 8; EP, 129th AR, 2003, p. 9.

98. EP, 125th AR, 1999, p. 5; EP, 129th AR, 2003, p. 13.

99. EP, 132nd AR, 2006, p. 13.

100. EP, Minute Book, EP2/1/20, 9 Oct 2001, p. 48.

101. EP, 134th AR, 2008, p. 5.

102. Written testimony, Linda Gray, 17 Aug 2023.

103. Oral testimony, Linda Gray, 17 Aug 2023.

104. EP, 135th AR, 2009, p. 9.

105. EP, Minute Book, EP2/1/31, 8 Sep 2009, p. 4.

106. East Park Report and Financial Statements for the Period Ended 31 March 2010, pp. 5–6.

107. EP, Minute Book, EP2/1/32, 11 May 2010, p. 2.

108. Oral testimony, Linda Gray, 17 Aug 2023; written testimony, May Henderson, 7 Jun 2023.

109. Written testimony, May Henderson, 7 Jun 2023; EP, Minute Book, EP2/1/31, 11 Aug 2009, p. 6; EP, Minute Book, EP2/1/32, 11 May 2010, p. 2, Report of the Directors for the period ended 31 March 2010.

110. EP, Minute Book, EP2/1/35, 10 Jan 2012, p. 5.

111. EP, Minute Book, EP2/1/35, 12 Jun 2012, p. 1.

112. EP, Minute Book, EP2/1/38, 21 Oct 2014, p. 2.

113. EP, Minute Book, EP2/1/14, 12 Aug 1997, p. 16.

114. EP, 125th AR, 1999, p. 5.

115. EP, Minute Book, EP2/1/15, 10 Mar 1998, pp. 63–4.

116. EP, 125th AR, 1999, p. 5.

117. EP, Minute Book, EP2/1/16, 11 May 1999, p. 29.

118. EP, 128th AR, 2002, pp. 6–7.

119. EP, 129th AR, 2003, p. 7.

120. EP, 130th AR, 2004, p. 4.

121. EP, 132nd AR, 2006, p. 6.

122. CALM Training, https://calmtraining.co.uk; 132nd AR, p. 6.

123. Build Progress Report and Opening Event Update, Judy Cromarty, 10 Aug 2016; written testimony, Karen Ferguson, 16 Oct 2023.

124. Oral testimony, Barbara Simpson and Carol Kerr, 31 Aug 2023.

125. Inclusion and Achievement Committee Meeting, 6 Dec 2016, in EP, Minute Book, EP2/1/40, 29 Nov 2016, p. 25.

126. Written testimony, Karen Ferguson, 16 Aug 2023.

127. The Independent Care Review, *The Promise*, 2020, p. 4, https://thepromise.scot/what-is-the-promise/independent-care-review [accessed 2 Nov 2023].

128. Ibid.

129. Ibid., p. 73.

130. Safespace® is designed for individuals who require safe surroundings at home or in a school environment. The flexible sides and soft floor reduce the risk of injury from hard surfaces, https://safespaces.co.uk/safespace/ [accessed 2 Nov 2023].

131. Oral testimony, Liam Feeney and Karen Ferguson, 11 Oct 2023.

132. Ibid.

Chapter 17

1. EP, 124th AR, 1998, p. 5.

2. EP, 125th AR, 1999, p. 5.

3. Written testimony, Linda Gray, 23 Nov 23; EP, 125th AR, 1999, p. 6.

4. EP, 125th AR, 1999, p. 5; EP Minute Book, EP2/1/16, 12 Oct 1999, p. 54.

5. EP, 125th AR, 1999, p. 5.

6. SMART is an acronym used over the years when setting targets, objectives or outcomes of interventions. The Care Inspectorate write that SMART principles can be used when tracking progress in achieving outcomes and to guide setting objectives. Traditionally, SMART outcomes have been classified according to the first set of definitions provided below. Various alternatives

are used and the Care Inspectorate suggests an alternative set of definitions more compatible with a personal outcomes approach and consistent with the ethos of appreciative inquiry and more relational approaches to care and support. These alternatives are included in brackets.

S: Specific (or Significant)

M: Measurable (or Meaningful)

A: Attainable (or Action-oriented)

R: Relevant (or Rewarding)

T: Time-bound (or Trackable)

Oral testimony, Karen Ferguson, 1 Dec 2023.

The Care Inspectorate Guide for providers on personal planning: Children and young people (Dundee: The Care Inspectorate, 2021), p. 20, https://hub.careinspectorate.com/media/4673/personal-plans-guide-cyp-final-07102021 .pdf [accessed 23 Nov 2023].

7. EP, 133rd AR, 2007, p. 6; EP, Minute Book, EP2/1/8, 9 Jun 1992, p. 2; EP Meeting with SOED, 1 Dec 1992, p. 2; East Park, Proposed restructuring, Feb 1995, p. 5.
8. Caledonian Awards, https://www.edubuzz.org/whatson/2011/08/10/the-caledonian-family-of-awards/ [accessed 18 Oct 2023].
9. Written testimony, David Traynor, 8 Nov 2023.
10. Ibid.
11. Oral testimony, Amy Little and Ailie Davie, 21 Nov 2023.
12. Written testimony, Linda Gray, 17 Aug 2023.
13. EP, 133rd AR, 2007, p. 5.
14. Ibid.
15. Written testimony, Linda Gray, 20 Sep 2023; EP, Minute Book, EP2/1/27, 13 Feb 2007, p. 5.
16. EP, 133rd AR, 2007, p. 5.
17. EP, 134th AR, 2008, p. 5.
18. Ibid.
19. EP, Minute Book, EP2/1/37, 16 Apr 2013, p. 6.
20. EP, Minute Book, EP2/1/38, 29 Apr 2014, pp. 6–7.
21. EP, Minute Book, EP2/1/38, 29 Apr 2014, p. 7.
22. EP, Minute Book, EP2/1/36, 8 May 2012, p. 3.
23. The University of Edinburgh, *East Park iPad Project*, https://dart.ed.ac.uk/research/east-park-ipad-project/ [accessed 3 Nov 2023].
24. EP, Board Minutes, EP2/1/38, 29 Apr 2014, p. 6.
25. Sinead O'Brien, *East Park iPad Project Report 2013/14*, Moray House School of Education (University of Edinburgh, 2014), p. 3.
26. EP, Minute Book, EP2/1/39, 24 Feb 2015, p. 12.
27. Ibid.
28. EP, Minute Book, EP2/1/16, 14 Sep 1999, p. 48; EP, Minute Book, EP2/1/15, 11 Aug 1998, p. 31; oral testimony, Geraldine O'Neill, 17 Oct 2023.
29. Oral testimony, Carol Kerr, 31 Aug 2023.
30. EP, Minute Book, EP2/1/15, 15 Feb 2012, p. 6.
31. EP, 133rd AR, 2007, p. 5.
32. EP, Minute Book, EP2/1/38, 29 Apr 2014, p. 2; East Park Patter, *Chickchickchickchickchicken*, Issue 18, Nov 2019, p. 3.
33. Ibid.; Written testimony, Catriona Campbell, 24 Oct 2023.
34. The Children's Wood and North Kelvin Meadow, https://www.thechildrenswood.co.uk [accessed 15 Oct 2023].
35. EP Board Minutes, 24 Sep 2013, p. 7.
36. East Park Patter, *We met the Queen and Princess Anne*, Issue 22, Oct 2021, p. 1.
37. Oral testimony, Jay McInally, 5 Jun 2023.
38. Scottish University Insight Institute, *Getting it Right for Looked After Disabled Children*, https://www.scottishinsight.ac.uk/Programmes/OpenCall201213GettingitRightforLookedAfterDisabledChildren.aspx [accessed 3 Nov 2023]; loosely based on the theme of Getting

Right for Every Child, the Scottish Government's commitment to provide children, young people and their families with the right support at the right time so that every child and young person in Scotland can reach their full potential, https://www.gov.scot/policies/girfec/ [accessed 3 Nov 2023].

39. EP, Minute Book, EP2/1/37, 15 Jan 2013, p. 3; EP, Minute Book, EP2/1/37, 21 May 2013, p. 8; East Park Patter, *Dramatic Success – Alisha's Surprise*, Issue 1, Nov 2013, p. 2.

40. EP, Minute Book, EP2/1/37, 21 May 2013, p. 8.

41. EP, Minute Book, EP2/1/37, 21 May 2013, p. 8, Annual Care Report.

42. Ibid.

43. Hear My Music, https://www.hearmymusic.org.uk/about [accessed 3 Nov 2023]; EP, Minute Book, EP2/1/38, 21 Oct 2014, p. 5.

44. EP, Minute Book, EP2/1/38, 15 Jul 2014, p. 4.

45. EP, Minute Book, EP2/1/38, 18 Mar 2014, p. 9, Annual Care Report, 2013–14.

46. EP, Minute Book, EP2/1/38, 29 Apr 2014, p. 5; East Park Patter, *East Park's Commonwealth Celebratory Adventure*, Issue 3, Jun 2014, p. 2.

47. EP, Minute Book, EP2/1/38, 20 May 2014, p. 5; written testimony, David Pool, 4 Oct 2023.

48. Written testimony, David Pool, 4 Oct 2023.

Chapter 18

1. EP, Twenty-fourth AR, 1898, pp. 5–6.

2. EP, Fifteenth AR, 1889, p. 3.

3. EP, Sixteenth AR, 1890, cover.

4. Ward & Lock Ltd published a range of guides to towns and cities in the British Isles and some parts of Europe.

5. Anon., *Ward & Lock's Popular History of and Illustrated Guide to Glasgow and the Clyde* (London: Ward & Lock, 1880).

6. On this topic, see Jaipreet Virdi, *Hearing Happiness: Deafness Cures in History* (Chicago: Chicago University Press).

7. Anon., *Ward & Lock's Popular History of and Illustrated Guide to Glasgow*.

8. NRS, Ordnance Survey map, Maryhill Parish, Lanarkshire, Sheet V1.2, 1861. On this map, Gairbraid Street is shown as Garscube Road.

9. NRS, Ordnance Survey map, Lanarkshire, Glasgow and its Environs, Sheet VI.2, 1896.

10. Ibid.

11. NRS, Ordnance Survey map, Lanarkshire, Sheet VI.2, 1913.

12. Ibid.

13. EP, Forty-seventh AR, 1921; Forty-eighth AR, 1922.

14. NRS, Ordnance Survey map, Lanarkshire, Sheet VI.2, 1935.

15. EP, Minute Book 1909–12, EP2/1/3, 15 Oct 1909, p. 40.

16. T J Dowds, *The Forth and Clyde Canal: A History* (East Linton: Tuckwell Press, 2003), pp. 62–3.

17. EP, 16-page supplement to Fifty-fourth AR, 1928, p. 6.

18. EP, Minute Book 1874–92, EP2/1/1, 25 Oct 1880, p. 103.

19. Ibid., 5 May 1881, p. 105.

20. GML, EP Eighth AR, GC362.7809.4.1443EAS, 1882, pp. 5–6.

21. EP, Minute Book 1874–92, EP2/1/1, 11 Apr 1882, p. 111.

22. EP, Minute Book 1874–92, EP2/1/1, 23 Sep 1887, p. 127.

23. Ibid.

24. EP, Minute Book 1874–92, EP2/1/1, 23 Sep 1887, p. 128.

25. Ibid.

26. EP, Minute Book 1874–92, EP2/1/1, 21 Jan 1888, p. 131.

27. Ibid.

28. *Glasgow Herald*, 2 Feb 1888.

29. Ibid.

30. Ibid.
31. EP, Minute Book 1874–92, EP2/1/1/1, 21 Mar 1888, p. 133.
32. EP, Minute Book 1874–92, EP2/1/1/1, 20 Oct 1888, p. 135.
33. EP, Minute Book 1874–92, EP2/1/1/1, 2 Mar 1889, pp. 137–8; 13 Apr 1889, pp. 139.
34. GML, EP Fifteenth AR, GC362.7809.4.1443EAS, 1889, p. 3.
35. Ibid., p. 5.
36. EP, Minute Book 1874–92, EP2/1/1, 11 Aug 1893, pp. 152–3.
37. EP, Minute Book 1893–1908, EP2/1/2, 6 Sep 1893, pp. 2–3.
38. EP, Minute Book 1893–1908, EP2/1/2, 6 Sep 1893, pp. 4–5.
39. Ibid., p. 5.
40. EP, Minute Book 1893-1908, EP2/1/2, 30 Nov 1893, p. 9.
41. EP, Twenty-seventh AR, 1901, p. 3.
42. EP, Twenty-eighth AR, 1902, p. 3.
43. EP, Twenty-ninth AR, 1903, p. 3.
44. EP, Minute Book 1893–1908, EP2/1/2, 6 Nov 1902, p. 99.
45. EP, Forty-sixth AR, 1920, p. 10.
46. Munro became particularly well known for his narration of the adventures of puffer captain, Para Handy. For more on Munro, see Leslie Lendrum, *Neil Munro: The Biography* (Colonsay: House of Lochar, 2004).
47. EP, Fifty-third AR, 1928, p. 3.
48. Oral testimony interview with Amy (pseud) on 13 Sep 1999.
49. EP, Seventy-third AR, 1947, p. 5.
50. For example, 63 at 31 Dec 1949, 58 at 31 Dec 1953, 50 at 31 Dec 1956, 37 at 31 Dec 1957, but 49 at 31 Dec 1959.
51. EP, Eighty-fifth AR, 1959, p. 8; Eighty-ninth AR, 1960, p. 8.
52. EP, Eighty-fourth AR, 1958, pp. 3, 5.
53. EP, Ninety-fifth AR, 1969, p. 10; 102nd AR, 1976, p. 6.
54. EP, 114th AR, 1988, p. 4.
55. EP, 113th AR, 1987, p. 11; 115th AR, 1989, p. 8.
56. EP, 121st AR, 1994, p. 11.
57. EP, 128th AR, 2002, p. 6.
58. Ibid., p. 7.
59. EP, 130th AR, 2004, p. 5.
60. EP, 132nd AR, 2006, p. 4.
61. EP, 134th AR, 2008, p. 5.
62. Ibid.

Chapter 19

1. Liam Feeney, 'Turning Ordinary Love into Extraordinary Outcomes at East Park', *Scottish Journal of Residential Child Care*, 19.2 (2020), pp. 146–59.
2. Much of this chapter is informed by Moyra Hawthorn's experience of spending time in East Park School and the residences as part of her research for this publication.
3. Oral testimony, Peter McLanachan, 21 Sep 2023.
4. Written testimony, Catriona Campbell, 24 Aug 2023.
5. Ibid.
6. Oral testimony, Amy Little and Ailie Davie, 21 Nov 2023.
7. Ibid.
8. Oral testimony, Bryan Tolland, 15 Sep 2023.
9. Oral testimony, Jay McInally, 5 Jun 2023.
10. Oral testimony, Bryan Tolland, 15 Sep 2023.
11. Written testimony, Karen Ferguson, 1 Dec 2023.
12. Written testimony, Lesley Gray, 7 Mar 2023.
13. Oral testimony, Lauren Black, 5 Oct 2023.
14. EP, Seventy-sixth AR, Jan 1950, p. 10; Lesley Fox, *As Long as We've Got a Voice: The Life of Jimmy*

McIntosh (Edinburgh: Thirsty Books, 2022), pp. 23–4; written testimony, May Henderson, 7 Jun 2023.

15. Oral testimony, Keith Greene, 5 Oct 2023.
16. Written testimony, Julie Breadner, specialist speech and language therapist, 11 Dec 2023.
17 Written testimony, Geraldine O'Neill, 12 Dec 2023.
18. Written testimony, Gerry Wells, 25 Oct 2023.
19. Ibid.
20. Ibid.
21. Andrew Kendrick, Moyra Hawthorn, Samina Karim and Julie Shaw, 'Scotland: Historic Abuse in Care and Human Rights', in Johanna Sköld and Shurlee Swain (eds), *Apologies and the Legacy of Abuse of Children in 'Care'* (Basingstoke: Palgrave Macmillan, 2015), pp. 124–33.
22. Scottish Child Abuse Inquiry, https://www.childabuseinquiry.scot message from Lady Smith, https://www.childabuseinquiry.scot/news/message-lady-smith-approach-work-inquiry [accessed 16 Dec 2023].
23. Scotland's Redress Scheme, https://www.gov.scot/collections/financial-redress-for-survivors-of-child-abuse-in-care/ [accessed 6 Nov 2023].
24. The Scottish Government, Redress Scheme, information for organisations, https://www.gov.scot/publications/redress-scheme-information-for-organisations/pages/background/ [accessed 6 Nov 2023].
25. Written testimony, Kieron O'Brien, 4 Aug 2023.
26. Scotland's Redress Scheme: combined annual report 2023 6.7, East Park School, https://www.gov.scot/publications/scotlands-redress-scheme-2023-combined-annual-report/pages/13/ [accessed 23 Nov 2023].
27. Written testimony, Gerry Wells, 10 Nov 2023.
28. Written testimony, Lesley Gray, 7 Mar 2023.
29. Written testimony, Kieron O'Brien, 4 Aug 2023.
30. Andrew Powell, Brigid Francis-Devine and Harriet Clark, *Coronavirus: Impact on the Labour Market* (House of Commons Library, 9 Aug 2022, p. 4, https://researchbriefings.files.parliament.uk/documents/CBP-8898/CBP-8898.pdf [accessed 13 Nov 2023].
31. Oral testimony, Liam Feeney and Karen Ferguson, 11 Oct 2023.
32. Ibid.
33. Personal testimony, Kieron O'Brien, 4 Aug 2023.
34. EP, Minute Book, Jan–Nov 2015, EP/1/39, 21 Jul 2015, p. 5.
35. Helen Glenn, East Park, School Enhancement Group Proposal, 2020.
36. Written testimony, Kieron O'Brien, 4 Aug 2023.
37. Ibid.
38. Oral testimony, Liam Feeney and Karen Ferguson, 11 Oct 2023; Laura Steckley, Lee Hollins, Sarah Deeley and Michael Bettencourt, *An Appreciative Inquiry into Holding in Residential Child Care: Pilot Report*, University of Strathclyde, 22 Jun 2023.
39. Mandy Rhodes, 'In announcing a review of the care system Nicola Sturgeon knows she has made a big commitment', *Holyrood*, 22 Oct 2016, https://www.holyrood.com/editors-column/view,in-announcing-a-review-of-the-care-system-nicola-sturgeon-knows-she-has-made-a-big-commitment_12557.htm [accessed 23 Nov 2023]; Independent Care Review, *Launch of 'root and branch review'*, https://www.carereview.scot/launch-of-the-root-and-branch-review/ [accessed 23 Nov 2023].
40. *The Promise*, 2020, p. 4, https://www.carereview.scot/wp-content/uploads/2020/02/The-Promise.pdf [accessed 23 Nov 2023].
41. East Park Patter, Issue 19, March 2020, p. 1.
42. Written testimony, Lesley Gray, 7 Mar 2023.
43. Written testimony, Dr William Livingstone, 8 Oct 2023.
44. These vignettes are based on Moyra Hawthorn's experience visiting the East Park residences on 23 and 24 Oct 2023.
45. Henry George Liddell and Robert Scott, *An intermediate Greek–English lexicon: Founded upon the seventh edition of Liddell and Scott's Greek–English Lexicon* (Oxford: Oxford University Press, 2010), p. 4.

46. Liam Feeney, 'Turning Ordinary Love Into Extraordinary Outcomes in East Park', *Scottish Journal of Residential Child Care*, 19.2 (2020), p. 149.
47. Ibid., pp. 157–8.
48. Oral testimony, Liam Feeney, 7 Nov 2023.
49. Written testimony, Geraldine O'Neill, 28 Nov 2023.
50. East Park Values are CARING:

    Collaborative: We work together with the children and young people, our staff, with families and carers, with external partners and teams to provide the best experiences, opportunities and services, to enable the children and young people to thrive into adulthood.

    Ambitious: We celebrate the strengths and abilities of the children and young people and encourage and support each person to communicate and achieve their ambitions. We will do all we can to support each individual in achieving his or her independence. We actively reject the soft discrimination of low expectation often experienced by the children and young people we work with, instead offering a new cycle of positive experiences, high aspirations and achievements.

    Respectful: We have unconditional positive regard for each child and young person, understanding that each person has a right to dignity and respect. This value and right extends also to staff and is reflected in our daily interactions and collegiate support, appreciation and respect of the roles undertaken by each of our colleagues in all departments across the organisation.

    Inclusive: We believe that the children and young people at East Park have the same right as their peers to be included and have access to positive experiences, to equality of opportunity, and to high-quality services, inside and outside East Park. On behalf of the children and young people of East Park, we are tenacious in our advocacy to access their rights.

    Nurturing: We have a holistic approach to supporting the emotional, intellectual and physical development of the child and young person, and the priority in this is the person's safety. We understand the need for constant positive, consistent and caring communication, tailored to each individual's mode of communication, in supporting each person's development within a calm and encouraging environment.

    Growth: All of our values are underpinned by growth – as a collaborative, ambitious, respectful, inclusive and nurturing organisation, we ensure that all our children and young people can flourish and achieve their potential.
51. Oral testimony, Jay McInally, day pupil at East Park, 2017–22.

Bibliography

Primary sources

Archdiocese of Glasgow Archives
    Smyllum Orphanage

East Park School
    Annual reports
    Minute books
    Combined Admissions and Lefts Register – East Park Home Special School, EP4/1
    Constitution of East Park, 1912, EP1/1
    1874 Centenary 1974 East Park Home (1974)
    East Park Home for Infirm Children (1988)
    'Supplement to Annual Report [1888?], East Park Home for Infirm Children, Extension of Premises'

Glasgow & Clyde Health Board Archive
    Glasgow Royal Infirmary, Medical Committee, 1939, HB14/1/46
    Royal Hospital for Sick Children annual reports

Glasgow City Archives
    East Park Free Church of Scotland, Deacon's Court Minute Book 1879–97, CH3/1669/2/2/1
    East Park Free Church of Scotland, Session Minute Book 1878–1909, CH3/1669/1/1
    Education Endowments (Scotland) Commission – Marshall Trust, MP13.137
    Poor Law records
        Calton
    Schoolmaster's Log 1866–1901, Inchinnan Parish
    Western Necropolis
        Proprietors' Register of Lairs/Registers of Lair Owners
        Registers of Interments
        Registers of Lairs

Mitchell Library – Glasgow Room
    Dill, Bessie, 'Sunshine and Shadow' (1921), ref. 99261
    East Park Home annual reports, ref. GC362 7809 41443 EAS
    Report upon the Vital, Social, and Economic Statistics of Glasgow for 1877

National Records of Scotland
    ScotlandsPeople
        Decennial Census returns, 1841–1921
        Old Parish Records
        Registrations of Births, Deaths and Marriages
        Valuation Rolls
        Wills

North Ayrshire Council
    Register of Lairs, Haylie Bank Cemetery, Largs

University College London
    Centre for the Study of the Legacies of British Slavery

University of Dundee Archives
    Baldovan Asylum annual reports
    Baldovan Asylum minute books

Wellcome Collection
    Clugston, Beatrice, *Missing Links in Scotland's Charities and how the chain may be repaired* (Glasgow: David Bryce, 1880)

Oral and written testimony

Amy (pseud.)	Henderson, May	Orr, Margaret
Billinghurst, Elena	Hunter, Elizabeth	Pool, David
Breadner, Julie	Kaur, Maura Morran	Simmons, Tim
Davie, Ailie	Kerr, Carol	Simpson, Barbara
Devlin, Michelle	Lalley, Stephen	Smyth, Mairi
Elizabeth (pseud.)	Little, Amy	Thompson, Elizabeth
Feeney, Liam	McChlery, Ken	Tolland, Bryan
Ferguson, Karen	McCreadie, Michael	Traynor, David
Foster, Ruth	McDermott, Jim	Tristan (pseud.)
Gray, Lesley	McLanachan, Peter	Watson, Lesley
Gray, Linda	Mellan, Evelyn	White, Jean
Greenhow, Pamela	Mullaney, Tommy	

Secondary sources

Government reports

House of Commons, Westminster

Committee of Enquiry into the Education of Handicapped Children and Young People, *Special Educational Needs* [The Warnock Report] (London: HMSO, 1978).

Her Majesty's Inspector of Schools, *The Education of Pupils with Learning Difficulties in Primary and Secondary Schools in Scotland* (Edinburgh: HMSO, 1978).

Ministry of Health, *The welfare of children in hospital* [The Platt Report] (London: HMSO, 1959).

Report of the Committee on Children and Young Persons – Scotland [The Kilbrandon Report] (Edinburgh: HMSO, 1964).

Report of the Prevention of Neglect of Children: Report of the Committee of the Scottish Advisory Council on Child Care [The McBoyle Report], Cmnd.1966 (Edinburgh: HMSO, 1963).

Report from the Departmental Committee on Habitual Offenders, Vagrants, Beggars, Inebriates, and Juvenile Delinquents [for Scotland] (Edinburgh: HMSO, 1895).

Social Work and the Community, proposals for reorganizing local authority services in Scotland (Edinburgh: HMSO, 1966).

Social security and allied services (Beveridge Report) (London: HMSO, 1942).

The Clyde Valley regional plan, 1946: a report. Clyde Valley Regional Planing Advisory Committee Report to the constituent local authorities, 1947, prepared for the Clyde Valley Regional Planning Committee by Abercrombie, P and R H Matthew (Edinburgh: HMSO, 1949).

Scottish Parliament

A Fairer Scotland for Disabled People: Our Delivery Plan to 2021 for the United Nations Convention on the Rights of Persons with Disabilities (Edinburgh: Scottish Government, 2016, updated Jan 2017).

Children and Families Directorate, *Progressing the Human Rights of Children in Scotland: A Report 2015–2018. Report to the Scottish Parliament under part 1 of The Children and Young Person (Scotland) Act 2014.*

Cross-Party Group on Scottish Gypsy/Travellers, 25 Mar 2022.

Historic Abuse Systemic Review, 'Residential Schools and Children's Homes in Scotland 1950 to 1995', The Scottish Government (2007).

Make my Day! The same as you? National Implementation Group, Report of the Day Services Sub Group (Edinburgh: Scottish Executive, 2006).

National Guidance for Child Protection in Scotland, Part 4: Specific Support Needs and Concerns, Protection of Disabled Children (2021, updated 2023).

The Same as You (Edinburgh: Scottish Executive, 2000).

United Nations

Convention on the Rights of the Child (1992).

Books and journal articles

Abel-Smith, Brian, *A History of the Nursing Profession* (London: Heinemann, 1960).

Abrams, Lynn, *The Orphan Country: Children of Scotland's Broken Homes from 1845 to the Present Day* (Edinburgh: John Donald, 1998).

Alston, David, *Slaves and Highlanders: Silenced histories of Scotland and the Caribbean* (Edinburgh: Edinburgh University Press, 2021).

Anderson, R D, *Scottish Education since the Reformation* (Economic & Social History Society of Scotland, 1997).

Anon., 'A K Chalmers MD LLD', *British Medical Journal*, 7 Feb 1942, p. 202.

Anon., 'Dr A K Chalmers', *Nature*, 7 Mar 1942, pp. 266–7.

Anon., *Helping the Helpless: Some Pictures of Broomhill Home* (n.d.).

Anon., 'Obituary: Sir Vivian Fuchs', *The Economist*, 19 Nov 1999.

Anon., 'Sir William Tennant Gairdner KCB, MD, FRCP Edin, FRS', *British Medical Journal* 2 (2427), 6 Jul 1907, pp. 53–9.

Anon., *Ward & Lock's Popular History of and Illustrated Guide to Glasgow and the Clyde* (London: Ward & Lock, 1880).

Baden-Powell, Robert, *Scouting for Boys* (London: Boy Scouts, 1908).

Baines, Dudley, 'The Onset of Depression', in Paul Johnson (ed.), *Twentieth-Century Britain: Economic, Social and Cultural Change* (Harlow: Longman, 1994), pp. 169–87.

Baines, Dudley, 'Recovery from Depression', in Paul Johnson (ed.), *Twentieth-Century Britain: Economic, Social and Cultural Change* (Harlow: Longman, 1994), pp. 188–202.

Baker, Richard, *Old Time Variety: an illustrated history* (Barnsley: Pen & Sword, 2011).

Boulton-Jones, Michael, *Glasgow Works: An account of the economy of a city* (Thatcham: Dolman Scott, 2009).

Bowden, Sue, 'The New Consumerism', in Paul Johnson (ed.), *Twentieth-Century Britain: Economic, Social and Cultural Change* (Harlow: Longman, 1994), pp. 242–62.

Bowlby, John, 'The Nature of the Child's Tie to his Mother', *International Journal of Psycho-Analysis*, 39 (1958), pp. 350–73.

Brown, Callum G, 'Religion and Secularism', in Tony Dickson and James H Treble (eds), *People and Society in Scotland III, 1914–1990* (Edinburgh: John Donald, 1992).

Brown, Callum G, *Religion and Society in Twentieth-Century Britain* (Harlow: Pearson, 2006).

Bruce, Steve, *No Pope of Rome: Anti-Catholicism in Modern Scotland* (Edinburgh: Mainstream, 1985).

Bruce, Steve, Tony Glendinning, Iain Paterson and Michael Rosie, *Sectarianism in Scotland* (Edinburgh: Edinburgh University Press, 2004).

Butler, A R and J L Hogg, 'Exploring Scotland's influenza pandemic of 1918–19: lest we forget', *Journal of the Royal College of Physicians of Edinburgh*, 37:4 (2007), pp. 362–6.

Chalmers, A K, *The Health of Glasgow, 1818–1925: An Outline* (Glasgow: Glasgow Corporation, 1930).

Checkland, Olive, *Philanthropy in Victorian Scotland: Social Welfare and the Voluntary Principle* (Edinburgh: John Donald, 1980).

Checkland, Olive, 'Clugston, Beatrice (1827–1888)', in H C G Matthew and Brian Harrison (eds), *The Oxford Dictionary of National Biography*, Vol. 12 (Oxford: Oxford University Press, 2004), pp. 224–5.

Cleall, Esme, *Colonising Disability: Impairment and Otherness Across Britain and Its Empire, c.1800–1914* (Cambridge: Cambridge University Press, 2022).

Climie, J, *William Quarrier, the Orphan's Friend* (Glasgow: Pickering & Inglis, c.1905).

Clugston, Beatrice, *Missing Links in Scotland's Charities and how the chain may be repaired* (Glasgow: David Bryce, 1880).

Connolly, Billy, *Windswept and Interesting: My Autobiography* (London: Two Roads, 2021).

Connolly, Billy, *Rambling Man: My Life on the Road* (London: John Murray, 2023).

Cooke, Anthony, *A History of Drinking: The Scottish Pub since 1700* (Edinburgh: Edinburgh University Press, 2015).

Cree, Viviene, *From Public Streets to Private Lives: The Changing Task of Social Work* (Avebury: Ashgate, 1995).

Crimmens, David and Ian Milligan (eds), *Facing Forward: Residential child care in the 21st century* (Lyme Regis: Russell House Publishing, 2005).

Cronin, Jenny, 'Beatrice Clugston', in Elizabeth Ewan, Sue Innes and Siân Reynolds (eds), *Biographical Dictionary of Scottish Women* (Edinburgh: Edinburgh University Press, 2007).

Crawford, Scott, *The History of Broomhill and Lanfine Homes* (Kirkintilloch: Scott Crawford, 2018).

Davis, Steve and Harry Lance, *Interesting: My Autobiography* (London: Ebury Press, 2016).

Devine, T M, *Scotland's shame?: bigotry and sectarianism in modern Scotland* (Edinburgh: Mainstream, 2000).

Devine, Tom, 'The Sixties in Scotland: A Historical Context', in Eleanor Bell and Linda Gunn, *The Scottish Sixties: Reading, Rebellion, Revolution* (Amsterdam: Rodopi, 2013), pp. 23–46.

Divine, David, *Aberlour Narratives of Success* (Durham: Durham University School of Applied Sciences, 2013).

Dixon, Stephen, Jimmy Logan obituary, *The Guardian*, 14 Apr 2001.

Dowds, T J, *The Forth and Clyde Canal: A History* (East Linton: Tuckwell Press, 2003).

Duguid, Charles, *Macewen of Glasgow: a recollection of the chief* (Edinburgh: Oliver & Boyd, 1957).

Dunbar, Helen, *History of the Society for the Blind in Glasgow and the West of Scotland* (Glasgow: Glasgow and West of Scotland Society for the Blind, 1989).

Dunbar, William MacLean, 'Quarrier, William (1829–1903)', in H C G Matthew and Brian Harrison (eds), *The Oxford Dictionary of National Biography*, Vol. 45 (Oxford: Oxford University Press, 2004), pp. 664–6.

Eliot, Marc, *Paul Simon: A Life* (Toronto: John Wiley, 2010).

Emond, Ruth, 'An outsider's view of the inside', in David Crimmens and Ian Milligan (eds), *Facing Forward: Residential Child Care in the 21st Century* (Lyme Regis: Russell House, 2005), pp. 127–36.

Ewan, Elizabeth, Sue Innes and Siân Reynolds, *The Biographical Dictionary of Scottish Women* (Edinburgh: Edinburgh University Press, 2006).

Feeney, Liam, 'Turning Ordinary Love into Extraordinary Outcomes at East Park', *Scottish Journal of Residential Child Care* 19.2 (2020), pp. 146–59.

Fell, Robert, '"It happened at the berry-time when Travellers came to Blair": Traveller Voices in *Tobar an Dualchais/Kist o Riches*', *Scottish Archives*, 28 (2022), pp. 16–33.

Fox, Lesley, *As Long as We've Got a Voice* (Edinburgh: Thirsty Books, 2022).

Fuchs, Vivian, *Of Ice and Men: the story of the British Antarctic Survey 1943–73* (Oswestry: Anthony Nelson, 1982).

Fulton, Kate, *Rikki & Me* (Edinburgh: Black and White Publishing, 2004).

Fulton, Rikki, *Is It That Time Already?* (Edinburgh: Black and White Publishing, 1999).

Gammie, Alexander, *William Quarrier and the Story of the Orphan Homes of Scotland* (London: Pickering & Inglis, 1937).

Goffman, Erving, *Asylums: Essays on the Social Situation of Mental Patients and Other Inmates* (London: Pelican, 1968).

Gregory, Adrian, *The Last Great War: British Society and the First World War* (Cambridge: Cambridge University Press, 2008).

Hall, Catherine and Sonya O Rose, *At home with the empire: Metropolitan culture and the imperial world* (Cambridge: Cambridge University Press, 2006).

Hanley, Clifford, *Dancing in the Streets: the classic account of a Glasgow upbringing* (London: Hutchinson, 1958).

Haraldsson, Haraldur Thor Hammer, 'Fictive Osteobiographical Narrative – The Missing Puzzle Pieces', in Hanna Björg Sigurjónsdóttir and James G Rice, *Understanding Disability Throughout History: Interdisciplinary Perspectives in Iceland from Settlement to 1936* (London: Routledge, 2022), pp. 163–80.

Harris, Bernard, 'Unemployment and the Dole in Interwar Britain', in Paul Johnson (ed.), *Twentieth-Century Britain: Economic, Social and Cultural Change* (Harlow: Longman, 1994), pp. 203–20.

Hay, J R, *The Origins of the Liberal Welfare Reforms* (Basingstoke: Palgrave, 1983).

Hazley, Barry, Lynn Abrams, Ade Kearns and Valerie Wright, 'Place, Memory and the British high rise experience: negotiating social change on the Wyndford Estate, 1962–2015', *Contemporary British History*, 35:1 (2021), pp. 72–99.

Hendrick, Harry, *Child Welfare: Historical dimensions, contemporary debate* (Bristol: The Policy Press, 2003).

Holman, Bob, *Champions for Children: The lives of modern childcare pioneers* (Bristol: Policy Press, 2001).

Hughes, Annmarie, *Gender and Political Identities in Scotland, 1919–1939* (Edinburgh: Edinburgh University Press, 2010).

Hutchison, Iain, 'Institutionalization of mentally impaired children in Scotland, c.1855–1914', *History of Psychiatry*, 22:4 (2011).

Hutchison, Iain, *Feeling our History: The experience of blindness and sight loss in Edwardian Edinburgh, the Lothians and the Scottish Borders* (Edinburgh: RNIB, 2015).

Hutchison, Iain, Malcolm Nicolson and Lawrence Weaver, *Child Health in Scotland: A History of Glasgow's Royal Hospital for Sick Children* (Erskine: Scottish History Press, 2016).

Jenkinson, Jacqueline, Michael S Moss and Iain Russell, *The Royal: the history of the Glasgow Royal Infirmary, 1794–1994* (Glasgow: Glasgow Royal Infirmary NHS Trust, 1994).

Johnson, Niall, *Britain and the 1918–19 influenza pandemic: a dark epilogue* (London: Routledge, 2006).

Kelly, Christine, 'Reforming Juvenile Justice in Nineteenth-Century Scotland: The Subversion of the Scottish Day Industrial School Movement', *Crime, Histoire & Société / Crime, History & Society*, 20:2 (2016), pp. 55–75.

Kendrick, Andrew, Moyra Hawthorn, Samina Karim and Julie Shaw, 'Scotland: Historic Abuse in Care and Human Rights', in Johanna Sköld and Shurlee Swain (eds), *Apologies and the Legacy of Abuse of Children in 'Care'* (Basingstoke: Palgrave Macmillan, 2015), pp. 124–33.

Knox, W, 'The Political and Workplace Culture of the Scottish Working Class, 1832–1914', in W Hamish Fraser and R J Morris (eds), *People and Society in Scotland II, 1830–1914* (Edinburgh: John Donald, 1990), pp. 138–66.

Laing, Dave, 'Kenneth McKellar obituary', *The Guardian*, 12 Apr 2010.

Lawrence, Jon, 'The First World War and its Aftermath', in Paul Johnson (ed.), *Twentieth-Century Britain: Economic, Social and Cultural Change* (Harlow: Longman, 1994), pp. 151–68.

Lendrum, Leslie, *Neil Munro: The Biography* (Colonsay: House of Lochar, 2004).

Liddell, Henry George and Robert Scott, *An intermediate Greek–English lexicon: Founded upon the seventh edition of Liddell and Scott's Greek–English Lexicon* (Oxford: Oxford University Press, 2010).

Livesay, Daniel, *Children of Uncertain Fortune: mixed race Jamaicans in Britain and the Atlantic Family, 1733–1833* (Williamsburg: Omohundro Institute of Early American History and Culture/Chapel Hill: University of North Carolina Press, 2018).

Lockhart, Douglas G, 'The Queen of all Bazaars', *Scottish Local History*, 111 (Spring 2022).

Logan, Jimmy, *It's a Funny Life* (Edinburgh; Black and White Publishing, 1998).

Longmore, Paul K and Lauri Umansky (eds), *The New Disability History: American Perspectives* (New York: New York University Press, 2001).

MacDonald, Helen J, 'Boarding-Out and the Scottish Poor Law, 1845–1914', *Scottish Historical Review*, LXXV, 2:200 (Oct 1996), pp. 197–220.

Mackie, Albert David, *The Scotch Comedians: from music hall to television* (Edinburgh: Ramsay Head, 1973).

MacQueen, Loudon and Archibald B Kerr, *The Western Infirmary 1874–1974: a century of service to Glasgow* (Glasgow: John Horn, 1974).

MacSporran, Graham, 'Influenza Epidemic in Glasgow, 1918–19: Source, Impact and Response', *Journal of Scottish Historical Studies*, 42:1 (2022), pp. 92–117.

Magnusson, Anna, *The Village: A history of Quarriers* (Bridge of Weir: Quarriers Homes, 1984).

Magnusson, Anna, *The Quarriers Story* (Edinburgh: Birlinn, 2006).

Maier, Charles S, 'Overcoming the Past? Narrative and negotiation, Remembering and Reparation: issues at the Interface of History and the Law', in John Torpey (ed.), *Politics and the Past: On Repairing Historical Injustices* (Oxford: Rowman and Littlefield, 2003), pp. 295–304.

Maloney, Alison, *Something for the Girls: The Official Guide to the First 100 years of Guiding* (London: Constable, 2009).

Marwick, Arthur, *The Home Front: The British and the Second World War* (London: Thames and Hudson, 1976).

Mathams, Robyn, 'Anne Mathams: A pioneer who spent her life helping physically disabled children to excel academically', *Times Educational Supplement*, 1 Apr 2011.

Maver, Irene, *Glasgow* (Edinburgh: Edinburgh University Press, 2000).

McGann, Susan, 'No Wonder Nurses Quit! What the New Health Service meant for Nurses in 1948', in Chris Nottingham (ed.), *The NHS in Scotland: The legacy of the past and the prospect of the future* (Aldershot: Ashgate, 2000).

McLarty, Marion and Moyra Hawthorn, 'Special Educational Needs: Working with Children and Families', in Baillie, Deborah, Kathryn Cameron, Lesley-Anne Cull, Jeremy Roche and Janice West (eds), *Social Work and the Law in Scotland* (Basingstoke: Palgrave Macmillan, 2003), pp. 191–202.

Milne, Ida, *Stacking the Coffins: Influenza, War and Revolution in Ireland* (Manchester: Manchester University Press, 2018).

Mitchell, William, *Rescue the Children (or Twelve Years of Dealing with Neglected Boys and Girls)* (London: William Isbister, 1885).

Moore, Tamanna, Enid M Hennessey, Jonathan Myles, Samantha J Johnson, Elizabeth S Draper, Kate L Costeloe and Neil Marlow, 'Neurological and developmental outcomes in extremely preterm children born in England in 1995 and 2006: the EPICure studies', *British Medical Journal*, 4 Dec 2012.

Nicol, James, *Glasgow 1881–1885: Vital, Social, and Economic Statistics of the City* (Glasgow: Town Council of the City of Glasgow, 1885).

Ó Catháin, Máirtin, '"Dying Irish": eulogising the Irish in Scotland in *Glasgow Observer* obituaries', *The Innes Review*, 61:1 (2010).

Oliver, Michael, *Understanding Disability: From Theory to Practice* (Basingstoke: Palgrave Macmillan, 2009).

Patience, Jan, 'Galleries: Scope of Jolomo's work surprises and delights our critic', *The Herald*, 5 Jul 2021.

Peden, George C, *British Economic and Social Policy: Lloyd George to Margaret Thatcher* (London: Philip Allan, 1985).

Peter, D. Cameron, *The Kenneth McKellar Story: 'Don't look at the Wallpaper'* (Johnstone: Linn Publishers, 2011).

Phillips, Robert W, *Roy Rogers: A Biography* (Jefferson: McFarland, 1995).

Philo, Chris and Jonathan Andrews, 'Introduction: histories of asylums, insanity and psychiatry in Scotland', *History of Psychiatry*, 28:1 (2009).

Proctor, Tammy M, 'Beyond God, Country, and Empire: The United Kingdom and the Transnational Turn in the First World War', *Britain and the World*, 16:2 (2023).

Quarrier, William, *A Narrative of Facts relative to Work done for Christ in connection with the Orphan and Destitute Children's Emigration Homes, Glasgow* (Glasgow, 1872).

Rafferty, Anne Marie, Marguerite Dupree and Fay Bound Alberti (eds), *Germs and governance: The past, present and future of hospital infection, prevention and control* (Manchester: Manchester University Press, 2021).

Reilly, Brian, *Up and Down the Hill, A History of Maryhill Football Club* (Lulu Press, 2009, https://www.lulu.com).

Rogers, Roy and Dale Evans, *Happy Trails: Our Life Story* (New York: Simon and Schuster, 1994).

Ross, David, *Scotland: History of a Nation* (Glasgow: Geddes and Grosset, 2000).

Ross, James, *The Power I Pledge* (Glasgow: Glasgow University Press for Quarrier's Homes, 1971).

Sandbrook, Dominic, *Never Had It So Good: A History of Britain from Suez to the Beatles* (London: Little Brown, 2005).

Sanderson, Helen, Jo Kennedy, Pete Ritchie and Gill Goodwin, *People, Plans and Possibilities: Exploring Person Centred Planning* (Edinburgh: SHS Limited, 1997).

Sawyer, Eva May, *William Quarrier and his Homes* (Glasgow: Pickering & Inglis, 1962).

Scotland, J, 'The Centenary of the Education (Scotland) Act of 1872', *British Journal of Educational Studies*, 20:2 (1972), pp. 121–36.

Scott, Ronnie, *Death by Design: The True Story of the Glasgow Necropolis* (Edinburgh: Black & White Publishing, 2005).

Shadow [Alexander Brown], *Midnight Scenes and Social Photographs being sketches of life in the streets, wynds, and dens of the city* (Glasgow: Thomas Murray, 1858), second edition published as *Glasgow, 1858: Shadow's Midnight Scenes and Social Photographs* (Glasgow: University of Glasgow Press, 1976).

Shakespeare, Tom and Nicholas Watson, 'The Social Model of Disability: An Outdated Ideology?', *Research in Social Science and Disability*, 2 (2002), pp. 9–28.

Sigurjónsdóttir, Hanna Björg and James G Rice (eds), *Understanding Disability Throughout History: Interdisciplinary Perspectives in Iceland from Settlement to 1936* (London: Routledge, 2022).

Steckley, Laura, Lee Hollins, Sarah Deeley and Michael Bettencourt, *An Appreciative Inquiry into Holding in Residential Child Care: Pilot Report* (Glasgow: University of Strathclyde, 2023).

Stevens, Tim and Brian Beacom, *The Adventures of Tiger Tim: The Authorised Biography of Tim Stevens* (Edinburgh: Black and White Publishing), 2000.

Strathclyde Regional Council, *Room to Grow* (Glasgow: SRC, 1979).

Sturdy, Harriet and William Parry-Jones, 'Boarding out insane patients: the significance of the Scottish system 1857–1913', in Peter Bartlett and David Wright (eds), *Outside the Walls of the Asylum: The History of Care in the Community 1750–2000* (London: Bloomsbury, 1999), pp. 86–114.

The Newsroom, 'Obituary: Johnny Beattie, much-loved Scottish Comedian and actor', *The Scotsman*, 14 Jul 2020.

Thompson, E P, *The Making of the English Working Class* (London: Penguin, 1963, 1968, 1980).

Tibballs, Geoff, *The Secret Life of Sooty* (Letchworth: Ringpress Books, 1990).

Tucker, Anthony, 'Obituary: Sir Vivian Fuchs', *The Guardian*, 12 Nov 1999.

Urquhart, John, *The Life Story of William Quarrier* (London: S W Partridge, 1900).

Van der Horst, Frank C P and René van der Veer, 'Changing attitudes towards the care of children in hospital: A new assessment of the influence of the work of Bowlby and Robertson in the UK, 1940–1970', *Attachment & Human Development*, 11:2 (2009), pp. 119–42.

Virdi, Jaipreet, *Hearing Happiness: Deafness Cures in History* (Chicago: Chicago University Press, 2020).

Watson, J M West, *Report upon the Vital, Social, and Economic Statistics for Glasgow for 1877* (Glasgow: James McNab, 1878).

Wilson, Brian, 'Obituary. Calum Kennedy: Gaelic singer whose career ranged from the Bolshoi to the village hall', *The Guardian*, 22 Apr 2006.

Wilson, Davie with Alistair Aird, *Wilson on the Wing: the Davie Wilson Story* (Chichester: Pitch Publishing, 2020).

Withers, Charles, 'The demographic history of the city, 1831–1911', in W Hamish Fraser and Irene Maver (eds), *Glasgow, Volume II: 1830–1912* (Manchester: Manchester University Press, 1996), pp. 141–62.

Wood, Ian S, '"Be Strong and of Good Courage": the Royal Scots' Territorial Battalions from 1908 to Gallipoli', in Catriona M M Macdonald and E W McFarland, *Scotland and the Great War* (East Linton: Tuckwell, 1999), pp. 103–24.

Wright, David, *Downs: The History of a Disability* (Oxford: Oxford University Press, 2011).

Young, Andrew, 'Empire on which the sun did set', *Glasgow Herald*, 9 Sep 1989.

Newspapers

Charity Organisation Review

Glasgow Herald/The Herald

Glasgow News

Glasgow Observer

Holyrood

Largs and Millport New

Supplement to the London Gazette

The Bailie

The Economist

The Guardian

The London Gazette

The Scotsman

Dissertations and theses

Cronin, Jenny, 'The Origins and Development of Scottish Convalescence Homes, 1860–1939', PhD thesis, University of Glasgow (2003).

Hawthorn, Moyra, 'Looking Back and Moving Forward: An Exploration of Survivors' Narratives of Historical Institutional Child Abuse', PhD thesis, University of Strathclyde, (2018).

McFarlane, Hazel, 'Disabled Women and Socio-Spatial "Barriers" to Motherhood', PhD thesis, University of Glasgow (2004).

Thomson, Andrea, 'Marriage and marriage breakdown in late twentieth-century Scotland', PhD thesis, University of Glasgow (2004).

Winters, Richard, '"The Empire of Learning": The School Board of Glasgow and elementary education, 1872–1885, with particular reference to the work of William Mitchell', PhD thesis, University of Glasgow (1997).

Online sources

Anchor Line, RMS *Caledonia V, 1948*, http://ssmaritime.com/MS-Circassia-Cilicia-Caledonia.htm

András Petö Faculty, Semmelweiss University, About Conductive Education, https://semmelweis.hu/pak/en/#:~:text=Conductive%20education%20is%20a%20comprehensive,learn%20through%20normal%20life%20experiences

Burgon, Jenny and Don Martin, 'An Appreciation of Beatrice Clugston, 1827–1888', presentation at a joint meeting of the Kirkintilloch Soroptimists and the Kirkintilloch & District Society of Antiquaries, 16 Mar 2022, www.youtube.com/watch?v=oSD7_duaink

CALL Scotland, https://www.callscotland.org.uk

Care Inspectorate, *The Care Inspectorate Guide for providers on personal planning: Children and young people* (Dundee: The Care Inspectorate, 2021), p. 20, https://hub.careinspectorate.com/media/4673/personal-plans-guide-cyp-final-07102021 .pdf

Cerebral Palsy Scotland, 'What is Cerebral Palsy?', https://cerebralpalsyscotland.org.uk/get-information/what-is-cerebral-palsy/

Daniel, Brigid and Jane Scott, *50th Anniversary: Social Work Scotland Act* (Social Work Scotland), https://socialworkscotland.org/sws-projects/50th-anniversary-of-the-social-work-scotland-act-1968/

East Park School, https://www.eastpark.org.uk/school/

ERIC, *The Children's Bowel and Bladder Charity*, https://eric.org.uk

Gentle Teaching – A Summary, https://www.gentleteaching.nl/gentle/en/wat-is-en/sum

Glasgow Taxi Outing Fund, *Goin tae Troon since 1945*, https://gtof.org.uk

Hope, S, 'The Luftwaffe bomb Kilmun Street, Maryhill', https://www.maryhillburghhalls.org.uk/blog/2020/5/8/1941-the-luftwaffe-bomb-kilmun-street-maryhill

Independent Care Review, *Launch of 'root and branch review'*, https://www.carereview.scot/launch-of-the-root-and-branch-review/

Kendrick, Andrew, Erin Lux, Sharon McGregor and Richard Withington, *Development of Children's Care Services in Scotland: Report for the Child Abuse Inquiry* (2021), https://pureportal.strath.ac.uk/en/publications/development-of-childrens-care-services-in-scotland-report-for-the

National Bobath Cerebral Palsy Centre (2022), https://bobath.org.uk/about-us/ourfounders

Kenneth McKenzie Norrie, *Legislative Background to Children Living Apart from their Parents* (2017), https://www.childabuseinquiry.scot/sites/default/files/2023-03/norrie_legislative-background-to-the-treatment-of-childrenyoungpeople-bmd-181017.pdf

O'Brien, Sinead, *East Park iPad Project Report 2013/14*, Moray House School of Education (University of Edinburgh, 2014).

Office of the High Commissioner for Human Rights, *Convention on the Rights of the Child*, Adopted and opened for signature, ratification and accession by General Assembly resolution 44/25 of 20 November 1989. Entry into force 2 September 1990, in accordance with article 49. https://www.ohchr.org/sites/default/files/Documents/ProfessionalInterest/crc.pdf

Powell, Andrew, Brigid Francis-Devine and Harriet Clark, *Coronavirus: Impact on the Labour Market* (House of Commons Library, 9 Aug 2022, p. 4), https://researchbriefings.files.parliament.uk/documents/CBP-8898/CBP-8898.pdf

Rhodes, Mandy, 'In announcing a review of the care system: Nicola Sturgeon knows she has made a big commitment', *Holyrood*, 22 Oct 2016, https://www.holyrood.com/editors-column/view,in-announcing-a-review-of-the-care-system-nicola-sturgeon-knows-she-has-made-a-big-commitment_12557.htm

RMS Caronia Timeline, https://caronia2.info/home.php_

Scotland's Redress Scheme, https://www.gov.scot/collections/financial-redress-for-survivors-of-child-abuse-in-care/

Scottish Child Abuse Inquiry, https://www.childabuseinquiry.scot/news/message-lady-smith-approach-work-inquiry

Scottish Government, 'Keeping the Promise' Implementation Plan (2022), https://www.gov.scot/publications/keeping-promise-implementation-plan/pages/2/

Scottish University Insight Institute, Getting it Right for Looked After Disabled Children, https://www.scottishinsight.ac.uk/Programmes/OpenCall201213/GettingitRightforLookedAfterDisabledChildren.aspx

Scouts, 'How Scouting Grew' (2023), https://www.scouts.org.uk/about-us/our-history/how-scouting-grew/

The Glasgow Story, https://www.theglasgowstory.com

The Glasgow University Story, http://www.universitystory.gla.ac.uk/

The Independent Care Review, *The Promise* (2022), https://www.carereview.scot/wp-content/uploads/2020/02/The-Promise.pdf

University of Edinburgh, East Park iPad Project, https://dart.ed.ac.uk/research/east-park-ipad-project/

World Association of Girl Guides and Girl Scouts (2023), https://www.wagggs.org/en/about-us/our-history

Radio, television, film
BBC, *Who do You Think You Are?* Series 1, Episode 6 – Moira Stuart

Robertson, J A, *Two Year-Old Goes to Hospital* (1952), http://www.robertsonfilms.info/2_year_old.htm

Miscellaneous sources
Hewitson, Wendy, Joyce Hawthorn, Moyra Hawthorn and Carolyn Johnson, 'The Famous Five Adventures', presentation at the World Down Syndrome Congress Conference, Glasgow, 24–27 Jul 2018

Programme, *Scottish National Orchestra Royal Gala Charity Concert in aid of East Park Home for Infirm Children*

Maps
Ordnance Survey, Maryhill Parish, Lanarkshire, Sheet V1.2 (1861)

Ordnance Survey, Lanarkshire, Glasgow and its Environs, Sheet VI.2 (1896)

Ordnance Survey, Lanarkshire, Sheet VI.2 (1913)

Ordnance Survey, Lanarkshire, Sheet VI.2 (1935)

Selective Index